Corinth in Contrast

Corinth in Contrast

Studies in Inequality

Edited by

Steven J. Friesen, Sarah A. James,
and Daniel N. Schowalter

BRILL

LEIDEN • BOSTON
2014

This paperback is also published in hardback under ISBN 978-90-04-22607-4 as volume 155 in the series NTS.

Cover illustration: A selection of imported and local fine wares and other objects from a floor deposit dated to between 125–75 BCE in the Panayia Field, Corinth (see James in this volume). From left to right: an Eastern Sigillata A bowl, an iron scythe, and a bowl with an outturned rim, a flat rim plate, a mold for making ceramic moldmade bowls, three loomweights, and a saucer. Photo by S. James and J. Herbst.

Library of Congress Cataloging-in-Publication Data

Corinth in contrast : studies in inequality / edited by Steven J. Friesen, Sarah A. James, and Daniel N. Schowalter.
    pages cm. — (Supplements to Novum Testamentum, ISSN 0167-9732 ; VOLUME 155)
    Includes bibliographical references and index.
    ISBN 978-90-04-22607-4 (hardback : alk. paper) — ISBN 978-90-04-26131-0 (e-book : alk. paper)
1. Corinth (Greece)—History. 2. Corinth (Greece)—Social life and customs. 3. Corinth (Greece)—Social conditions. 4. Corinth (Greece)—Religion. 5. Corinth (Greece)—Antiquities. 6. Equality—Greece—Corinth—History. I. Friesen, Steven J., editor of compilation.

DF261.C65C667 2013
938'.7—dc23

2013031395

This publication has been typeset in the multilingual "Brill" typeface. With over 5,100 characters covering Latin, IPA, Greek, and Cyrillic, this typeface is especially suitable for use in the humanities. For more information, please see www.brill.com/brill-typeface.

ISSN 0167-9732
ISBN 978-90-04-26186-0 (paperback)
ISBN 978-90-04-26131-0 (e-book)

MIX
Paper from
responsible sources
FSC® C109576
www.fsc.org

Printed by Printforce, the Netherlands

CONTENTS

PART ONE

ELITES AND NON-ELITES

PART TWO

SOCIO-ECONOMIC INEQUALITIES IN CORINTH

PART THREE

INEQUALITIES IN GENDER AND RELIGION IN ROMAN CORINTH

LIST OF ILLUSTRATIONS

All drawings and photographs are courtesy of the American School of Classical Studies at Athens Corinth Excavations unless otherwise noted.

James

Figures

Nasrallah

Figures

Lepinski

Figures

Sanders

Tables

Figure

Graphs

Caraher

Figures

Schowalter

Figures

Stroud

Figures

Friesen

Figure

Table

Maps

ACKNOWLEDGEMENTS

The editors are grateful to the many people who contributed to the development of this volume. Ann Morgan and Aubrey Hooser provided indispensible assistance for the execution of the conference in which participants first presented their research. At that conference there were several official discussants who helped us see some of the strengths, weaknesses, and interconnections of our preliminary arguments. These interlocutors included: John Lanci, Adam Rabinowitz, Betsey Robinson, Barbette Spaeth, Rabun Taylor, Christine Thomas, James Walters, L. Michael White, and Antoinette Wire. The following units at the University of Texas at Austin lent their support to the conference: the Institute for the Study of Antiquity and Christian Origins; the Department of Religious Studies; the Department of Classics; and the College of Liberal Arts.

As the project moved from conference to publication there were others who joined in the work. Carl Holladay facilitated the placement of the volume in the Supplements to Novum Testamentum series. Louise Schouten and Mattie Kuiper of E.J. Brill helped us interface with the publisher. A special debt of gratitude is owed to James Herbst and to Ioulia Tzonou-Herbst for their assistance with images, objects, questions, and tasks too numerous to recount. G. Anthony Keddie worked on the early editing of the papers, and Jin Young Kim labored over the final stages, finishing the component parts and bringing them together as a volume.

The editors also wish to recognize the generous financial support of the Foundation for Biblical Studies, whose vision for the contextualized study of Christian origins made this work – and many other projects – possible. Finally, we could never have gotten this project off the drawing board nor could we have brought it to its conclusion without the support, encouragement, and advice of Guy Sanders.

Thanks to all of you, and to the many others who assisted us at every step along the way.

LIST OF ABBREVIATIONS

Note: All abbreviations of ancient authors and biblical texts use the standards of Hornblower and Spawforth (2012) and Alexander et al. (1999). All journal abbreviations follow the standards of the *American Journal of Archaeology* and the *Journal of Biblical Literature*.

ACO   *Acta Conciliorum Oecumenicorum.*
III = E. Schwartz and R. Schieffer. Berlin, 1940.

Agora   *The Athenian Agora: Results of Excavations Conducted by the American School of Classical Studies at Athens.*
XXIV = A. Frantz, *Late Antiquity: A.D. 267–700*, Princeton, 1988.
XXVII = R.F. Townsend, *The East Side of the Agora: the Remains Beneath the Stoa of Attalos*, Princeton, 1995.

CCxt   *Corinth in Context: Comparative Studies on Religion and Society*, edited by S.J. Friesen, D.N. Schowalter, and J.C. Walters, Leiden, 2010.

CID   *Corpus des Inscriptions de Delphes*. Paris. 1977–.
IV = F. Lefévre, *Documents amphictioniques*, Paris, 2002.

CIL   *Corpus Inscriptionum Latinarium*. Berlin. 1863–.

Corinth   *Corinth: Results of Excavations Conducted by the American School of Classical Studies at Athens.*
I.1 = H.N. Fowler and R. Stillwell, *Introduction, Topography and Architecture*, Cambridge, 1932.
I.3 = R.L. Scranton, *Monuments in the Lower Agora and North of the Archaic Temple*, Princeton, 1951.
I.4 = O. Broneer, *The South Stoa and Its Roman Successors*, Princeton, 1952.
I.5 = S. Weinberg, *The Southeast Building, the Twin Basilicas, the Mosaic House*, Princeton, 1960.
I.6 = B.H. Hill (ed.), *The Springs: Peirene, Sacred Spring and Glauke*, Princeton, 1964.
II = R. Stillwell, *The Theater*, Princeton, 1952.
V = T.L. Shear, *The Roman Villa*, Cambridge, 1930.
VI = K.M. Edwards, *The Coins: 1896–1929*, Cambridge, 1933.
VIII.1 = B.D. Meritt, *Greek Inscriptions: 1896–1927*, Cambridge, 1931.

VIII.2 = A.B. West, *Latin Inscriptions: 1896–1926*, Cambridge, 1931.

VIII.3 = J.H. Kent, *The Inscriptions: 1926–1950*, Princeton, 1966.

X = O. Broneer, *The Odeum*, Cambridge, 1932.

XII = G. Davidson, *The Minor Objects*, Princeton, 1952.

XVIII.2 = K.W. Slane, *The Sanctuary of Demeter and Kore, The Roman Pottery and Lamps*, Princeton, 1990.

XVIII.3 = N. Bookidis and R.S. Stroud, *The Sanctuary of Demeter and Kore: Topography and Architecture*, Princeton, 1998.

XX = C.K. Williams and N. Bookidis (eds.), *Corinth, the Centenary: 1896–1996*, Princeton, 2003.

Délos   *Exploration archeologique de Délos faites par l'École française d'Athènes.*

VIII = J. Chamonard, *Le Quartier du théâtre; Étude sur l'habitation delienne à l'epoque hellenistique*, 1922–1924.

Ephesos   Forschungen in Ephesos veröffentlicht vom Österreichischen Archäologischen Institut in Wien.

VIII.1 = K.V. Strocka, *Die Wandmalerei der Hanghäuser in Ephesos*, Vienna, 1977.

FD   *Fouilles de Delphes.* Paris. 1908-.

IG   *Inscriptiones Graecae.* Berlin. 1873–1927.

IGLSyr   *Inscriptions grecques et latines de la Syrie*, edited by L. Jalabert and R. Mouterde, Paris, 1929.

ILLRP   *Inscriptiones Latinae Liberae Rei Publicae*, edited by A. Degrassi, vol. 1^2 (1965), 2 (1963).

Isthmia   *Isthmia: Excavations by the University of Chicago under the Auspices of the American School of Classical Studies at Athens.*

II = O. Broneer, *Topography and Architecture*, Princeton, 1973.

V = T.E. Gregory, *The Hexamilion and the Fortress*, Princeton, 1993.

Kenchreai   *Kenchreai. Eastern Port of Corinth. Results of Investigations by the University of Chicago and Indiana University for the American School of Classical Studies at Athens.*

I = R.L. Scranton, J.W. Shaw, and L. Ibrahim, *Topography and Architecture*, Leiden, 1978.

IV = K. Adamscheck, *The Pottery.* Leiden, 1979.

NPNF   *Nicene and Post-Nicene Fathers.*

NRSV   *New Revised Standard Version Bible.*

PG   *Patriologia graeca*, edited by J.-P. Migne. Paris, 1857–1886.

PGM   *Papyri graecae magicae*, edited by K. Preisendanz et al., *Papyri Graecae Magicae: Die griechischen Zauberpapyri*, 2 vols., 2nd ed., 1973.

RP   I = *Roman Peloponnese I: Roman Personal Names in their Social Context (Achaia, Arcadia, Argolis, Corinthia and Eleia)*, edited by A.D. Rizakis and S. Zoumbaki, Athens, 2001.

RPC   I = *Roman Provincial Coinage, Volume I: From the death of Caesar to the death of Vitellus (44 BC to AD 69)*, edited by A. Burnett, M. Amandry, and P.P. Ripollès. London, 1992.

SEG   *Supplementum Epigraphicum Graecum.* Amsterdam. 1923–.

URRC   *Urban Religion in Roman Corinth: Interdisciplinary Approaches*, edited by D.N. Schowalter and S.J. Friesen. Cambridge, 2005.

LIST OF CONTRIBUTORS

WILLIAM CARAHER, Department of History, University of North Dakota.

STEVEN J. FRIESEN, Department of Religious Studies, The University of Texas at Austin.

CAROLINE JOHNSON HODGE, Department of Religious Studies, College of the Holy Cross, Worcester, MA.

SARAH A. JAMES, Department of Classics, University of Colorado Boulder.

SARAH LEPINSKI, Visiting Scholar, Bard Research Center, New York, NY.

BENJAMIN W. MILLIS, Humanities Division, University of Oxford.

LAURA S. NASRALLAH, Faculty of Divinity, Harvard Divinity School.

DAVID K. PETTEGREW, Department of History, Messiah College, Grantham, PA.

GUY D.R. SANDERS, Director of Corinth Excavations, American School of Classical Studies at Athens.

DANIEL N. SCHOWALTER, Departments of Religion and Classics, Carthage College, Kenosha, WI.

RONALD S. STROUD, Department of Classics, University of California, Berkeley.

CHAPTER ONE

INEQUALITY IN CORINTH

Steven J. Friesen, Sarah A. James, and Daniel N. Schowalter

This volume is the third in a series of collaborative studies on the ancient city of Corinth. The first volume grew out of a conference held at Harvard Divinity School in 2002,[1] and the second volume developed from a conference at the University of Texas at Austin in 2007.[2] The third conference took place between September 30 and October 2, 2010, again at the University of Texas at Austin, and those papers and discussions became the foundation for this volume.

All three conferences were wide-ranging and crossed disciplinary lines. They included archaeologists, historians, ceramicists, epigraphists, New Testament scholars, art historians, and others. Some scholars have contributed to more than one meeting, but the cast of specialists has shifted with each iteration to incorporate new materials and theoretical orientations. Thus, participants have examined aspects of urban planning, elite rhetoric, hydrology, religious history, city magistrates, architecture, burial inscriptions, domestic space, ritual theory, gender roles, literary processes, coinage, house churches, imperialism, and more.

The topic for the third conference and volume grew directly out of its predecessors. The discussions of the second conference in particular highlighted three crucial themes: Greek and Roman aspects of Corinthian urban identity; social stratification; and local religious traditions. For each of these domains, the participants found themselves gauging various phenomena, weighing alternative facets of events, describing dissonant features of social systems, and re-conceptualizing problematic categories. These labors paid off in a volume that revised Corinthian social history and generated new insights about the roles of religion in that setting.

---

[1] *URRC* 2005.
[2] *CCxt* 2010.

In reflection on the second conference and volume, it seemed that a good deal of our deliberations were connected to different kinds of inequalities – social, economic, religious, political, and so on. In fact, we came to see more clearly the way in which inequalities provide much of the texture of social life. Thus, if society can be characterized in part as the unequal distribution of material, cultural, and spiritual resources, then a focused analysis of these unequal distributions should provide new insight into the socio-economic, religious, and political networks present in Corinth

The examination of ancient inequalities, however, faces a particular challenge, because these differentials affected not only ancient lives but also our access to those ancient lives. Those with less on any of these scales – political, religious, cultural, economic, etc. – tend to be the ones for whom we now have very little data. Thus, our modern analysis often focuses on those who had surpluses and not on those who were deprived, on the haves rather than the have-nots.

So, for the third conference, participants were asked to consider the polarities that we often use to characterize forms of inequality – urban/ rural, male/female, Greek/Roman, rich/poor, pagan/Christian, Jew/Gentile, monotheist/polytheist, slave/free, high/low status, etc. Participants were further encouraged to move beyond these polarities by bringing forward new data, by reexamining existing data, by showing connections between different forms of inequality, and/or by applying new methods or theories. Since inequality can be discussed from a number of perspectives, the specialists were invited to select an approach that suited their ancient data and their research goals. They were also encouraged to take up topics dealing with Corinthian religion and topics related to continuities and discontinuities between the Roman imperial period and earlier periods.

As a result, there is no one theory of inequality that guides this volume. All of the contributors would agree that inequalities permeated Corinthian society, but that does not mean that we agree on the sources of these inequalities or on the ethical evaluation of inequalities. In fact, if the eleven contributors had been asked whether inequality is a healthy or unhealthy phenomenon (they were not asked), they probably would have produced at least eleven different answers. So, no particular evaluation of inequality was presupposed for participation in this volume. Indeed, careful readers will note degrees of difference among the ideologies of inequality endorsed by the various contributors.

We are, however, all participants in Western academic traditions that promote democratic values and that privilege egalitarian goals over hierarchical ones. So the analyses in this volume tend to lean toward a negative evaluation of inequality. It is important to recognize this general bias toward egalitarian values as a Western discursive formation that is not shared by many people in the contemporary world, nor was it shared by any people in the ancient world.

Therefore, the goal of focusing on inequalities in these studies is not to find our own preferences in the ancient world, nor to convert our contemporaries to our own ideological commitments. Rather, the goal of focusing on inequalities is two-fold (or perhaps binocular). One goal is to understand better the distinctions between different social strata that characterized the ancient world. Such insights into Corinthian society can promote new approaches and interpretations of the data and, in doing so, bring us closer to seeing the 'invisible,' those poorest parts of the population who were present in every ancient city. The other goal is to help us reflect on the difficult question of why inequalities are so prevalent in human communities, and on the equally vexing issue of the extent to which such inequalities are morally acceptable. In other words, if some forms of inequality are healthy and others are harmful, how do we tell the difference and how should we respond? We do not expect unanimous answers to those questions and contemporary implications are not a focus of these studies. But all the authors in this volume have gone to great lengths to contextualize their analyses of ancient inequalities, so we should at least recognize that we also operate in specific historical contexts that have a bearing on our research. This volume, no less than the subjects it examines, has been affected by various forms of inequality.

In order to give shape to this collaboration of situated interdisciplinary studies, the editors have organized the chapters into three clusters. It seemed most appropriate to begin with research that emphasizes relationships between elite and non-elite groups. The second section contains studies where socio-economic inequalities come to the fore. The final group of chapters contains those in which gender and religion play prominent roles in the inequities.

Elites and Non-elites

The opening section focuses especially on distinctions between elite and non-elite Corinthians. In the first chapter, Sarah James recasts our knowledge of the so-called interim period – the century between the destruction of the Greek city of Corinth by the Roman general Mummius in 146 BCE and the refounding of Corinth as a Roman colony by Julius Caesar in 44 BCE. During this period Corinth did not exist institutionally as a city, but it is clear that there were people in the area. There is not yet agreement as to the character of that population but the chapter by James moves us toward some clarity. After a critique of the flawed arguments of specialists who think there was a complete decimation the population during this period, James argues for some degree of continuity in habitation. One sign of this continuity is that most of the important buildings in the city center appear to have remained intact even though their functions changed. Instead of public buildings, during the interim they became makeshift domestic space for Corinthians of mostly modest resources. Moreover, materials from recent excavations even provide us with some evidence for socio-economic distinctions within this population of modest means. Pottery finds show a wide range of imports during the interim period, including some elegant Eastern Sigilatta A for domestic use. But along with those impressive pieces there are many more examples of utilitarian coarse wares and cooking vessels. If we add the emerging evidence for local pottery production, transport amphorae, loom weights, and tools, it is clear that there was an ongoing presence in Corinth of inhabitants engaged in farming and small scale manufacturing during the interim period. James concludes that we should imagine a community in the range of 500–1000 inhabitants in the city center, mostly from the lower classes who could not afford to relocate after the destruction, and who probably provided part of the Greek substratum for the hybrid culture that developed in the early colony.

'Hybrid culture' was proposed by Benjamin Millis in the second volume of this series as a way of describing the early colony's mixed Greek and Roman heritage.[3] In his earlier paper, Millis argued that veterans played no significant role in the colony, which was dominated rather by freedmen from the Greek East. In this volume, Millis sets out to elucidate more precisely the character of the ruling elite, which he argues was composed of three types of men – Greek provincials, freeborn Roman citizens active in the Greek East, and freedmen from the Greek East. Examination of the inscriptions, coins, and literature shows that the freedmen were more numerous than both of the other two groups combined. Such analysis does not, however, support the claim – often found in the secondary literature – that these freedmen are evidence for a great deal of social

---

[3] Millis 2010a.

mobility at Corinth that would have allowed non-elites to enter the ruling class. On the contrary, the freedmen known to have filled magistracies in the colony's first century were already wealthy, powerful members of influential businesses before relocating to Corinth. Their main purpose in settling at Corinth and holding office appears to have been to extend those preexisting businesses to Corinth, where there were no entrenched interests already in power and where there was great potential for profit. Moreover, once in place, this newly formed Corinthian ruling elite closed ranks by appointing family members, clients, and allies to important positions, and so the colony's new elite quickly became self-perpetuating and allowed little social mobility. Thus, Millis encourages us to think of the colony's prominent freedmen not primarily as ex-slaves, but rather as wealthy men with powerful backing who happened to have been slaves at some point.

Laura Nasrallah integrates previously known Corinthian materials with the social history described in the previous two chapters by turning our attention toward the majority of Corinthian freedpersons, who were not so prominent. We have only fragmentary information about non-elite freedpersons in general and so Nasrallah surveys legal definitions and literary references to elucidate distinctions which had freedpersons straddling the divide between slave and free. Slavery itself was an ambiguous category that labeled slaves as human commodities, as 'things' that could be bought and sold. Prices for buying humans varied according to characteristics and skills, which emphasized the slave's similarity to a thing. Freedpersons were not released from that ambiguity and in fact had other complexities layered onto their lives, for manumission did not normally end one's affiliation with the former owner, who often became the freedperson's patron, boss, or even spouse. Moreover, the terms of manumission could mandate this ongoing relationship through continued service or through forced abandonment of one's children to slavery with one's former owner. Paul's letter known as 1 Corinthians is one of the only extant texts that addresses a Corinthian audience that included such slaves and freedpersons, and these complexities of manumission help us imagine the ancient receptions of Paul's slave imagery in that letter. Paul's description of a slave in the *ekklēsia* ("assembly") as "the Lord's freedperson" and a freeborn person as a "slave of Christ" (1 Cor 7:21) played off these complexities with paradoxical symbolic formulations. It required everyone in the audience to think of a slave simultaneously as manumitted, and an owner simultaneously as a commodity. So these statements by the apostle would have relativized the slave/free distinction in certain ways, but they would still have maintained the slavery framework for describing relations "in Christ." Believers were "bought with a price," which still required them to consider what sort of 'thing' they were.

In the final chapter of this section Sarah Lepinski integrates a new set of materials into the social history outlined by James and Millis. A large corpus of Corinthian wall paintings has been recovered from the Roman period, but systematic analysis of the materials, methods, and content is still in the early stages. Lepinski's chapter focuses primarily on the 1st to 3rd centuries CE and illuminates some material evidence related to the colony's hybrid culture. While these artistic traditions invariably drew on several sources, the wall paintings evince two distinct periods that reveal two different fusions of Roman and Greek traditions. In the early colonial period there is a complete adoption of Italic materials and technique, including thick layers of plaster finished in fresco (rather than the earlier use of thin hard layers of plaster in the Hellenistic period) and multiple examples of Third Pompeian Style murals from throughout the city. The stylistic details from this earlier period are especially close to Campanian examples, suggesting that the Corinthian artisans were trained in Italy and perhaps even in Pompeii. In the 2nd and 3rd centuries CE, however, the nature of Corinthian wall painting had clearly changed again. The materials shifted to thinner layers, making a fresco technique impossible, and dramatic pigments like cinnabar and Egyptian blue were deemphasized in favor of lead white and madder lake. Moreover, while Corinthian painting remained visually within the norm for Roman provinces during this later period, the themes and execution of specific objects shows an unusual influence of local monuments and traditions. In short, the visual culture of Corinthian wall painting went from a fusion that emphasized Italian connections in the early colonial period, to a fusion in the 2nd and 3rd centuries CE that emphasized regional and local nuance within a Roman imperial setting. While it is not yet clear whether these changes are due to economic, political, cultural, and/or other factors, there is no question that the visual culture of elite and non-elite Corinthians was the result of an evolving confluence of traditions, articulated in a Roman imperial framework.

Socio-economic Inequality in Corinth

The second section of the volume focuses on inequalities related to economy and society in the Roman colony of Corinth. Guy Sanders begins the section with an example of how we might examine the majority of the ancient Corinthians who left little or no evidence in the historical record. In other words, he addresses the conundrum of what we can learn from the material record about people who left little or no material data. His approach is to work with comparative materials from other better-documented periods of Greek history as a way of framing the possibilities in the Roman imperial period. Specifically, Sanders draws on sharecropping agreements in Greece from the Ottoman era and on oral histories of Greek farmers about the (still pre-industrial) early 20th century. These varied data support the conclusion that subsistence farming on the soil around Corinth required about eight hectares for an average family of five people before the advent of mechanized agriculture. Turning then to the ancient period, Sanders uses those observations along with site-specific archaeological data to estimate how many individuals the land around Corinth could support. Sanders then adds comparative material from global economic history to the mix in order to construct a heuristic model for socio-economic inequality in Corinth during the interim and colonial periods. His proposal is that the local and comparative materials suggest the following overall proportions. The monumental architecture and material remains at Corinth reflect the resources of the rich and super-rich, who made up no more than 2% of the population. At the other end of the spectrum are the Corinthians who lived at or near subsistence and whose lives have left little or no material evidence; they made up 65% or more of the population. Two middling groups together made up around 20% of the population. One of these middling groups lived at perhaps 3 to 4 times subsistence by renting out their land and/or engaging in haulage or trade. Their material remains include decorated ceramics, glass drinking vessels, storage pithoi, and refuse piles with some animal bones. The other middling group, living at a level above 4 times subsistence, is visible to us through artifacts such as mosaic floors, small scale sculpture, and wall painting. One of the implications of this model is that we need to revise radically our reconstructions of Corinthian society in order to correct the current bias toward the wealthiest fraction of the population.

One way to mitigate our wealth bias is to consider the range of participants in the Corinthian economy. David Pettegrew does this by focusing on one of the distinctive sectors of the Corinthian economy – the two harbors and the possibility of transshipment across the Isthmus. Academic writing about the Corinthian economy has been dominated by the idea that there was a road across the Isthmus called the 'diolkos' that allowed shippers to avoid sailing around the Peloponnese by hauling ships and/or cargo across the Isthmus. Pettegrew argues that this historical reconstruction comes from a misunderstanding of the ancient authors, who described only eight extreme situations where military vessels were hauled across the Isthmus in order to gain the element of surprise in battle. In fact, only one ancient writer uses the term diolkos for the Corinthia and it does not refer to the road that traverses the Isthmus. Ancient authors do, however, talk about the 'emporion' of Corinth as a source of its wealth. An emporion was a term for a site where wholesale commerce could expand due to favorable topography both for travel and for human settlement. Corinth's two main harbors – Lechaion and Kenchreai – allowed the city (and then the colony) to become just such a regional node for trade from the west (Italy and beyond) and from the east (the Aegean and beyond). Thus, while the city center housed normal urban economic activities, the emporion of the harbors added another sector to the Corinthian economy with hundreds of workers – haulers, accountants, buyers, sellers, etc. Ancient authors who wrote about this emporion and its workers reflected elite perspectives – that the emporion generated great wealth, but also attracted disreputable characters, offered temptations to luxury and immorality, and promoted unhealthy contact with foreigners. For most of those workers, however, the emporion was a source of seasonal employment and not a source of wealth. In the emporion of Corinth, then, we see institutions that generated great wealth for a few and thereby heightened local inequality. The unequal distributions from this sector of the economy must have had an ambivalent impact on the city as a whole, and also on those Corinthians who were attracted to the churches' claims about Jesus Christ.

William Caraher challenges our bias toward the wealthy by examining a different sector of the economy during the 6th century CE. Caraher's chapter looks at monumental architecture – churches and the city wall – that involved imperial funding and a great deal of manual labor. His thesis is that these projects were not simply projections of imperial power into the Corinthia by Justinian I, but also sites where imperial and local interests of officials and common people intersected and engaged each other in complex ways. From this perspective, the massive basilicas from 6th-century Corinth did not signify an increasing number of Christians so much as an infusion of new imperial funding for the building of monumental churches near the urban core. With these large projects came the need to negotiate imperial and local theological interests. For example, the Lechaion Basilica near Corinth's northern harbor tends to support the dominance of imperial theology and ritual, for it breaks with local ritual tradition by centering the ambo and by using a solea (balustrade near ambo) according to Constantinopolitan fashion. But the Kraneion Basilica undercut this imperial ritual setting by omitting the larger colonnade balustrades that separated congregants from the clergy's processional area. Justinianic inscriptions also suggest such an interplay of imperial and local interests. Two inscriptions – probably from the Hexamilion Wall or the city wall – used explicit Nicene-Constantinopolitan creedal language, but one of them also invoked the controversial title 'Theotokos' for Mary. These monumental projects also required some negotiation of elite and non-elite interests, for the labor needs gave opportunities to strengthen the position of workers and guilds in the city. Such examples suggest more than a binary struggle between empire and resistance. They reflect instead an interplay that involved imperial projections of power, local assertions of sovereignty, and the everyday lives of the laborers who actually built the structures. Such inequalities played out in a Corinthian arena that was simultaneously religious, economic, and political.

The chapter by Daniel Schowalter completes this section of the volume by examining two statue bases that suggest that the city's official attitudes toward the wealthy shifted over time. The two bases contain inscriptions indicating that they supported statues of Annia Appia Regilla Caucidia Tertulla. Regilla and her husband Herodes Atticus formed one of the wealthiest 'power couples' in 2nd-century CE Greece. Most of the secondary literature follows Kent in the conclusion that these two bases for an elite woman of the 2nd century were reinscribed and re-erected for her in the 4th century. One of the statues probably stood in the Peirene Fountain complex, and the other likened Regilla to Tyche. But why would a prominent benefactor like Regilla be memorialized so long after her death in the 2nd century? Schowalter examines the evidence and concludes that the Regilla bases were probably not re-inscribed in the 4th century. It is likely that the Peirene base was simply reused in the 4th century, and it is possible that the Regilla-Tyche base was also reused. Since it is likely that Regilla again became part of the public iconography in 4th-century Corinth, we can observe some important changes in her usefulness to the city. In the mid 2nd century Regilla and Herodes were among the most prominent figures in the eastern Mediterranean imperial elites who had family ties to Corinth. Thus, display in the 2nd century would have focused on Regilla as a specific benefactor for the city and region. In the 4th century, however, benefaction was no longer a factor in the display. In the 4th century, the city portrayed her not as a patron but rather as a sterling example of *sōphrosynē* ("moderation") from Corinth's past. Moreover, the use of the general cultural virtue of *sōphrosynē* in a 4th-century setting may represent an effort to find common ground between Christian and non-Christian interests in Corinth through the choice of a term that neither side would find objectionable. But these finely tuned distinctions were for people who could read the inscription and who were concerned with the machinations of elite politics. For the majority of Corinthians in either century, the sculpted statue would have served as an image that reinforced fundamental inequalities of the time.

Inequalities in Gender and Religion in Roman Corinth

The first chapter in this final section surveys curses in Corinthian religion and then provides details about gendered cursing associated with one particular site. Ronald Stroud begins by reminding us that religion, in the ancient world as today, includes negation, coercion, revenge, and destruction. For example, in Corinth there was a statue of Terror that commemorated Medea's vengeful slaughter of her own children, and a famed haunted house. The richest body of physical evidence for practices of magic and retribution, however, comes from lead tablets and other curse inscriptions found in several places throughout the urban area. The largest source of curse tables so far comes from the Sanctuary of Demeter and Kore, which had a special connection to women's rituals. This sanctuary had a long uninterrupted history stretching from at least the 7th century BCE until the Mummian destruction of 146 BCE, but it was not among the first religious sites to be rebuilt after the founding of the Roman colony. In fact, some of the earliest remains from the Roman period are curse tablets that predate the rebuilding of the site, suggesting that specialists in magic may have been among the first to reuse the sanctuary. While curse tablets have also been found elsewhere in the sanctuary, two rooms in particular seemed to have functioned as ritual centers – a slightly renovated dining room with two tablets and two incense burners used in rituals, and another dining room with ten tablets. The contents from all 18 of the curse tablets from the whole sanctuary await final publication.[4] Many of them, however, record curses by particular women or curses directed against particular women. The themes include love spells, destruction of enemies, and fertility. The supernatural beings invoked include deities of the underworld, Hermes,

---

[4] Stroud forthcoming.

Ge, the Fates who exact Justice, Necessity, and even Lady Demeter, and all of this comes from a site dedicated to Demeter and to Persephone/ Kore, the queen of the underworld. Thus, the lead curse tablets from this sanctuary and from elsewhere in Roman Corinth provide information on ritual practices and gendered concerns that are seldom addressed in the monumental remains, and add to our picture of the religious lives of women and men who populated the Roman colony.

The chapter by Steven Friesen shifts our attention from the mostly undocumented women who frequented the Sanctuary of Demeter and Kore to one very powerful woman – Junia Theodora – who made Corinth the center of her business and political interests in the early imperial period. Our information about Junia Theodora comes solely from an 85-line inscription discovered near Corinth in 1954.[5] The inscription probably comes from the second quarter of the 1st century CE, and it contains five texts from Lycia that praise Junia for her assistance to that region in southwestern Asia Minor. In recent secondary literature, Junia has been cited to support the idea that women were subject to less oppression in the Roman imperial period. Friesen argues that, on the contrary, Junia presents us with an example of a woman who used her resources to extend Rome's oppressive policies in the eastern Mediterranean. He analyzes her influence using two concepts: the 'structural parameters' such as legal status, wealth, gender, family, and ethnicity that set limits and expectations for an individual; and the 'subject position' that results from an individual's interactions in relation to those parameters. In the case of Junia Theodora, the picture that emerges is that of a woman who had considerable resources and who used them to help Roman authorities control the region of Lycia. Thus, her agenda and subject position aligned well with those of the men in Corinth's ruling elite in the early colonial period. Moreover, her political and economic network illuminates the way in which Corinth functioned both as a bridgehead for Roman power in the region and also as a competitor with other cities for regional resources.

In the final chapter of the volume, Caroline Johnson Hodge examines a particular example where gender, family ideologies, and religious commitments helped shape inequalities in Corinth and beyond. The object of inquiry here is the Christian phenomenon of 'mixed marriages' between believers and nonbelievers. This was an issue from the earliest period,

---

[5] An appendix to the chapter contains a new translation of the inscription.

starting as soon as someone converted without being joined by a spouse, but our evidence is again fragmentary and dominated by the authorized literature that has survived to our day. So Johnson Hodge begins by looking at the evidence from 'published Christians' whose literature still survives. The first known text about this topic is 1 Corinthians 7, but Paul's advice was somewhat opaque: believing Corinthians were to remain in mixed marriages if the unbelieving spouse was willing, since the believing spouse sanctified the unbelieving spouse and children. Later published Christians – mostly male writers like Tertullian (ca. 200 CE) and Cyprian (ca. 250 CE) – had to reinterpret Paul's advice because they disagreed with his practice in two ways: they thought that mixed marriages were wrong; and they thought women were the focus of the problem. So these later writers replace Paul's advice to husbands and wives with arguments directed primarily at the perceived dangers for believing wives in mixed marriages. This focus on believing wives probably reflects a greater commitment on the part of these published Christian leaders to hierarchical, male-dominant families and churches. But their written admonitions allow us to begin to reconstruct the views of the 'unpublished Christians' who have been silenced by the inequities of their time and by the biases of history. We can safely assume that some of these unpublished Christians – mostly female – would have wanted to leave their mixed marriages and others would have wanted to remain. The counsel of the published male Christians, however, allows us to recover some of the strategies used by those believing wives in order to regularize their mixed marriages. The strategies included: finding spiritual directors who approved of such arrangements; categorizing marriage to an unbeliever as a sin of low significance; justifying mixed marriage by the low number of appropriate prospective husbands; making the sign of the cross over one's body or over the shared bed; and blowing one's hand with spittle as a symbolic cleansing of the whole body. There were no doubt other strategies for remaining with an unbelieving husband, and also for exiting such a marriage. But attention to the published and unpublished Christians from the early centuries CE helps us begin to fill in some details regarding the interlocking and overlapping inequalities that characterized life in the Roman Empire. This particular example also helps us see the way in which a letter written to Corinth in the mid 1st century CE by a Jewish apostle for Jesus Christ soon had ramifications for communities throughout the eastern Mediterranean, and eventually influenced the structures of inequality throughout the world.

As we conclude this introduction, the editors would like to remind readers that the chapters that follow are not only the result of intensive work by individuals, but also the result of years of conversations and collaborations. Two senior scholars from the Corinthia have played crucial roles in this evolving cross-disciplinary engagement over the course of decades. In honor of their years of generous advice and leadership, this volume is dedicated to Elizabeth Gebhard and Timothy Gregory.

PART ONE

ELITES AND NON-ELITES

CHAPTER TWO

THE LAST OF THE CORINTHIANS?
SOCIETY AND SETTLEMENT FROM 146 TO 44 BCE

Sarah A. James

Introduction

A long-standing and crucial matter of debate both for archaeologists and New Testament scholars has been to what degree aspects of Hellenistic or pre-Roman Corinth survived into the Roman colony. In order to address this issue it is vital to determine what happened during the interim period, that time between the sack of Corinth by Mummius in 146 BCE and the foundation of the new colony in 44 BCE. While today there is little doubt that there was some presence in the city during this more than 100 year period, the precise nature of the activity and the identity of the actors has been more difficult to ascertain.[1] This has not stopped scholars from positing various theories, but until now such hypotheses were made on rather tenuous grounds.

The question of who was living in Corinth during the interim period is an important one because these inhabitants probably were absorbed into the new colony. The presence of such persons who were culturally Greek and retained knowledge of pre-Roman Corinth would presumably have facilitated continuity from the Greek to Roman period in religious and social practices. This 'Greekness' in the early Roman colony is often discussed in studies of Corinth in the 1st century CE, since it impacts our understanding of the socio-cultural context of both material remains and texts as papers in the two previous conferences in this series have demonstrated.[2] Such studies inevitably, and perhaps inadvertently, have also generated the same kinds of polarities, in regard to indigenous and foreign cult and burial practices and the impact of the 'Roman' elite class,

---

[1] See Gebhard and Dickie 2003, Bookidis 2005, and Millis 2006 for recent summaries of archaeological scholarship on the interim period. For the argument in New Testament studies, see for example Willis 1991 and Gill 1993.

[2] Millis 2010a; Thomas 2010; Wikkiser 2010; Bookidis 2005; Robinson 2005; Thomas 2005; Walters 2005.

that the overarching theme of inequality in this conference aimed to explore more thoroughly.

With these issues in mind, this chapter will examine the topic of Corinth during the interim period using all currently available evidence. First, I will update the state of research on the interim period. Over the past several years there have been rapid developments relating to the recent excavations in the Panayia Field and new arguments for the nature of the interim period settlement and its inhabitants. Next, based on new evidence, I will argue for continuity from the interim period into the late 1st century BCE and explore its implications for the early colony. Although the archaeological record does not directly attest to activity in the generation or so before the foundation of the colony, the material record indicates strong connections between the late Hellenistic and Augustan periods.[3] Lastly, I will suggest how some members of the interim period community may have been incorporated into the fabric of the early colony.

Land Use during the Interim Period

After 146 BCE, Corinth ceased to function as a political entity with a centralized civic organization. Other cities in the region, however, were left relatively independent. Corinth's largest neighbour, Sikyon, was considered a 'free' city in the settlement after 146 BCE, which meant that it was not directly subject to Roman taxes. While Tenea certainly survived the events of 146 by siding with the Romans, it is likely that other small settlements in the Corinthia were also largely untouched.[4] As for the local population, Pausanias tells us that many Corinthians were able to leave the city during the three day period before the sack and it is possible that some refugees were harboured in these small towns.[5]

---

[3] The issue of farm labor during the interim period and earliest years of the colony is discussed in a chapter by Sanders in this volume.

[4] Strabo on Tenea 8.6.22. Gebhard and Dickie (2003) and Wiseman (1978) propose that other towns survived as well. It is probable that the sanctuary of Poseidon at Isthmia was at least pillaged by Roman troops.

[5] In regard to the possible fate of some of these individuals, Cassius Dio tells us that Mummius convened all the people of the region and seized the Corinthians present and sold them into slavery (21.72). This same source says that this act marked the end of persecution of Corinthians. It is therefore likely that many Corinthians remained in the area of the city and those not present at that particular event remained thereafter. Inscriptions found in Egypt, Athens, and Delos record individuals identifying themselves as 'Corinthian' in the later 2nd and 1st centuries BCE and demonstrate that some of the population, presumably from the wealthier echelons of society, escaped the Mummian sack (for a full discussion, see Millis 2010b).

Between 146 and 44 BCE, the land of Corinth was officially designated as *ager publicus*, or Roman public land, which was subject to taxation by the Senate for the benefit of the Roman people.[6] We know that the ager publicus of Corinth was producing considerable revenue for Rome as of 63 BCE and that perhaps a portion of it was sold for profit in 111 BCE.[7] Since Sikyon was given control of Corinthian territory and the Isthmian Games after 146, it was probably also responsible for ensuring that the taxes of the ager publicus of Corinth were delivered to Rome.[8] How these taxes were collected is unclear, but we can speculate that Sikyon as the *possessor* of Corinthian lands facilitated its cultivation in order to pay the appropriate *vectigal* (property tax) to the Senate.[9] Some tantalizing evidence for this suggestion is provided by the references in Vergil and Pausanias to Sikyonian olive oil.[10] As there is no indication that Sikyonian olive oil was of any note in the Mediterranean before the 1st century BCE, and yet Corinthian olive oil was widely exported since the Archaic period, it is tempting to credit Sikyonian control of Corinthian olive orchards with this new reputation.[11]

Perhaps a greater question to ask is who was doing the agricultural labor on the ager publicus. Since the final siege of Corinth in 146 was relatively brief, it is unlikely that the countryside was decimated to the point that those tied to it left in large numbers; those who were small landholders or tenant farmers likely remained or returned quickly. Otherwise we have to postulate a rather large and rapid influx of people to cultivate even

---

[6] Evidence for Corinth's status is based on the *lex agraria* of 111 BCE (*CIL* I² 585) which implies that Corinth was to be measured and boundary markers set before being sold or leased. The possibility that the land of Corinth was centuriated more than once during the interim period has been hotly debated; see most recently Walbank 2002 and Romano 2003.

[7] Cic. *Leg. agr.* 1.2.5.

[8] Paus. 2.2.2; Strabo 8.6.23. See also Romano 2003, 280, n. 12.

[9] Cicero refers to the taxable ager publicus of Corinth (*Leg. agr.* 1.2.5, 2.18.51; *Tusc.* 3.22.53). Walbank (1998, 96–97, esp. n. 11) also suggests that the Sikyonians controlled the agricultural production of Corinthian lands to pay Roman taxes, although this does not seem to have been a beneficial arrangement for them given their perilous financial situation in the 1st century BCE. Letters of Cicero record that Sikyon borrowed money from his friend Atticus and was struggling to repay the debt (Cic. *Att.* 1.19.1, 1.31.1, 2.21.6).

[10] Verg. *G.* 2.519; Paus. 10.32.19; cf. Stat. *Theb.* 4.50.

[11] Finds of kiln sites by the Sikyon Survey Project and material from rescue excavations show that a new type of transport amphora, for either wine or olive oil, was produced during the interim period and suggest that the local agricultural economy expanded in the later 2nd century BCE. There are literary references to Sikyonian olive oil after the foundation of the Roman colony in 44 BCE and Sikyon did continue to produce their own transport amphoras suggesting that production continued; see Lolos 2011, 40.

a small portion of 130 sq km of Corinthian territory in order to supply Roman demands for taxes.[12]

Those few Pauline scholars of the last two decades who have chosen to engage with the subject of Corinth's population during interim period have largely relied on James Wiseman's synthetic 1979 article and more recently Donald Engel's book on Roman Corinth.[13] Wiseman presented the hypothesis that during the interim period some of the original inhabitants returned to Corinth and lived there until the foundation of the Roman colony.[14] From the perspective of historiography, the idea that Corinthians returned to Corinth was Wiseman's own interpretation of the evidence and not the consensus of the archaeological community at the time. In fact, still today there is considerable disagreement among archaeologists working at Corinth not only about the identity but also the very existence of any interim period occupants.[15] Since Wiseman's article has been so widely used by Religious Studies scholars, the current 'middle ground' on the subject in that field is that Corinth was re-inhabited after 146 BCE and that some of these people made up a small minority in the new Roman colony.[16] The fact that this interpretation has been traditionally considered the 'middle ground' is quite remarkable, since until recently there has been very little archaeological or literary evidence to support such a stance.

---

[12] Bookidis (2005, 150) implies that slaves were brought in to farm the territory for the Romans during the interim period. Taxes levied at Corinth's main harbors may also have generated revenue for the Romans, but it is very difficult to demonstrate that this would have been enough to pay Roman taxes, and even if it was sufficient, it remains unlikely that Corinthian agricultural lands lay completely uncultivated for more than 100 years. See the chapter by Pettegrew in this volume for a discussion of the economic role of Corinth's harbors during the Roman period.

[13] Wiseman 1979. Engels (1990) is widely cited, in part, because it assembled a wide variety of evidence on Roman Corinth into an accessible format, but his conclusions have been repeatedly challenged by archaeologists since its publication.

[14] This is reiterated by Engels (1990, 92).

[15] Romano (1994, 62–63) suggests that the occupants in the city center may have been Roman surveyors, but that Corinthians continued to farm the *chora* of Corinth. Williams (1979, 21) mentions squatters but without reference to their identity. Bookidis (2005, 149–51) argues against the presence of Corinthians because of the lack of evidence for interim period activity in cult places in the city.

[16] For example, Hull 2005, 9–11.

Evidence for the Destruction

One challenge to Cicero's account and the likelihood that the lands of Corinth were cultivated and inhabited after 146 BCE has been raised by the idea that Mummius performed a *devotio* in 146 BCE. A devotio is a ceremony performed by a Roman general (either before or after battle) during which the land of a conquered city is dedicated to Dis Pater and the gods of the underworld.[17] This act of dedication made the land in question ritually polluted. So if Mummius had "cursed" the land of Corinth in 146 BCE, this would have made it uncultivable and thus would have precluded the existence of an interim period community. But the evidence that a devotio was performed in Corinth (as is well-documented for Carthage) is very tenuous.[18] Of the many accounts of the ruin and destruction of Corinth, only Macrobius's *Saturnalia*, written in the early 5th century CE, records that such a ceremony was performed in the city. Macrobius's work is principally a treatise on astrology and ritual magic presented as dialogues and not intended as a historical work. There are, however, many other reasons to question this source. Firstly, the context of Macrobius's reference to a devotio at Corinth is embedded in his account of Scipio Aemilianus's performance of the same rite at Carthage in 146 BCE.[19] Other evidence for a devotio at Carthage is extensive. According to Stevens, Carthage was under a religious taboo such that parts of it were excluded from the agrarian law of 111 BCE.[20] She further cites a passage in Tertullian that alludes to a reconsecration of the land of Carthage to the infernal gods in 81 BCE.[21] Also, Cicero notes specifically that the ager publicus of Carthage included those lands 'consecrated' by Scipio Aemilianus.[22] Similar evidence for a devotio at Corinth simply does not exist. This should raise considerable doubts about the validity of Macrobius's account for modern scholars since Corinth is also mentioned in the same passage as Carthage in both the agrarian law of 111 BCE and in *De legibus agraria* but without any references to excluded or consecrated lands.

---

[17] Versnel 1976, 376–78. For a more recent discussion, see Gustafsson 2000.

[18] For an account of the ritual performed by Scipio Aemilianus in Carthage, see Macrob. *Sat.* 3.9, 9–13.

[19] Macrob. 3.9.13.

[20] *CIL* 1.200.81; see also Stevens 1988, 39.

[21] Tert. *De Pallio* 1.

[22] Cic. *Leg. agr.* 1.5.

Secondly, in the Macrobius passage, Corinth is listed with six other cities where he believed that a *devotio* had taken place. As noted by Versnel, this list of cities is quite unusual. The existence of one city, Stonios, is only recorded in this passage, and two others (Gabii and Fidenae) may not have been destroyed at all in this period, which leaves four cities (Corinth, Fregellae, Carthage, and Veii) where recorded conflicts occurred.[23] Of the last three cities, only for Carthage (and possibly Veii) can other ancient sources be mustered to support Macrobius's statement that a devotio was performed there.[24] We therefore have cause to doubt the veracity of Macrobius's list of seven cities, since the rite was probably not performed at two or more of them. It is also possible to question the presence of Corinth in this list, as it is mentioned in the same clause as Carthage and later authors habitually equated events in the two cities as a matter of course.[25]

Most importantly, if a devotio had been performed by Mummius at Corinth in 146 BCE, we would expect that it would have been recorded in at least one other source.[26] The fact that the closely contemporary accounts of the sack of Corinth fail to mention that such a notable ceremony occurred should cast serious doubt onto Macrobius's much later and far more casual report. Vital in this respect is the account of Livy, who states that a devotio was performed at Carthage, but does not record one at Corinth.[27] Certainly, if it was considered an event worth mentioning at Carthage it would seem very odd that Livy would omit it from his account of Corinth if one actually occurred. Furthermore, Cicero explicitly states that Mummius gave the land of Corinth to the Roman people.[28] If Mummius had performed a devotio and dedicated Corinth's land to the underworld gods, thereby cursing it, it is doubtful that he would have given these same lands to benefit the people of Rome.[29] Since this is in the same

---

[23] See also Versnel 1976, 380.

[24] For Carthage, see above. For Veii, Livy (5.21.2) records that an *evocatio* occurred, which was the necessary preliminary to a devotio according to Versnel (1976, 382).

[25] For a discussion of this phenomenon, see below.

[26] Other sources that reference or describe the complete and deliberate ruin of Corinth and its territory and do not mention a devotio are Antip. Sid. (Greek Anthology ix.51), Antipater of Thessalonike (Greek Anthology vii.493), Vell. Pat. (1.13.1), Diod. Sic. (32.27), Strabo (8.6.23), Paus. (7.16–17), Cic. (*Tusc.* 2.33.53, *Leg. agr.* 2.87–90; *Fam.* 4.5.3–4), Oros. (5.3.6), and Zonar. (in Cassius Dio 9.31.6).

[27] Livy *Per.* 52.

[28] Cic. *Leg. agr.* 1.5.

[29] One further possibility is that if a devotio was performed by Mummius, it only applied to a portion of the land, thereby freeing him to gift the remainder to Rome. If this

passage noted above in respect to the 'consecrated' lands of Carthage, the fact that he does not describe any Corinthian lands as 'consecrated' is very curious if a devotio occurred. In short, it can be concluded that there is no evidence to support Macrobius's report. Thus, we should treat his brief and very late reference to a devotio at Corinth as an anomaly and disregard it in the face of overwhelming evidence to the contrary. This severely limits the value of Macrobius's reference in the debate regarding occupation of Corinth and its hinterlands during the interim period.

In regard to the physical damage that occurred in Corinth in 146 BCE, an eyewitness account of the looting by Mummius's troops is provided by Polybius.[30] He reports that he saw soldiers throwing paintings on the ground and playing dice among them. In a similar account, Strabo states that many of the greatest artistic works in Rome were taken from Corinth.[31] If true, then our best literary source indicates that some of the public buildings were stripped of their valuables. Polybius's description does not, however, imply that the city was completely razed to the ground.

Although we know that Corinth was destroyed as a political entity in the fall of 146 BCE, the question of the degree to which Corinth was physically ruined is an important one when considering arguments for occupation in the interim period. Many Greek and Roman writers describe a ruined and abandoned Corinth, and while there can be little doubt that the city was burnt and plundered, these accounts are contradicted by the archaeological evidence that most major public buildings were left structurally intact.[32] We therefore should consider other reasons why the image of a ruined Corinth is so pervasive in ancient literature.[33] Letters of Cicero provide some of the earliest images of a ruined Corinth: the first from Cicero himself, who visited Corinth sometime between 79–77 BCE, and described how he spoke to people (*Corinthioi*) living amongst

---

is the case, however, we might expect it to be made explicit which lands were given by Mummius as in the case of Scipio Aemilianus at Carthage. Regardless, there is no positive literary evidence that, if a devotio did occur, it rendered the chora of Corinth uninhabitable and uncultivable up to the period of the colony.

[30] Polyb. 39.3.

[31] Strabo 8.23.6. Pausanias also describes how works of art from Corinth were taken to Rome and Pergamon by Mummius and Philopoemen (Paus. 7.16.8; cf. Livy *Per.* 53). It should be noted that the account of Polybius was used as source material for these later descriptions of the sack.

[32] For example, Paus. 7.16.8, 2.1.2 and Strabo 8.6.23. See below for a discussion of the archaeological evidence of Mummian destruction.

[33] This topic has also been treated extensively in Wiseman 1979 and Gebhard and Dickie 2003.

the ruins; the second of Servius Sulpicius Rufus written in 45 BCE, referred
to Corinth as a city in ruins.[34] Wiseman has argued that most of the references to Corinth's total destruction and abandonment occur in later
sources and in poetic or rhetorical texts where exaggeration would be
expected.[35] As evidence that such rhetorical license was commonplace,
he points out that Rufus lists in his letter Aegina, Megara, and Piraeus
along with Corinth as ruined cities, even though they were all inhabited
at the time of his visit.[36] This example and others illustrate the fact that
ancient authors commonly used words like *diruere* ("destroy"), *perdere*
("ruin, waste"), and *delere* ("expunge, annihilate") to describe cities conquered or controlled by Rome that were neither physically ruined nor
abandoned. Such a tendency suggests that there was some fluidity in the
meaning of these and related terms and cautions against taking ancient
accounts of total destruction too literally. As Gebhard and Dickie rightly
point out, Corinth was destroyed as a functioning *polis* in 146 BCE and it is
therefore possible that these literary references allude to this political and
economic reality rather than to physical ruin and human abandonment.[37]

Further indications that descriptions of a ruined and abandoned Corinth
are the result of a historiographical trope can be found by examining the
literary and archaeological evidence for the destruction of Carthage.[38]
While the punishment inflicted on Carthage appears to have been more
extreme than for Corinth, and the city itself was not re-inhabited, in
terms of the literary treatment of both cities reasonable parallels can be
drawn.[39] At Carthage, scholars have argued against the historical tradition

---

[34] *Tusc.* 2.33.53 and *Fam.* 4.5.4. Cicero makes an additional reference to the destruction
of Corinth in *Leg. agr.* 2.87. See also Gebhard and Dickie (2003, 263) and Bookidis (2005,
40) for a discussion of these works and the possible use of '*Corinthioi*' as a locative rather
than an ethnic descriptor.

[35] Wiseman 1979, 493. Rizakis (2001, 77–78) argues that the same is true for descriptions
of conditions in the wider Peloponnese after 146 BCE.

[36] Wiseman 1979, 492–93. He also notes that Livy uses the same language to describe
the fate of Corinth (*diruit*) and Chalcis and Thebes (*dirutae*) (*Per.* 52).

[37] Gebhard and Dickie 2003, 262–64.

[38] Carthage was a city that Rome 'destroyed' after many years of conflict (Plut. *Cat. Mai.*
26–27). Corinth did not have a similar history with Rome and therefore its treatment in
defeat was surely somewhat different. This, however, did not stop ancient authors from
equating events in the two cities, since they occurred in the same year and were both
restored by Julius Caesar.

[39] Wiseman (1979, 492) noted that ancient authors often describe Carthage and Corinth
collectively using the same language. For examples, see Plut. *Caes.* 57.8, Cass. Dio 43.50.3–
5, and Paus. 7.16.7–8.

of a total destruction for many years, citing literary and archaeological evidence.[40] Beginning in the 1920s, Kelsey wrote that the main monuments of Carthage were primarily made of stone and, drawing an analogy to cities bombed in the First World War, that complete destruction would have been nearly impossible.[41] More recently, Ridley has argued that the story of Romans plowing over the city and 'salting the earth' at Carthage is an early 20th-century invention.[42] If such is even the case for Carthage, which surely received the harshest treatment of all Rome's enemies, then we should perhaps not place too much weight on the literary evidence for the razing and abandonment of Corinth.

Archaeological evidence for the destruction of Corinth in 146 BCE is similarly slight. It has been argued that only buildings related to the functioning of the city as a political entity were badly damaged in the sack of 146 BCE.[43] The Columned Hall, which may have functioned as a tax office, was destroyed and portions of the city walls were dismantled.[44] Other buildings possibly damaged in 146 BCE are the North Stoa, which seems to have served as an armory, and the Theatre, which may have been a meeting place for civic or military councils.[45] Numerous official public inscriptions were also smashed.[46] Other major public buildings, however, survived largely intact including the South Stoa and the Temple of Apollo.[47] The water supply of the Peirene Fountain also remained open and usable for at least part of the interim period.[48] This selective destruction means that significant portions of the later Forum area were still habitable throughout the interim period.

---

[40] Most recently, see Ridley 1986, 141–43.

[41] Kelsey 1926, 16–17. He also cites Plutarch's description of Marius Gracchus sitting among the ruins of Carthage as evidence that parts of the city remained standing after 146 BCE (*Mar.* 40.4).

[42] Ridley 1986. Stevens (1988) suggests that the story of the salt was a conflation of historical fact and later embellishments.

[43] Walbank 1997, 96; Kallet-Marx 1995, 86.

[44] Williams 1977, 52–58 (Columned Hall); Zonar. 9.31, Oros. 5.3.6 and *Corinth* III.2, 126 (dismantling of walls). Arguably the destruction of the tax office alone would have effectively 'destroyed' Corinth because all official records of land ownership would have been lost.

[45] On the North Stoa as an armory and its destruction, see de Waele 1931, 408–11. Evidence shows that by the period of the early colony, the Theater's *skene* had lost its roof and superstructure, but whether this occurred in 146 BCE or afterwards in a scavenging operation is unclear (*Corinth* II, 135).

[46] Walbank 1997, 96.

[47] *Corinth* I.4, 100–102.

[48] Robinson 2011, 150.

Aside from Cicero's oft quoted eyewitness account of squatters in the Forum area, considerable archaeological evidence has been amassing for habitation in the central part of the city. Most recently, my own research on the fills of the South Stoa wells has reinterpreted the deposits that were once thought to be Mummian destruction debris that was cleaned up in the early years of the colony.[49] While these fills do contain a small amount of architectural fragments from the South Stoa that may be associated with a disturbance, and some wells have Roman pottery and coins that dates their final deposition to the early colony period, most of the material is debris that accumulated during the interim period. These interim period deposits are characterized by the presence of large quantities of cooking and coarse wares, a wide range of table wares and numerous loom weights, all of which suggests that this material is most likely refuse from people living in the shops of the South Stoa and perhaps the immediate Forum area. One reason for this interpretation is that the nature of these fills is strikingly different from the debris from the public drinking activity that occurred in the South Stoa prior to 146 BCE.[50] These interim fills therefore indicate that activities within the South Stoa changed dramatically after 146 BCE and evidence for similar changes can be seen in other parts of the Forum.

New constructions in the Forum area, such as the so-called miserable huts built behind the West Shops and traces of rubble walls near the Sacred Spring and at the southwest and northeast ends of the Hellenistic race course are dated to the interim period. The presence of these simple structures in and around formerly prominent civic monuments marks a significant break from the first half of the 2nd century BCE and suggests that

---

[49] Although some of the fills in question were deposited in the early years of the Roman colony, others, on the basis of their stratigraphy, can be shown to have accumulated during the interim period. The timing of an individual fill's deposition, however, does not impact significantly the type and date of the material that they contain from well to well. The fact that almost all of these fills contain imported objects and local pottery that can be dated externally to the late 2nd and 1st centuries BC strongly argues against the interpretation that all of the debris in all of these fills is Mummian destruction debris from the sack of Corinth in 146 BC (James 2010).

[50] During the early 2nd century BCE, many of the South Stoa wells had small fills (approximately 1 m deep) that consisted primarily of large numbers of drinking cups and transport amphora fragments which had been dumped into the wells to block off their water channels. The general absence of domestic material, such as table wares (plates and bowls), cooking vessels, and loom weights, from these early 2nd-century fills indicates that activity in and around the South Stoa in that period and slightly earlier involved large-scale public drinking.

the ancient descriptions of people living amongst the ruins were correct.[51] Other evidence that indicates a change in the nature of occupation from the early 2nd century BCE is the presence of new pathways attested by cart tracks at the east and west ends of the South Stoa. Several new roads were also arguably created, possibly as short-cuts, between the Lechaion Road and the Theater to areas on the west side of the city. A possible western focus indicated by these roads may be related to traces of occupation in the area of Anaploga on the western edge of the city. Although this apparent emphasis on communication with the west may be the result of bias in excavation, it may also show a reorientation towards Sikyon.[52]

New Evidence for the Interim Period

Certainly, the most compelling body of evidence of interim occupation consists of the hundreds of non-local table wares, amphoras, and coins, which date to between the late 2nd and early 1st century BCE, that have been found at Corinth.[53] These objects attest to a remarkable degree of outside contact during a time when Corinth was traditionally thought to have been abandoned. The question of who was responsible for bringing these imports to Corinth is a difficult one. Charles Williams, in discussing the presence of so many imported amphoras, suggested that the Forum area was used as a kind of way station, where the contents of these amphoras were repackaged for transportation inland.[54] An alternative suggestion,

---

[51] Two inscriptions found in the area of Corinth's Forum have arguably been dated to the period between 146 and 44 BCE and are often cited as proof of activity in the city. One inscription refers to a dispute between Athenian and Isthmian artisan guilds that can be dated externally to 134–112 BCE (Corinth Inventory No. I 1885; Corinth VIII.3, 12–3, no. 40 (dated pre-146 BCE based on letter forms); CIL I² 2662; ILLRP 342; see Gebhard and Dickie 2003, 270–72 for a summary of the historical arguments for a later date). The other inscription describes a crossing of the Isthmus in 102 BCE (Corinth Inventory No. I 788–791; Corinth VIII.2, no. 1; Corinth VIII.1, no. 31; see also Gebhard and Dickie 2003, 272–75, who suggest an interim date). If we believe that these inscriptions were found close to their original setting and not brought from elsewhere, then they suggest that the Forum area was at least occasionally occupied during the interim period as there is no reason to place expensive inscribed stone documents in Corinth if there was no one to see them until 44 BC (a conclusion also reached by Gebhard and Dickie 2003, 275–76).

[52] The modern village of Ancient Corinth occupies a large area immediately east of the Forum and because of this American archaeologists have systematically explored the western and southern portions of the ancient city more extensively.

[53] In 2003, Gebhard and Dickie (2003, 266–68) tabulated a group of approximately 300 objects. This number has since grown and of 2010 more than 350 imported objects can be dated to the interim period.

[54] Gebhard and Dickie 2003, 267 n. 50.

by Irene Romano, is that some of the objects may have been brought as heirlooms by the early colonists or are debris from short-term visitors such as Roman surveyors.[55]

My own work on these imports shows that they represent almost every region of the Mediterranean, but that contacts with the eastern Aegean and Italy appear to have been the most substantial. Knidian amphoras and East Greek moldmade bowls, including those from Ephesos and Pergamon, are two of the largest classes of objects found in interim deposits in Corinth. Finds of late 2nd and early 1st century BCE Knidian amphoras and other eastern table wares at Sikyon further support the suggestion that a fairly constant flow of traffic destined for cities on the Corinthian Gulf was passing through the Isthmus from the Aegean.

From the region of Antioch, numerous Eastern Sigillata A (henceforth ESA) vessels that may date to the interim period have been found both at Corinth and its eastern port of Kenchreai.[56] This type of pottery is very common throughout the Mediterranean in the 1st century BCE and may have come to Corinth with the Knidian amphoras and other eastern products.[57] When these vessels were recognized at Corinth and Kenchreai decades ago and they were interpreted as 50 or 75 year old heirlooms brought with the first colonists. Identification of heirlooms in the archaeological record, however, can be very problematic. There are indeed heirlooms but these tend to be ritual or special purpose shapes that are infrequently used. In general, ancient table wares tend to break fairly easily if used daily. For example, Roman pottery made at Sagalassos, near Antioch, is estimated to have a maximum use-life of 5–7 years but modern ethnographic studies put breakage rates much lower at 6–12 months for an average pot.[58] It is therefore very unlikely that any of the imported table wares dated to

---

[55] Romano 1994, 62–63.

[56] Most recently, Lund 2005, 235–37. See Schneider (2000, 352) for chemical analysis confirming the general location of production as between Tarsus and Antioch. There are at least six examples of early ESA vessels found in Corinth and an additional eight from Kenchreai. From Panayia Field: Corinth Inventory No. C 2006–37 (bowl), Corinth Inventory No. C 2006–38 (plate); from Anaploga (Corinth Inventory No. C 1965–96); from the Forum area Corinth Inventory Nos. C 1967–53, C 1967–49, C 1961–115 (based on early forms listed in Slane 1978). From Kenchreai, *Kenchreai* IV, nos. 15 to 22. Adamsheck acknowledges that the shapes belong in the early period of ESA production, but she rejects them as having been brought to Kenchreai or Corinth in the interim period because of the destruction in 146 BCE.

[57] Lund 2005, 240–41. At most sites from Cilicia to Alexandria to Berenike between 100–25 BCE almost 40% of the fine ware was ESA. It is likely that the ESA vessels came as part of trade with the eastern Aegean.

[58] Klynne 2002, 36–38.

the interim period are heirlooms; they simply would not have survived in such large quantities to be brought by the colonists.

Western imports, both transport amphoras and table wares, are also well represented in interim deposits.[59] Although not the most common type of imported amphora at Corinth, numerous intact Italian amphoras have been found in interim period deposits in the Forum area. Italian table wares, such as Campana A and B wares and thin walled wares, are also relatively common. As was the case for eastern imports, finds from Sikyon show a similar range of western products as Corinth.

Even though Corinth was no longer a viable political entity, its geographic location and two ports meant that it remained in contact with commercial traffic from the east and west that was moving through the Gulf during the later 2nd and 1st centuries BCE.[60] The fact that some of these imports found their way into Corinth indicates the presence of a relatively stable population large enough to absorb hundreds of objects over several generations.

Cumulatively then, the evidence suggests the presence of a small, loosely organized community that took advantage of the remaining buildings and benefitted from proximity to the Isthmus. The actual size of the population is difficult to estimate, but a loosely organized community of 500–1000 or more would not be unreasonable given the evidence at hand.[61] Individuals or small groups were able to accomplish minor construction projects and create new routes of communication through the Forum area. The inhabitants also had access to a significant quantity of imported objects whether as intermediaries or consumers from just after 146 to at least 75 BCE. Such a wide chronological range for these imported objects indicates that there must have been at least a semi-permanent resident population for almost 75 years. This evidence therefore casts serious doubt on the suggestions that the objects dated to the interim period were brought to Corinth by Italian surveyors or other short-term occupants. At the same time, the fact that certain members of the community

---

[59] Greco-Italic Will type 1C amphoras: C 1948–235, C 1948–236, C 1948–237, C 1948–238, C 1948–239, C 1948–240, C 1948–241 and C 1947–939; Lamboglia 2 amphoras: C 1947–839, C 1947–840, C 1947–841, C 1947–842, C 1947–843, C 1947–844 and C 1947–845 (all Corinth Inventory Nos.). Will type 3 amphoras probably contained wine and began production in the third quarter of the 2nd century BCE (Will 1982). Similarly the more popular Lamboglia 2 amphoras begin appearing in late 2nd-century BCE contexts in the Aegean, notably at Athens and Delos as well as Corinth (Lawall 2006, 272–74).

[60] A similar pattern of eastern imports is visible at Argos (Abadie-Reynal 2005, 37–41).

[61] For a less conservative estimate, see the chapter by Sanders in this volume.

were able to purchase imported and local pottery and the contents of imported amphora suggests that there was a degree of economic disparity within the small interim community. We may perhaps hazard that the individuals responsible for the importation of foreign goods were among those who consumed them. Although the idea of upper-class 'squatters' in the Forum area is a bit strange, those families who lived in the area of the South Stoa clearly had enough resources to access these kinds of goods as well as local pottery. Those individuals and families who were working the land were presumably less affluent and remain archaeologically invisible.

At the same time, the varying amounts of imports indicate that activity within Corinth gradually increased after 146 and then steeply declined after about 75 BCE.[62] But does this decrease and cessation of imported objects actually mean that Corinth was abandoned during the generation or so before the foundation of the colony? Probably not. Rizakis has noted that the number of imported goods at Peloponnesian sites declines after the Sullan sack of Athens in 87/86 BCE because of the economic disruption caused by the First Mithridatic War and its aftermath.[63] Such an explanation may account for the pattern at Corinth. However, the question still remains of who was responsible for this activity.

A clue to the identity of some of the interim-period inhabitants was found in 2006 in the Panayia Field, where a floor deposit dated to the late 2nd or early 1st century BCE was discovered in a room of the Hellenistic 'long building' (fig. 2.1).[64] Earlier in the Hellenistic period this entire area appears to have been primarily residential with some evidence of industrial activity in the form of metallurgy and the production of cooking pots. The floor deposit represented the contents of a storeroom that was probably used by a single household. This is a unique deposit in Corinth and the first one to give direct evidence of activity during this period, because the finds are *in situ* rather than in secondary refuse fill. The deposit included a

---

[62] One problematic body of evidence is the East Greek moldmade bowls. Although research is ongoing at Knidos, Ephesos, and other sites, there have been few published reports to date. It is possible that once the bowls found in Corinth have been re-dated, there may be imports that date to later in the 1st century BCE. Based on Delian parallels, the latest East Greek moldmade bowls are as late as the first half of the 1st century BCE (Edwards 1981, 198–99). The three bowls reported by Edwards appear to be the basis for the statement of Gebhard and Dickie (2003, 266) that there are imports that date right up to the foundation of the colony.

[63] Rizakis 2001, 87.

[64] The Hellenistic and earlier phases of the Panayia Field will be published in Sanders et al., 2014.

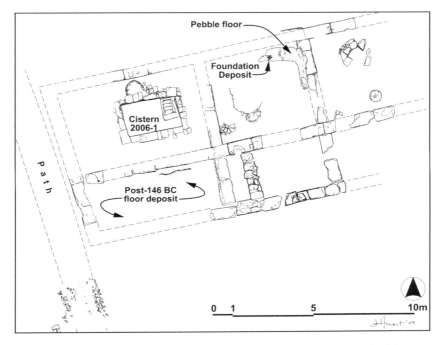

Fig. 2.1. Plan of the post-146 BCE floor deposit in the Hellenistic 'long building' in the Panayia Field. Drawing by J. Herbst.

wide range of local and imported table wares, cooking pots, and transport amphoras, as well as a lead weight, nine loom weights, an iron scythe, a bronze spade, a grinding mill, and a mold to make ceramic bowls (Corinth Inventory No. MF 2005–32, fig. 2.2). In short, the objects in this storeroom would have facilitated a wide range of activities. The imported pottery provides the date of 125–75 BCE for the time of deposition.

This deposit clearly attests to the fact that life resumed in the city during the interim period and offers some clues as to its nature. Since it is unlikely that this room was used as a storeroom in its initial phase because it was in one of the main entrances to the building, here we see an earlier building re-occupied and put to a new use – as appears to have occurred in the later Forum area. Agriculture and food processing were primary concerns, as shown by bronze and iron tools and the hopper mill, while small-scale industry is represented by the loom weights and the terracotta mold. The presence of the lead weight hints that some form of exchange was being conducted beyond the household.

Equally important in this deposit are the locally made table wares that fit within the tradition of Corinthian Hellenistic pottery. My research

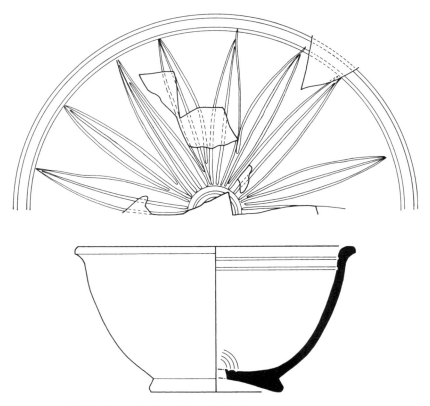

Fig. 2.2. Mold for linear leaf moldmade bowls (MF 2005–32) from the Panayia
Field floor deposit. Drawing by C. Kolb.

included a re-evaluation of Hellenistic Corinthian fine ware and it is very
clear that the pottery from the floor deposit is virtually identical in type
and fabric to that made immediately before 146 BCE.[65] As I have argued
elsewhere, there are good reasons to believe that this pottery was in fact
made during the interim period and is not a random collection of heirlooms that survived the sack.[66] Moreover, the explanation often put forward that some interim pottery may be from Sikyon can be dismissed
in the case of the floor deposit, as my recent work at Sikyon shows that
there are distinct and recognizable differences between Corinthian and

---

[65] There are strong parallels to Manhole 1986-1 (ca. 160–150 BCE), which is Deposit 29
in the study, see James 2010.
[66] James forthcoming.

Sikyonian table wares and other ceramic objects.[67] Instead, the table wares in the Panayia Field floor deposit were almost certainly made by Corinthian potters using Corinthian clays. These craftsmen must have returned to the city soon after the sack and the presence of their products shows that they were part of the interim community.

Millis's study of the grave markers of Corinthians who escaped the events of 146 BCE and died in other cities confirms that some citizens survived and thrived.[68] It seems likely, however, that those who were able to escape to places like Athens and Delos were among Corinth's wealthier and more mobile classes. The resumption of the ceramic industry would seem to suggest that those with less means, such as potters, did not go very far afield and returned to the city fairly quickly. Since it has been argued that much of Corinthian pottery was produced by part-time specialists who were also engaged in agriculture, the presence of this group fits well with the argument for sharecropping in the interim and early colony as presented by Sanders in this volume.

Evidence for Continuity and Assimilation into the Roman Colony

As mentioned above, there was a strong connection between Corinth and Sikyon during the interim period. Although Sikyon may have been struggling financially in the early 1st century BCE, my studies show that the local ceramic industry was still vital, producing imitations of Italian and eastern Aegean table wares as well as continuing to make shapes in the local Hellenistic tradition.[69] While there can be little doubt that the pottery in the floor deposit from Panayia Field is Corinthian, some pottery that was made in Sikyon does occur in the interim deposits of the South Stoa wells.

The most recognizable interim period products that were made in Sikyon and found in Corinth are lamps. Kilns found on the Sikyon survey and wasters found both on the survey and in rescue excavations clearly show that type X lamps were made at Sikyon.[70] On the basis of finds from

---

[67] I am currently preparing a manuscript on Sikyonian Hellenistic pottery, which will include a detailed discussion of its relation to Corinthian pottery and the nature of the local late Hellenistic assemblage (James in preparation).

[68] Millis 2010b.

[69] See above, n. 66.

[70] For a detailed discussion of the kilns, see the final publication of the Sikyon Survey Project by Yannis Lolos et al. (in preparation). I thank Dr. Lolos for permission to mention them here.

contexts at Corinth, this type of lamp began to be produced in the late 3rd century BCE and continued into the 1st century BCE.[71] Finds of hybrid lamps at Sikyon suggest that the type X lamp developed into the type XVI lamp in the early 1st century BCE and type XVI lamps made in cooking fabric are ubiquitous at Sikyon into the early Roman period. This is a significant point because type XVI lamps are associated with the early colony at Corinth and it was assumed that they were a local Corinthian product.[72] Type XVI lamps, made in grey or brown cooking fabric, are found in interim deposits of the South Stoa wells as well as early Augustan deposits at Corinth. Clearly, this was a popular type of lamp that was used in the city during the late Hellenistic and early Roman periods. This popularity eventually resulted in Type XVI lamps being made in Corinthian fine ware clays in the 1st century CE.[73] Although these finds could be explained as simple continuity in trade between Corinth and Sikyon from the interim to early colony period, proof that such a relationship existed opens the door to other possibilities, such as sustained contact with Sikyonians living in the city.

Perhaps not surprisingly, the strongest archaeological evidence of continuity between the pre-Roman and Roman periods at Corinth is found in the area of pottery production, namely in humble cooking pots.[74] It has long been recognized that there are strong similarities between locally-made Classical/Hellenistic and very early Roman cooking wares.[75] In fact, there appears to be almost no break in tradition in the main shapes, and the minor variations in form and technique between Hellenistic and early 1st century CE Roman cooking wares are minimal (fig. 2.3).[76] These similarities are particularly striking when a cooking pot from a well, dated to

---

[71] They are found at numerous sites in the northeast Peloponnese and at Athens and Delos (Williams and Russell 1981). It is possible that their occurrence at these sites indicates that Sikyonian products were leaving through Corinth's Saronic harbors.

[72] *Corinth* XVIII.2, 9.

[73] *Corinth* XVIII.2, 9–10.

[74] S. Rotroff has also argued for continuity in some Hellenistic types of table wares, cooking wares, and lamps at Athens after the Sullan sack in 86 BCE (Rotroff 1997). Evidence for local production of Hellenistic shapes well into the 1st century BCE has been found at a number of sites including Argos (Abadie-Reynal 1995), Sparta (Pickersgill 2009, 294–95), Olympia (Martin 1997, 212) and Knossos (Sackett 1992, 162).

[75] The confusion in the cooking ware from the earliest deposits is illustrated by the inclusions of an early Roman stewpot in *Corinth* VII.3 chytra II; for correction see *Corinth* XVIII.2, 75.

[76] Distinctive characteristics in Roman cooking ware begin to develop by the mid 1st century CE. See *Corinth* XVIII.2, 72–77 for a discussion of local Roman cooking vessels.

Fig. 2.3. Interim and early colony cooking pots. Photo by author.

the last decade before the Common Era, is compared to cooking pots from the interim deposits of the South Stoa as figure 2.3 shows – the two on the left are from interim deposits and the one on the right is Augustan.[77]

In a publication on material from an early Augustan well, Kathleen Slane also noted a typological connection to Hellenistic traditions in locally-made stewpots of the late 1st century BCE.[78] From collecting the raw materials to forming the shape and firing the finished product, the process of making pottery requires knowledge and a specific skill set that excludes the possibility that these similarities are the result of chance. At the same time, much like the table ware, it is highly unlikely that any of these cooking pots are heirlooms. Instead, we appear to be seeing continuity in tradition wherein the same style and manufacturing techniques were maintained through the transition to the early colony.

If the similarities in late Hellenistic and Roman cooking pots indicate continuity, then it would appear that we have substantial evidence of Corinthian ceramic traditions that were maintained through the turbulent 1st century BCE. However, there are problems with the data, namely the gap in the archaeological record at Corinth between about 75 and 10 BCE. Based in part on analogy to Sikyon, this is the period in which local table wares would have undergone significant changes and begun to develop into a more recognizably Roman assemblage.[79] On the other hand, because the shape of cooking wares is determined by function, their shapes tend to change much more slowly than table wares and one would not expect any significant developments over such a short

---

[77] From left to right, Corinth Inventory Nos. C 1948 120, C 1948 37, and C 1960 220.
[78] Slane 1986, 305–6.
[79] One of the first steps in this process at Sikyon is the local imitation of popular foreign table ware shapes; James (in preparation).

period of time. It is therefore reasonable to suggest, despite the gap in Corinthian evidence, that the manufacturers of pottery and lamps in the interim period may have interacted with and supplied the new colonists. Craftsmen and workers in various fields would surely have been needed in the new colony and it is only a question of how they were absorbed into the community.[80]

Conclusions

Although debates about the identity of the early colonists have seldom gone beyond the question of veterans or freedmen, the archaeological data adds a new dimension to these arguments and suggests that the incorporation of long-term local inhabitants from the region is certainly a possibility. Millis showed that the idea of a veteran's colony is untenable, especially when compared to the evidence for the colony at Patras. Instead, he agreed with Spawforth and Walbank, who argue that it was more likely to have been a colony with a significant, if not dominant, component of freedmen.[81]

The geographic origin of the colonists, or at least those elite members whose names were recorded, has been another contested issue. The use of Latin in early colony inscriptions has been used to argue that most of the colonists were Latin speakers of Italian stock. Scholars, however, have hastened to point out that most of the inscriptions were for public display and that the use of any other language in a Roman colony would have been unacceptable. In the realm of private inscriptions, however, the dominant language was Greek. Millis's study of graffiti on personal objects and manufacturer's marks on everything from buildings to tiles and pottery from the early colony shows that they are commonly written in Greek.[82] Arguably, this is evidence for a lower class of Greek speaking laborers who, although they were perhaps not Roman citizens, were actively engaging with the colony and colonists at some level.

Spawforth has argued on the basis of the names of early colonists that there was a strong connection to merchant families of the Greek East.[83] But in examining the whole of the literary and epigraphic evidence, Millis stressed the hybrid nature of the early colonists – people who could move

---

[80] A suggestion also put forward by Millis (2010a, 30–35).
[81] Spawforth 1996, 170–71; Walbank 1997, 97; Millis 2010a.
[82] Millis 2010a, 26–29. See also n. 3 in the chapter by Millis in this volume.
[83] Spawforth 1996.

between the two languages – with an elite class composed of freedmen Roman citizens and a lower class with local or at least Greek origins.[84] This resulted in a dynamic society that could interact with both the Greek East and Roman West.

Crucial archaeological evidence can now be added to these conclusions. Ceramic evidence shows that Corinthian potters were among the interim period inhabitants of Corinth. In combination with the likelihood that Corinthian farmers returned to their land after 146 BCE, we can imagine that they too formed part of the interim period community. At least a portion of Cicero's 'squatters' were therefore locals who returned to the city early in the interim period, mostly from the lower echelons of society, who perhaps lacked the ability to build new lives elsewhere. An argument can also be made that there were strong contacts with Sikyon and perhaps even that some Sikyonians were among the interim period inhabitants of the city. Almost certainly, these Corinthians and Sikyonians would have been in the lower class of craftsmen and workers required by the early colonists. It may well be that some of these people were responsible for the graffiti noted by Millis. Certainly, the integration into the colony of those who populated the interim community at Corinth is a definite possibility given the apparent continuity in cooking ware and certain types of lamps. On the other hand, Sikyon clearly had continuous contact with both Roman and pre-Roman Corinth. This evidence for continuity and connections between Hellenistic and Roman Corinth means that part of the 'Greekness' in the early colony was indigenous to the Corinthia. As Sanders points out in his paper in this volume, a large portion of the population of the early colony were probably farm laborers or sharecroppers who worked the land for the new colonists. The likelihood that these early laborers were many of the same individuals who farmed the Corinthia during the interim period is made stronger by the presence of local ceramics and Greek graffiti in the heart of the city. While this Greek-speaking element may not have constituted the elite of colonial society, they did make a visible impact on the material fabric of the city and their influence on religious and social practices of early Roman Corinth may have been similarly distinctive.

---

[84] Millis 2010a.

CHAPTER THREE

THE LOCAL MAGISTRATES AND ELITE OF ROMAN CORINTH

Benjamin W. Millis*

Introduction

Colonia Laus Iulia Corinthiensis, founded ca. 44 BCE on the site of the ancient Greek city of Corinth, may well have begun on a rather small scale,[1] but it expanded quickly over the waning years of the 1st century BCE. By the middle of the Julio-Claudian period, Corinth was a bustling merchant city and seaport, as well as, presumably, the thriving capital of the province of Achaia.[2] The city's burgeoning population was composed of a number of disparate groups, and the opportunities available in Corinth would have attracted people from a variety of economic and social backgrounds throughout the wider region, particularly from the Greek East. As has long been recognized, literary and epigraphic evidence shows clearly that freedmen were a major element within this mix of settlers, and recent scholarship has argued that freedmen were not just a dominant group, but the predominant group, at least among the colony's elite.[3]

---

* As always, I owe a debt of gratitude to Sara Strack for careful reading of an earlier draft and helpful comments. Mouritsen 2011 contains much that is generally relevant to many of the men discussed below, and I regret that it appeared too late for me to make systematic use of it.

[1] The number of original colonists is normally estimated to have been ca. 3,000, largely on the basis of that figure being given for Carthage at Appian *Pun.* 136; for example, Engels 1990, 22; Stansbury 1990, 125, 145 n. 98; and Brunt 1971, 259–61 for a discussion of the size of various colonies.

[2] The evidence that Corinth was the provincial capital is not quite conclusive, although the identification is generally accepted: Wiseman 1979, 501–2 with n. 244, Stansbury 1990, 166–69.

[3] For analysis of the evidence and for earlier bibliography (of which the most important is Spawforth 1996), see Millis 2010a. I would like to take this opportunity to draw attention to two problems in that paper (see also below, 41). Adams (2003), although not adducing evidence from Corinth, discusses in detail much that is directly relevant, especially for the picture I attempted to draw of how the Roman Corinthians mediated between the sometimes conflicting claims of the two societies and languages and reference to this important work should have been made throughout. Despite Adams's major contribution, however, a thorough collection and analysis of the use in Greek of Latin terms, with all their orthographical and morphological variants, remains to be done. Second, my collection of the

The Career of Cn. Babbius Philinus

The status of freedmen and the opportunities afforded to them at Corinth is perhaps best illustrated by the case of Cn. Babbius Philinus. Babbius, clearly recognizable as a freedman by his Greek cognomen and his lack of filiation,[4] was a Corinthian notable and prominent benefactor from the early Julio-Claudian period.[5] He held a range of civic magistracies and priesthoods; those attested are aedile, duovir and pontifex maximus.[6] The source of his wealth is unknown but presumably came from commerce.[7] He is perhaps best known among modern scholars for his crucial role in the architectural development of the west end of the Forum, where he donated the Fountain of Poseidon and the so-called Babbius Monument, although these may not have been his only major benefactions to the city. Williams offers a convenient thumbnail sketch of his career in terms of his architectural benefactions.

> [The Fountain of Poseidon] seems . . . to be more the type of monument that fits within the cursus honorum of a man at the time when he is serving as aedile of the city. The circular aedicule [i.e. the Babbius Monument] . . . may have been ordered from Athens and imported to Corinth from Athens already carved. An expense of this sort might imply the gift of a man who has arrived at the peak of his career.[8]

Finally, West notes that "the name of Cn. Babbius Philinus appears more frequently than any other in Corinthian inscriptions,"[9] although this verdict may not be entirely correct since some of the inscriptions probably do not refer to Babbius himself but to one of his descendants.

---

graffiti on early Roman pottery at Corinth was incomplete; complete collection of this material would present a somewhat different picture. The conclusions I drew from the graffiti are therefore too extreme, as is the resultant depiction of the strata of Corinthian society that produced the graffiti, and ought to be softened. I do, however, stand by my conclusions regarding the city's elite. I thank Kathleen Slane for helpful discussion of this issue; for further comment, see Slane 2012.

  [4] This universally accepted observation was first made by West in *Corinth* VIII.2, no. 132.

  [5] The evidence for Babbius is collected at *RP* I COR 111 (for other Babbii, many probably related, see *RP* I COR 106–10, 112; cf. 659–60); Spawforth 1996, 169. Stansbury (1990, 254–58) provides a narrative account of Babbius' career.

  [6] *Corinth* VIII.2, no. 132; *Corinth* VIII.3, no. 155.

  [7] Thus *Corinth* VIII.3, 100 (on no. 232), for example.

  [8] Williams 1989, 162 n. 14.

  [9] *Corinth* VIII.2, 5 (on no. 2).

Despite having reached the pinnacle of the Corinthian hierarchy, and
unlike many similar figures, a number of whom will be considered below,
Babbius has no obvious connections with Romans prominent in the East
such as the numerous mercantile families or generals. His lack of discern-
ible origins,[10] aside from his previous servile status, and his steady upward
progression through the local cursus honorum create the impression of a
man succeeding and prospering in spite of humble beginnings. What is
more, Babbius is hardly an isolated case. Despite the great strides made
by Anthony Spawforth in identifying possible origins for many of Roman
Corinth's elite,[11] the origins of many such men remain obscure, and much
work can still be done. The career of Babbius, and that of others like him,
lends itself to a simple narrative: an ex-slave makes his way to the new
colony at Corinth; he perhaps sees opportunities for advancement and a
better life; his hard work and industriousness pay off; and he eventually
succeeds beyond his wildest dreams. This rather crudely stated 'rags to
riches' story of the Corinthian freedmen occurs occasionally in the rhetoric of antiquity, most notably in the sneering epigram of Crinagoras (*Anth.
Pal.* 9.284) that laments the fact that repeatedly sold slaves now hold sway
where the Bacchiadae once ruled.[12] While Crinagoras clearly presents the
success story of the ex-slaves as a very bad thing, modern scholars have
tended to do exactly the opposite, finding the potential for social mobility
a compelling and appealing narrative that resonates strongly with the ide-
als promoted by modern Western, and particularly American, society.[13]

Even when scholars have specifically warned against viewing Corinthian
society in this manner, they have often found this characterization difficult to avoid altogether. So, for example, Stanbury rightly notes that "the
tendency to view Corinthian settlement as somewhat egalitarian or having
broad political opportunity should be guarded against."[14] Yet subsequently
he describes the career of Babbius in terms reminiscent of precisely this
tendency: "Philinus came to the colony as a freedman, developed his local

---

[10] On the basis of the cognomen [I]talic[us] of a possible son of Babbius (*RP* I COR 110),
Stansbury (1990, 256) tentatively, and dubiously, suggested that Babbius's patron, i.e. his
former master, might be located in Italy.

[11] Spawforth 1996.

[12] See also Appian's characterization of the colonists as ἄποροι (*Pun.* 136) and Strabo's
description of them enriching themselves by plundering old graves; possibly relevant is
Alciphro 3.60 (cf. 3.51).

[13] For example, Meeks 1983, 48; Engels 1990, 68–69. Friesen (2010, 232–35) provides an
instructive, and critical, examination of this trend in scholarship concerned with Erastus.

[14] Stansbury 1990, 120; see also 143 n. 82.

business and political connections, and then gained office."[15] As a final example, see one of the more hyperbolic such assertions:

> There was no impediment, legal, social, or otherwise, to freedmen partici-
> pating in and even dominating the political structure of the early colony....
> Monuments throughout the city proclaimed the servile origins of their erec-
> tors, ...but such origins seem to have imposed no impediments, social or
> otherwise, to advancement to the highest levels within the community.[16]

While such formulations are accurate enough on their face, since freed-men really did advance to the highest magistracies in Roman Corinth, they are also deeply misleading in that they imply that social origins played a negligible role in determining success and standing within the colony. A contributing factor to such uncritical and contradictory descriptions of the society of Roman Corinth is precisely the position of many of the elite as freedmen. This status has been treated as the dominant characteristic of the elite and so has engendered confusion by dictating the terms in which these people are discussed. A more profitable course might be instead to examine the origins and careers of individual members of Roman Corinth's elite, while paying particular attention to possible connections with succeeding generations, to see if a general picture emerges which can explain both the unusual prominence of freedmen at Corinth and whether or not their status as freedmen was in fact the defining characteristic of this group.

Composition of the Elite Class in the Early Roman Corinth

Roman Corinth's elite, known to us primarily through the holders of the various magistracies there, is composed of three main strands: freedmen, almost exclusively of Greek origin; Romans, i.e. Roman citizens from the West, usually members of the Roman elite and normally already active or settled in the East, sometimes having been so for several generations; and members of the Greek provincial elite.[17] Each of these groups can be examined in more detail, taking them in reverse order and proceeding from the smallest to the largest.[18]

---

[15] Stansbury 1990, 258.

[16] Millis 2010a, 34–35.

[17] Members of the provincial Greek elite may or may not have been widely considered to be Corinthian citizens and, in any case, are perhaps best viewed as more akin to foreign benefactors than as members of the local elite.

[18] In view of the prominence of veterans throughout the scholarship on the subject (Walbank 1997, 97 is a notable exception), it is worth emphasizing again that veterans played no significant role whatsoever in the colony at Corinth; see Millis 2010a, 19–21.

The smallest of these three constituent parts is composed of the
Greek provincial elites and is exemplified by M. Antonius Aristocrates.[19]
Aristocrates was an Argive notable who presumably owed his enfran-
chisement to Marc Antony, with whom he sided in the latter's struggles
against Octavian.[20] At some point after Actium, probably in the 20s BCE,
Aristocrates seems to have switched his allegiance to Octavian, if one can
judge by his involvement in Corinth and the success of his later career.
Aristocrates may never have been duovir at Corinth, as he seems to have
been at the contemporary colony of Dyme further along the coast of
the Corinthian Gulf, but probably fairly soon after Actium he did hold the
agonothesia, the highest magistracy at Corinth.[21] His tenure as *agonothetes* was presumably mutually beneficial: Corinth found a wealthy
benefactor to underwrite the considerable expense associated with the
Isthmian Games, and Aristocrates found a convenient means of expressing his pro-Augustan bona fides and of elevating his status within the
province more widely. As a non-Corinthian co-opted into the governing
structure of Corinth, Aristocrates is an early example of a phenomenon
that became more common only late in the Julio-Claudian period and
thereafter.[22] The only major difference is that, unlike some similar figures,
such as the Cornelii of Epidaurus and the Euryclids of Sparta, he seems
not to have been part of a dynasty, and thus his family did not reinforce
its association with Corinth over multiple generations. In any case, men
like Aristocrates did not form a normal part of the Corinthian elite and
must always have appeared to a certain extent as outsiders, since their
connection with the city and its governance tended to be sporadic. They
would provide benefactions and occasionally hold office, although one
suspects that the latter was mostly honorific and, on a smaller and more
local scale, analogous to the honors awarded to emperors. Their importance in this context is in showing the kind of men being sought out by
the Corinthians and, in turn, the men who saw Corinth as a suitable stage

---

[19] New evidence for Aristocrates has rendered obsolete all existing accounts of the man
(e.g. *RP* I ARG 19); the entirety of the evidence, together with a reappraisal of the man and
his career, will appear in Balzat and Millis forthcoming.

[20] Plut. *Ant.* 69.1.

[21] The evidence for the magistracies of Aristocrates at Corinth and Dyme, all of which
is either unpublished or previously not connected with Aristocrates, will be discussed in
full in Balzat and Millis forthcoming.

[22] Spawforth (1996, 173–74) gives a generally accurate picture of the phenomenon of
non-Corinthians holding office at Corinth but does require some revision in light of the
new evidence concerning Aristocrates.

for distributing largesse and gaining prestige as one step on the rungs of the imperial service.

A second group, which was involved in Corinth more intimately and in greater numbers than the Greek provincial elites, is formed from Romans active in the Greek East.[23] Their motives may often have been similar to those of men like Aristocrates, but there may have been important differences as well. Ti. Claudius Dinippus, for example, one of the best-attested Roman Corinthians and one who perhaps rivals Babbius in the frequency of occurrences of his name, seems in many ways not dissimilar from Aristocrates. Dinippus, a Roman knight, appears to belong to a family of Hellenized *negotiatores* that had been established in the East for nearly two centuries.[24] He held all the high magistracies at Corinth as well as several priesthoods and various other offices. Dinippus differs from Aristocrates mainly in the number of offices held, and thus presumably also in his benefactions to the city (commemorated by a large number of honorific monuments erected to him in Corinth), but like Aristocrates also saw benefit to himself in his involvement at Corinth, in this case presumably by establishing his family in a position of prominence in a vitally important commercial center. Earlier Ti. Claudii are attested at Corinth, and it is possible that Dinippus is descended from them and thus is a second or third generation Corinthian continuing, rather than establishing, his family's prominence there. Even so, he remains akin to Aristocrates in that his position among the elite of the province and even further afield seems to concern him as much as his place within the city's elite. While hardly neglecting Corinth and its magistracies, he uses them as means of realizing his wider ambitions.[25]

Following in much the same vein are a number of other duovirs of non-freedman origin. Men like L. Castricius Regulus,[26] L. Furius Labeo,[27] and

---

[23] A very good and recent overview of the 'Roman diaspora' is Purcell 2005a. Some older work, such as Wilson 1966 and Hatzfeld's important study of 1919, remain useful.

[24] *RP* I COR 170; Spawforth (1996, 177–78) discusses the family more generally.

[25] M. Insteius Tectus would be an obvious and important figure to discuss in this context, but an inscription discovered forty years ago on Temple Hill seems to upset basic facts in the reconstruction of his career. Until this inscription is finally published and account can be taken of its contents, any discussion of Tectus is futile. For Tectus, see *RP* I COR 320; Amandry 1988, 36; Spawforth 1996, 179 (all writing without knowledge of the inscription from Temple Hill). Once the Temple Hill inscription is published, Spawforth's concerns about "whether a Roman senator would be found sharing a provincial IIvirate with a partner of lower social status" may prove to be irrelevant (1996, 179).

[26] *RP* I COR 146; Spawforth 1996, 177.

[27] *RP* I COR 284; Spawforth 1996, 178.

A. Vatronius Labeo[28] all came from powerful and well-established families of negotiatores, as may have M. Novius Bassus.[29] Similar also, although apparently of lesser status even if not obviously of freedmen origin, are men such as L. Arrius Peregrinus[30] and L. Rutilius Plancus.[31] These men, and others like them, presumably attracted to Corinth because of its commercial possibilities, certainly succeeded at Corinth and probably did improve the fortunes of their families there,[32] but for them Corinth was not necessarily their only opportunity. They were already successful members of the eastern elite, albeit sometimes relatively minor members. Stated more bluntly, they are exactly the type of people, with the same level of social standing, who formed the local elite in towns and cities across the empire. Though a minority of Corinth's elite, they do nonetheless form a significant core of that elite. As such, they offer no evidence that opportunities for social mobility were greater at Corinth than elsewhere but in fact suggest the opposite.

Before proceeding further, one group ought to be mentioned briefly as a subset of Romans active in Corinth. This small group, poorly attested and perhaps even illusory, is composed of members of powerful Roman families who would have been at the top of the hierarchy nearly anywhere. Possible examples include C. Pinnius[33] and P. Tadius Chilo,[34] although the status and identification of both, especially the latter, have been doubted. The handful of possible cases of high-ranking Romans holding a magistracy in early Roman Corinth have been explained away on various grounds, all of which are based at least in part on the assumption that a high-ranking Roman would want nothing to do with the relatively low status Corinthian elite.[35] Although many members of the Corinthian elite

---

[28] *RP* I COR 611; Spawforth 1996, 181.

[29] *RP* I COR 432; Spawforth 1996, 180. Grant (1946, 267) seems to explicitly connect Bassus with Novii active on Delos, perhaps as bankers.

[30] *RP* I COR 86; Spawforth 1996, 176.

[31] *RP* I COR 543; Spawforth 1996, 181.

[32] Spawforth (1996, 176 and 181) argues that the Corinthian Arrii and Rutilii only gained full Roman citizenship after their arrival in the colony.

[33] *RP* I COR 475; Spawforth 1996, 180.

[34] *RP* I COR 579; Spawforth 1996, 181.

[35] For both Pinnius and Tadius Chilo, see Spawforth 1996, 172–73. Regarding the latter, who has been linked with P. Tadius, a senatorial-class Roman living in Athens in 79 BCE, Spawforth (1996, 173) argues that "the status of Chilo is unclear.... His duoviral colleague, the freedman C. Heius Pamphilus, seems an unlikely partner for a Roman of senatorial family; so Chilo was probably himself of freedman stock." Spawforth's view underestimates the status of Pamphilus, at least locally; additionally, if Chilo is connected with the senatorial Tadius, his tenure as duovir may have been little more than honorific. The possible

and the holders of magistracies at Corinth were probably not of such low status or dubious origin as their position as freedmen might imply, unfortunately there is as yet no clear cut case of a truly high-ranking Roman holding office at Corinth. It is perhaps here more than anywhere that the case of Insteius Tectus might turn out to be crucial.[36]

Even if added together, all the various cases so far discussed are only a minority, albeit a significant one, of Corinth's elite. A third group comprised the majority and the real backbone of the elite at Corinth – the men of freedmen origin.[37] This fact has not always been completely appreciated, but recent work should have removed any lingering doubts.[38] If there is evidence of real social mobility to be found at Corinth, it is surely to be found among this group: these men were, after all, ex-slaves who subsequently found themselves in positions of great power and prominence, even if only at a local level. From one point of view, the bare fact that freedmen held high office at Corinth, and did so in large numbers, is by itself irrefutable proof of social mobility.[39] This opportunity, apparently commonly available at Corinth, was denied to freedmen throughout much of the empire.[40] It should, however, be noted that throughout the

---

identification of high-ranking Romans at Corinth is further complicated by the apparent phenomenon of recently enfranchised citizens taking the name of an entirely unrelated high-ranking Roman; see Spawforth (1996, 178) for examples, among which note especially Q. Caecilius Niger, an earlier duoviral colleague of C. Heiuis Pamphilus.

[36] For Tectus, see above n. 25.

[37] How long and how far they had been removed from the Greek East, both geographically and culturally, if indeed they had ever left it, are questions addressed in Millis 2010a. The aspect of primary importance here is simply their status as freedmen and the fact that at Corinth, as apparently in at least some other Caesarian colonies, they were eligible to hold local magistracies. Cn. Babbius Philinus, whose career was briefly outlined above, is representative of this group. Mouritsen (2011, 52) suggests that the devastating civil wars of the Late Republic resulted in a proliferation of patronless freedmen and that this loss of social ties enabled many such men to emigrate, for example to Corinth. Leaving aside other issues, as far as the elite at Corinth are concerned, Mouritsen's conclusion is at odds with the results of detailed prosopographical study (especially Spawforth 1996) and is a misunderstanding of both the origins of Corinth's elite and the workings of the colony.

[38] See especially Spawforth 1996; Millis 2010a.

[39] The basic discussion of the eligibility of freedmen for office is Treggiari (1969, 52–64; 63 for the practice in Caesarian colonies); cf. Stansbury 1990, 142 n. 78; Brunt 1971, 256. The most recent discussion of freedmen holding office in Caesarian colonies is Mouritsen 2011, 74–5. Brunt (1971, 254–59) gives a brief overview of the population of Caesarian colonies generally. Corinth does seem to differ from other contemporary colonies in the large number of freedmen holding office, but that apparent difference most likely reflects the state of our evidence rather than historical reality.

[40] The use of the word 'empire' here is perhaps somewhat anachronistic, since the colonies in which freedmen held office are limited largely, if not entirely, to the so-called 'Caesarian colonies' (see previous note) belonging to the Late Republic. Further, the practice

Roman world generally the descendants of freedmen did not normally face the restrictions on holding office that freedmen themselves did, but only the same difficulties that any *novus homo* might encounter.[41] The freedmen families at Corinth were, therefore, exceptional only in that they were able to advance a generation or two earlier than similar families elsewhere. Although a potential contributing factor for this exceptionalism will be suggested below, it remains questionable whether the early removal of a barrier to holding high office is evidence for real social mobility and whether holding these offices constitutes a real advancement in social status.[42]

A good starting point for examining the freedmen magistrates of Roman Corinth is the relatively well-documented father and son pair, M. Antonius Theophilus and M. Antonius Hipparchus, both of whom were duovirs.[43] Clearly enjoying both wealth and power, they resemble M. Antonius Aristocrates, another Antonine partisan, in their astuteness in sensing the prevailing political wind and being among the first to abandon Antony for Octavian. In the aftermath of Actium, Theophilus was Antony's agent in Corinth and was charged with protecting other Antonine partisans,[44] while during the same period, his son Hipparchus was in a position to

---

of freedmen holding office is generally assumed to have been curtailed during the Augustan period (see, for example, Treggiari 1969, 63–64). Regardless of what may have happened elsewhere, the practice seems not to have ceased at Corinth quite so early, although it certainly did lessen and eventually disappear there too later in the Julio-Claudian period; for possible reasons for its disappearance in Corinth, see below.

[41] For discussion of the evidence for the sons of freedmen holding office, see Treggiari 1969, 53–62; Wiseman 1971, 16, 70–71, 86.

[42] See Wiseman (1971, 86) for the conclusion (in a slightly different context) that an allegation of obscure birth "is not in itself evidence for social mobility except within the upper class itself, and sometimes not even that;" see also Syme 1958, 587.

[43] Theophilus: *RP* I COR 76; Hipparchus: *RP* I COR 63; for both see Spawforth 1996, 176. See the relevant entries in *RP* I for the evidence for the details of their careers mentioned below. In discussing M. Antonius Orestes (*RP* I COR 68) in the same context as Theophilus and Hipparchus, Spawforth (1996, 176) may well be correct that Orestes "too was one of Antony's freedman-agents" but he is mistaken in attributing this view also to Walbank (1989, 371 n. 27), who merely notes that "M. Antonius Orestes was probably enfranchised by Antony" without declaring whether she thought him a freedman or a Greek enfranchised by Antony (the latter view is asserted by Amandry 1988, 40).

[44] Grant (1946, 267) appears to view the career of C. Iulius Nicephorus (*RP* I COR 348; see also below), duovir in 43/42 BCE, as closely parallel to that of Theophilus: "C. Julius Nicephorus, like Theophilus, was a Greek who had profited by his association with the Caesarian party." Both men are clearly freedmen of Caesar and Antony respectively (for Nicephorus as a freedman, see Spawforth 1996, 179), not provincial Greeks, as Grant seems to imply, but what similarity or evidence Grant may have had in mind beyond this banal point is unclear.

enrich himself as a war profiteer. Simply labeling these men as ex-slaves is therefore clearly misleading. They already held positions of leadership and power prior to holding high office at Corinth; the magistracies merely legitimized and provided a public outlet for power and influence they already wielded. Similarly lofty connections can be seen, for example, in the cases of some of the colony's Claudii or the duovir P. Vipsanius Agrippa,[45] himself not a freedman but probably the son of a freedman of the famous Agrippa, with whom he shared his name. Outside the magistracies one might note a man like the freedman P. Licinius, cognomen unknown, whose favored position with the emperor was proclaimed by his epithet *philosebastos*, i.e. *amicus Augusti*.[46]

Obviously, not all freedmen at Corinth had connections that reached the highest echelons of Rome's elite. Nevertheless, a large number of Roman Corinth's magistrates can be plausibly identified as the freedmen, or the descendants of freedmen, from Roman families that were active and well-established in the East, often as negotiatores. Examples include C. Heius Pamphilus and his presumed descendants, C. Heius Pollio I and II,[47] and C. Heius Aristo;[48] a certain Licinius;[49] probably the father of C. Servilius Primus;[50] and so on. This nexus between eastern negotiatores, their freedmen, and Corinthian magistracies has already been extensively documented by Spawforth[51] and is nothing particularly new. The implications of this nexus and its meaning, however, seem not to have been adequately explored or even fully realized.

---

[45] *RP* I COR 650; Spawforth 1996, 180–81. Stansbury's suggestion (1990, 193) that this man was "perhaps the descendant of a soldier enfranchised by the general" (i.e. Agrippa) is very unlikely and ought not to have the prominence given to it in *RP* I. Since Agrippa is most likely descended from a freedman of the famous Agrippa, he is not a particularly good example (*pace* Spawforth) of the onomastic phenomenon discussed in n. 35 above.

[46] *RP* I COR 375; Spawforth 1996, 179–80. For the term *philosebastos*, as well as the related *philocaesar*, see Buraselis 2000, 101–10.

[47] Pamphilus: *RP* I COR 309; Pollio I: *RP* I COR 310; Pollio II: *RP* I COR 311; for all three, see also Spawforth 1996, 178–79.

[48] *RP* I COR 306; Spawforth 1996, 179 (where correct 'Aristio' to 'Aristo'). This man was both a freedman himself and most likely a generation or two younger than Pamphilus; the two men are thus very unlikely to have been related, although they may well both have been freedmen of the same family.

[49] *RP* I COR 372; Spawforth 1996, 179–80.

[50] *RP* I COR 565 (Primus himself is COR 569); Spawforth 1996, 181.

[51] Spawforth 1996.

Negotiatores and the Success of Freedmen in Roman Corinth

I have argued elsewhere that the colony at Corinth was founded largely with commercial purposes in mind.[52] The success of such a venture depended largely on men who could rebuild the transportation routes and trading networks that had deteriorated or fallen into disuse during the century following the sack of the Greek city of Corinth. The eastern negotiatores and their freedmen were precisely the men who had the necessary experience and contacts to carry out this rebuilding both successfully and quickly. This brief outline, while generally accurate in my opinion, does not sufficiently explain the role freedmen played in the new colony or Corinth's unusual openness to them. Whatever the precise motives – and there may have been several – for the availability of magistracies to freedmen in at least some Caesarian colonies, at Corinth wealthy Romans were able to exploit this openness to their advantage, probably with the complicity or foreknowledge of the colony's founder.[53] Numerous such families had established themselves in the East in order to take advantage of the area's wealth. Any astute businessman of the time would surely have realized that the colony at Corinth would enjoy tremendous geographical advantages for east-west trade and that with the right guidance the colony could quickly become one of the region's foremost commercial and transportation hubs. Furthermore, the same businessman would also have realized that failure to become involved in Corinth would mean not simply missing out on potential gain but also facing a dangerous rival eating into his own trade.[54] The negotiatores who made this realization and were in positions to act upon it did so. Some families, for example that of Ti. Claudius Dinippus, ensured that one of their own family members held positions of prominence in Corinth. Other families, in what amounts to nearly the same thing, used

---

[52] Millis 2010a, 33–34. See also Williams 1993 (especially 31–33); Engels 1990. Spawforth (1996, 175 n. 36) provides further examples of this view, although he himself disagrees, calling it "a confusing of aims with consequences" (1996, 75).

[53] Examination of Caesarian colonies generally is outside the scope of the present paper, as is an assessment of the extent to which they may have been a manifestation of deliberate economic or social policy. Nevertheless, trends such as the easing of social restrictions on magistrates that occur in a number of them are most naturally interpreted as the result of conscious policy or at least tacit acquiescence on the part of Caesar or other leading Romans, presumably for a variety of reasons.

[54] For a picture of how trade might have worked at the time, with wealthy and powerful backers behind various levels of middlemen, see Garnsey 1983 and Pleket 1983. Note, however, that neither deals with a civic population constituted in quite the same manner as at Corinth.

instead one of their freedmen, presumably one who had already displayed both loyalty and the capacity for success.

A further ramification of this process is that almost from the moment of Corinth's founding there was a ready-made governing class whose composition was largely predetermined by powerful interests. Treggiari observes the following concerning freedmen and magistracies.

> The qualifications for office were not legal, but social and economic: prestige, wealth, education, and support. Similarly, there was probably no ban on freedmen in office or in the Senate: the prohibition was not explicit and legal, but *libertini* lacked many of the prerequisites of political advancement.[55]

Wealth and powerful backers, however, were precisely the advantages possessed by the freedmen of negotiatores who settled in Corinth. By filling the elite and the governing class at Corinth, these loyal supporters provided their powerful backers with a place in Corinth's lucrative trade and transportation network. Furthermore, since the colony was a new foundation, there were few entrenched interests to oppose this imposition of an elite, and any competition the negotiatores faced was only among themselves. Although in my view the colony at Corinth was foremost a commercial concern, Corinth's location was also of obvious strategic value, and the appearance of a supporter of an outside vested interest as duovir exactly when the occasion demanded suggests strongly the degree to which manipulation of Corinth's magistracies was possible. Thus, for example, it is highly suggestive that one of the very earliest duovirs, probably one of the first pair, was a certain C. Iulius, identified by Amandry as a provincial Greek enfranchised by Caesar but more plausibly seen by Spawforth as one of Caesar's wealthy freedmen.[56] The same is presumably also true of C. Iulius Nicephorus, duovir in the following year.[57] Similarly, M. Antonius Theophilus, the partisan of Antony discussed earlier, was duovir in 30 BCE,[58] exactly the moment when Antony needed to be certain that Corinth was in loyal hands. At a somewhat later date, and in rather different circumstances, one might also note P. Memmius Cleander, duovir in 66/7 CE during Nero's trip to Greece.[59] Cleander had been priest of the *Sebastoi* at Delphi where a decade earlier in 54/5 CE he erected a monument in honor of Nero.[60]

---

55 Treggiari 1969, 63; cf. Syme 1958, 587.
56 *RP* I COR 330; Amandry 1988, 32; Spawforth 1996, 179.
57 *RP* I COR 348; Spawforth 1996, 179. See also n. 44 above.
58 For the date, see Amandry 1988, 42.
59 *RP* I COR 421; Spawforth 1996, 180. For the date see Amandry 1988, 14–22.
60 *CID* IV 138.

In this context of selected freedmen and their powerful backers, breaking into the elite at Corinth would have been tremendously difficult. The only clear cases are individuals such as M. Antonius Aristocrates, discussed above, who were already wealthy and powerful in their own right and were not so much breaking in as being invited in. Thus, the occurrence of social mobility seems not only extremely unlikely but actually counter to the way the system was designed. To be sure, one could advance from being wealthy, powerful, and well-connected to being wealthy, powerful, well-connected, and holding public office, but this distinction would have been meaningful to few outside the small group of the governing elite.[61] To the vast majority of people, the elite were part of a closed system that offered little to no hope of entrance. For this reason, to return to the example used at the outset, a man like Cn. Babbius Philinus is very unlikely to have been any kind of self-made man or to have come to Corinth with his fortune and reputation still to be made. Without wealth and, more importantly, without the backing of a powerful supporter, most probably his former owner, Babbius would never have been able even to begin his progress through Corinth's magistracies and offices.

Social Mobility in Roman Corinth?

The picture just presented may seem to offer a bleak outlook on social mobility in Roman Corinth, but examination of the composition of the Corinthian elite over the course of time provides an even clearer picture of exactly how little social mobility existed in this self-perpetuating system. Naturally, the particular families in power at any given moment changed over time as some formerly powerful families waned in importance while other previously obscure families increased their standing, but the system was remarkably stable and presumably lasted about as long as the empire itself. Few members of a ruling elite are content to watch themselves and their families be replaced by newcomers, and this is especially true for the family-based society of the Romans.[62] Mention has already been made of the father-son pair M. Antonius Theophilus and M. Antonius Hipparchus

---

[61] See the remarks of Wiseman in n. 42 above.

[62] That the appearance of even very wealthy and well-connected newcomers could provoke great anxiety is of course well known. The standard treatment of the subject for Rome itself is Wiseman 1971. Within a provincial context, Churchin's 1990 study of the magistrates of Roman Spain provides much useful material for comparison (see 125–26 for his conclusions about the lack of real social mobility).

and of the family grouping C. Heius Pamphilus, C. Heius Pollio I, and C. Heius Pollio II, who apparently all represent different generations of the same family, even if their precise relation to one another is uncertain. These sorts of relations abound, even when consideration is restricted to duovirs alone. To cite only a few further examples, the early duovir L. Castricius is presumably a forebear of L. Castricius Regulus, duovir in 21/2 CE;[63] the latter was the colleague of P. Caninius Agrippa, who was the forebear of a homonymous duovir of 68/9 CE.[64] C. Iulius Laco was duovir quinquennalis probably in 17/18 CE, while his son C. Iulius Spartiaticus was duovir quinquennalis probably thirty years later and again five years after that.[65] From the founding of the colony to the end of the Julio-Claudian period in 69 CE, we know the names of 69 duovirs. Among these 69 duovirs, there are only 33 different family names. While admittedly not every individual sharing the same name need be related,[66] especially in the case of common names, the amount of repetition is impressive and reinforces the notion of the restrictiveness of the Corinthian elite.[67]

Despite the limited and fragmentary state of our evidence, which often makes it very difficult, if not impossible, to trace family relationships,

---

[63] Castricius: *RP* I COR 142; Regulus: *RP* I COR 146; for both see Spawforth 1996, 177. Castricius is known only from coins, where his name appears in the abbreviated form L. Cas. The resolution Cas(tricius) was first suggested, surely correctly, by Edwards in *Corinth* VI, no. 18–19 on the basis of the existence of Regulus; Amandry (1988, 36) repeated the suggestion while remaining agnostic, and Spawforth (1996, 177) endorsed it. Bagdikian (1953, 31, 34 no. 3, followed by Kent in *Corinth* VIII.3, 24 and *RP* I) suggested instead L. Cas(sius). Bagdikian's rationale for rejecting the suggestion of Edwards is that it is "pure conjecture." In fact, the resolution of the name by Edwards, even if not conclusively provable, is a reasonable deduction from the evidence, while Bagdikian's counter proposal is little better than pulling a name out of a hat. Note also that the only Cassius attested at Corinth is a poet from Syracuse (*RP* I COR 144) who victorious at the Caesarea of 3 CE (*Corinth* VIII.1, no. 14 l. 85–86) and again some years later (*Corinth* VIII.1, no. 19 l. 11).

[64] Agrippa I: *RP* I COR 135; Agrippa II: *RP* I COR 134; for both see Spawforth 1996, 176–77.

[65] Laco: *RP* I COR 345; Spartiaticus: *RP* I COR 353. The exact dates of their magistracies are secure for neither father nor son; the dates followed here are those of Kent in *Corinth* VIII.3, 25–26 (following Bagdikian 1953, 32–33, 37 no. 20, 39 no. 34). Note that this father and son pair differs from the others in that they are members of the Spartan Euryclid dynasty, and thus foreign magistrates in the same vein as M. Antonius Aristocrates. But the point here is simply to emphasize the repeated appearance of members of the same family among Corinth's magistrates. For the Euryclids generally, see Bowersock 1961; Spawforth 1978.

[66] So, for example, C. Heius Aristo is almost certainly not related to the family of C. Heius Pamphilus (see n. 48 above), although the two may well have been freedmen of the same family and thus shared a patron in common.

[67] For brief discussion of the influence of C. Iulii and M. Antonii in the early colony, see Balzat and Millis forthcoming.

let alone to reconstruct lists of successive office-holders, the grooming of sons to follow fathers into high office seems to have been a pervasive and highly successful practice in Corinth, as indeed it was throughout the Roman world. Although the real evidence has to come from the identification of family relationships between office-holders like those mentioned above, various inscriptions concerned with the Isthmian Games demonstrate the workings of this phenomenon, even if they are somewhat later than the period primarily being addressed here. The agonothesia was the highest office in Roman Corinth and was usually held as the pinnacle of a long and distinguished career. By the time a man obtained the agonothesia in late middle age, he would likely have had sons of just the age to be in the early stages of their own careers. Interestingly, a number of these inscriptions show that the agonothetes in charge called upon a son for one of the junior offices.[68] It seems difficult to avoid the conclusion that these cases are examples of a father using his prestige and the power of his position to favor a son with a place on one of the lower rungs of the local cursus honorum.

Conclusions

To return to the issue raised at the outset, in one sense social origin did not matter regarding election to Corinth's highest magistracies, if all that is meant is that ex-slaves could, and did, obtain these offices. The problem, of course, with this statement is that obviously not all ex-slaves are the same, and thinking of Corinth's freedmen magistrates primarily as ex-slaves does little more than muddy the waters. It is much more useful to think of them as wealthy, successful, and powerful businessmen who had the strong backing and support of other similar, but even more successful and powerful, businessmen, all while happening to have once been slaves. Typical Greek slave names, which then normally appear as the cognomen of a freed and enfranchised ex-slave, are certainly not infrequent at Corinth, but in no way do they dominate. For this reason, together with their connections and obvious elevated status (aside from being freedmen),

---

[68] The clearest example is *Corinth* VIII.2, nos. 82 and 84 as restored by Geagan 1968, 78: during the reign of Claudius, C. Rutilius Fuscus (*RP* I COR 540) is *isagogeus* during the agonothesia of his father, L. Rutilius Fuscus (*RP* I COR 539). *Corinth* VIII.3 no. 224, dated to the Trajanic period, may be another example (cf. Geagan 1968, 80), while in 127 CE L. Gellius Iustus II (*RP* I COR 291) was *hellanodikes* when his father, L. Gellius Iustus I (*RP* I COR 290) was agonothetes (Biers and Geagan 1970, 79 l. 4–7).

a significant number of prominent Corinthian freedmen might possibly in origin have been prosperous Greek elites, or their descendants, who had been caught up in the wars raging across the East over the previous century. Partly on this basis, and partly because the Romans often proved themselves an eminently practical people who knew how to take advantage of opportunities, skepticism may be warranted in the case of attempts to explain away, as unrelated homonyms, apparently well-born Romans appearing as magistrates at Corinth on the grounds that they would have been squeamish about hobnobbing with freedmen.

As a new foundation, Corinth did not have behind it centuries or more of an evolving society and the gradual formation of an elite within that society; nevertheless, it needed men to run the city from the very beginning. This need was met, I argue, in essence by the imposition of a governing class formed by representatives of various interests, primarily commercial, throughout the Greek East, for whom involvement in Corinth could be very lucrative, and non-involvement could be very risky. Once established, this elite, like most aristocracies, quickly worked to perpetuate itself by filling the lower ranks of government with younger members of the families holding the more powerful positions. The younger generation would work its way to the top, and the cycle would begin again. There was no real social mobility simply because there was never meant to be any. The system was designed to concentrate power in the hands of a few and to discourage attempts at breaking into this select group. While the influence and numbers of freedmen at Corinth is indisputable, to think of it primarily as a freedmen colony with ex-slave magistrates is deeply misleading. Like most places in the empire and like Rome itself, Corinth was a city with an entrenched elite, in this case composed of men who happened to be freedmen, that was very hostile to newcomers and that did its best to maintain a closed system. It differed from other places only in that, as a new foundation, its elite had been imposed *en bloc* rather recently. In its social workings, Corinth bears out the essential truth of the famous statement of Aulus Gellius (*NA* 16.13) that colonies are miniatures of Rome.

CHAPTER FOUR

"YOU WERE BOUGHT WITH A PRICE": FREEDPERSONS AND THINGS IN 1 CORINTHIANS

Laura Salah Nasrallah

> Listen to things
> More often than beings...[1]

Humans have often been things, bought with a price. Sometimes they can escape this situation by buying their freedom or having it bought for them. This is true in our own day. We hear reports of slavery and sex trafficking. Reproductive industries functionally or explicitly buy and sell the human goods required to make future humans: a womb can be rented. Ethnographers report that the poor fear organ trafficking.[2] In each case, the human, the potential human (the ovum, uterus, and sperm that produce the human), or human body parts are bought, rented, exchanged, or sold, often in an unregulated market. We may also ask what would it mean to write history in light of a sliding scale of being in which distinctions not only between humans as persons and humans as commodities, but also between things, humans, animals, and other creatures, might not be clear.[3]

Our understanding of the concept of humans as things and commodities (slaves) or as former things and commodities (freedpersons) in Mediterranean antiquity is constrained by a lack of evidence in the literary and archaeological record and data that challenge attempts to quantify ancient slave populations, slave trade, and slave prices. Yet from the quantitative and qualitative data together, we glean an impression of a vast slave trade. Walter Scheidel concludes:

---

[1] Birago Diop "Spirits" 1989, l. 152. I am grateful to research assistants Katie Todd and Tyler Schwaller, and particularly grateful to the latter for allowing me to cite his unpublished work; to Katherine Shaner for her dissertation and for countless discussions of the topic; and to early readers Joan Branham, David Frankfurter, Andrew Jacobs, AnneMarie Luijendijk, Shelly Matthews, and Larry Wills.

[2] Skinner 2008; Spar 2006; Scheper-Hughes and Wacquant 2003; Brooten 2010.

[3] Bennett 2010; Haraway 2009; Anderson 2002.

During the millennium from the emergence of the Roman empire to its eventual decline, at least 100 million people – and possibly many more – were seized or sold as slaves throughout the Mediterranean and its hinterlands. In terms of duration and sheer numbers, this process dwarfs both the transatlantic slave trade of European powers and the Arabic slave trade in the Indian Ocean.... The modern observer must wonder how to do justice to the colossal scale of human suffering behind these bland observations.[4]

My chapter takes up the topic of slavery and manumission by focusing on three short sentences in 1 Corinthians. Twice in this letter, Paul and Sosthenes say to the *ekklēsia* ('assembly') of those in Christ at Corinth: "You were bought with a price" (1 Cor 6:20a; 7:23a). And 1 Cor 7:22a contains the only use within the New Testament canon of *apeleutheros* or its cognates, the technical Greek term for a freedperson: "For the person who is a slave at the time when s/he was called in the Lord is the freedperson of the Lord." My analysis has three purposes. First, it argues that language of being bought and of being a freedperson would have been particularly significant at Corinth, a colony largely ruled by freedpersons. Second, it shows the complexity of freedperson status and the pricing of slaves in antiquity.[5] Third, it seeks to shift New Testament scholarship away from the question of whether Paul advocated that slaves seek freedom or remain in slavery and toward the multiple ways in which those in the Corinthian assembly may have heard his injunctions.[6]

How would those who first received this letter have understood its use of terminology associated with slavery theologically and materially? We have no reason to assume that eschatological thought rendered Paul, his co-workers, and the ekklēsiai to which he wrote unconcerned about the reality of slavery – that their emphasis on an imminent end made them

---

[4] Scheidel 2011, 309.

[5] On historians' avoidance of the topic of freedpersons and manumission, see Mouritsen 2011, 1–9. I am indebted to Dale Martin's insistence that we interpret Paul's language of slavery not only in terms of the idea of the Isaianic "servant/slave of the LORD" (Martin 1990, xiii–xxiii; also Westermann 1948, 55–56), but also in light of epigraphic evidence regarding slaves in the Roman world (Martin 1990, 147). For Martin, Paul's references to himself as slave of Christ are best interpreted in light of the upwardly mobile *oikonomos* or *vilicus* who helps to manage his master's affairs.

[6] Jennifer Glancy asks how slaves and others might have interpreted 1 Corinthian's injunction that *porneia* ("prostitution, fornication") must be excised from the community, when slaves could be forced into prostitution or be sexually used by their masters; Glancy 2002, 21–24; Marchal 2011, 749–70. For slavery in New Testament studies: Martin 1990; Harrill 2006; Brooten 2010; Glancy 2000 and 2004; Shaner 2012. On the significance of the earliest reception of Paul's letters (rather than Paul's intention): Johnson-DeBaufre and Nasrallah 2011; Wire 1990; Schüssler Fiorenza 1999; and Kittredge 2000.

accepting of social inequalities. The letter's reference to the freedperson and its insistence that one is "bought with a price" demands that those who had risen in status despite being ex-slaves recall the price of freedom; those in the assembly who might own slaves are asked not only to consider the work of their slaves, but also to consider themselves as potential slaves; those who were slaves might recall their price and calculate the cost of manumission. Although it is difficult to reconstruct the exact nature of the discussion, 1 Corinthians 7 gives evidence of deliberation and debate over whether to replicate or revolutionize relations of domination naturalized by slavery and manumission practices in the 1st-century Roman Empire.

The Ambiguous Status of Freedpersons

Ancient philosophical and legal sources define the slave in terms of a piece of property or a tool. Such terminology helps us to consider how, through abjection and economics, human personhood can be ignored. Aristotle, for example, states clearly that the slave is a piece of property (κτῆμα), a tool (ὄργανον) (*Pol.* 1.1253b30–32), even if this tool is a complicated thing:

> There can be no friendship or justice in our dealings with inanimate things (τὰ ἄψυχα). We cannot even have it towards a horse or a cow, nor even towards a slave in his character of slave. For there is nothing in common: the slave is an animate tool, just as a tool is an inanimate slave. There can therefore be no friendship of a master for a slave as such, though there may be for him as a human.[7]

In Aristotle's taxonomy, the slave despite his or her soul (ψυχή) straddles the line between human and thing. We find similar attempts at taxonomy in Varro's *Res rusticae* (1st century BCE). Discussing the tilling of land, he sets slaves into two categories: among humans who work the land, both slave and free; and among instruments or aids to humans (*adminicula hominum*); slaves are articulate instruments (*instrumenti genus vocale*).[8] Gaius's *Institutiones* (mid 2nd century CE) offers a tripartite division of

---

[7] Arist. *Eth. Nic.* 1161b6; translation modified from Garnsey 1996, 119. Gardner (2011, 414–37) emphasizes that slaves were property (so also Mouritsen 2011, 13–14; Garnsey 1996, 1), but see Honoré 2002. On slaves and freedmen as friends, see Mourtisen 2011, 36–65; on foundlings and on the lack of clear boundaries "between sale, pawning, and lease" of minors, see Scheidel 2011, 298–99. Regarding whether Aristotle's thought was used in the early Roman period, see Harper's summary of scholarly debate (2011b, 160–68).

[8] Varro, *Rust.* 1.17. The Latin is from Hooper and Ash 1934.

the law: law pertains to persons, to things, or to actions. The category of persons involves human beings and human beings can be "either free men or slaves," in Gaius's words. Yet slaves can also fall into the category of things, named alongside other "corporeal or incorporeal" possessions such as land, gold, silver, and other such objects.[9]

Slaves evoke questions about the difference between person and thing and the freed slave (*apeleutheros, apeleuthera; libertus, liberta*), while not rare, was sometimes interpreted as confounding the categories of person and thing, free and slave. One form of Roman law regarding manumission created a fictive drama that denied that one moved from slave to free. The *manumissio vindicta* "took the form of a mock trial," which implied that "the person had been wrongly enslaved and was restored to his or her rightful status through the trial." With *manumissio censu* the slave entered the census record and thus slid quietly into the list of the free.[10]

Roman imperial law presented a range of approaches to the transitions between slave and free and the status of freedperson, as we can see from a few examples roughly contemporaneous with the first reception of 1 Corinthians. Augustan legislation, with its 'family-values' inclinations, both stigmatized freedpersons and provided opportunities for them to cross boundaries into freedom. On the one hand, legislation prohibited a senator or his male descendants from marrying a freedwoman (or actor) and a senator's daughter or the female descendants from his male line from marrying a freedman (or actor).[11] On the other hand, those who had been manumitted unofficially (Junian Latins) could obtain Roman citizenship "by entering into a marital relationship with a Roman or Latin woman ... and having a child who survived to the age of one year." The *lex Iulia de maritandis ordinibus* (18 BCE) and the *lex Papia Poppaea* (9 CE) gave freed slaves incentives to marry and to have children: a freedwoman who had four children could escape the guardianship of her patron (that is, her former owner or the person he had designated in his will).[12] Producing children for empire allowed some freedoms. The *Senatus Consultum Claudianum* (52 CE), much revised in later centuries, stated that a free woman who chose to cohabitate with a slave man could herself

---

[9] Gaius, *Institutiones* as cited in Garnsey 1996, 25. See also e.g. *P. Oxy.* XXXIII 2673, which lists *tetrapoda* and *andrapoda* as church property (with thanks to AnneMarie Luijendijk).

[10] Mouritsen 2011, 11.

[11] *Dig.* 23.2.16, 23, and 44 (cited in Treggiari 1991, 61–62).

[12] Gai. *Inst.* 1.194. Treggiari 1991, esp. 69. On Augustan marriage law in general, 60–80; Gardner 2011, 428–29.

be enslaved or could be reduced to the status of a freedwoman, a *liberta*.[13]
The Claudian regulation thus implied that slavery is a kind of contagion:
the free woman who associated with the slave herself is mildly infected
with the slave's condition and becomes neither free nor slave.[14] Women
who were border crossers of the lines of social status and property use
were, at least the law claims, regulated and punished.

Ancient literature often characterizes freedpersons as suspect, stained
by their former slavery (*maculis servitutis*), irrevocably flawed by the
tendency to flatter, and incapable of bravery. They were degraded and
degrading,[15] even if wealthy and prominent. Such freedpersons are often
satirized in the works of writers like Juvenal or Petronius.[16] And, except
in special cases like Corinth, the wealthy freedperson was not normally
eligible for civic office; still their prestige and power offered the hope that
the next generation could fully participate in elite society.

The problems of ambiguous freedperson identity were even more clearly
embodied by freedpersons who were only conditionally manumitted.
They likely could not afford the cost of full manumission, but remained
in servitude to their masters; a *paramonē* clause dictated a time period in
which they would continue to serve their master or mistress or their children. Others were freed but required to provide a child or children to
their masters or masters' offspring. Westermann and Finley have used the
paramonē inscriptions to argue that there was a range of statuses between
slave and free,[17] and Keith Hopkins, discussing manumission inscriptions at Delphi,[18] states: "In some...contracts, ex-slaves were explicitly
required to go on working after manumission, 'like slaves' (*douleuonta* –
FD 3.3.337; cf. 6.51). Such requirements...make nonsense of the conventional dichotomy, dominant in the sociological literature, between slave
and free."[19] Moreover, the continuing link between a former slave and his
or her former master in the form of a client-patron relationship, with all
its obligations, makes problematic any clear lines between the practices of
the free and those of slaves. For like slaves, freedpersons might continue

---

[13] Harper 2010b, 610. For original texts, see Mommsen and Krüger 1905; for translation,
see Pharr 1952; see also Mouritsen 2011, 22 citing Tac. *Ann.* 12.53.
[14] This regulation does not apply to men.
[15] Mourtisen 2011, 17–35.
[16] Peterson 2006, 1–13; Mouritsen 2011, 7, *passim*; see chapter by Millis in this volume.
Juv. *Sat.* 1.100–116; Petron. *Sat.*
[17] Westermann 1945; Finley 1964. On debate over the differences between debt labor by
the free and the work of slaves, see Harper 2010a.
[18] See fig. 4.1 for an example of a manumission inscription.
[19] Hopkins 1978, 153.

to serve as tools, whether for sexual use, as embodiments of their former master's opinions (carrying his or her letters and expanded upon them to the recipient),[20] or as powerful commercial brokers acting in the interest of their former masters.[21]

Freedpersons and Human Price in Corinth

Twice in 1 Corinthians Paul tells those in the Corinthian ekklēsia, "You were bought with a price" (ἠγοράσθητε γὰρ τιμῆς at 6:20a; τιμῆς ἠγοράσθητε at 7:23a), and thus, whether slaves or free or freedpersons, they are asked to imagine themselves as things or commodities. In 1 Corinthians 6 "you were bought for a price" is an emphatic conclusion to Paul's rejection of the Corinthian slogan "all things are permitted to me" (v. 12). It is likely that the Corinthians understood their new status in Christ to lead to social and spiritual liberation and spiritual gifts such as prophecy and glossolalia. In Paul's thought experiment, such liberation and the idea that "all things are permitted" could lead to male use of a prostitute (πόρνη, v. 15). In such an act, the 'members' of the individual body, tied into the one body in Christ, commingle with the members of another body and thus produce sin "against one's own body" (v. 18). Using language of purity, Paul insists that such actions pollute the body, which he argues is a *naos* or temple, housing a (or the) holy spirit from God. Paul concludes, "Shun *porneia*" (v. 18a; φεύγετε τὴν πορνείαν).[22]

This question of becoming 'one body' with someone else (v. 16) or with the Lord (v. 17) leads to the crescendo (vv. 19b–20a): "Do you not know that ... you are not your own? You were bought for a price" (ἢ οὐκ οἴδατε ὅτι ... οὐκ ἐστὲ ἑαυτῶν; ἠγοράσθητε γὰρ τιμῆς).[23] It is likely that for the early hearers of 1 Corinthians, at least two slaves are evoked in this passage. The first is the slave who is forced into porneia – because s/he is a thing, an instrument to be used or rented out – and then excluded by Paul's injunction from the possibility of community in Christ because s/he is the agent of porneia.[24] The second slave evoked in this passage is the Corinthian who reads or hears this letter and, whether slave or free, is

---

[20] See Marchal 2011, 756–57; Mouritsen 2011, 48, 279–99.
[21] See chapter by Millis in this volume.
[22] On issues of purity, pollution, and porneia, see also the chapter by Johnson Hodge in this volume.
[23] Mason 1971, 160–65 exemplifies scholarship that sees Paul's reference to porneia as an accurate reflection of Corinthian vice.
[24] Glancy 2002, 65–67; Marchal 2011, 759.

confronted with the idea that s/he is bought for a price and thus rendered a slave, required to glorify God in his or her body. The passage raises the question: Who has the power to control the purity of his or her body? To whom does one belong?

Paul again brings the Corinthians into the *statarion* or slave market in a section on manumission and freedom in 1 Corinthians 7: "You were bought for a price; do not become slaves of humans" (v. 23). Papyrological evidence shows that the use of τιμῆς with a verb (as in 1 Cor 6:20 and 7:23) highlighted the issue of cost, whether of grain or, in this situation, of people.[25] Such terminology would have confronted those Corinthians familiar with the language of trade and purchase with the question of human pricing. The ability *to be bought*, to become a slave of the Lord, liberates the Corinthians from the condition of being slaves to humans (but only) by rendering them slaves of God. The mechanics and material realities of this transfer of sale are unclear, but in 1 Corinthians 7 it is linked to manumission: the preceding verse contains the only use in the New Testament of the technical term for freedperson (ἀπελεύθερος, v. 22).

It may not be coincidental that the only reference in the New Testament to the status of freedperson occurs in 1 Corinthians. Numismatic evidence indicates that a mix of freedmen and traders became leaders in Corinth upon the founding of the new colony.[26] Although freedpersons were not usually eligible for magistracies, Caesar made exceptions for colonies he founded, and at Corinth ex-slaves, not military veterans, joined the Greek community that still inhabited the city.[27]

Because Corinth was a freedperson's colony, some saw it as populated by "a mass of good-for-nothing slaves," in 1st-century BCE poet Crinagoras's language.[28] Spawforth explains that these were "the 'men without means', ἄποροι with whose demands for land Appian linked Caesar's foundation of Corinth (*Pun.* 136)."[29] Yet the rhetoric of low-status freedpersons may be precisely aimed to discredit the high-status freedpersons who emigrated to Corinth to take advantage of this commercial hub. Prominent ex-slaves, tied by the patronage system to their masters, could conduct business for

---

[25] Arzt-Grabner et al. 2006, 241–42.

[26] Spawforth 1996, esp. 169.

[27] Treggiari 1969, 63–64; Millis in this volume; Millis 2010a, 17–21; Williams 1993, 33. On Jewish slaves at Corinth, see Josephus *BJ* 3.540; on continuity of inhabitation, see the chapter by James in this volume.

[28] Harrill 1995, 71.

[29] Spawforth 1996, 169; Millis (in this volume; and 2010a, 22, 34) is more sanguine about the Corinthian freedperson's social status.

their masters (often wealthy, powerful *negotiatores*) and themselves at an important port between west and east.[30] Corinth rose as a crucial business center in the 1st century CE,[31] perhaps even emerging as a key site of the eastern slave trade.[32]

Some freedmen in Corinth monopolized high civic positions and thus the key city center of the Forum was marked by freedperson benefactions.[33] Perhaps the most famous example of a freedman civic leader and benefactor is Cn. Babbius Philinus, pontifex, aedile, and duovir who thrived in Corinth in the first half of the 1st century CE and left significant monuments, including the Fountain of Poseidon in the Forum.[34] We also find freedmen at the Tiberian-period monument of the *Augustales*; its base indicates that at least two freedmen participated – clearly so marked because of the inscription 'L' (for *libertus*) – and onomastic evidence suggests that an even greater number of freedmen were involved. Participation in the *Augustales* was in part a means for freedpersons and their children to advance socially and to exhibit wealth.[35] The placement of dedications from Cn. Babbius Philinus and the *Augustales* thus locate freedmen in a prominent place, within the Forum, at a key center of politics, religion, and history.[36]

Thus, at the time of Paul's visits to the city, Roman Corinth was run in part by freedpersons, and prominent freedpersons continued to be visible in the public square through their benefactions and the monuments that honored them. The lives of poorer freedpersons and of slaves at Corinth are harder to reconstruct, although we have some evidence in 1 Corinthians. It is clear in 1 Corinthians 7 and implicit elsewhere in the letter that slaves were participants in the assembly in Christ.[37]

---

[30] Millis in this volume; Williams 1993; Slane 2000. Regarding onomastic evidence, see Millis 2010a, 22. For a discussion of the literary evidence for Corinth as an emporion, see the chapter by Pettegrew in this volume.

[31] Slane 2000, 310. Trade probably continued during the period between Mummius's sack and Caesar's refoundation of Corinth as colony (James in this volume).

[32] Harrill 1995, 73. See Millis in this volume on the business hazards of ignoring Corinth's potential.

[33] See the chapter by Millis in this volume.

[34] Koester 2005; Laird 2010; Millis in this volume.

[35] The *Augustales* were largely a western phenomenon and, so far as we know, existed only at Patrae and Corinth in Achaia (Laird 2010).

[36] Robinson 2005.

[37] Primary discussants in the debate concerning the social and economic status of the ekklēsiai to which Paul traveled include Deissmann 1927; Meeks 1983; Friesen 2004; Meggitt 1998 (critiqued in Martin 2001). For a fairly optimistic view of the economy and access to food in the early empire, see Jongman 2003. The reference in 1 Cor 11:22 to "those

Short but difficult-to-understand passages like 1 Cor 7:17–24 challenge us to think about the impact of this letter on those slaves and freedpersons at Corinth who first received it. First Corinthians 7:17–24 forms a *digressio* or *parekbasis* to the chapter's discussion of married or unmarried status and Paul's advice neither to divorce nor to marry unless the latter is perceived to be absolutely necessary.[38] In the digressio, identities of circumcised/uncircumcised and slave/free become thought experiments in the question of whether one can change or choose one's status.[39] Paul begins:

> Εἰ μὴ ἑκάστῳ ὡς ἐμέρισεν ὁ κύριος, ἕκαστον ὡς κέκληκεν ὁ θεός, οὕτως περιπατείτω. καὶ οὕτως ἐν ταῖς ἐκκλησίαις πάσαις διατάσσομαι.

> Nevertheless, as God has called each, as the Lord has allocated to each, let each walk in this manner. So also, I make arrangements in all the assemblies (v. 17).

Elsewhere in the passage we find the verb μενεῖν ("remain"), which offers a similar concept to the one found here in v. 17: keep living (περιπατεῖν) in a certain way. By saying that he orders all the ekklēsiai in this manner, Paul conjures a larger set of assemblies whose behavior the Corinthians should match.[40] Given the preponderance of freedpersons in Corinth, and given the way in which manumission might already be on their minds, the Corinthians could have understood their situation to be exceptional. Paul insists that they temper their exceptionality. In addition, their status as "called" (κλῆσις, καλεῖν), which earlier in the letter indicated their chosenness and transformation (e.g., 1 Cor 1:2), here marks only their social status as "called" while un/married, un/circumcised, or un/free.

Verse 20 comes at the midpoint of chapter 7 and summarizes Paul's argument: "Let each remain (μενέτω) in the calling in which s/he was called." The verb 'remain' (μενεῖν) is an injunction and a refrain in the

---

who have not" may indicate that some in the community were living below subsistence levels (Friesen 2005). Reference to "those of Chloe" (1 Cor 1:11) provides possible evidence of a slave-holding woman; so too, reference to the "household of Stephanas" may indicate a slave-holding household (1:16). Such references may indicate a few with wealth within the early Corinthian ekklēsia and that male and female owners and their slaves participated together within the community.

[38] Dawes 1990, 683; see the overview in Fitzmyer 2008, 306. On these verses as pertaining to ethnicity, see Johnson Hodge in this volume and Cohen 2011.

[39] See Harrill 1995, 108–28 on the philology and context of 1 Cor 7:21. On the question of whether slaves could reject an offer of manumission, see Bartchy 1973.

[40] See 1 Cor 11:16; Wire 1990, 32–33.

chapter (vv. 8, 11, 20, 24, 40).[41] The digressio has a clear structure: verse 17 contains the concept of remaining as one is; this is echoed at verse 24 and appears at the midpoint in verse 20.

If we think of this chapter as functioning in part as a discussion of the three categories that occur in the baptismal formula in Gal 3:28 (Jew/ Greek, slave/free, male/female), we see that Paul offers, in the midst of a discussion of marriage (thus involving male and female), first a comment on the condition of circumcision or uncircumcision (thus involving Jew and Greek). He states clearly: do not seek circumcision, and do not hide circumcision. What challenges the interpreter is the ambiguity of the second comment, involving slave and free:

> δοῦλος ἐκλήθης, μή σοι μελέτω· ἀλλ' εἰ καὶ δύνασαι ἐλεύθερος γενέσθαι, μᾶλλον χρῆσαι. ὁ γὰρ ἐν κυρίῳ κληθεὶς δοῦλος ἀπελεύθερος κυρίου ἐστίν, ὁμοίως ὁ ἐλεύθερος κληθεὶς δοῦλός ἐστιν Χριστοῦ. τιμῆς ἠγοράσθητε· μὴ γίνεσθε δοῦλοι ἀνθρώπων. ἕκαστος ἐν ᾧ ἐκλήθη, ἀδελφοί, ἐν τούτῳ μενέτω παρὰ θεῷ.

> Were you a slave when called? Don't let it concern you. But even if you can gain your freedom, rather[42] use it. For s/he who was called in the Lord as a slave is a freedperson of the Lord. Likewise s/he who was free when called is a slave of Christ. You were bought with a price; do not become slaves of humans. So, brothers and sisters, in whatever state each was called, remain with God. (vv. 21–24)

Paul again frames his discussion of slave/free status in light of calling (ἐκλήθης, κληθείς). But here calling has lost its quality of privilege and has become a stasis in status: Stay as you were called.[43]

Whether Paul insists that people 'remain' in the situation of slavery has been – and continues to be – debated. In 1 Cor 7:21, in the midst of his passage on slave, free, and freedman, we stub our interpretive toe on an unfinished ellipsis, as other scholars and interpreters have for centuries. "Were you a slave when called? Don't let it concern you. But even if you can gain your freedom, rather, use it." Scholars debate which noun belongs after the infinitive. Does one go back to the closest noun, ἐλεύθερος, and thus supply 'freedom' after μᾶλλον χρῆσαι? Does one look

---

[41] See the conceptual equivalents of μενεῖν in vv. 17, 26. Fitzmyer (2008, 305) entitles 7:17–24 as "Basic Principle: Remain in the Status in Which You Were Called."

[42] Harrill 1995, 108–21. Llewelyn (1989, 67–70) instead reads μᾶλλον as "all the more." Fitzmyer (2008, 309) translates it "take advantage of."

[43] Harrill (1995, 76) explains that those who follow a philological analysis usually conclude that Paul meant "use freedom" while those who follow a contextual analysis normally conclude that Paul meant "stay as you are."

to the larger theme of the passage, with its banging repetition of μενέτω, and instead supply δουλεία ("slavery")? The grammatical uncertainty is not a matter of our weak grasp of 1st century-*koinē*: roughly three centuries after the writing of 1 Corinthians, John Chrysostom's community debated whether to supply 'freedom' or 'slavery' in the phrase μᾶλλον χρῆσαι.[44] The Corinthians who received this letter – in the absence of further or prior discussions in their own ekklēsia – were likely as baffled as we are about the meaning of these words. We may wonder whether they sought clarification from the carrier of Paul and Sosthenes's letter, who was likely a freedperson or slave; such letter carriers were often expected not only to deliver their masters' correspondence, but also to voice and to interpret its contents.[45]

Many scholars, in the face of such translational and interpretive uncertainty, attempt to neutralize the passage's revolutionary idea of seeking freedom, on the one hand, or its horrifying quietism of staying enslaved, on the other. They do so by reading the passage as 'merely' eschatological or theological. Conzelmann, for example, arguing that the passage should be read as an injunction to stay within slavery and to use it, entitles his analysis of 1 Cor 7:17–24 "Eschatological Freedom."[46] He and many other commentators impute to Paul (and thus to 'his' churches) a disinterest in material conditions on account of expectation of an imminent parousia (διὰ τὴν ἐνεστῶσαν ἀνάγκην, 7:26) or popular Stoic injunctions to be free philosophically, no matter your legal status. Conzelmann's conclusion is, "No change of status brought about by myself can further my salvation. . . . In the Church worldly differences are already abrogated."[47] Richard Horsley, a prominent liberationist interpreter, argues that Paul is a social revolutionary.[48] Yet he, like Conzelmann, misses the opportunity to think about material and social realities of slavery at Corinth. Horsley reads Paul's "bought with a price" not in light of the commodification of humans as σώματα ("bodies," sometimes with the meaning "slaves") but as a cosmological concept having to do with God's redemption, a metaphorical purchase (ἐξαγοράζειν) of the person into an apparently immaterial

---

[44] Harrill 1995, 77–78.

[45] Mouritsen 2011, 48. "Chloe's people" reported something to Paul, and presumably Paul sends messages through people who function as his clients, if not slaves.

[46] Conzelmann 1975, 125; Fitzmyer 2008, 309. In contrast, Harrill 1995 and others supply *eleutheria*, i.e., "take advantage rather of (such) freedom."

[47] Conzelmann 1975, 126.

[48] Horsley 1998, 100–3; see Harrill 1995, 74–75 on scholars' misunderstandings of social conservatism in antiquity.

liberation: "Paul's point is to check what he sees as a self-centered empowerment of certain Corinthians, not to present the new life as 'slavery' to
God."[49]

The phrase "bought with a price" had caught the scholarly interest of
Adolf Deissmann at the turn of the 20th century. Deissmann argued that
manumission inscriptions at the precinct of the god Apollo at Delphi were
relevant for reading 1 Corinthians 6–7. Deissmann interprets the reference
in 1 Cor 7:22 to being "the Lord's freedperson" as similar to the mechanism
by which slaves were manumitted at Delphi, where thousands of inscriptions say that slaves were sold to the god Apollo.

> St. Paul is alluding to the custom referred to in these records when he speaks
> of our being made free by Christ. By nature we are *slaves* of sin, of men, of
> death; the Jew is furthermore a *slave* of the law, the heathen a *slave* of his
> gods. We become *free men* by the fact that Christ *buys* us. And He has done
> so: –
> "Ye were bought with a price,"
> says St. Paul in two places, using the very formula of the records, "with a
> price."[50]

Conzelmann and others have argued against Deissman's use of the
Delphi inscriptions to interpret this passage in Corinthians. Indeed,
they are correct insofar as we cannot clearly establish that Paul or the
Corinthians have the Delphic formulation in mind: are those in Christ
at Corinth analogous to slaves manumitted at Delphi by being sold to
the god?[51] But Conzelmann and others who dismiss Deissmann are also
wrong. Deissmann reminds us that those who point to 1 Corinthians 7 as
having only an "eschatological" force miss the opportunity to consider
the alternative: the Corinthian responses to the resounding injunction to
"remain as you are," and the responses to the puzzling (to us and to them?)
statement μᾶλλον χρῆσαι.

The inscriptions at Delphi and elsewhere that fall under the scholarly
category 'sacral manumission' expand the possibilities of interpretation
by giving us a larger, if not local, context for the Corinthian response. They
help us to understand the pricing of humans, the value of their labor and
of their selves and their kin as things. These, along with scant evidence
from Egyptian papyri, are nearly the only evidence we have of the price

---

[49] Horsley 1998, 63. Note that Horsley nonetheless recognizes (103) that slaves likely
participated in the Corinthian community, pointing to two in Stephanas's household
whose names hint at slave status: Fortunatus (Lucky) and Achaicus (the Achaian).

[50] Deissmann 1927, 323–24.

[51] Conzelmann 1975, 128.

of slaves.[52] Looking at the transaction of humans – a bare transaction that occurs under the eyes of and even with the help or by the agency of (the) god – helps us to understand the range of knowledge and experience that Corinthian believers may have brought to Paul's letter and to concepts of being a slave of this new God, in a new assembly in Christ.

A Market for People and Things

Although we have some evidence of high-status freedpersons at Corinth in the 1st century CE, we unsurprisingly have scant local evidence about slaves. Yet Paul's twice-repeated phrase, "You were bought with a price," calls attention to the material reality that humans can be things to be purchased and sold, leading us to search more broadly through evidence for slave prices and slave markets in antiquity, in Delphi and elsewhere.[53] I began by citing Scheidel's comments about the number of humans – σώματα – bought and sold in the Roman Empire (cf. Rev 18:13). What these bodies were worth varies, and that variation and its causes are difficult to trace.[54] Here I survey evidence about slave price, including matters that affect price and sale, such as legal debate concerning potential defects, *paramonē* clauses which require the now former slave to stay and 'slave' for the master, and contractual obligations to leave behind one or more children for the master's family.

Ephesos, Rome, and Delos were famous for their slave markets, but other cities perhaps had occasional markets or, in the case of evidence from Baetocaece in Syria, bi-weekly markets.[55] Monika Trümper's collection of inscriptions about *stataria* and other possible locations for slave markets helps us to glimpse the slave market at Ephesos,[56] a city in which Paul stayed and likely from which he penned 1 Corinthians. Fragments of a statue base found in the vicinity of the Tetragonos Agora in the lower city honor the proconsul of Asia (42/43 CE), C. Sallustius Crispus Passienus, for his role as "a patron of those who do business in the slave market (*qui in*

---

[52] Straus 2004; Hopkins 1978, 139; Harper 2010a, 214; Mouritsen 2011.

[53] Harper 2010a; Scheidel 2011.

[54] Along with scholars like Scheidel, see Hopkins 1978 and Jongman 2003. On the interchangeability and mutual influence of free wage labor and slave labor, see Harper 2010a, 213–14; and Temin 2004, 513–38. On manumission as incentive, see Harper 2010a, 214.

[55] Scheidel 2011, 301.

[56] Trümper (2009, 73) finds no evidence of a building constructed as a slave market, she cites Coarelli's argument that the Serapion served this purpose. Stat. Silv. 2.1.72 hints at a rotating platform on which slaves stood.

statario negotiantur)."[57] This same group dedicated a statue to freedman Tiberius Claudius Secundus in the Tetragonos Agora in ca. 100 CE.[58]

The prices of slaves in those markets elude scholars. As those who study the economy of slavery in the Roman world admit, attempts to translate the costs recorded in inscriptions to 'real dollar value' are difficult. But references to slave prices accumulated from the Delphi manumission inscriptions, from papyri recording the Egyptian census, and from other sources indicate that from the 1st to the 3rd centuries CE, a young adult slave with moderate skills would be worth approximately four tons (plus or minus 50% [!]) of wheat equivalent,[59] which is slightly more than three years' survival for a peasant family at subsistence levels.[60] In addition, a slave's *timē* or price varied according to at least four different attributes: age, sex, ethnic origin, and skills.[61]

A primary source of data comes from the precinct of Apollo at Delphi where, from the 2nd century BCE to the 1st century CE, slave prices were recorded in roughly 1,000 inscriptions, mentioning more than 12,000 slaves.[62] The inscriptions, neatly written and tightly packed (figs. 4.1 and 4.2), cover the polygonal masonry that forms the retaining wall of the famous Temple of Apollo and are scattered elsewhere along the Sacred Way. They creep past that temple into the theater above it, lining *parodoi* and the seats and steps of the *cavea*.

Hopkins and others after him have mined these inscriptions to construct a diachronic, thick analysis of slave prices, even if trends are hard to explain. From the manumissions at Delphi, it is clear that the price of freedom increased from the 2nd century BCE to the 1st century CE. In the case of male slaves, the cost for full freedom doubled, and the cost of conditional release (i.e., freedom with a *paramonē* clause) rose 10%; for female slaves, the cost of full freedom rose 28%, and the cost of conditional release 14%.[63] Intimacy brought few rewards. There is no significant

---

[57] Trümper 2009, 22.

[58] Trümper 2009, 22–23. Archaeological evidence for slave traders is scarce (Scheidel 2011); for two examples, see Trümper 2009, 23 (Thyatira); and Duchêne 1986 (briefly discussed in Morris 2011, 191) for a freedman-turned-slave-dealer who also depicts a gang of chained slaves (Amphipolis).

[59] Scheidel 2011, 303.

[60] Using Hopkins (1978, 146) for conventional wheat prices: 400 drachma (commonly paid for *paramonē*) = 3.5 tons of wheat = 3 years of food for peasant family.

[61] Harper 2010a, 211 (versus the 34 attributes assessed from evidence from slavery in the ante-bellum United States); Harper 2011b. On ethnicity, see, e.g., *Dig.* 21.31.21.

[62] Hopkins 1978.

[63] Hopkins 1978, 161.

Fig. 4.1. Close-up of manumission inscription on the polygonal masonry of the retaining wall of the Temple of Apollo, Delphi. Photo: J. Gregory Given and the Harvard Archaeology of the New Testament World Project.

Fig. 4.2. Stoa of the Athenians and retaining wall, looking up to the columns of the Temple of Apollo. Sanctuary of Apollo, Delphi. Photo: J. Gregory Given and the Harvard Archaeology of the New Testament World Project.

reduction in the price of one's freedom if one is home-born (*oikogenēs*) or bought from outside (6% cheaper if home-born); nor, in one case, is one's freedom less dear if one is a slave who is also (likely, given that they share the same name) the master's son.[64]

In addition to the increasing expense of manumission, other ancillary costs were high. At both Delphi in the 1st century BCE and Kalymna (opposite the island of Kos) in the 1st century CE, it seems to have been "increasingly common for masters to make explicit provision in the manumission contract about the status of children born during service."[65] Sometimes one was required to leave a child, and rarely two, to the master or the master's offspring (e.g., *FD* 3.6.38). Contracts stipulate that these children would have to be one to two years old; such age requirements served as a minor guarantee of the product, since the child would have passed one significant hurdle of mortality.[66] Sometimes one could pay a fee if unable to provide a child.[67]

Two inscriptions exemplify the complexities of manumission, especially of *paramonē* agreements and slave children. The first, from Delphi, dates to the first half of the 1st century CE.[68] It is completely preserved, carved into a block on the podium of the Theater.

> ... Sophrona with the consent of her son Sosandros gives over to the Pythian Apollo for freedom a home-born female slave (σῶμα) by the name of Onasiphoron, for the price of three *mnae*, and he has received the entire price. So also Onasiphoron entrusted the contract to the god, by whom she is free and no one can claim her as slave, nor does she belong at all to anyone in any way. Eukleidas Aiakida is the guarantor according to the laws.... But let Onasiphoron remain (παραμείνατο) with Sophrona all the years of her life, doing what is commanded uncomplainingly, but if she does not do it, let Sophrona have the authority to lay a penalty upon (her) in whatever way she wishes. Let Onasiphoron give a child (βρέφος) to Sosandros. It is executed according to law, which is engraved in the sanctuary of Apollo...[69]

---

[64] Hopkins 1978, 154. Mouritsen attempts to answer the question of who paid for manumission (2011, 162–66, 170). Scheidel (2008, 123), finding slaves more expensive in the Roman Empire than in classical Athens, argues that they were a luxury item in the Roman period.

[65] Hopkins 1978, 155.

[66] See Bagnall and Frier 1994.

[67] Hopkins 1978, 155–56.

[68] The twenty-seventh priesthood, ca. 20–46 CE.

[69] *FD* 3.6.36, accessed online through Packhard Humanities Institute. I thank Tyler Schwaller for pointing me to these 1st-century CE inscriptions. A scan for *breph** in *FD* (3.3 and 3.6) reveals 10 inscriptions demanding at least one child. See also *FD* 3.3.313 and Hopkins 1978, 143 regarding Euridika.

Another example from the first half of the 1st century CE comes from
Kalymna. The almost half-meter square slab of white marble, found in
secondary use as pavement in a Christian church, reads:

> In the reign of Claudianos, the twentieth of the month of Dalios. Epicharis
> daughter of Zoilos freed her own slave Isidotos on the condition that he
> remains with (παραμένει) her and her husband Neikephoros for the rest
> of their lives. After their death, he shall rear for her children Doras and
> Onesimes each a little male nursling, or give as payment 50 denarii for
> use.... But if he does not stay, let him give every day...[the daily payment
> is missing].[70]

"She is free," says the inscription from Delphi; "she has freed her own slave,"
says the inscription from Kalymna. In both cases, we may sense promise –
a hope of freedom – soon compromised, we may feel, both by *paramonē*
clauses and by the demand that the slaves Onasiphoron and Isodotos leave
behind children in slavery or raise children to be slaves.

Complexities regarding manumission or sale were not limited to
paramonē agreements or the requirement to leave an enslaved child; 'disease and defect' also affected slave price. With the sale of slaves as of
livestock, buyers and sellers wondered how to guarantee the quality of the
thing sold.[71] Justinian's *Digest* 21 treats this topic of worth and information in legal rulings and debates, including materials from the 1st and 2nd
centuries CE. Recorded within it is the Edict of the Curule Aediles, which,
according to Ulpian, concerns "the sales of things immovable as much
as of those movable or animate" (*Dig.* 21.1.1).[72] Many such edicts seek to
secure the buyer against what we could call a 'lemon,' a thing that looks
useful but turns out to be broken once you get it home: "This edict was
promulgated to check the wiles of vendors and to give relief to purchasers
circumvented by their vendors" (*Dig.* 21.1.2). The slave vendor needed to
disclose the slave's 'defect and disease.'[73]

Debates of subsequent legal experts on what constitutes defect and
disease – and whether this formulation is merely pleonastic – help one
to imagine the slave as an item with a subinventory. Defects and diseases
which Roman legal experts debate include what we would call mental

---

[70] Segré 1944–45, 188: *Tituli Calymnii* 171 (accessed online through Packard Humanities
Institute); the inscription dates to ca. 14–54 CE and is likely from the Temple of Apollo.

[71] Ratzan 2011, on *sortes* as an attempt to glean business information. See Gardner 2011,
416 on injury and cost.

[72] All translations are from Watson 1985.

[73] Crook 1967, 181.

illness, learning disorders, speech defects (*Dig.* 21.1.10, 12), loss of fingers and toes (21.10), women who produced stillborn infants (21.1.14), those who had suicidal tendencies (21.1.23.3), slaves who had previously attempted to run away (21.1.17),[74] those missing teeth (21.1.11) or who had had the tongue cut out (21.1.8), criminality, and even those tending to religious fanaticism (21.1.1.9) – an accusation that could have been directed toward those first hearing 1 Corinthians.[75] A slave's value could decrease not only because of age or injury, but also for moral and ethical causes.[76] If a slave has a "bad habit, cavorting around the shrines and uttering virtually demented ravings," it is a mental defect "and so constitutes no ground for rescission," according to Vivianus (*Dig.* 21.1.1.10), a conclusion further confirmed by Pomponius, who explained:

> [A] vendor is not required to produce a slave of full intellect, still if he sell one so silly or moronic that he is useless, there is a defect under the edict. Generally, the rule which we appear to observe is that the expression 'defect and disease' applies only in respect of physical defects; a vendor is liable in respect of a defect of mind, only if he undertake liability for it. ... Hence, the express reservation for the wandering or runaway slave; for their defects are of the mind, not physical. It is for this reason that there are those who say that animals prone to shy or kick are not to be accounted diseased; for such defects are of the mind, not the body. (*Dig.* 21.1.4.3)

Aulus Gellius (*NA* 6.4) cites the 1st-century jurist Caelius Sabinus, who states that some slave traders put felt caps on those slaves whom they would not guarantee. Even as we might curse a car warranty that expires just before the transmission gives out, so too in antiquity there were guarantees against slaves' defects, but limited ones. Garner states, "The buyer was protected against the appearance of additional defects for six months, or for two if the slave was sold without warranty, by the *actio rehibitoria* (action for cancellation of sale), and for a year, or six months if bought 'as seen', by the *actio quanti minoris* (action for reduction in value)."[77]

---

[74] Runaways, if savagely used by masters, are not runaways if they return (Vivianus in Justinian *Dig.* 21.1.17.3). Galen *Aff. Dig.* 8 mentions slaves' mistreatment: "My mother, however, was so very prone to anger that sometimes she bit her handmaids."

[75] Neronic era tablets from Herculaneum guarantee payment if something goes wrong. So too do Transylvanian tablets; one from Dacia (142 CE) ensures that the slave is free from theft and wrongdoing (Crook 1967, 183–84).

[76] The slave's price can also be affected by the purchaser, who reduces the value perhaps by "the purchaser's cruelty making him a fugitive" (*Dig.* 21.1.23); see Ulpian on "deterioration in the slave" (21.1.25). A friend of Galen, traveling from Corinth, perhaps reduces his slaves' value by beating them, nearly to death, with a sword blade (*Aff. Dig.* 5).

[77] Gardner 2011, 417; Crook 1967, 182.

While it is impossible to determine with certainty the price of a given slave at Corinth in the 1st century CE, the phrase "bought with a price" might evoke common knowledge regarding the marketability and monetary value of a slave. This monetary valuation not only happened at the moment of sale, but also often at the moment of manumission, when the slave paid for his or her own freedom or it was paid for him or her. As we have seen, slave value varied not only according to race or ethnicity, gender, age, and skills, but also in light of multiple factors of disease and defect, and freedom was increasingly expensive. Even if the manumission price was reduced by ancillary clauses, such as a *paramonē* clause or the requirement to leave behind or to produce a thriving child for the *kyrios* or his family, we can wonder whether such discounted manumission was, in emotional terms, incalculably dear.

Conclusions

"You were bought with a price." "Do not be a slave to humans." The language of slavery abounds in the New Testament and in the Pauline letters. Paul refers to himself often as *doulos Christou*, slave of Christ (e.g., Rom 1:1; Phil 1:1; Gal 1:10). Despite references in Paul's letters to freedom and even to the act of freeing in a sense that seems to be explicitly about the freeing of slaves (Gal 5:1; 1 Cor 7:21–22; Gal 3:13), Paul's ambiguous statements elsewhere about slavery and manumission allowed his pseudepigraphers to assume that it was appropriate for members of communities in Christ to own slaves and to insist that Christian slaves must be subject to their masters (1 Tim 6:1–2, Col 3:22, Eph 6:5).[78]

Slavery, as Harrill and others have discussed, is so endemic to the Roman world that Paul, like other writers, not only referred to slaves, but also used slavery as a way to think through philosophical and theological problems. But what of the reception of such slave/free language? How might the early ekklēsia at Corinth have heard such language of buying and selling, of price, of being a freedperson?

Whether or not Paul so intended, his comment, "You are bought with a price," asks the hearers or readers to think of themselves as things on the market. A community of freedpersons would already have considered the issue of human price. Such a comment directs the free and the freed

---

[78] On 1 Timothy and the possibility of slaves as religious leaders, see Shaner 2012.

to consider what price they are worth, what it means to be bought, and perhaps how they might slip so easily from the status of person to the status of thing. Indeed, Paul's words briefly render the ekklēsia a kind of statarion – a location where God or Christ moves into the marketplace to purchase humans. One effect of hearing 1 Cor 7:17–24 might be to relativize free/slave status in this ekklēsia by rendering God or Christ as lord (*kyrios*), with all the potentially disturbing undertones of a divine master.[79] Even if one is trading up masters, the structure is the same.

"You are bought with a price" might remind freedpersons to calculate how much their still-enslaved children or spouses would cost. It might evoke in the freedperson or the person earning his or her *peculium* (money or property managed by a slave which could be used to purchase manumission) the memory or concrete consideration of his or her valuation: I was bought with a price; I bought or hope to buy myself. They might recall how much it had cost to jump from the status of nearly freed (with a *paramonē* clause) to completely freed – the Kalymna inscription mentions a daily tax upon freedom. They might haggle over the price of their own slaves, even as they wondered if the vendor's claims regarding the slave's health and usefulness would hold true. And finally, and most radically, some Corinthians may have heard the text as demanding that free and slave and freedperson alike think about the slave owner as commodity. What is s/he worth? You too, the letter insists, are bought with a price. What is the value of the thing that you are?

---

[79] Briggs 1989 explores the opposite, the enslaved God.

CHAPTER FIVE

PAINTING PRACTICES IN ROMAN CORINTH: GREEK OR ROMAN?

Sarah Lepinski*

The most significant challenges facing a study of Roman-period mural paintings from Greece result from preservation, chronology, and academic traditions. These issues have constrained the study of Roman-period mural paintings in Greece (and elsewhere in the eastern Mediterranean) and have limited the potential contribution of painting studies to general archaeological and historical narratives in the ancient Mediterranean, and more specifically to cultural and material stratification in Ancient Corinth.

Research into the large corpus of Roman-period paintings at Corinth, however, demonstrates that the study of ancient paintings has much to offer to our understanding of cultural practices. This paper presents specific groups of paintings from Corinth that illustrate the patterns in painting techniques, material-use, and visual representations from the 1st to the 3rd centuries CE. It traces these patterns diachronically, integrating discussion of technical and iconographic facets with the consideration of the artistic associations of the painters, the interests and cultural resources of Corinthian patrons, and the networks of exchange in which Corinth participated during these centuries. This perspective highlights the manner in which paintings reflect cultural practices and the dynamic and multifaceted nature of artistic production in the Roman Mediterranean.

Roman and Corinthian Painting: Research Challenges

Few Roman sites preserve painted walls like those found in the cities and suburban villas in Campania. In fact, mural paintings from most sites throughout the Roman world are found in much less pristine conditions – sometimes adhering to walls, but in many cases found in fallen positions on floors or re-deposited within construction fills and pits. Often the arduous task of documenting, cleaning, and conserving fragmentary paintings

* I am indebted to the Corinth Excavations and the Department of Greek and Roman Art at the Metropolitan Museum of Art in New York for facilitating my research for this chapter; and to Christopher Lightfoot and Joan R. Mertens for their helpful comments on earlier versions.

remains unrealized. Thus in many situations, owing to strained resources both in terms of money and time, paintings from archaeological contexts are left unstudied, and at best, perhaps only briefly mentioned in archaeological reports. Despite the challenges presented by issues of conservation and lack of resources, however, research on provincial paintings (particularly those found *in situ*) is expanding, although the majority of this work focuses on paintings in the western Mediterranean and Europe.[1]

Modern political interests and academic traditions are principally responsible for this discrepancy. In contrast to the northwestern Roman provinces, particularly Britain and Gaul,[2] for instance, where modern national interest has played a large role in preserving, studying and publishing Roman-period sites, other former Roman provinces, such as Greece, have histories in which modern nationalistic connections are aligned with other cultural periods, particularly those that are not colonial in nature.[3] For Greece these cultural connections belong with the Classical and Byzantine pasts and they play a significant part in the current paucity of scholarship on Roman paintings from Greece.[4]

The strict division between the study of Greek and Roman paintings further contributes to the present state of scholarship. While these two subfields overlap at points chronologically and geographically, they remain distinct.[5] This separation is maintained by academic traditions – by the evolutionary armature of history writing and the common application of the binary Greek or Roman. As the paintings from Corinth demonstrate, the classification of artistic characteristics as either Greek or Roman misrepresents the ethnic and cultural diversity inherent in the Roman Mediterranean.[6] The duality of Greek or Roman also misrepresents the intensive cultural interactions predating the Roman period that fostered mutual borrowing and adaptation of artistic methods and visual forms among various Mediterranean cultures. The combination of technical

---

[1] Barbet 1981; Delplace 1986, 1989; Moormann 1993; Béarat et al. 1997; Bóhry 2004; and the bibliographies published by the Association Internationale pour la Peinture Antique (www.peintureantique.net).

[2] Woolf (2004, 220) uses France as an example of how the Roman past is adopted by a modern nation, as is illustrated by the slogan ". . . nos ancestres les gaulois."

[3] Woolf (2004, 223) cites North Africa.

[4] Kostakis 1998; Osborne and Alcock 2007; Hurst 2007, 73–75.

[5] A synthetic study of the specific attributes of painting traditions in various regions of the ancient Mediterranean does not exist, although Kakoulli's recent work (2009) on Greek painting techniques and materials integrates Roman practices.

[6] See Alcock (2005, 325–26) for discussion of the dualist conceptions of Greek versus Roman within the Roman provincial studies.

and visual facets evident in later Hellenistic painting, particularly in the examples from Delos that show affinities with earlier painting practices of the Italian peninsula, Northern Greece, and Egypt (which, in turn, draw from traditions in Asia Minor, Southern Italy and Egypt), demonstrate that early Imperial Italian practices are very much a part of international Mediterranean painting traditions.

Owing to the large size of the corpus as well as its range in date (over four centuries), Roman-period paintings from Corinth present an unparalleled opportunity to consider cultural practices and networks of interaction from the perspective of artistic production. Ongoing study of the paintings' materials, techniques, and visual traits reveals complex patterns of shifting practices and cultural interactions.[7] These patterns demonstrate a striking discontinuity with earlier Hellenic painting tradition following the city's founding as a Roman colony in 44 BCE and a wholesale adoption of Italian painting practices at this time. These practices change, however, in the late 1st or very early 2nd century CE when painting techniques and material-use shift away from Roman practices, integrating methods and materials that were common in earlier Hellenistic painting tradition. Iconographically and stylistically, however, the later Corinthian paintings continue to draw from a Roman repertory. This complex pattern reflects the dynamism present in many artistic media during these centuries highlighting both the fusion of Greek and Roman characteristics in Roman art and the distinction of regional technical traditions.

Investigations into the techniques and materials employed in mural paintings inform on multiple levels. For instance, the materials used in the plaster support may indicate the geological sources exploited for sand and other aggregates and they may also tell of the economic resources of the patron since, for example, multiple layers of lime plaster can be costly. Similarly, the use of marble flakes in the final layer of plaster likely signals investment in materials, and in turn, the type of plaster (and the number of layers) employed dictates what painting techniques can be used.[8] In specific cases, the painting techniques also determine the pigments that can be used. Some pigments, such as lakes and copper-based pigments, for instance, are chemically incompatible with fresco technique.[9] Particular

---

[7] Apostolaki et al. 2006; Lepinski 2008; Lepinski and Brekoulaki 2010.

[8] For example, fresco (wet) technique requires multiple layers of lime plaster whereas *secco* or tempera technique frequently necessitates the use of a binding material to help the pigment adhere to the plaster support. Ling 1991, 198–211; Kakoulli 2009, 7–16.

[9] Kakoulli 2009, 40, 75, 80; Lepinski and Brekoulaki 2010.

pigments and binders can also denote specific cultural associations, economic circumstances, and perhaps the geographic origin of the materials. Finally, painted representations reflect artistic and social choices, as well as the aesthetic intentions and tastes of both artisans and patrons. Placed within a larger contextual framework, the study of paintings, their materials, and representations, offers insight into various cultural facets.

Corinthian Mural Paintings in the 1st Century CE

While not overtly visible to the modern visitor to Corinth, mural paintings once covered the walls in most Roman buildings. Both the American School of Classical Studies and the Greek Archaeological Service have recovered vast amounts of fragmentary paintings, as well as *in situ* murals in excavations in and around Corinth. These paintings adorned buildings of all types – civic, commercial, domestic, and funerary.[10] In fact, currently it is possible to associate specific schemes with at least twenty different structures, including civic buildings such as Peirene Fountain and the Roman Theater, commercial structures in the South Stoa and the western shops, domestic areas, such as the villa at Kokkinovrysi and the Panayia Domus, and tombs, particularly in the northwestern section of the city around the hill of Cheliotomylos (Map 1). Corinthian paintings depict a range of subjects and themes, including isometric masonry-style walls, painted imitation stonework, and paneled ensembles with framed schemes, including small-scale architectural elements, vegetal and animal motifs, and large-scale figures.[11]

---

[10] Known Corinthian wall paintings in civic and religious buildings include the following. Julian Basilica: *Corinth* I.5, 49. South Stoa: *Corinth* I.4, 100, 110, 134–35; Williams 1980, 119. Central Shops: *Corinth* I.3, 114. Odeum: *Corinth* X, 62–63. Theater: Shear 1925, 383–87; *Corinth* II, 87–94; Williams and Zervos 1984, 97, 104–106; 1986 15–151; 1988 pl. 43. Peirene Fountain: *Corinth* I.6, 110–115; Robinson 2001, 85–90; 2011, 601–15. Fountain of the Lamps: Wiseman 1970, 130–37; 1972, 13–17. East of Theater: Williams and Zervos 1984, 104–7; 1988, 123–24, 128–29; 1989 13–19; Gadbery 1993; Hykin 1993. Southeast Building: Meggiolaro, Pappalardo, and Vergerio 1995; Meggiolaro et al., 1997, 105–06; Pappalardo 2000, 358–59. Corinthian wall paintings in domestic structures are also attested. Roman Villa at Kokkinovrysi (Shear Villa) Shear 1925, 395–96; *Corinth* V, 4–5. Panayia Field Domus: Sanders 1999, 443; Lepinski 2008; forthcoming. Painted Tombs have also been examined. Painted Tomb: Robinson 1963, 77–80; 1965, 289–305. Tomb with Painted Walls: Shear 1931, 224–41. Charitonidis tomb: Charitonidis 1966, 122. Pallas tomb: Pallas 1969, 121–34; 1975, 1–19.

[11] Forthcoming publication of a group of funerary paintings by Barbet and Monier from Koutsongila, north of the port of Kenchreai, will facilitate further study of Corinthian paintings on a regional level (Rife et al. 2007) and incorporate all other extant groups of

As noted above, 1st-century CE Corinthian paintings demonstrate a complete adoption of Italic painting techniques following the city's founding as a Roman colony in 44 BCE. These Italic traits are strikingly different from those preserved in earlier Hellenic painting at Corinth. Paintings from Classical Greek and, to the extent that we can tell from the scant evidence, from Hellenistic structures in Corinth are executed on thin and hard mortar layers, whereas the Roman paintings employ thick layers in which the penultimate layer usually contains transparent aggregates such as quartz or marble flakes.[12] This plaster technology is associated with fresco painting technique, in which pigment is applied to the final layer of plaster (*intonaco*) when it was still wet. While fresco technique was used in Aegean mural paintings as early as the Bronze Age, it was not employed extensively until the Hellenistic period.[13] Mural paintings in Macedonia, Egypt, Delos, as well as in Rome and the towns and villas in Campania in Italy were executed with this technique.[14] We do not find this type of mural painting at Corinth before the mid 1st century BCE, however, that is, before Corinth became a Roman colony.[15]

The earliest known Roman period wall décor at Corinth decorated the South Stoa. The masonry-style walls (isometric blocks molded with stucco relief to imitate monumental ashlar masonry) belong to the early colony renovation phase of the South Stoa in the late 1st century BCE, during which time the eastern eight rooms of the Greek building were converted into larger spaces (A, B, C, D).[16] This renovation was part of a larger program that transformed of the older Greek sacred area of the city into the center

paintings from Kenchreai (Pallas 1957, 54, fig. 1; 1990; and *Kenchreai* I) and Isthmia (Daux 1968, 782–85, fig. 15–16; *Isthmia* II, 63).

[12] The transparent aggregates create an overall brightness or sheen when the pigment color is burnished into the final plaster layer. Pappalardo 2000, 351 and n. 12; Strocka 2007, 304 and n. 3. Vitruvius *De Arch* 7.6. For general discussion of techniques, see also Klinkert 1957, 124; Barbet and Allag 1972, 969–70; and Mora, Mora, Philippot 1984.

[13] See Kakoulli 2009, 7–16, and citations therein. Minoan Crete and Thera: Asimenos 1978; Sotiropoulou, Andrikopoulos, and Chrissikopoulos 2003. Olympia and Delphi: Eibner 1926, 60–61. For Hellenistic Macedonia, see the Tomb of Lyson and Kallikles at Lefkadia: Miller-Collett 1993; Brekoulaki 1997, 15; Tomb II at Aineia: Brekoulaki 1997, 15; Delos: Kakoulli 2009, 29.

[14] It should be noted, however, that most true fresco paintings also contain pigments that were applied when the plaster had dried, executed in a tempera or secco technique over fresco-painted backgrounds.

[15] Corinth may not have participated in the same networks of artistic exchange as the cities in Macedonia, Delos and Campania in the 3rd and 2nd centuries BCE.

[16] It is uncertain whether the stucco was painted or left with a lime-white finish. *Corinth* I.4, 100, 110 and pls. 27, 28 4. Scahill (2012) presents a new reconstruction of the South Stoa in the Greek period.

of Roman civic and commercial activity. In terms of artistic influence, the practice of fashioning of isometric blocks with plaster relief was widespread in the Hellenistic and late Republican Mediterranean and it was absorbed into Roman painting tradition, influencing the First Pompeian Style in Campanian mural painting.[17] Its application in the civic rooms of the colony's newly reconstructed Stoa was certainly appropriate for the Corinth's colonial status, with its décor drawing from a pan-Mediterranean visual tradition, referencing monumental architecture and what was by this time, Italian artistic forms.

Dating later, to around the first half of the 1st century CE, paintings from the area East of Theater also show close stylistic and iconographic affinities with Italic examples, particularly with those from Campania. These affinities further support the technical evidence for an importation of western painting traditions to Corinth in the 1st century BCE. Both Charles Williams and Laura Gadbery have discussed stylistic connections between paintings from the area East of Theater and examples in Campania.[18] In particular, Gadbery associates an early 1st-century architectural scheme that depicts Corinthian columns and capitals painted in perspective on a bright red ground (fig. 5.1) with schemes from cubiculum M in the Villa of Fannius Synistor at Boscoreale, in Campania, which are now on exhibit in the Metropolitan Museum of Art in New York.[19] Despite the more modest rendering of the capitals from the area East of Theater, as Gadbery notes, stylistic similarities between the Corinthian scheme and the example from Boscoreale suggest a direct artistic connection between Campania and Corinth in the early 1st century CE (fig. 5.2).[20]

A second scheme illustrating the direct connection between Italic and Corinthian paintings depicts a decorative frieze with alternating half-rosettes and lotus-palmettes on a yellow-ochre band; these fragments

---

[17] Ling 1991, 12–22. The style is well known in Hellenistic Greece. Moreno 1979a, 1979b; Miller 1989; Miller-Collett 1993; Brekoulaki 2006. Pella, Stuccoed House: Siganidou 1981, 48–50 fig. 4 (plans), pls. 58, 59 b; 1982, 34, figs. 4–5; 1990 173; Calamiotou, Siganidou, and Filippakis 1983 (pigment analyses). Eretria: Reber 1998, 115–120. Delos: Bulard 1908; *Délos* VIII; Bezerra de Menezes 1970, 1983, 1999; Alabé 1987, 1991, 1995, 1999. Athens: Wirth 1931; Bruno 1969; *Agora* XXVII, 115. For general discussions of masonry style walls in Greece, see Andreou (1989) and Wesenberg (1990).

[18] Williams and Zervos 1988 123–24, 128–29; Gadbery 1993.

[19] The capital, which is one of five preserved examples, has been reconstructed from fragments found in fill deposits within the road that runs north to south, east of the Theater. Gadbery 1993, 51–52, fig. 3; Williams and Zervos 1988, 123, pl. 40 a–d. Bergmann et al. 2010.

[20] Gadbery (1993, 52–53) suggests that the designs were taken from a Campanian copybook.

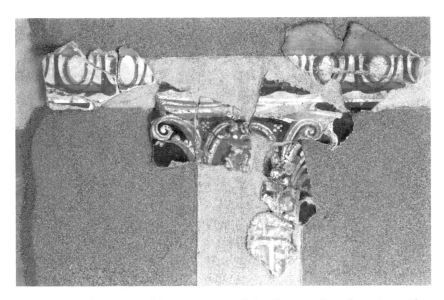

Fig. 5.1. Corinthian Capital from area East of the Theater. Photo by I. Ioannidou and L. Bartzioti.

Fig. 5.2. East Wall, Room M, villa of Fannius Synistor in Boscoreale. Courtesy of the Metropolitan Museum of Art, New York.

originally decorated a small room in an early Roman house on the west side of the excavated area in Panayia Field at Corinth (fig. 5.3).[21] A number of motifs related to the frieze, including a water bird, lotus blossoms with multi-colored petals, rosettes, and columns painted to imitate diamond-encrusted mosaic, likely filled other decorative bands and zones on the walls of this room (fig. 5.4). Together these motifs show close affinities with Third Pompeian style ensembles in Campania and Rome, particularly in rooms that contain Egyptianizing themes, which were popular in the later 1st century BCE and the early decades of the 1st century CE.[22]

The décor in Room 15 in the Villa of Agrippa Postumus at Boscotrecase, also in the Metropolitan Museum collections, depicts features typical of the Third Pompeian Style, including birds, fantastical creatures, floral motifs and stylized friezes supported by slender columns and candelabra (fig. 5.5). A frieze of palmettes and lotus blossoms on the entablature in the central panel on the rear wall is remarkably similar to the Corinthian scheme, although as with the Corinthian capital the Corinthian frieze is more modestly painted; the stylized lotus palmette and volute are shaded.[23] The paintings from Boscotrecase date to the beginning of the last decade of the 1st century BCE, while those at Corinth were painted at least a decade later.[24] This temporal discrepancy illustrates a measured rate of diffusion for the transference or adoption of the Italic motifs in Corinth.

Paintings from a number of sites in Roman Gaul and Hispania follow similar patterns to those present in the 1st-century paintings from Corinth.[25] Most prevalent in these regions, as at Corinth in the 1st century, are schemes and motifs associated with Third Pompeian-style paintings in

---

[21] The architecture of the Roman phases in Panayia Field are in preparation. For publication of the phases of the Roman road bordering the Domus see Palinkas and Herbst 2011. The date of the early Roman structure to which this room belonged is likely post-Augustan.

[22] The motifs are associated with Roman 'Egyptomania' following the annexation of Egypt in 30 BCE by Octavian. For other similar friezes see Ehrhardt (1987, taf. 108–18), especially Casa del Bell' Impluvio (I 9, 1) and Villa of the Mysteries. The decorative elements of this style – the stylized floral friezes, small-scale animals and birds, as well as ornamented architectural elements – both within an overall system and independent of one another, offered opportunity for innovation for the painter and multiple choices for a patron. Leach 1982, 155; Clarke 1991, 64–65; Leach 2004, 156.

[23] Von Blanckenhagen and Alexander 1990, pl. 6, 7 for entablature frieze, pl. 65.6 for stylized palmette on bright green ground, and pl. 21 for similar frieze from north wall of Room 16.

[24] Von Blanckenhagen and Alexander 1990, 3.

[25] Abad Casal 1982.

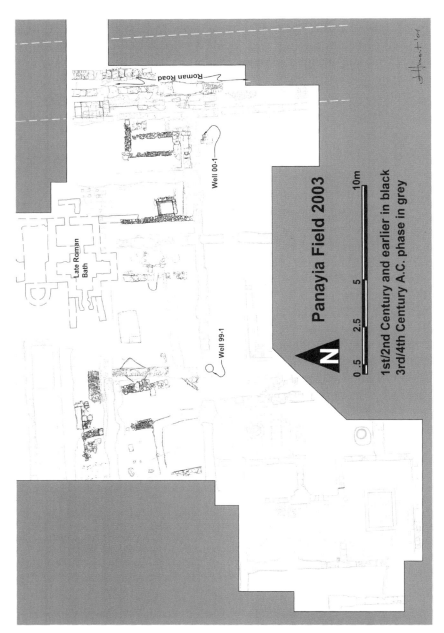

Fig. 5.3. Plan of Panayia Field. Drawing by J. Herbst.

Fig. 5.4. Wall of pre-domus room, Panayia Field, with Egyptianizing scheme.
Drawing by author.

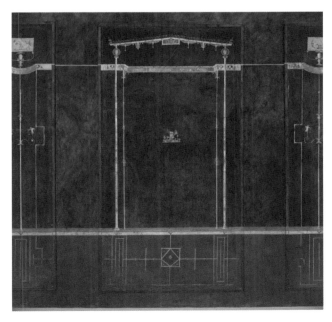

Fig. 5.5. North Wall, Room 15, Villa of Agrippa Postumus at Boscotrecase. Courtesy
of the Metropolitan Museum of Art, New York.

Campania. In her study of paintings from Roman sites in Gaul, Barbet has also traced the transmission of the motifs, the artistic style and technical traits to within about a decade of their development in Campania.[26] The close parallels between the paintings from Panayia Field at Corinth and contemporary examples in Gaul connect Corinth to the same sphere of artistic exchange as metropolitan centers in the western Roman provinces in the 1st century CE. This artistic connection corresponds to evidence for commercial ties between Corinth, Italy, Gaul and Hispania in the 1st-century ceramic assemblages at Corinth.[27]

The widespread application of the Third Pompeian Style in the provinces raises questions regarding the specific modes of transmission for the represented schemes and motifs. It is generally accepted that books of various types and function were partly responsible for the wide circulation of images in the Roman period, although there is little physical evidence to support this supposition, at present.[28] One can speculate that during the early decades of the 1st century CE, a period of intensive Roman colonization, painting styles and motifs were spread with the movement of artists and their sketchbooks to various cities in the Empire.[29] Also, it is likely that artists used these books in a number of ways, both in formal situations such as apprenticeships, special commissions, and collaborations with artists working in other media, as well as through more informal interchanges of ideas and technical know-how.

That Corinth had direct artistic ties with the Italian peninsula in the 1st century is apparent in the technical and aesthetic characteristics of the Corinthian paintings. These facets support the assertion here that the painters in 1st-century Corinth were trained in Italy; in fact, the close affinities between the Corinthian and Campanian examples perhaps point to Pompeii as the city in which the painters were trained or once worked.

---

[26] Barbet 1982a, 1982b, 1983, 1987.

[27] Slane 1989, 221–22; 2000, 229–300.

[28] Allison's (1991, 82) list includes illustrated texts; picture books; separate cartoons (perhaps to scale drawings), which were thematically accurate copies of the originals, created to transmit motifs; pattern books which were manuals, designed specifically for artists and possibly containing such cartoons or drawings; individual sketches, kept and added to over the years; and working sketches made on site as study. Recently discovered late Hellenistic papyri contribute significantly to the on-going discussion of copybooks used in mosaic design: Donderer 2005; Gallazzi, Kramer, and Settis 2008. For general discussion of copybooks: Weitzmann 1970; Blanck 1992; Small 2003.

[29] Traveling artists (*pictori peregrini*) were also a well-known phenomenon in the Roman world. Kleiner 1977, 661–96; Davey and Ling 1982, 48; Toynbee 1951, 43–50; Mckenzie 1990, 11 (for Petra); Rozenberg 1996; 2004, 28.

While it is not possible to determine the ethnic identity of the 1st-century painters in Corinth, gauging from evidence regarding artisans in the Roman world in general, it is highly probably that most were of east Greek descent and likely of freedman status.[30] East Greek cultural associations for the 1st-century painters fit well with the general ethnic make-up of Corinth's population in the early colony, which also consisted primarily of freedmen of Greek origin.[31] In this light both the Corinthian patrons and the artists shared a general cultural heritage.

The economic success of 1st-century Corinth and the renovation of the city center, with its public edifices, temples, and commercial structures certainly attracted numerous artisans and craftsmen to Corinth.[32] Together with the monumental facades with large-scale sculptural assemblages, the paintings augmented the general Roman appearance of 1st-century Corinthian buildings. Monumentalizing isometric masonry-style paintings in the official rooms of the South Stoa from the early decades of the colony and later, the Third Pompeian Style paintings with Egyptianizing themes in domestic buildings placed the Corinthian commissions alongside those in the Italic west and other provincial regions.

While the majority of 1st-century painted schemes demonstrate the Roman tastes of the Corinthian patrons, three related paintings reference mythologies that are specific to Corinth's Hellenic heritage. These paintings include fragments of a horse, identified as the immortal winged Pegasos, and two accompanying fragmentary inscriptions in Greek that identify (the now missing figures) Briareus (BPIA<PEΩΣ>) and Posideon (ΩΝ) (figs. 5.6 and 5.7).

As part of a larger decorative program with architectural vistas and megalographic figures, these fragments adorned the Southeast Building in a short-lived phase dated to the early 1st century CE. Situated on the southeastern side of the Roman Forum, between two monumental basilicas, the building has been tentatively identified as a library or a depository for civic documents.[33] Themes of Corinth's mythologies fit well in a public building. Pegasos and Bellerophon have a long association with Corinth since, according to myth, Peirene Fountain at Corinth was the place where

---

[30] Stewart 2008, 16–18.
[31] Millis 2010a; Spawforth 1996, 175.
[32] See Shoe (1964, 300–3) for identification of Italian masons; Millis (2010, 26–30) for consideration of other crafts in the early colony.
[33] The building forms part of Paul Scotton's ongoing study of the Roman basilicas and other structures in or near the Roman Forum. *Corinth* I.5, 9–10; Williams 1979, 107 n. 2; Pappalardo 2000, 358–59 and n. 40.

Fig. 5.6. Painted Pegasos on red ground from Southeast Building. Drawing by author after Pappalardo (2000, fig. 12).

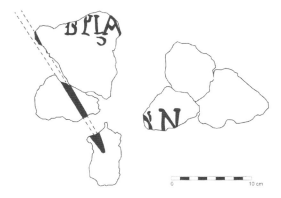

Fig. 5.7. Briarius Inscription from Southeast Building. Drawing by author after Pappalardo (2000, fig. 13-14).

Pegasos was captured and tamed by the hero Bellerophon. In a later version, the headwaters of the Peirene Spring miraculously appeared where Pegasos struck his hoof.[34]

The painted inscriptions identifying Briarius and Poseidon likely refer to the myth of the contest between Helios and Poseidon for control of Corinth, in which Briareus awarded Acrocorinth to Helios and the Isthmus

---

[34] Statius, *Silv.* 1.4.25–30; 2.7.2–4; *Theb.* 4.51–69. Amandry 1988, 38–39, 42 and 7; Robinson 2001, 159–60.

to Poseidon.[35] Painted implements, such as a sword or a shaft, and perhaps also a wand or a trident, further support the identification of the reference to Poseidon.

The paintings reflect visual themes that are also found on contemporary Corinthian coins. The image of Bellerophon mounted on Pegasos was placed on the reverse of the first coin minted in colonial Corinth, and slightly later, in an issue dated 43–42 BCE, which depicts Bellerophon leading Pegasos on the reverse and a seated archaic-style Poseidon on the obverse (fig. 5.8).[36] The paintings from the Southeast Building, like the coins, reference Peirene Fountain, itself refurbished in the early colony as a Roman monument that had been and continued to be synonymous with Corinth and the Isthmian games, the cultural institution that was re-established in the later 1st century BCE.[37] They complement the monumental expressions of Greek legacy, such as the renovated Archaic Temple as well as Peirene and Glauke Fountains, which reflect in Thomas's words the "fusion of Roman practice with an appeal to Greek cultural heritage."[38]

0 ⊢————————⊣ 1 cm

Fig. 5.8. Corinthian coin with Bellerophon leading Pegasos on reverse; seated archaic-style Poseidon on the obverse. Photo by B. Robinson.

---

[35] Paus. 2.1.6, 2.5.1, 2.4.6; Dio Chrys., *Orat* 37, 11. Pappalardo 2000, 335, tav. 10b, no. 28 a–g; Robinson 2001, 160.

[36] Howego 1989, 199–200. According to custom, the head of Julius Caesar, the colony's founder was placed on the obverse. Amandry 1988, 23–36, P. 1–4; *RPC*, no. 1116–23; Robinson 2005, fig. 4.7; Walbank 2010, 152.

[37] Robinson 2001; 2005, for Pegasos in particular see 116–28; Bookidis 2005, 164. Cultural institutions were also re-established, such as the Isthmian Games, around 40 BCE (Gebhard 1993).

[38] Thomas 2010, 137 and 139.

Corinthian Mural Paintings in the 2nd and 3rd Centuries CE

A fusion of Greek and Roman elements also characterizes the later (2nd and 3rd centuries) paintings at Corinth, although here particular technical aspects exhibit Hellenic influence while aesthetic qualities show sustained associations with Roman types. After the 1st century the techniques and materials employed in Corinthian mural paintings reveal a striking departure from earlier Roman painting practices. The most recognizable change is found in the mortar support. At this time, the thick laminations of multiple layers of densely prepared plaster that were employed in the 1st-century paintings are replaced at Corinth by a new technique that uses a very thin final layer of plaster or intonaco. This type of plaster precludes the use of fresco technique, which needs multiple layers of lime plaster; the background pigments were therefore applied in a secco technique, in which the pigments are mixed with a binding material and applied to a dry plaster face.[39] Ongoing chemical analyses of the paintings from Corinth (with chromatography) have determined the existence of organic binders in the later paintings, although the specific proteins (egg or gum arabic, for example) have yet to be identified.[40]

It is unclear what prompted the change in mortar plaster techniques, but economic factors likely played a role. Thinner layers of plaster require fewer materials and less preparation time than the multiple plaster layers for mural paintings, which require large amounts of calcined lime. This new mortar technique may also be related to the common use of mud brick or pisé in Corinthian walls after the late 1st century CE, such as those in the Domus in Panayia Field and the buildings bordering the street East of Theater.[41] Similar changes in plaster layers are also evident at Ephesos in the 2nd century CE, demonstrating that the shift in plaster technology at Corinth may be part of a larger trend, perhaps impacted by shifting economic conditions and commercial ties in the Mediterranean.[42]

Changes in painting practices at Corinth are also apparent in pigment-use, particularly with the less-accessible and vibrant materials like cinnabar and Egyptian blue. Both pigments have a long history of use in the

---

[39] Kakoulli (2009, 7–16) for overview of technique.
[40] Apostolaki 2006; Lepinski and Brekoulaki 2010.
[41] Domus: Sanders 1999; Lepinski 2008. East of the Theater: Gadbery 1993, 54; Williams and Zervos 1984, 107.
[42] Personal communication, Norbert Zimmermann, September 2010. Corinth and Ephesos share many similarities (Thomas 2010) and participated in the same social networks.

Mediterranean and were employed extensively in Imperial paintings in Rome and Campania. Cinnabar is attested earlier on Greek marble funerary reliefs and in Etruscan and Greek Hellenistic mural paintings as well as other objects, while Egyptian Blue was employed in mural paintings, particularly in Egypt and the Aegean, as early as the Bronze Age.[43] In Roman Corinth, the two pigments are used liberally as backgrounds in 1st-century paintings such as those from East of Theater, but they are employed primarily for details in later representations.[44]

Patterns of cinnabar-use similar to those at Corinth are also apparent in Italian and Gaulish paintings beginning in the later 1st century CE, and it has been suggested that the pigment's uneven use was a result of fluctuations in commercial and trade patterns.[45] While cinnabar and Egyptian blue are considered by ancient and modern sources alike to be less readily available and more expensive than naturally occurring earth pigments, from a geological and technological perspective, both pigments are widely accessible throughout the Mediterranean.[46] Certainly, this is the situation at Corinth in the Roman period, although it is unclear whether these resources were exploited. In the case of cinnabar, it is likely that the raw material from specific areas (such as the famous sources in modern-day Spain or Turkey) was valued over that from others during the Roman period. Certain qualities, such as texture, intensity of color, or its resistance to alteration probably drove the desire to procure cinnabar from one source over another.[47]

As for Egyptian blue, the expertise required for its preparation was widespread throughout the Mediterranean during the Hellenistic period. Its manufacture was certainly feasible at Corinth, as glassmaking took place throughout the Roman period.[48] Not enough is known about the manufacture and trade in ancient pigments in general, to either determine the specific sources of cinnabar used in Corinthian paintings or to

---

[43] Cinnabar: Calamiotou, Siganidou, and Filippakis 1983, 120; Wallert 1995, 178. Egyptian Blue: Chase 1971, 80–91; Filippakis, Perdikatsis, and Paradellis 1976, 147–51; Jaksch et al. 1983, 525–35.

[44] Williams and Zervos 1988, pl. 43; 1986, 150–51, pl. 35 a–d; 1984, 97, 104–6, pl. 30 d–e.

[45] Barbet 1990, 260; Barbet and Lahanier 1983; Gee 2010.

[46] Theophrastus (De Lapidibus, 57–59) mentions cinnabar from sources in Spain, Asia Minor, and the Caucasus (Colchis, in what is now part of Western Georgia); Caley and Richards 1956, 57–58; Eastaugh et al. 2004, 105. Ephesian sources are not known to modern geologists. Pliny (NH 33:117 and 35: 30) and Dioscorides (De material medica V: 94) both discuss the valuable attributes of cinnabar.

[47] Kakoulli 2009, 68; Lepinski and Brekoulaki 2010.

[48] Glass production in Corinth: Corinth XII, 78–86; Whitehouse 1991.

establish whether Egyptian blue was fabricated in certain glassmaking centers and shipped abroad with other exports, either in final powder form or in solid-glass form (to be pulverized by artisans on-site), or if it was produced in local or regional centers, such as Corinth.[49] What does seem apparent from the study of pigment-use at Corinth, however, is that these two pigments were less-readily available in the 2nd and 3rd centuries than they were in the 1st century.

When Peirene Fountain was remodelled in the 2nd century CE, the interior walls of the Spring Chambers were repainted with scenes of marine life swimming in waters rendered with Egyptian blue.[50] The extensive use of Egyptian blue in this case is likely associated with the significance of the fountain's civic function, and its use may have served as a vivid statement of the benefactor's generosity to the city.[51]

While the use of both cinnabar and Egyptian blue becomes less frequent after the 1st century, other pigments are integrated into the painter's palette at Corinth at this time. The most distinctive of these are lead white and pink madder lake. Lead white, which was used as the background color in the series of figural paintings from Building 7 in the East of Theater (fig. 5.9), is derived from metallic lead that has been corroded by acetic acid (vinegar).[52] It was used only in secco painting, either unmixed to produce an opaque pigment or in combination with other colors to make lighter tones.[53] Madder lake, which is extracted from the madder plant Rubia Tinctorum, is a dye rather than a pigment (like those derived from mineral sources), which is prepared by precipitation of the organic dye on a calcium carbonate inorganic inert substrate.[54] It is found in the 3rd-century paintings from the Panayia Field.

The use of the two pigments in the 2nd and 3rd-century paintings at Corinth is significant because both madder lake and lead white are common in Greek Hellenistic painting tradition (in mural paintings executed in secco technique and on marble grave stele) but are not found in

---

[49] Complexities involved in ancient pigment-use certainly warrant further study. For general overview see Kakoulli (2009) and bibliography therein.

[50] Robinson 2001, 68–85; 2011, 223–8.

[51] *Corinth* I.6, 113; Robinson 2001, 60–85.

[52] Williams and Zervos 1989 14–18; Gadbery 1993, 58 fig. 7. Corinth Inventory No. A 1990 06).

[53] Pliny *NH* XXXV.45, 49; Kakoulli 2009, 44.

[54] Gettens and Stout 1966, 126.

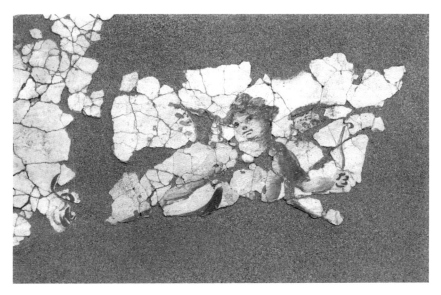

Fig. 5.9. Eros from Room 7, area East of the Theater (A 1990 06). Photo by
I. Ioannidou and L. Bartzioti.

the early Roman paintings at Corinth.[55] These pigments are incompatible with fresco painting technique, and their use is inextricably linked
with the change in plastering technique at this time. The integration of
these materials into the painting palette at Corinth demonstrates that
Corinthian artistic influences or relations shifted to regional centers in
Roman Greece (or in the eastern Mediterranean at large) after the turn of
the 1st century. Whether this shift reflects changing interaction between
specific artisans or workshops or shifting economic and political circumstances awaits further research.

While Corinthian painting practices break with Italian traditions technically after the late 1st century CE, the later paintings visually maintain
stylistic and compositional affinities with Roman types. These types were
ubiquitous throughout the Roman world by the 2nd century and formed
part of the widespread repertory of themes and motifs that, while based
on earlier Greek forms, constituted the core of Roman art. The manner
in which these types were depicted in the middle and late Imperial period, both in the Italian peninsula and throughout the provinces, is vastly

---

[55] Kakoulli 2009; Lepinski and Brekoulaki 2010.

divergent and regionally distinctive. The multiplicity of styles and visual choices as well as varying artistic competence and aesthetic inclinations are a hallmark of later Roman art.

At Corinth, paintings such as the Eros and its associated figures from Room 7 in the area East of Theater, which are dated to the late 1st century or early 2nd century, show close similarities with Campanian examples, which were executed at least thirty years earlier (fig. 5.9).[56] The figure is twisting to face the viewer and holds a bow in his left hand a long, flaming torch in his right hand.[57] The sustained aesthetic demonstrates the traditional taste of the Roman Corinthians, and the stylistic affinities show that despite the shift in painting techniques, Corinthian painting workshops retain well-trained painters adept in rendering naturalistic styles according to Roman forms.

The figural paintings that decorated a 3rd-century Domus in the Panayia Field also show close stylistic affinities with earlier Italic types (fig. 5.10). Two large-scale painted Victories originally stood on the northern wall of Room A12 and were part of an extensive painted program, which includes a maenad as well as floral and vegetal decorative schemes.[58]

The Victories are painted in an expressive, quick, and deft manner and each carries a palm frond and a wreath. Certain visual characteristics, such as their round 'Severan' eyes and associated illusionistic cornices reflect contemporary 3rd-century trends in the west, suggesting that there may have been direct artistic interaction between Corinthian and Italian artisans during this time (fig. 5.11).[59] Other traits, however, particularly the naturalistic rendering and traditional poses of the Victories exhibit what I am identifying as a local predilection for stylistically 'old-fashioned,'

---

[56] Gadbery 1993, fig. 1; Williams 2005, 237. I would like to thank Charles Williams for his permission to cite the figures here and for his helpful suggestions regarding close comparisons with Pompeian examples. The figural program in Building 7, which includes figures of Herakles, Hera, Zeus, Athena, Aphrodite, and Artemis, is dated by Williams to around or slightly after 100 CE. His publication and detailed interpretation of these paintings is forthcoming.

[57] Williams and Zervos 1989 17–18, pl. 5; Gadbery 1993, 63 fig. 14.

[58] Victories: Corinth Inventory No. A 1996 08 and A 1997 05. The maenad (Corinth Inventory No. A 1997 04) decorated room A7 and the paneled decorative schemes were found in rooms A12, A9, and A5.

[59] The organization of figures within painted panels on a single wall with separate cornices forming the upper frame of the panels is common in Late Antonine-Severan paintings in the western Roman Empire. Rome: See Mielsch (2001, abb. 125) for building under S. Crisogono (Piazza Sonnino), now in the Musei Comunali; Miesch (2001, abb. 128 and n. 6) for paintings in the Cryptoporticus in the Via Friuli Baiae; see Mielsch (2001, abb. 147) for paintings in the peristyle of the Sosandra Baths.

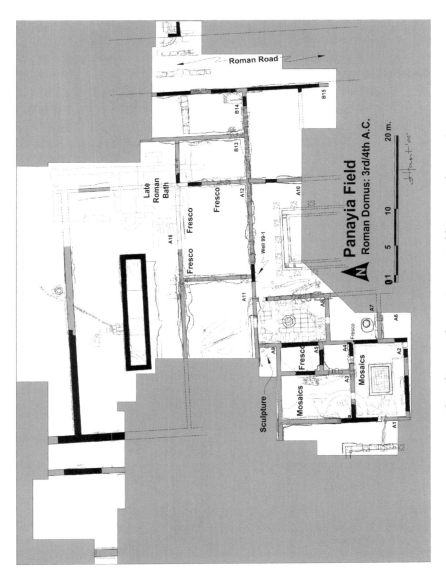

Fig. 5.10. Plan of Roman domus, Panayia Field. Drawing by J. Herbst.

Fig. 5.11. Victory on red ground from Room A12, domus, Panayia Field (A 1996 08).
Photo by G. Sanders and drawing by J. Herbst.

i.e. early Imperial, forms.[60] These traits distinguish Corinthian paintings from contemporary paintings, both in Italy and elsewhere, which are rendered, in general, with less dimensionality.

The corporality of the figures and the sense of movement of the garments of the Corinthian Victories are reminiscent of earlier Italic painted examples, but the closest comparable forms are found in contemporary Roman sculptures from Corinth, suggesting that while the form is based on earlier prototypes, the artist found inspiration locally. For example, a sculpted Victory (Corinth Inventory No. S 1932) recovered in the excavations by the American School of Classical Studies in the Forum area (one figure of a pair that originally decorated the South Basilica in the 2nd century CE, probably as acroteria) resembles the painted Victories in a number of respects (fig. 5.12).[61] The figure moves forward with her weight on her front left leg, and she wears a high-girted chiton that opens to reveal her right leg, which is bent at the knee, and swells slightly at her waist before falling in loose vertical planes below her belt.

The stylistic and compositional similarities between the painted Victories and the sculptures from the South Basilica support an argument for cross-media influence, although the common depiction of Victory on many types of objects, including gems, coins, and lamps, leaves a specific source or even a particular medium of transmission unknown.

The painted figure of a maenad from Room A7 in the Domus in Panayia Field may also draw from visual sources in other media (fig. 5.13). This figure is slightly smaller than the Victories and is painted in a much tighter manner on a deep-red background. She stands in a largely static stance, her upper legs and torso are frontal and there is a slight indication of movement in her garment and right lower leg. She holds a thyrsus behind her head and a drum in her left hand, her head is turned in sharp profile to the left, and she gazes past her outstretched left arm and hand.

---

[60] Smith 2006, especially 40–74, for discussion of various applications of Hellenistic and Roman forms (both iconographic and stylistic) in portrait statuary at Aphrodisias from local cultural and historical perspectives.

[61] Stillwell 1936, 41; *Corinth* I.3, 68–69, pl. 25 1, 2. The statue was found near the Temple of Tyche. It has attachments for wings (Edwards 1994, 280, pl. 67 and fig. 6). For the base see *Corinth* VIII.2, no. 11. Victory S 1932: Broneer 1935, 68, pl. 20c; *Corinth* I.5, 73–74, 76 pl. 46:1; Ridgway 1981, 435 n. 57. Scranton tentatively associates the cult of Fortuna-Victoria citing numismatic evidence (*Corinth* I.3, pl. 26:1). He states that the earliest notice of the cult on coins is on one issued by A. Vatronius Labeo and L. Rutilius Plancus (*Corinth* VI, 20, no. 46, pl. II) that is dated shortly after 22–23 CE. This coin represents a Victory on a globe holding a wreath and a palm; *Corinth* I.3, 69 pl. 26:1a.

Fig. 5.12. Victory (S 1932) from South Basilica.

Fig. 5.13. Maenad from Room A7, domus, Panayia Field (A 1997 04).
Photo by author.

Unlike the painted Victories from the Domus, the maenad does not find close parallels in monumental Corinthian sculpture. Furthermore, to the best of my knowledge, her stance is unparalleled in contemporary paintings and it may represent a unique addition to the corpus of intact Roman paintings. In fact, the maenad's form appears to be an amalgam of types, perhaps drawing from the poses preserved in neo-attic Tolmeta-type relief sculpture in terms of her profile head and bent right arm, and from images on widely circulating objects, such as molded terracotta lamps, which depict a maenad holding the thyrsus behind her head with one hand and a drum in the other.[62] The linear rendering of the maenad's garments, however, is strikingly similar to the abstraction of folds preserved on a second statue of Victory (Corinth Inventory No. S 2073) from the Corinthian Forum (fig. 5.14).[63] The fusion of these compositional and stylistic aspects in the painted maenad, therefore, seems to signify innovation on the part of the Domus owner or the artisans.

Unique elements are also evident in other decorative media in the Domus. For example, a statue of Roma found within a cache of small-scale sculptures in Room A9 may also allude to a local Corinthian monument, as there are no direct parallels in contemporary assemblages.[64] Sweetman and Sanders identify a number of distinctive designs and unusual features in the mosaic floors in the Domus, which may indicate originality on the part of the mosaicist and/or owner of the Domus.[65] Outside the general Dionysian connotations of the maenad and Victories, the paintings give little further insight to the specific interests of this particular patron. Overall, however, the décor of the Domus, which integrates mosaic and opus sectile floors, marble fountains, small-scale sculpture and paintings,

---

[62] Hauser 1889, pl. II for original types; Caputo (1948, pls. IV, XIV) for Antonine-period reliefs from Tolmeta (Ptolemais) in Cyrenaica, known as the Tolmeta-type. As Donohue (1998–1999, 27) notes the Tolmeta type "looks as though it has been assembled from elements of several Hauser types." An early Roman lamp in the Metropolitan Museum Cesnola Collection (74.51.2154) shows a maenad in this pose but with her head facing frontally. A second from Nikopolis (now on display in the new museum) portrays the same visual type but on a later lamp-type with a handle and short plain nozzle, likely dating to the middle or late Imperial period (I was unable to identify an inventory number).

[63] This sculpture (S 2073) was found at the west end of the Forum; *Corinth* I.3, pl. 25.2.

[64] Stirling 2008, 112–13. The assemblage includes two figures of Artemis (one smaller and one larger), two figures of Asklepios (one seated and one standing), a Dionysos, a weary Herakles, a Europa/Sosandra, and a Satyr (Pan).

[65] Sweetman and Sanders 2005, 359–60.

Fig. 5.14. Victory (S 2073) from west end of the Forum.

vividly showcases the owner's status in Roman Corinthian society and likely also in a larger Mediterranean-wide community.[66]

One final example illustrates the vast expanse of such a community. The vertical vegetal motif from a paneled ensemble in Room A12 of the Domus is found in many renditions throughout the Roman provinces dating from the early Imperial period through late antiquity (fig. 5.15). Contemporary examples, however, come primarily from the Eastern provinces. Two schemes with remarkably similar compositions to the Corinthian schemes are from the sites of Ephesos in Asia Minor and Zeugma on the western bank of the Euphrates. These schemes display the geographic extent of the shared visual repertory during 2nd and 3rd centuries.[67] The variation

---

[66] Stirling (2005b), and regarding heirloom pieces dating to the 1st century, personal correspondence, May 2003 and January 2004; Stirling 2008, 112–13, 156.

[67] Ephesos: *Ephesos* VIII.1, 43–68; Zimmerman 2005, taf. 85.14, 85.12, 85.6 and 85.8 (phase II) 86.4, 86.6., 87.7 (phase IV); Zimmermann and Ladstätter 2010, Abb. 146, 1–3, Abb. 183, 1–9. Zeugma: Barbet 2005, 110–19, 144–57.

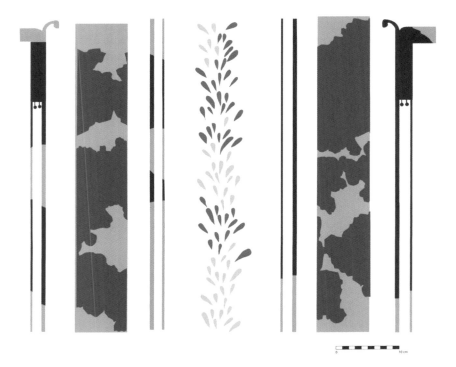

Fig. 5.15. Vertical vegetal motif from Room A11, domus, Panayia Field. Drawing by author.

of stylistic execution between these examples, which is apparent even in the contemporary schemes from different houses at Zeugma, shows a diversity of artistic conception, which is common within later Roman painting. These schemes draw from common sources but they are painted according to local tastes by local artisans and workshops.

Conclusions

The patterns in painting practices and aesthetic preferences at Corinth say more about larger Corinthian societal trends and cultural interactions than individual status or the specific interests of particular segments of the population. The paintings reinforce the current scholarly perspective of Corinthian cultural practices in the 1st century BCE and 1st century CE as a fusion – in terms of the city's architectural landscape as well as its social milieu – of Roman cultural practices and Greek historical legacy. Corinth's painting practices and artistic tastes generally adhere to Italic trends following its foundation as a colony in 44 BCE and show close connections with western provincial painting, particularly in Gaul and Hispania. The 1st-century CE paintings that reference Corinthian mythologies, however, directly correspond with other overt statements of the city's Greek past that are expressed both in small-scale media, such as the coins struck in the early colony, and in monumental form, like the refurbishment of the Archaic Temple.

After the 1st century CE, the changes in painting techniques and material-use show a break, technically, from western influence and an integration of earlier Hellenic traditions. The break with western technical practices, however, is not reflected in either the subject matter or the stylistic rendering in the later Corinthian paintings. Instead the later paintings display a sustained aesthetic preference for early Roman forms. This preference is shared with other metropolitan centers in the Eastern Mediterranean, such as Ephesos and Aphrodisias and demonstrates Corinth's participation in broad networks of social and economic exchange in the eastern Mediterranean during the 2nd and 3rd centuries CE.

The distinction, however, between the later Corinthian paintings and those preserved in other Roman cities – even those with which Corinth shares networks of exchange – lies in the manner in which the paintings are executed both compositionally and stylistically. The later paintings from Corinth show that Corinthians adhered to widespread Roman visual types, but that their paintings were likely influenced by local monuments and other well-circulated and readily available media. These forms were skillfully fashioned by Corinthian painters in the 2nd and 3rd centuries, sometimes as composite representations such as the maenad, into dynamic schemes.

In Roman Corinth, painting practices reflect both the general interests of its population as it changed from the 1st century BCE through the 3rd century CE as well as the economic and social networks in which the city participated during these centuries. Consideration of the complex patterns in painting techniques, material use, and visual representations in Corinthian paintings reveals that technical practices are not always congruent with sources of visual influence. At no time in its Roman history do Corinthian paintings draw from a single source of influence and therefore the characterization of practices as either Greek or Roman falls short. Instead, these patterns illustrate fusions of visual, technical, and cultural traditions and underscore the multifaceted nature of artistic production in the Roman Mediterranean.

PART TWO

SOCIO-ECONOMIC INEQUALITIES IN CORINTH

CHAPTER SIX

LANDLORDS AND TENANTS: SHARECROPPERS AND SUBSISTENCE FARMING IN CORINTHIAN HISTORICAL CONTEXT

Guy D.R. Sanders

As historians, archaeologists, and art historians we tend to spend our academic lives studying the careers and monuments of the richest echelons of society. Even those archaeologists who revel more in examining mundane ancient waste than describing civic monuments are enjoying the refuse of those who could afford to generate it. One reason for our inability to see the poorest echelons of society is rooted in the "Ricardo-Malthusian Trap." This universal economic law of nature states that at any given time, everywhere, except in parts of Europe and North America after the Industrial Revolution, the great majority of humanity has lived at a level at or near subsistence.[1] Subsistence is a state where a family has only sufficient resources to pay taxes, to feed itself, and to replace such necessities as tools and livestock. Before the Industrial Revolution their material culture was ephemeral: their houses may not have had proper foundations or solid walls, they did not eat off delicate ceramic plates but durable wooden platters, and their storage bins were more likely to have been mud plastered wicker than expensive ceramic jars.[2] Their diet was enough cereals, pulses, vegetables, fruit, oil, and wine to survive on but not to get fat. With the exception of an occasional chicken or a lamb, eaten on special days, their animals were for traction and milk. Only when the working life of their livestock had ended were they used for their meat,

---

[1] Boserup, 1965, 1981.

[2] Ceramics are so common in the archaeological record that we tend to consider them of low value even though substantial effort actually went into their production. At the beginning of the 20th century a new Korone storage pithos cost 15 drachma, and the daily wage of a laborer was 1 drachma. In today's terms when an immigrant, uninsured day laborer in Greece is paid $35 a day, the pithos would cost $1,400. This fact probably explains why, in the archaeological record, pithoi were repaired or removed for use elsewhere and why built storage containers were used. Similarly ceramic tiles were frequently recycled. For a breakdown of ceramic production and costs, see Sanders 2000 and Blitzer 1990a. For reuse of ceramics in the Roman period, see Peña 2007.

hooves, horns, bones, blood, and pelt, all of which, efficiently used, can be reduced to an archaeological minimum.

If the material remains of the majority of human beings are insignificant when compared with the monuments, dedicatory inscriptions, and imported fine ware pottery of their masters and landlords, then for generations we have perversely treated the latter as the norm for the ancient societies we study. We are, therefore, more historians of the literati and glitterati than true social historians. If we are truly interested in past societies, we must try harder to understand how the majority lived. For Greece, in less well-documented historical periods, we can do much worse than looking at the conditions in which the poorest rural Greeks lived in better-documented periods.[3] We have, for instance, more information about the landless and subsistence farmers during the period of Ottoman rule and after the formation of the Greek state. The details of these people's lives provide insights into the more remote past, for instance the living conditions of those who remained living on the Isthmus after the sack of Corinth by Lucius Mummius Achaicus and when Gaius Julius Caesar re-established the city.

Living memories of subsistence lifestyles survive in both archives and anecdotes. Over 50 Ottoman documents pertaining to Corinth and Corinthia are preserved in the state archive in Istanbul. These contain data on the property and taxes of individuals, rich and poor, in Corinthia between the mid 15th and early 19th centuries.[4] Unfortunately, translation and analysis of these documents have only recently begun and the size of the data set is so great that it will be some time before the process is complete. The anticipated data should resemble those documents recently published for part of Messenia.[5] Messenian tax surveys record individual holdings and assess the expected taxes due in detail. An example is the property of Ali Hoca at Palaiopirgos near Chora. Ali owned two houses, a vineyard, an oil press, a barrel and two pithoi. His estate consisted of about 27 ha of cultivated land, which was plowed using six yokes of oxen by four sharecroppers, who themselves owned 120 sheep. The expected yield on wheat was 4:1 and that on barley was 5:1. Ali also had about 3 ha

---

[3] Blitzer forthcoming is a multi-volume publication on traditional Greek practice and production. For two aspects of this series see Blitzer 1990a and 1990b.

[4] Copies of these documents are now in the hands of Dr. Y. Lolos, Dr. M. Panahi, and myself. Panahi has started on the translation of a set of documents pertaining to Corinth in the early 17th century, a period for which we have a representative sample of human skeletal material belonging to the poorest echelons of Ottoman society; see Rohn, Barnes, and Sanders 2009.

[5] Zarinebaf, Bennet, and Davis 2005, 56–58.

of vineyards, 400 olive, 15 pear, 9 fig, 6 almond, 5 mulberry, two lemon, and a single orange tree. Ali Hoca's houses and those of the sharecroppers were probably similar to one in Lakonia described by William Martin Leake at the beginning of the 19th century:

> The house is constructed, in the usual manner, of mud, with a coating of plaster; the roof is thatched, which is not a very common mode of covering the cottages of Greece. There is a raised earthen semicircle at one end for the fire, without any chimney; towards the other, a low partition, formed of the same material as the walls, separates the part of the building destined for the family from that which is occupied by the oxen and asses used on the farm, one door serving for both apartments. The usual articles of furniture of a Greek cottage are ranged, or hung around, namely, a loom, barrel-shaped wicker baskets, plastered with mud, for holding corn, a sieve, spindles, some copper cooking-vessels, and two lyres. The floor is bare earth covered, like the walls, with a coat of dried mud. An oven attached to the outside of the building, and in the garden some beans, artichokes, and a vine trailed over the roof, indicate a superior degree of affluence or industry ... While I was at dinner five oxen entered, and took up their abode for the night behind the low partition.[6]

In the absence, for now, of local archival data we can consider another precious but rapidly disappearing source – the living memory of traditional agricultural life. Such accounts preserve evidence that the simple level of existence described by Leake continued in the Greek countryside well into the 20th century. Aristomenes Arberores clearly remembered life before mechanization and artificial fertilizers as a boy growing up in Ancient Corinth in the 1940's.[7] His family was certainly not one of the wealthiest in the village, but neither were they among the very poorest. With their property and stock, they were not as fortunate as Ali Hoca of Messenia but better off than his tenants. The Arberores household consisted of three generations, his grandmother, his parents and their six children. They lived in a traditional two-story village house with a stable for the livestock below and three small rooms, without plumbing, for the family above. The house was built of stone bonded by clay mixed with lime cement, a tiled roof and windows with shutters but no glass. The family income from all sources,

---

[6] Leake 1830, 222–24. Houses fitting this description still exist in Ancient Corinth today. When I purchased my house in the village, all the movable property of the former elderly owners was still in place with the addition of photographs, beds, glassware, and ceramic plates. There were no lyres, but all the other articles described by Martin Leake were present. They also had a bread oven, a kitchen shed, an outhouse, a wine press, and a well.

[7] Personal communication, Jan. 22, 2003. Mr. Arberores was the foreman of the American School excavations at Corinth for many years and was known for his quick intelligence, honesty, and excellent memory.

including the value of their produce, was probably in the region of $200 to $400 per annum. At the time, 60% of all Greek families had an income of less than $500. This was a large proportion compared with contemporary rural, non-white family incomes in the US. In 1947, only 10% of farming and 4% of non-farming American families had an income of under $500.[8] Altogether, the Arberores family owned about 6.65 ha on the terraces immediately around the village cultivated in a three-year rotation of wheat, pulses and fallow.[9] They possessed a further 0.35 ha of olives in Elaiona and 0.85 ha of currant vines in the plain below the village. The household stock was comprised of a horse, a donkey, two oxen, three goats, about 50 sheep, 80 turkeys, and a number of chickens.[10] The family's oxen were one of fifteen yokes in the village and, at their peak, they could plow 0.35 ha in a day. The family plow was a wooden ard with an iron shoe, and family members followed the plow using tools to break up the clods. They expected wheat yields on the lower terraces at Ancient Corinth of about 4 or 5:1. Aristomenes could recall one memorably bad year when they harvested less than 2:1 and one particularly good year when their fields gave over 6:1. Different varieties of wheat were sown depending on the quality of the land. In the mid 20th century, farmers sowed 200 *okes* of *eretria* (a variety of wheat) per ha on the terraces near the village and 30 okes of *mavrogani* (a different variety of wheat) per ha on the coastal plain below.[11]

---

[8] Allbaugh 1953, 463 table 31; Department of Commerce 1949, 16 table 2. The US dollar sums above are not adjusted for cost of living. Subsistence farmers lived largely on what they produced; many services were exchanged for services in kind or produce, for instance to the priest for a baptism, wedding, funeral or memorial. Cash was primarily required to pay taxes. Many agricultural and household tools such as plows, harrows, baskets, sieves, cradles, looms, chests, plates and spoons were made of wood at home. Many items such as plows, millstones, storage pithoi and copper kettles were dowry items and required an initial outlay of cash but were well treated and survived to be inherited by another generation. The main difference between the Greek subsistence farmer and the rural poor of the United States was that the Arberores family held title to their land whereas sharecropping Americans did not. Greeks had capital investments but low incomes whereas Americans paid share rents but seem to have had relatively high incomes.

[9] Every year one third of their land was sown with wheat, one third with pulses, and one third lay fallow. Little barley was sown and then only for animal fodder. Pulses planted included *lathouries, vikou, koukia* and *revithia*. Lathouries were for animal fodder and never eaten except by the very poorest in the occupation during the Second World War and are held to have been responsible for their lifelong physical impairments.

[10] Every family had at least 40 sheep except the few families with no land on which to graze them. All households kept at least 50 turkeys and several chickens.

[11] An oke is 1.27 kg. Eretria and mavrogani are both varieties of wheat and their differential use reflects their qualities, the quality of the land on which they were sown, and the ability of the farmer to judge what should be sown where. Engels (1990, 27 n. 30) cites

Three documents from the early 19th century spell out the precise arrangement between landlord and tenant in Greece. One document is published in an obscure Greek regional journal, the second is an entry in the diary of an American philanthropist, and the third is from a letter of complaint to the Greek government from disgruntled tenants.[12] They are pertinent to earlier periods of Greek history because they document agricultural arrangements in Greece rather than some far-flung part of the world. The issue of their modernity is mitigated by the fact that patterns of wealth distribution and agricultural practices in Greece probably changed less in the three millennia before ca. 1950 than in the sixty years since.[13] These three documents demonstrate that sharecropping was not simply a contract between landlord and tenant. Instead, the state and other individuals took a substantial share leaving the main stakeholders with a small proportion of the crop for their own use. The documents present an opportunity to explore how much land a family of Corinthian subsistence farmers required in order to survive.

Sharecropping Documents for Greece

The first of the three early 19th-century documents was written in Italian by someone present at a threshing floor in Boeotia. It states:

> Throughout Boeotia the common contract between landowners and cultivators is as follows: the *aga* gives the cultivator two cattle and the cultivator provides another two because four cattle are required to cultivate a yoke of land.[14] If the cultivator has the means he provides another two cattle to make a total of six. They keep two in reserve to replace the first pair when they tire. The aga gives them 30 *koila* of wheat and 10 koila of barley for

---

Salmon (1984, 130, who cites Jardé 1925, 31–60) to justify his pessimistic wheat yields of 3:1 and a sowing rate of 188 okes/ha for wheat.

[12] After surveying five decades of sharecropping literature in some detail, these and certain Egyptian papyri are the only documents I have found which offer any detail, but doubtless there are others.

[13] Ethnographical analogy is much weakened with geographical and chronological distance from the subject. Hence a comparison of sharecropping arrangements in India under British rule in the early 19th century is less valid for comparison with Greek situations in the Roman imperial period than a comparison with arrangements in 19th century Greece under Ottoman rule. The form of colonialism, languages, history, cultures, and land in British India in no way relate to Roman Greece. In the Ottoman Empire, however, the language, history, and culture were all linear descendants of the Roman Empire and the productive capacity of the land was, of course, the same.

[14] An aga was a landowner.

sowing.[15] They don't give them other seed. Usually 200 stremmata makes up a yoke of land; that is 100 stremmata (about 10 ha) for the first year and other 100 stremmata (left fallow) for the second year.[16] The cultivator is responsible for (organizing) the harvest, the threshing and the winnowing of the wheat and barley. During the winnowing the *spahi* and the aga, the *kehaya* or the *soumbasi* are present along with the secretary.[17] They measure the crop and calculate division as follows:

Assuming they have counted (a yield of)	300 koila
they subtract the tithe	30
for reaping	30
threshing with a mare at 5%	15
food for the reapers at 2%	6
for soumbasi's salary	5
for use of threshing floor	2
for the *protoyeros* and secretary's salary (excluding the share of the bishop and priest)	2
for the rural guard's salary (and) for the summery animal keeper's salary	2
for the spahi's salary	1
for seed	30
the expenses are:	123
remaining from the 300 measured	177

This sum should be shared in two equal parts by the aga and the cultivator. For each village yoke they are required to sow 2 k. of wheat and 2 k. of barley separately for the soumbasi. The soumbasi gives to them the seed and they (the cultivators) are required to undertake the reaping and the threshing for him.[18]

The document is most informative about the rent relationship between the tenant and the landowner. It is a sharecropping contract wherein the tenant paid an agreed proportion of the harvest rather than a fixed rent to the landowner. Most economic geographers tend to believe that the division was a simple 2:1 division, if one or other of the parties undertook the 'risk' or 1:1 if the investment was equal. In the Boeotian case, the situation

---

[15] Doursther (1840, 185–86) values 1 Constantinopolitan kilo of wheat = 22 okes = 35.11 liters, where 1 oke = 1.2829 kg. The Peloponnesian unit was the same as that at Constantinople.

[16] Today the *stremma* is measured as 1000 m² but the pre-metric unit in Greece existed in several forms depending on location (and perhaps fertility of the land) between about 900 and 1,270 sq m.

[17] A kehaya and soubasi were terms used for the landowner's agent; a sipahi was a mounted soldier.

[18] Christopoulou 1971–2, 464–65.

is transparent: the contract was a 1:1 contract whereby traction, fees, labor, seed and taxes were deducted before the landlord and tenant divided the remainder. Ten percent was set aside for seed and a full 30 percent went for taxes, fees, and labor. The tenant and landlord each retained about 30 percent. From this, if the landlord and tenant were both Christians, they also paid head tax and a sum to the local priest (table 6.1).

Two of the surprising points raised by this document are the number of plow teams required to work a yoke of land and the yield. We have become accustomed to understand that a yoke of land was the extent which a single team of oxen could plow in a year. Here we are told that two teams were considered essential and three teams were preferable suggesting that we should redefine the word yoke in reference to land measurement. Rather than measure a yoke in terms of ox stamina, we should consider it as the amount of land a farmer could plow in a season.

Plowing season in Greece is short. It begins after the first good rains in September and ends when farmers sowed their beans and winter wheat. Land sown with grain required a single plowing but the fallow, often sown with beans, vegetables and vetch (for animal fodder), required two successive plowings. Plowing thus formed a major part of a farmer's year. In Greece a plow team plowed more or less one third of a hectare a day, depending on the soil and the age of the oxen, and the Boeotian sharecroppers cited above required 25 days to plow their wheat fields and 50 days for their fallow. At three plowed furrows per meter, this represents

Table 6.1. Actual Boeotian cereal sharecropping case, with 1:1 tenant – landlord division: taxes, costs and gains (based on Christopoulou 1971–2)

	Tenant	Shared	Landlord	Tenant	Shared	Landlord
Harvest		100%		8468 kg		
Dhekatia		10		847		
Police and guards		2.3		195		
To the harvesters		10		847		
Harvesters' board		2		169		
Fee for threshing		5.7		483		
Seed		10		847		
Legal fees		1		85		
Crop remaining		59		4996		
1:1 division	29.5		29.5	2498		2498
To the priest	?		?			
Other payments	?		?			
Share	<29.5		<29.5			

a linear distance of nearly 900 km, the equivalent of walking from Austin, Texas to Memphis, Tennessee.

The given yield of 10:1, a harvest of 300 koila from 30 sown, is much greater than the average 6:1 most economic geographers tend to estimate for Greece. Greek wheat yields, of course, vary greatly by region and our pre-modern sources for southern Greece give a range of between 3:1 high on Mount Taygetus to more than 20:1 on irrigated land in the Messenian plain.[19] On poor land in the Mani, sowing took place after the first rains in September and October but on good soil at Gastouni in Elis and Sparta, and in Messenia the sowing season was between November and January.[20] Until comparatively recently, when new strains of cereals were introduced, the density of sowing depended on rainfall, altitude and the quality of the soil. Modern farmers in the Peloponnese sow wheat comparatively heavily. In Arcadia, for instance, 120 okes/ha is usual on high land in the mountains, 150 okes/ha on the lower slopes and between 150 to 200 okes/ha in the Alpheios and Ladon River plains.[21] The 19th-century Boeotian farmers sowed only 66 okes/ha (85 kg) which is consistent with lighter sowing regimes described by other 19th-century sources.[22]

There are practical reasons for sowing at a lower density. Simply stated, in areas of low rainfall in the growing season, the net harvest from fields sown at higher rates will be only slightly greater than more lightly sown fields but the return on the investment of seed will be significantly less. Clayey soils, such as those at Corinth, required denser seeding because germination and rooting was less efficient than in loamy soils. Densely sown crops show greater variability in output but the most important consideration is that they develop fewer tillers (side shoots) with flowering heads and the seed yield ratio is thus much lower than less densely sown cereals.[23]

Logically, the amount of land required to feed a family varied according to location. In the case of the Boeotian farmers, the ample land cultivated and the harvests reaped ensured that they had sufficient returns to meet their taxes and rent, feed the family, and still have a considerable surplus for sale. If we accept the figure given for the harvest as realistic, we can estimate the size of the harvest. From the document, we see that the

---

[19] Leake 1830, 322.
[20] Leake 1830, 13–14, 147, 322.
[21] Tsotsoros 1986, 128–29.
[22] Leake 1830, 13; Zarinebaf, Bennet, and Davis 2005, 194, n. 168.
[23] Gallant 1991, 46–48.

farmers reaped 8,500 kg (300 koila, where 1 *koile* = 22 okes = 28.226 kg) of which both landlord and farmer received 2,500 kgs (table 6.1). From the contemporary Corinthian contract which follows below, we see that the Boeotian sharecroppers were much more than subsistence farmers.

The second document is preserved in the diary of Samuel Gridley Howe, the Bostonian doctor, who founded Washingtonia after the Greek War of Independence as a model farm and settlement for Greek refugees.[24] Howe had asked the Greek government for a grant of 500 ha that had once been part of the local Ottoman magnate's estate and ended up receiving 1,000 ha tax-free for five years.[25] Howe's original colony consisted of a church, a school converted from Kiamel Bey's country residence, and 36 families: in all 200 people. By the end of January 1830, the number of families had grown to about 50 who cultivated the land as sharecroppers. Howe's plan was that they pay their half share rents to a community bank. This bank, in turn, would provide funds to establish new colonists, staff the school, and provide community services such as a hospital.[26] Howe recounted the local Corinthian system of share rent as follows:

> Others continue to come, and at last the [former] inhabitants of this place showed themselves, and asked if they might come and build here again. From thirty three families they are reduced to fifteen, who are living in the caves about here, not having dared to abide in the village for six years for fear of the Greek soldiery, who took from them their substance and at last pulled the houses to pieces. The inhabitants have contrived to save among them five pair of oxen with which they wish to go to work under my protection, as they express it. The best-informed man among them, and the best off, had a long confab with me this morning, and amused me much. "*Effendi*" (my lord), said he, "we have been accustomed to obey one, as our fathers did before us; we know that nothing goes well without a head, and we pray that you will grant us the same privileges that you are going to give others."
>
> The old fellow then began to descant on the advantages of their situation under the Turks, and said it was better than their present one in theory.

---

[24] Washingtonia is now the village called Hexamilia located a few km east of Ancient Corinth. Howe also established the renowned Perkins Institute for the Blind in Watertown, Massachusetts, while his wife Julia Ward Howe won greater and longer lasting acclaim for writing "The Battle Hymn of the Republic" and for advocating the establishment of "Mother's Day."

[25] Richards 1909, 339, 341, 365. Washingtonia included the villages of Upper and Lower Hexamilia which he extended over to the port of Kenchries (361). Kiamel Bey of Corinth had formerly owned the land between Hexamilion and Kenchries, and had warehouses at the port of Kenchries.

[26] Richards 1909, 363.

This led me to examine the affair, and after much cross-questioning and difficulty, I made out the relative situation then and now.

The Bey gave them their house, land to cultivate, seed to sow it with, and loans without interest; they cultivated the earth in their own way, and at harvest time made the following division:

Suppose a peasant reaped one hundred bushels: he had first to subtract –

The seed he had received, say	20 per cent
He paid to the priest	½
Blacksmith per annum	½
Tax for Sultan	10
To labourers for the harvest	5
To the Kehaya, or agent	10
Horse for beating out (threshing)	5
	51 per cent

But the Bey made a present apparently in this way: when the harvest was stocking, the peasant took one sheaf or bundle in every ten for his family, which taken from 51 leaves 41. Then from 41 to 100 we have 59 per cent, which was divided between the Bey and the peasant, leaving [the latter] 29½ per cent. But then the Kehaya, or agent of the Bey, made every peasant sow, cultivate, and reap for him 3 kilo of grain, making 111 okes; so that the peasant [actually] received about 25 per cent. Now, under the Government, he has land, and pays-

One third of the crop, making, say	33 per cent
He pays the priest	½
Blacksmith	½
Expenses of harvesting, say	10
Expenses of his house	3
	47 per cent

Taking 47 from 100 leaves 53 per cent, while before he had only 25.

They could always borrow money from the agent of the Bey, the first time without interest, afterwards by paying eight per cent.[27]

Howe was a doctor and was used, as part of his management of American post-war relief in Greece, to making proper accounts but his account presents a few problems. The agent's salary is double that of the Boeotian agent's but, as in Boeotia, the Washingtonia sharecroppers had to sow and reap a portion for the agent separately from the crop to be shared. Although Howe accounts for this in the calculation of Kiamel's gift, it does not appear as part of his tabulation. Thirdly, Howe makes the equation 3 kilo = 111 okes whereas in the Peloponnese we would expect the Constantinopolitan

---

[27] Richards 1909, 352–54.

equivalent of 3 kilo = 66 okes. Alas, we cannot suppose that the 111 okes was the harvested quantity from the 3 kilo sown. This would infer a yield of less than 2:1 where Howe (and others) estimated average yields of 5:1 in the region. I suspect the original figure the peasants were to sow for the agent was 5 kilo = 110 okes which compares with the total of 4 koila sown by the Boeotians for their soubasi. Finally, Howe neglects to deduct seed from the portion remaining to the peasant under the new Greek government – this would reduce the amount remaining to him for his personal use to only 33%.

If we accept the figure of 111 okes as the portion planted for the agent and Howe's inference that this was about 4.5% of the total crop, then we can estimate the amount of seed and the size of the total crop (table 6.2). At 1.283 kg/oke of wheat, 111 okes are 142.413 kg, which is 4.5% of a 3,164.7 kg harvest, and both landlord and tenant each received 790 kg. With a yield of 5:1, the amount of seed required was 633 kg. If we assume a sowing density of 90 kg/ha, then the cultivator was cultivating about 7 ha every year which, if they farmed a two-year rotation with fallow or beans and vetches, implies they rented a total extent of 14 ha. Had these cultivators been independent property owners they could have lived, like Mr. Arberores senior and his family, on a 7–8 ha plot.

After the War of Independence, the Greek state confiscated property belonging to the Ottoman magnates and rented it out. The state received rent and tax on the land leaving the tenant with a portion of the harvest almost identical to that he received under Kiamel Bey. A letter of complaint from Corinthian cash croppers, the third document, summarizes their yield, rent, taxes and expenses (table 6.3).[28]

Table 6.2. Washingtonia case, with 1:1 tenant – landlord share: taxes, costs and gains (based on Richards 1909)

	Tenant	Shared	Landlord	Tenant	Shared	Landlord
Harvest		100%		3165 kgs		
Dhekatia		10		316.5		
Expenses		20		633		
Seed		20		633		
Crop remaining		50		1583		
Share	25		25	791		791

---

28 Andreades 1996, 198–99.

Table 6.3. Corinthian cash croppers' costs and gains from agriculture ca. 1835
(based on Andreades 1996)

	Cash cropper
Harvest	100
Demosio tax	25
Demotiko tax	2
Rent	4
Upkeep of oxen	2
To the priest	2
Police and guards	2
To the harvesters	10
Harvesters' board	3
Fee for threshing	5
Seed	20
Cultivator's share	25

These three documents show how much the state, various administrators and landlords could extract from the harvest while leaving the cultivator enough to subsist and to maintain a minimum of livestock. For the purposes of making land grants of confiscated property, the Greek government in 1835 determined that a family would require 4 ha of irrigated land in the plain (which was a rare commodity), 8 ha of un-watered land in the plain, or 12 ha of land on hill slopes.[29]

With the figures for Corinthian sowing density and yields we can make an independent estimate of how much land was required to feed (and no more) a single Corinthian subsistence farmer, whether sharecropper or owner cultivator. These estimates are based on a staple diet of wheat, barley, and legumes. They suggest that a family of four adult and young adult owner cultivators required over 5 ha, and a family of sharecroppers required twice as much to feed themselves and no more (tables 6.4 and 6.5).[30] From this, we can conclude that the Greek government was essentially correct in its calculations and that the Arberores family and both Kiamel's and Howe's Washingtonia sharecroppers literally lived at subsistence level cultivating 8 ha and 14 ha respectively.

---

[29] McGrew 1986, 170.

[30] In order to keep the mathematics uncomplicated, I have used figures for post-war Crete in 1947 when the average annual consumption of cereals and vegetables was 107 kg of wheat, 29.2 kg of barley, and 108.5 kg of vegetables and fruit. Potatoes in the modern Greek diet obviously should be substituted with cereals when dealing with periods predating their introduction; see Allbaugh 1953, 107 table A51.

Table 6.4. Number of cultivators supported if 1 ha is planted exclusively with a single crop using average Ancient Corinth yields. S = Share cropper, O = Owner cultivator. The tax figure is that of the Peloponnese in the early 19th century (Leake 1830, 11)

		Produce kg/ha	Seed reserve	Tax 1/7	Deductions 23.3%	Owner	Cultivator	Calories	People supported
Wheat 5:1	S	450	90	64.3	104.9	95.4	95.4	295,740	0.56
	O	450	90	64.3	104.9		190.9	591,480	1.12
Barley 6:1	S	540	90	77.1	125.9	123.5	123.5	327,275	0.62
	O	540	90	77.1	125.9		247.0	654,550	1.24
Legumes 2.6:1	S	442	170	63.1		104.5	104.5	137,870	0.26

Table 6.5. Amount of land required in Ancient Corinth to support one adult male (S = Share cropper or O = Owner cultivator) based on local yields and consumption in post-war Crete (Cretan data from Allbaugh 1953, 107 table A51)

	Consumption kg/year	Available kg/ha	Area required ha/person	Area required 2 yr rotation w/ pulses
S				
Wheat	107.0	95.4	1.12	2.24
Barley	29.2	123.5	0.24	0.47
Pulses	108.5	104.5	1.04	0.00
Total			2.40	2.71
O				
Wheat	107.0	190.9	0.56	1.12
Barley	29.2	247.0	0.12	0.24
Pulses	108.5	208.9	0.52	0.00
Total			1.20	1.36

Rich and Poor in Antiquity

Our figures from Ottoman and more recent pre-modern agricultural sources consistently indicate that about 7 to 8 ha of unirrigated land in the plain were sufficient to support a subsistence farmer in southwestern Messenia and the area immediately around Corinth. Many farmers in other parts of the Peloponnese will have required much the same, while others in less fertile areas would have required more. Those living in the well-watered plains of Helos, Messenia and Elis, for instance, certainly required less. These figures are somewhat in excess of the 4 to 5 ha suggested by other scholars.[31] If we infer that similar techniques and conditions existed in the past, we may consider the disparity between the very poorest and more affluent members of society in, for example, early Roman Corinth.

We now know that after Mummius's sack in 146 BCE, there were sufficient resident Corinthians remaining to warrant the local production of fine ware pottery.[32] We can estimate with a reasonable degree of certainty that the agricultural land within an hour walking distance of Corinth could support about 700–800 families of independent subsistence farmers, say between 2,500 to 4,000 people. The best land was *ager publicus* and although provision for the sale of all or part was included in the *lex agraria* of 111 BCE,[33] at least part of it remained unsold in 63 BCE.[34] Apparently, this land was still available nineteen years later for the creation of the new colony. Strabo (8.6.23) says that the Sikyonians obtained most of the Corinthian land although they could not have had title to the ager publicus if it retained this status in 63 and 44 BCE. Individuals could have had usufruct rights, that is, the right to cultivate in return for rent, to the Corinthian ager publicus if it was designated *ager censorius* although there is no surviving evidence that it was so designated. As such, Sikyonian and other individuals may have purchased the rights to collect rent from cultivators of the ager publicus for renewable periods of five years.[35] It is conceivable that such arrangements took the form of fixed and share rents of the kind discussed above for the early 19th century. In such a case, the population of post-Mummian Corinth will likely have been closer to 400–500 families and about 1600 to 2,500 people living alongside several other small Corinthian communities on the Isthmus, inland and to the west.[36] Many, if not most, of these people will have identified themselves as Corinthians and will have preserved at least some of the traditions and

---

[31] Gallant 1991, 82–87; Walter and Schofield 1989, 13.

[32] See the chapter by James, this volume.

[33] Walbank 1997, 99–100.

[34] Lintott (1992, 281) commenting on line 101 of the *lex agraria* refers to Cicero (*leg. agr.* 1.5, 2.51) concerning the land law proposed by Publius Servilius Rullus.

[35] Roselaar 2008, 128–33. Roselaar offers a very full discussion of ager publicus, which is clearly a much more complex subject than commentators on Corinth to date have appreciated.

[36] See the chapter by James in this volume for a lower estimate, based on known usage of buildings and extant pottery finds.

identity of Hellenistic Corinth. Even in a community of this scale there will have been a hierarchy of cultivators, artisans, merchants, and overseers, and perhaps even a few of the richer echelons of society. Many of those providing services or engaged in a profession will have lived in close proximity to one another, for instance in the former city of Corinth. This center of population may not have had a magistrate or a tax collector but there may well have been a need for administrators and supervisors of some kind and the framework of a local religious hierarchy, albeit junior. Quite possibly there was an agricultural market, corn merchants, stables, inns, and a smithy, and Corinth will have had some of the services of a small town rather than those of an agricultural village. It still had access to those resources that had once made Corinth a prospering city such as its location at the hub of regional land and sea communications, abundant water, stone and clay beds. Moreover, enough of the city center stood to frame and orient the Roman colony's forum and its monuments, for instance a building below the Julian Basilica and the South Stoa.[37]

Before he died in March 44 BCE, Gaius Julius Caesar arranged for a colony on the Corinthian ager publicus. The authorities presumably assessed how much land each colonist required to survive in this environment by canvassing the locals and inspecting tax registers.[38] Doukellis, Walbank, and Romano have independently established that the coastal plain from the slopes of Mt. Geranion westwards was centuriated between the late 2nd and mid 1st century BCE (fig. 6.1).[39] Doukellis recognized blocks of 256 (16 × 16) and 400 (20 × 20) *actus*, while Romano believes they were units of 384 (16 × 24) actus. The simplest division of these two units is 16 (8), 32 (16), and 64 (32) actus (*iugera*) of about 2, 4, and 8 ha plots respectively. Assuming that the Roman officials thought in terms of these convenient multiples, and that they had assessed the supportive capacity of the land (table 6.6), I suggest each colonist was to receive a tract or several smaller plots amounting to 64 actus (8 ha).

---

[37] *Corinth* I.5, 37–39; *Corinth* I.4, 100–102.
[38] Caesar's *lex Campana* allocated plots of 10 iugera in the *ager Campanus* (Cic. *Att.* 2.16.1; Suet. *Caes.* 20.3). Evans (1981, 432) observes that, having been ager publicus for so long, it was well known that 10 iugera plots would suffice.
[39] Doukellis 1994; Walbank 1997, 100–103; Romano 2005, n. 66.

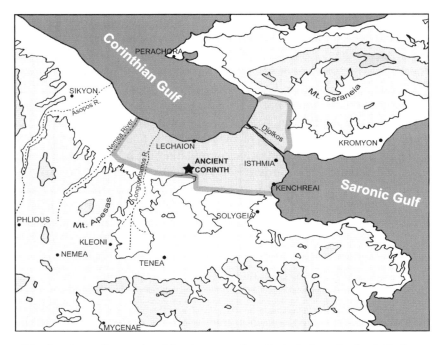

Fig. 6.1. Area of centuriated land surrounding Corinth. Drawing by J. Herbst.

Table 6.6. Allotment size at the colonies of Vibo, Thurii, Bononia and Aquileia
(based on Gargola 1995, 90)

Colony	Date BCE	Colonists	*Iugera Pedites*	*Iugera Equites*
Vibo (Livy 35.40.5)	192	3,700 + 300	15 (3.80 ha)	30 (7.59 ha)
Thurii (Livy 35.9.7)	193		20 (5.06 ha)	40 (10.12 ha)
Bononia (Livy 37.57.8)	189	3,000	50 (12.65 ha)	70 (17.71 ha)
Aquileia (Livy 40.34.2)	181/80		50 (12.65 ha)	140 (35.42 ha)

The plain from the Isthmus to the Sikyonian border amounts to about
130 sq km of centuriated land with Corinth located pretty much at the
mid-point of the strip. If, as the evidence of Mr. Arberores in the mid
20th century and of the other cases presented here suggest, we may allow
each ordinary Corinthian colonist a plot of 8 ha without being overly generous. This extent of centuriated land is, therefore, sufficient for a total
of about 1,600 allotments of 8 ha for an equal number of colonists and
their families. These figures suggest that the agricultural population of
the colony was somewhat smaller than that suggested by Engels, and that

Walbank's estimate of 2,000–3,000 families was closer to the mark.[40] It is possible that the previous cultivators of the ager publicus also formed part of the colony as what in medieval Greece were called *paroikoi*, agricultural laborers (*incolae*) without the same privileges as the colonists.[41] They may have continued to farm as laborers, tenants, or as landholders on the margins of the colonial allotments. It is also possible that the merchants who formed part of the colony received tax and trade concessions instead of land.

Walbank has rightly suggested that life in the early colony was hard and the community was initially small and living close to, if not at, subsistence levels. The early colony of Corinth almost certainly did not generate a significant surplus for export besides taxes paid in kind. Walbank also envisaged that Corinth's location ensured a steady growth in the local economy that presented opportunities for the colonists to earn day wages to supplement their farm income. The very existence of the colony also ensured that there was a local market for the small agricultural surpluses and there were certainly magistrates and tax collectors within the community. I imagine that some of the original colonists may have sold a portion of their land to invest in a craft or in business. I also imagine that careful farmers gradually acquired enough extra cash to acquire land that they then rented to others and engaged in other business while being partially supported by their tenants. Outside the plowing season, farmers may have used their oxen to haul loads over the Isthmus or from the ports of Lechaion and Kenchreai to the city thereby earning a valuable supplement to his income.[42] Someone who actually invested in haulage, working every day of the year, may have earned a maximum income of 5,000 kg of wheat per yoke of oxen in a year. Although such full employment is highly optimistic, the pre-tax earnings of someone working two thirds of the year was twice what he would gain by cultivating an 8 ha plot.[43]

---

[40] Engels 1990, 22; Walbank 1997, 105.

[41] Roselaar 2008, 77. According to Pomponius D.50.16.239.2, an *incola* was "someone who has established his domicile in any region; the Greeks call such a person a *paroikos*. Nor are those who stay in a town the only people who are *incolae*, but also those who hold land within the territory of any town in such a way that they establish themselves there as if in a fixed abode."

[42] David Pettegrew, this volume. argues differently. He understands the harbors of Corinth to have been emporia and I understand them to have been entrepôts.

[43] From Diocletian's price edict (17.3), Clark and Haswell (1967, 184–89) calculate that overland haulage cost 4.6 kg/ton/km. The median rate of the 34 examples cited by Clark and Haswell is 0.34% per km. At the lower median rate, hauling a half ton load of wheat

A growing town and market would also change the nature of agricultural production favoring higher value crops, such as vegetables, over subsistence staples like wheat in the immediate hinterland of the city and its ports.[44] Within a generation, Corinth was a market town and some of the original colonist families, and possibly even some of the paroikoi, were no longer subsistence farmers but solidly established with business interests and supportive of other much poorer agricultural families. By the close of the century, Corinth had a vital economy attracting immigrants and its population had perhaps doubled. It was a town of regional significance and had a fully developed social hierarchy. Within a hundred years of the formation of the colony, Corinth was a city of empire-wide significance with two dependent harbor towns acting as both entrepôts and emporia.[45] At the time of Paul's visit, international commerce was of major significance to the city, so much so that within two decades, Nero sought to facilitate the passage of cargoes by cutting the diolkos canal with slaves brought from Jerusalem for the purpose. Fortunately for, or perhaps because of, those employed in the docks and in haulage this initiative was quickly abandoned.

The Evolution of Inequality in Early Roman Corinth

Although this paper is presented as if there were few primary or secondary sources for the rural economy in Greece or for the Roman Empire at large, this is certainly not the case and the bibliography is extensive.[46] But the historical sources are limited and patchy while the secondary literature by necessity is a mosaic assembled from estimates and both primary and ethnographic sources. Economic studies of the Roman Empire tend

---

8 km across the Isthmus road earned the haulier 13.6 kg of wheat ($0.0036 \times 500 \times 8$). If repeated every day, the maximum annual income was $13.6 \times 365 = 4,964$ kg. Calculated at this rate, transport across the Isthmus added only 2.7% to the cost of the cargo if we assume the haulier also undertook the unloading and loading at either end. For haulage across the Isthmus, see Sanders 1996 and 2005b.

[44] So, paraphrasing Cato (Agr. 8.2), "Close to the City [grow] all kinds of vegetables, and plants for wreaths;" and Varro (Rust. 1.16.3), "Near to a city, it is profitable to have gardens of violets and roses and produce for which there is a demand but there would be no gain to cultivate the same things on a farm far from a market."

[45] For a Graph Theoretical analysis of the central place of Corinth within the communications network of southern Greece in the Roman period, see Sanders and Whitbread 1990.

[46] For bibliography on the Roman Empire at large, see Scheidel and Friesen 2009. For Greece in particular, see Gallant 1991; Garnsey 1988; Sallares 1991.

to deal with the big picture and generally have to find some common currency such as gold- or wheat-equivalents to homogenize data drawn from chronologically and geographically diverse parts of the empire. The intent here was not to ignore this mass of excellent scholarship, but to avoid the imposition of an average Roman world economy view on one small part of Southern Greece. By looking at data specific to the region, it is possible to get a more nuanced idea of the local economy and to focus on the agricultural potential of Corinth's immediate hinterland and those who cultivated it.

We can catch a glimpse of the contrast of wealth that may have existed in Greece through time. The so-called Ricardo-Malthusian trap is an economic model that has survived two centuries. It holds that the sum total of wealth is directly proportionate to the land resources available; in periods of lower population, this wealth is divided between fewer people, which leads to an increase in population and to relative impoverishment, which in turn leads to higher mortality and lower population. Worldwide this pattern held until the Industrial Revolution when average wealth and total population in industrialized countries, such as Britain and later Germany and France, increased dramatically. Statistics for wealth distribution for pre-industrial economies are rare and problematic, but figures from more recent undeveloped economies are illuminating. Arguably, the economies of Brazil and India were not industrialized on the scale of 18th-century England, even in the late 19th and mid 20th centuries respectively. Over 60% of the population of these countries had an annual income at or close to subsistence and only 2% earned more than 7 to 14 times subsistence level (graph 6.1).

These figures are compatible with the conclusions of Walter Scheidel and Steven Friesen who made the reasonable assumption that between 65 and 88% of the Roman Empire's population earned subsistence incomes and less, and that 97% earned less than five times subsistence level.[47] What the Brazilian and Indian data do suggest is that the number of people in the income group immediately above those living at subsistence may have been a little larger than Scheidel and Friesen estimate (graphs 6.1 and 6.2). Graphically, these actual and assumed percentages very likely resemble the income structure of Greece at any time in its past between the Mycenaean period and the mid 20th century. The two thirds of the population who lived at or near subsistence levels were perhaps small

---

[47] Friesen 2005, 364–69; Scheidel and Friesen 2009.

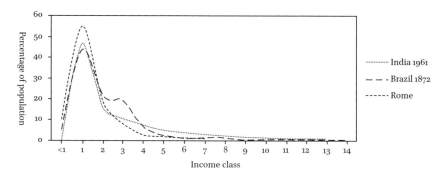

Graph 6.1. Income inequality in the Roman Empire, Brazil 1872 and India 1961 (adapted from Scheidel and Friesen 2009, Milanovic, Lindert, and Williamson, 2007b, 36–43, and Sreenivasa and Ram Jain 1974, table 4a). 1 = subsistence or near subsistence income.

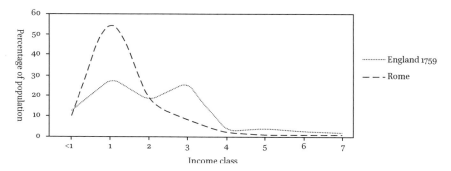

Graph 6.2. Undeveloped (Roman Empire) vs. developed (England & Wales 1759) (from Scheidel and Friesen 2009 and Milanovic, Lindert and Williamson 2007b).

landowners, tenant farmers, and day laborers. The 20% or more in the next bracket were perhaps artisans, landlords, and tradesmen. The richest two percent had an annual income eight and more times the income of the poorest and doubtless had investments well beyond the regional level.

Milanovic, Lindert, and Williamson have suggested that income inequality is a variable determined by the complexity of the economy.[48] In theory, a simple economy, in which a large majority of the population lives at subsistence levels, has less of a surplus to support elites and therefore inequality between richest and poorest is limited. The early

---

[48] Milanovic, Lindert, and Williamson 2007a, 4–5.

colony of Corinth was such a society, consisting of subsistence farmers and a core of administrators who sent tax revenues to the capital. The ratios of rank and inequality in such a situation resembled 89 cultivators: 10 managers: 1 administrator where the cultivators lived at a subsistence level and the managers and administrators had incomes of multiples of subsistence level. The graph of income inequality in the early colony must have looked like the empire-wide distribution proposed by Scheidel and Friesen.[49]

As the colony grew, different opportunities arose which changed the shape of the local economy and while the empire-wide distribution of wealth did not change significantly, on the local scale at Corinth income inequality at the lower levels became more complex. It may have more resembled 60 cultivators: 30 tradesmen and managers: 1 administrator with a much larger gap between the poorest and the richest elements. The graph of incomes may have more resembled that of mid 18th-century England and Wales, that 'nation of shopkeepers,' where a significant proportion of individuals had incomes two and three times greater than subsistence and where there was a larger managerial and administrative echelon (graph 6.2).[50] Corinth at the time of Paul may have had quite a substantial consumer class, as did Brazil in 1872 (graph 6.1), especially when compared with the average income distribution of the Roman Empire.

A plethora of data helps us to identify the super-rich echelons of Greek society. Just one measure – land – shows that the richest had resources equivalent to the combined wealth of hundreds or even thousands of the poorest. For instance in 8 BCE, Gaius Caecelius Isidorus, a wealthy freedman somewhat impoverished by the Civil Wars, bequeathed 60,000,000 sesterces, 3,600 yokes of oxen, herds numbering 257,000 head, and 4,116 slaves in his will.[51] If Columella's figures are taken as an indicator, the oxen were sufficient to plow an estate of ca. 90,000 ha.[52] Lucius Domitius Ahenobarbus at Corfinium, in 49 BCE, promised 40 iugera to each of his soldiers from his own estate. Since his army numbered some 10,000 soldiers, he committed about 400,000 iugera or 100,000 ha and more since the officers were to receive more *pro rata parte*.[53] The extent of his estate was equivalent to the Julian colony at Corinth.

---

[49] Scheidel and Friesen 2009, table 10.
[50] Milanovic, Lindert, and Williamson 2007b, 53–54.
[51] Plin. *NH* 33.135.
[52] Columella, *Rust.* 2.12.7.
[53] Caes. *B Civ.* 1.17.4.

Conclusions

As observed in the introduction, these rich and super-rich individuals are quite visible in the written, monumental, and archaeological record but their thousands of dependents living at subsistence levels are not. And who were those whose incomes lay somewhere between sufficiency and opulence? One group documented here is the Boeotian farmers who rented land for cash cropping wheat. This group retained three to four times the amount of wheat kept by the Hexamilia sharecroppers. In my brief speculation on lower income groups in the early Roman colony of Corinth, one group consisted of the colonists and agricultural laborers (*paroikoi*) who separated themselves from the land by a degree and engaged in trades such as haulage. I would suggest that this income group is visible in the archaeological record as living on 3 to 4 times the subsistence level. They may be recognized in the archaeological record as those who had decorated local and imported ceramics, glass drinking vessels, expensive storage pithoi, and a garbage midden containing animal bones. If so, we can detect another middling group with an income greater than 4 times subsistence whose archaeological legacy consisted of mosaic floors, small scale sculpture, and wall painting. This is a standard of living seen in the 4th-century Panayia Field Domus at Corinth.[54]

The poorest echelons, approximately 65+% (Scheidel and Friesen 85%) of the population, including the landless farmers living close to or at subsistence level, had few non-perishable material possessions that survived in the archaeological record and so they remain invisible in the world's museums and libraries. It is not surprising, then, that their means of existence has escaped the attention of archaeologists and historians who are data-blind below a certain high threshold of material wealth. It is high time that archaeologists and historians changed their focus and began studying human physical remains more systematically and exca-vating in places where we will find the urban and rural poor rather than their employers and rulers. In terms of the physical anthropology, we need to excavate, study, and publish the graves of individuals with few or no 'grave goods.'[55] In terms of domestic archaeology, we need to dig urban and rural sites where there are low expectations of 'finds' beyond those we can recover in a sieve, water sieve, or soil sample. These sorts of

---

[54] Sanders 2005a; Sweetman and Sanders 2005.
[55] Rohn, Barnes, and Sanders 2009.

investigations would build up new data about a mute segment of ancient Corinthian society. Since this group made up the majority of the population, a better understanding of these Corinthians will require us to alter significantly our reconstructions of Corinth before, during, and after the colonial period.

CHAPTER SEVEN

THE DIOLKOS AND THE EMPORION: HOW A LAND BRIDGE FRAMED THE COMMERCIAL ECONOMY OF ROMAN CORINTH

David K. Pettegrew

Introduction

Territory has always formed a common theme in explanations of the wealth and power of the city of Corinth.[1] Thucydides was the first to connect Corinthian wealth to the city's situation on the Isthmus and its commercial facility (1.13.5). When the Greeks developed navies, he noted, the Corinthians built a fleet, suppressed piracy, and provided a trade market making their city wealthy and powerful. Roman writers repeated, expanded, and reinterpreted the explanation of Thucydides about the commercial facility of the Isthmus and its relationship to Corinthian wealth.[2] By the end of antiquity, Corinth was inextricably associated with the image of a maritime city whose Isthmus fostered commerce, prosperity, and power.[3]

In the 18th and 19th centuries, when Corinth became the subject of historical study, scholars again invoked territory to make sense of the city. Historians drawing on ancient texts regularly remarked on two factors in particular that influenced the city's historical fortunes.[4] They noted firstly that the commercial facilities of the Isthmus and the harbors created markets that generated revenues in the form of duties on imports and exports, and profits through trade. They pointed secondly to the commercial flow of ships and cargoes over a trans-Isthmus portage road called the diolkos that created revenues for the city through traffic and services, transit duties, and transport fees. According to the first assertion, a commercial emporion made the Isthmus a market for merchants arriving from east

---

[1] I am grateful to the participants in conference in Austin and to the others in attendance for their questions, comments, and suggestions. Thanks also to Melissa Hogan for her valuable feedback on this paper.

[2] E.g., Strabo 8.20; Ael. Arist. *Or.* 27; Favorinus [Dio Chrys.] 37.8 and 36.

[3] E.g., John Chrys. *Hom. 1 Corinthians*, Preface 1–2; Libanius *Decl.* 25.2.46.

[4] Chandler 1776, 240; Dodwell 1819, 191; Lemprière and Anthon 1831, 408; Curtius 1852, 521, 539, 545–46, 596; Curtius 1868, 270–74; Wyse 1865, 326–27.

and west; according to the second, a portage road called the diolkos made the Isthmus a thoroughfare for maritime traffic and shipping between Italy and Asia. These arguments, which were already present when the first archaeologists began work in the Corinthia in the early 20th century, were quickly absorbed into scholarship related to Paul and the Corinthian epistles.[5] Each has also reappeared in recent discussions of the social and economic background to the ancient city and Paul's problematic assemblies.[6] The arguments for the diolkos and the emporion have constantly influenced interpretations of the city.

My goal in this paper is to reconsider each of the explanations about the commercial facilities of the Isthmus in light of the extant textual evidence. As I shall argue, the second of these ideas (the thoroughfare thesis) has no basis in ancient texts while the first (the commercial emporion) is found in an array of textual evidence. The ancients had little conception of the Isthmus as an actively used commercial thoroughfare but they did view it consistently as a commercial destination and marketplace for the exchange and redistribution of goods. In the conclusion of this paper, I will offer some thoughts on the implications of an emporion for addressing the economy of Roman Corinth, the social opportunities, and forms of inequality.

The Diolkos of Corinth and the Thoroughfare Thesis

At the center of the thoroughfare thesis is the diolkos of Corinth. Scholars today use the term to refer to the paved limestone portage road that runs across the narrowest part of the Isthmus.[7] This road, which was partially excavated by Nikolaos Verdelis in the late 1950s, was made of poros slabs 3.5–6.0 m wide and had deep parallel grooves spaced 1.5 m apart suggesting rails for moving heavy loads.[8] Verdelis argued that the road was constructed by the tyrant Periander in the late 7th century BCE, subsequently refurbished after the late 5th century BCE, and used repeatedly throughout antiquity.

---

[5] E.g., Davies 1877, 165–66; Farrar 1879, 555–56; Linton 1881, 3–4.

[6] Wiseman 1979, 438–47; Engels 1990, 59; Hafemann 2000, 22–25; Murphy-O'Connor 2002, 61–62; Horrell and Adams 2004, 1–8.

[7] For overviews of the archaeology of the road, see Verdelis 1956a, 1956b, 1957, 1958, 1960, 1966a and 1966b; Raepsaet 1993; Papafotiou 2007; Pettegrew 2011b; Lohmann forthcoming; and Koutsoumba and Nakas forthcoming.

[8] Lewis 2001.

Since the investigation of the portage road in the 20th century, archaeologists, historians, and New Testament scholars have used the diolkos to
explain the city's economy. The common view today is that ships arriving
in the small harbor of Schoinos at Kalamaki Bay, or at Poseidonia in the
Corinthian Gulf, were set on carts and ferried over the bridge where they
continued their journeys to destinations further afield. In another version,
cargoes were unloaded from ships, carted overland, and restacked in sailing vessels in the opposite gulf. In either variant, the diolkos made the
Isthmus a transient medium in maritime traffic between Italy and Asia
Minor and created revenues and wealth for the city through transport fees
and transit tolls. According to some scholars, merchants could cross the
Isthmus with ships or cargo and continue on their way within the span
of only a few hours.[9]

If modern writers have universally adopted one or the other version
of the thoroughfare thesis, several new studies have called for a careful
rereading of the relevant texts and offered alternate interpretations. A
forthcoming article by Hans Lohmann has reached very different conclusions about the date, function, and purpose of the road. In Lohmann's
view, ships were carried over the Isthmus only a few times during military
expeditions; when ships were transferred, they were dragged via wooden
rollers, not the diolkos; and the physical limestone road called the diolkos
was probably constructed in the late Hellenistic or Early Roman period
reusing cut stone from abandoned monumental buildings after the 146 BCE
destruction.[10] Another study, by this author, argues that the Isthmus was
not the grand thoroughfare scholars have imagined it to be. My aim in the
remainder of this section is to summarize briefly the part of this study that
has reexamined the textual sources.[11]

Despite current scholarly consensus, there is actually no ancient textual
evidence for a road called the diolkos. The only writer of antiquity
to apply the term diolkos to the Corinthia (Strabo) refers to a land

---

[9] For example, Davies 1877, 165–66.
[10] In the analysis of Lohmann (forthcoming), the ship portages of ancient literature have
nothing to do with the limestone portage road used for carting freights over the Isthmus.
I learned of the valuable study of Koutsoumba and Nakas (forthcoming) regarding the
diolkos too late to incorporate in this chapter.
[11] The reader who seeks a fuller version of the evidence and argument may consult
Pettegrew 2011b, which details logistics of portaging, the archaeology of the road, ceramic
evidence against the thoroughfare thesis, and the ancient texts. The following summary
briefly reviews the texts that have been central to the thoroughfare thesis. To access all
the texts discussed here, see http://corinthianmatters.com.

strip – "the narrowest part of the Corinthian Isthmus" – and not a physical road.[12] The one ancient writer, Pseudo-Skylax, who does refer to a road across the Isthmus, does not connect it to portaging episodes or name it as the diolkos, but only remarks, "There is a road of 40 stades that runs over the Isthmus from one sea to the other."[13] These are the only texts that relate anything about an ancient trans-Isthmus road, or a place in the Corinthia called 'diolkos'.

We are in no better position when the evidence for a trans-shipment operation over the land bridge is considered. Scholars have often referred to seven recorded episodes of portaging ships between the 5th century BCE and the 9th century CE in the context of war,[14] and suggested that the absence of evidence reflects the ancient biases against mundane economic activities and monuments.[15] In this view, these 'military episodes' represent the most visible instances of a regular undercurrent of ship portaging that included commercial vessels especially. This argument from silence, however, falters with scrutiny. Comparative evidence, firstly, stands against it. One can contrast, for example, the total absence of evidence for commercial portaging over the Isthmus with the relatively good evidence for commercial ships rounding Cape Malea.[16] Furthermore, a consideration of the practical aspects of portaging (see below) severely erodes confidence in the argument from silence. How could ancient authors have so systematically ignored what could only have been one of the greatest engineering feats of classical antiquity, the regular movement of sizable (10–30 m long) and weighty (20–50 tons) ships across a land bridge six km in length? Why would ancient writers have nothing to say about the "largest trackway in ancient times," as one scholar titled the road?[17]

The absence of evidence actually has a simpler explanation: carting ships across the Corinthian Isthmus marked an extraordinary tactical

---

[12] Strabo 8.2.1, 8.6.4, and 8.6.22. The later Roman writer Hesychius also mentions the diolkos but is only summarizing Strabo.

[13] Pseudo-Skylax, *Periplus* 40.4.

[14] The episodes occurred in 412 BCE, 220 BCE, 217 BCE, 172 BCE, 102/101 BCE, 30 BCE, and 872 CE. There is also an eighth portage that should be dated to the late 3rd century BCE.

[15] E.g., *Corinth* I.1, 49–51.

[16] In contrast with the few instances of portaging ships over the Isthmus, there are two dozen relevant Greek and Latin passages recording voyages of military galleys and merchant ships around the southern coast of Greece. See, for example, *Hymn to Pythian Apollo*, 388–439; Hdt. 7.168; Alciphron *Letters of Fishermen* 10; Arrian *An.* 2.1.2; Diod. Sic. 11.15.1; 11.84; 16.62; Dion. Hal. 1.72.2–3; Heliodorus *Aeth.* 4.16.7.1.

[17] Werner 1997.

maneuver, a brilliant stratagem, that rarely occurred.[18] The exceptional nature of portaging is evident from the explanations ancient historians provide for it. In some cases, writers note why the portage occurred. Thucydides, for example, describes transferring ships as a stealth naval offensive that the Peloponnesians planned against Athens only twice, in 428 BCE when weakened by disease and rebellion, and in 412 BCE after the disastrous Sicilian expedition.[19] Polybius's description of the portage of Demetrius of Pharos in 220 BCE explains the transfer of ships as aiding the Macedonians and catching the Aetolians by surprise in the Corinthian Gulf.[20] And Cassius Dio has Octavian transfer his ships across the Isthmus because it was winter and the sea was too choppy to sail around Malea; the sneak move and rapid sail catch Mark Antony and Cleopatra completely off guard.[21] In these cases, the historians represent portaging events as covert, brilliant, and decisive stratagems carried out in the context of exceptional military circumstance.

The textual sources also explain how portaging occurred by noting the complexity, expense, or dangers of the crossing. The Peloponnesians, Thucydides says (3.15–16), "set to work zealously" on the preparations of the road in 428 BCE. Demetrius transferred over his fleet in 220 BCE only after the Macedonians agreed to front the expense of the operation.[22] The extraordinary nature of ship portaging is most explicit in the famous inscription of Marcus Antonius, the paternal grandfather of the triumvir who fought Octavian at Actium.[23] As proconsul, Marcus Antonius had ships transferred across the Isthmus in 102/101 BCE and then had the deed commemorated in Latin verse as epic achievement and athletic accomplishment.[24] The inscription notes that the remarkable transfer occurred with little confusion, no injury, and in only a few days' time.

If these passages highlight the extraordinary reason for or nature of military ship transfers, what about the three authors whose brief comments have suggested to scholars that ship carting was regular and frequent?

---

[18] For a fuller consideration of the literary nature of portaging episodes, see Pettegrew 2011a and 2011b.

[19] Thuc. 3.15–16; Thuc. 8.7–10.

[20] Polyb. 4.19.7–9.

[21] Cass. Dio 51.5.

[22] Polyb. 4.19.7–9.

[23] *Corinth* VIII.2 no. 1, 1–4, also published in Taylor and West 1928, and subsequently improved in *CIL* 1².2 no. 2662 and Dow 1951. For discussion of this inscription, see Gebhard and Dickie 2003, 272–77.

[24] Gebhard and Dickie 2003.

In fact, it is easier to read Aristophanes, Strabo, and Pliny as allusions to the same remarkable military stratagems discussed above than as random references to a regular commercial transshipping operation. When the playwright Aristophanes makes one of his characters say, "You have an Isthmus, man; up and down you're dragging your member more frequently than the Corinthians,"[25] he is referencing not a constant commercial operation but the recent transfer of military vessels that occurred the year before the production of the play (411 BCE), when the Peloponnesians drew a fleet of 21 ships over the Isthmus. The event nearly caught the Athenians off guard and would have been on their mind the year of the play's production.[26] When the geographer Strabo describes the diolkos as the place "where ships are transferred overland,"[27] he is not commenting on a portage operation of the late 1st century BCE but is noting for his readers the strip of land where the famous portages had occurred in ancient times. And when Pliny the Elder suggests in the later 1st century CE that smaller ships were drawn over the Isthmus on trolleys instead of sailing around Cape Malea, he is not making a contemporary observation but is summing up an historical tradition of famous ship-crossing episodes.[28] Strabo and Pliny mention portaging because of its importance within the historical narratives that were famous in their own day, especially Thucydides and Polybius.

The overland conveyance of ships rarely occurred because it marked an extraordinary logistical feat that required a tremendous investment of material resources and traction power.[29] A military ship like the Greek trireme was some 35 m long, 5 m wide, and nearly 4 m high, weighing, when dry and without its movable equipment or crews, about 25 tons, or 50,000 pounds,[30] about the height and weight of a modern tractor-trailer truck but double the length and width. The typical coastal trading vessels of the Hellenistic and Roman era were smaller than the trireme but carried loads weighing 20–70 tons, while long-distance freighters were significantly wider and commonly transported cargoes of 100 tons or more.[31]

---

[25] Ar. *Thesm.* 647–48.

[26] Sommerstein 1994, 196.

[27] Strabo 8.2.1.

[28] Pliny *NH* 4.9–10.

[29] See Raepsaet 1993, 2008; Lewis 2001; Pettegrew 2011b.

[30] These figures for weight are based on Morrison and Coates 1989, 20, 68; Morrison, Coates, and Rankov 2000, 277.

[31] For the size and weight of merchant ships, see Casson 1971, 160–63 n. 17 and 36, 169–73, 189–90; Houston 1988.

Transferring even the lightest of these vessels by wheeled cart over a ridge
80 m above sea level through an average grade of 2% would have required
hundreds of men and created extreme dangers to the ship and the crew.
While it was possible to transfer military galleys and very small merchant
vessels over the Corinthian Isthmus, it was also very difficult and did not
occur frequently. The ancient historians who narrated these portages represented them as extraordinary in some way.

Scholars recognizing the logistical difficulties of ship dragging have
long advanced an alternative interpretation of the diolkos road.[32] If it was
difficult to transport commercial vessels, it would have been possible to
unload and transfer their cargoes apart from the ships. While there is no
space here to outline the arguments against this thesis, we can summarize the major objections that have been explored more fully elsewhere.[33]
The archaeological evidence of ceramic distributions does not support the
notion of consistent overland transshipment of cargoes as the eastern and
western sides of the Isthmus show, respectively, clear eastern and western
orientations in trade. Logistically, the diolkos lacks the necessary harbor
facilities on the Corinthian and Saronic Gulfs to accommodate a major
overland shipping business.[34] Not only are there no harbor installations,
moles, or broad quays, but there are no warehouses, hostels, restaurants,
and settlements – in short, none of the facilities found at serious Greek
and Roman harbors.[35] Transshipment would have required considerable
time: several days of unloading, moving, and reloading, not the few hours
sometimes envisioned.[36] The operation would also have depended on an
enormous supply of bovines as hundreds of ox-drawn carts were needed
for each commercial ship. Finally, the costs to the merchant would have
been enormous: harbor taxes, cargo duties, expenses of porters, drivers,
and oxen or mules. Could a merchant have counted on profiting from his
cargo at inflated costs?

There is no question, of course, that goods could be and were carted
across the Isthmus in antiquity either fully or in part. Such transfers, how-

---

[32] MacDonald 1986.
[33] See Pettegrew 2011b for further discussion.
[34] Sanders 1996.
[35] For useful overviews of built harbors, see Casson 1971, 361–70; Shaw 1972; Blackman
1982, 2008. It is true that small-scale coastal traders did not necessarily require well-built
facilities to unload goods – a simple beach or wooden quay would sometimes do just fine
(Houston 1988; Hohlfelder and Vann 2000) – but a road designed to facilitate a major shipping business would have required considerable infrastructure.
[36] Pomey and Tchernia 1978; Rickman 1985, 112, 114 n. 57.

ever, do not add up to the kind of major portage operation envisioned by modern scholars. While the archaeological evidence is beyond the scope of this paper, the imported Roman pottery distributed across the Isthmus does suggest that the region functioned more as a terminus to eastward and westward commercial flows than a conduit.[37]

Corinth and the Emporion

If the diolkos road did not contribute greatly to Corinth's commercial facility, how did the Isthmus make Corinth wealthy? Here, ancient writers agreed that Corinth had a major emporion, a trading center that concentrated maritime and terrestrial traffic via land and sea. Thucydides was largely responsible for this interpretation of the city in arguing (1.13.5) that the control of an emporion since ancient days had brought revenues and power. Others followed. Corinth was called wealthy, Strabo explained (8.6.20), not "because of its commerce" as one translator translated emporion, but because of its "place of commerce" that facilitated the exchange of goods between Italy and Asia.[38] Aelius Aristides characterizes the Corinthia as a kind of *agora* and meeting space common to all Greeks.[39] Libanius, the greatest Greek orator of the 4th century CE, describes Corinth as the common emporion of Greece.[40] And his famous student John Chrysostom, in the preface to his commentary on Paul's first epistle to the Corinthians, explains the Corinthian community's strife in terms of the wealth and pride resulting from the city's commercial foundation on the Isthmus.[41]

What did the ancient concept of emporion entail? First, the Greek word ἐμπόριον denoted a place of commerce situated in a convenient location for travelers and traders. The term was used consistently from classical times to denote a mart or trading-center, a settlement or part of a

---

[37] Pettegrew 2011b.

[38] The Loeb version of Strabo's *Geography* mistranslates the phrase Ὁ δὲ Κόρινθος ἀφνειὸς μὲν λέγεται διὰ τὸ ἐμπόριον as "Corinth is called 'wealthy' because of its commerce." As this translation has been promulgated through two widely-used books on Roman Corinth (Engels 1990 and Murphy-O'Connor 2002), scholars have not fully understood Strabo's specific point. Corinth was wealthy not because of exchange itself but because of its particular place of exchange, the trading station in the Isthmus.

[39] Ael. Arist. *Isthmian Oration* 23. See De Ligt 1993, 101–2.

[40] Libanius, *Decl.* 25.2.46.

[41] In *epistulam 1 ad Corinthios*, Argument.

settlement where maritime traffic and commercial flows concentrated.[42] These nodes of heightened connectivity were sometimes maritime cities but more frequently substantial harbors situated on the sea or the mouths of rivers with easy access to trading flows.[43] Emporia are so common to discussions of world geography and *periploi* ("voyages around") in the early Roman era precisely because so many are associated with ports. Strabo, for example, who names some 48 different emporia in his geography, uses the term for populous and highly-trafficked trading centers and ports that facilitated the exchange of products for peoples or regions separated from one another by long distances.[44]

Second, in its reference to a particular place, emporion also denoted the nature of trade and the kinds of goods available at that place. Emporia were centers of wholesale trade of merchandise between regions and peoples, not urban and rural markets serving only the inhabitants of a region. In some cases, emporia functioned as regional ports for the exchange of inland products with goods imported by sea, or as trading centers for neighboring tribes.[45] Other emporia functioned as entrepôts for the trade of materials imported from regions separated from one another by long distances: Classical Athens in the Aegean and Apamea in Syria for goods from Italy and Greece.[46] Writers like Strabo suggest that the sorts of goods exchanged at these emporia included food stuffs (grain, olive oil, wine, and honey), construction materials (timber, wax, and pitch), animals and their products (cattle, hides), slaves, plants (silphium), clothing, and other merchandise.[47] Pliny the Elder describes the emporion of Adulis on the Red Sea where slaves, apes, tortoise shells, and ivory and hides from

---

[42] Liddell and Scott 1996. Definitions and discussion are numerous: Rougé 1966, 108; Casson 1971, 365–70; Bresson and Rouillard 1993, including Casevitz 1993, 10, Étienne 1993, 30–34, Rouillard 1993, 46; and Counillon 1993; Frayn 1993, 10, 15–16; Hansen 1997, 2006; Petropoulos 2005; Rosenfeld and Menirav 2005, 16–17, 29–31.

[43] Casevitz 1993; Rouillard 1993; Counillon 1993. Emporia are more commonly the harbors of substantial cities than maritime cities themselves, but an emporion was not always a port, and a port not always an emporion. Xen. *Hell.* 5.2.16 and Plut. *Fab. Max.* 17.3 juxtapose but do not conflate the two terms 'limena' (harbor) and 'emporion.' Moreover, inland emporia disconnected from waterways did exist even if they were not common: Dion. Hal. 7.20.2 distinguishes between inland and maritime emporia; and Livy describes (38.18.12–15) Gordion in Crete as an inland emporion, but has to explain that it received more visitors than an inland city normally does.

[44] Cf. Étienne 1993; Rouillard 1993.

[45] Strabo 3.4.6 (New Carthage); 5.1.8 (Aquileia); 11.2.3, 11.2.16, 11.2.17 (Tanais, Dioscurias, and Phasis on the Black Sea); 11.2.16 (Dioscurias).

[46] Athens: Isoc. *Paneg.* 42; Apamea: Strabo 12.8.15; Delos: Strabo 10.5.4; 14.5.2; Paus. 8.33.2.

[47] See n. 45–46 above. For silphium, see Strabo 17.3.20.

hippopotami and rhinoceri were brought in large quantity and traded.[48] In fact, these ancient lists of merchandise traded at emporia are not meant to be comprehensive but represent the most important, unique, or exotic forms of commodities; local agricultural products, especially grain, wine, and olive oil would have been the standard imports and exports for much of the Mediterranean.[49]

Third, emporia were consistently linked with wealth and abundance. Some writers suggested that the great numbers of foreign traders and travelers generated this prosperity.[50] Strabo, for example, notes that Corinth, Comana, Ephesos, Delos, and Alexandria were all made wealthy by the traders that passed through the harbors.[51] The real reason for wealth, of course, was revenue from duties on goods imported and exported through the ports;[52] state and local civic bodies actually invested in harbor facilities for this reason.[53] But emporia also created 'wealth' locally through employment of traders and service workers. Dio Chrysostom, for example, explains the wealth of the town of Celaena in Phrygia resulting from the periodic markets that occurred when the provincial governor visited.[54] Moreover, Greek and Roman writers describe the wealth of trading centers in terms of the abundance of goods that their ports brought into the region. Isocrates describes the Piraeus as an emporion in the center of Greece that brought rare merchandise to Athens from all over the world, addressing the problem of regional deficits and surpluses.[55]

Finally, ancient writers had long regarded emporia with suspicion and caution. Since the days of Plato, the consistent philosophical critique was that despite all their advantages for cities, harbors fostered lust for wealth, encouraged deceit through exchange, corrupted the civic fortitude and loyalties of the inhabitants, and led citizens away from good occupations like agriculture.[56] Aristotle, for example, recognizes the value of a port in meeting deficiencies in goods and foods, but recommends keeping

---

[48] Pliny *NH* 6.173.

[49] Rouillard 1993.

[50] Etienne 1993, 30–34; Rouillard 1993.

[51] See, respectively, Strabo 8.6.20; 12.3.36; 14.1.24; 14.5.2; and 17.1.13. For additional examples of the association of port, traders, and wealth, Polyb. 10.1.9; Diod. Sic. 2.11.3; Livy 39.25.9; Dio Chrys. *Or.* 32.36.10.

[52] Purcell 2005b.

[53] Morley 2007b, 55–60.

[54] Dio Chrysostom notes (35.14–16) that the market created work for peddlers, porters, artisans, and prostitutes. Wherever the great crowds are found, money is abundant and the people of the place thrive.

[55] Isoc. *Paneg.* 41–42.

[56] See Cristofori 2001, with sources; Morley 2007b, 79–89, on trade and morality.

the emporion at a safe distance from the town center.[57] Athenaeus, citing Theopompus, describes the detrimental and corrupting consequences of the Byzantinians and Chalcedonians spending too much time in their waterfront emporia in the midst of their luxuries.[58] One could also note here Juvenal's satirical quip at the "scented sons of Corinth" and the "unwarlike Rhodians," two cities made effeminate by excessive luxury resulting from their trading centers.[59] As centers of exchange, these emporia were also considered problematic in introducing foreigners into the region who mixed with the citizen populations.[60] Emporia were for this reason restricted ideally to the harbors, or districts within the harbors where the foreign populations could be closely supervised by officials.[61] Piraeus in Athens with its metic and foreign trading populations provides a good example of this 'world apart,'[62] as wares imported by sea were displayed right on the water in a district known as the *Deigma*, the "sample market" or "bazaar," for immediate purchase.[63]

Corinth possessed an emporion of the kind outlined above at its two harbors flanking the Isthmus. Thucydides says (1.13.5) that in his own day, Corinth furnished an emporion for maritime trade on the Isthmus, which capitalized on traffic by land and sea. Strabo's interpretation of Thucydides linked the concept emporion with specific places, the two harbors on the Isthmus (8.6.20). Livy refers to Kenchreai as an emporion (32.17.3), and Roman descriptions of Kenchreai highlight the constant flow of commercial traffic in and out of that port.[64] Lechaion too was a trading depot although there are fewer explicit ancient testimonies about the harbor and settlement there.[65]

Archaeological work over the last century has revealed that the harbors described by ancient texts were, indeed, substantial ports in the Roman

---

[57] Arist. *Pol.* 1327a.

[58] Ath. 12.526d–e.

[59] Juv. *Sat.* 8.112–16.

[60] Dem. 35.2. On the 'mixed' and foreign populations of harbors and emporia, see Etienne 1993, 30–34; Cristofori 2001; Blackman 2008, 653–54.

[61] Arist. *Pol.* 1327a. See Cristofori 2001, Möller 2007, 368, 373–74.

[62] Von Reden 1995.

[63] Garland 1987, 83–95; Xen. *Hell.* 5.1.21; Dem. 35.29; 50.24. These kinds of spaces are also known elsewhere. See, for instance, the *Deigma* mentioned in Aen. Tac. 30.2; Polyb. 5.88.

[64] Cf. Apul. *Met.* 10.35; Favorinus 37.8.

[65] The panhellenic sanctuary site of Isthmia, situated on the principal artery in and out of the Peloponnese, was also recognized as a major center of trade and meeting point between east and west. Thucydides' reference to it (1.13.5) as an emporion, however, seems to be exceptional. See Casevitz 1993, 17–18.

era well equipped for large-scale trade. Lechaion is located only 3 km from the city, built as an artificial installation in the sandy beach at the point where the *cardo maximus* from the Roman colony intersected the shore. The harbor works at Lechaion that are visible in the coastline today represent the most dramatic physical vestiges of the harbor built in the mid to late 1st century CE,[66] which was clearly an impressive undertaking and major development of the landscape. The coastal lagoon was drained away and an extensive inner harbor of 10 ha was excavated to create several interconnected basins connected to the Corinthian Gulf by a long and narrow channel (150 m × 12 m wide) lined with cut blocks. Three mounds rising as high as 15 m above sea level at the entrance to the inner harbor indicate the volume of gravel and sand moved during the construction and subsequent dredging; two stone structures of Roman date on one of these mounds perhaps represent ancient lighthouses. The Roman builders at Lechaion also constructed two rectangular outer quays with protective moles that projected into the seas and created an additional 5 ha of shelter from waves and currents. The inner and outer harbors together provided up to 15 ha of sheltered area, making it a very substantial constructed harbor indeed, in the same league as Sebastos (Caesarea Maritima) with its 20 ha basin.[67] A settlement surrounded Lechaion but we know very little about its extent or size.

Kenchreai was the city's eastern port that lay 10 km east of the city in one of the natural coves of the Saronic Gulf.[68] The Roman harbor is located in a natural indentation of the coast where a small bay is defined by a pair of promontories that project the coast seaward at the north and south; artificial breakwaters and moles now submerged extend the promontories to create a sheltered cove of 3 ha with a depth up to 25 m.[69] The investigations of Kenchreai in the 1960s revealed in great detail the physical remains and plan of the harbor itself, which was developed in the course of the 1st and 2nd centuries CE and had phases of refurbishment as late as the 7th century. Limited excavations on the inner quay of the harbor uncovered warehouses, commercial buildings, and shops that were constructed sometime between the late 1st century BCE and

---

[66] For this overview, see Rothaus 1995. There remain questions of chronology that can only be settled through excavation.

[67] Raban et al. 2009.

[68] See publications in *Kenchreai, Eastern Port of Corinth* series; Hohlfelder 1985. For a recent summary and overview of Roman Kenchreai, see Rife 2010.

[69] *Kenchreai* I, 14–17.

1st century CE.[70] Excavations on the north side of the harbor brought to light stores (*tabernae*), an open square and stoa (1st century CE), a mole constructed of earth and rubble (1st century CE), and a Roman villa used throughout the Roman period.[71] The south pier produced a similar array of commercial buildings and warehouses (early 1st century CE) and even fish tanks (*piscinae*) that were constructed in the later 1st century CE, as well as a Roman nymphaeum (post 2nd century) that produced over 120 glass panels of opus sectile still packed in their wooden shipping crates.[72] A very large town surrounded the harbor proper in the Roman era.

In Strabo's view, the wholesale trading centers at Kenchreai and Lechaion and not the urban center itself formed the emporion in the Corinthia. The urban center had substantial market spaces, of course, as Williams has shown in his survey of the excavated fora and macella,[73] which would have retailed products of the countryside (e.g., meat) for purchase by city dwellers. In other Roman cities, such macella and fora were permanent building spaces for retailing specialty food products like grain, vegetables, meat, and fish – the sort of expensive goods available to people with resources.[74] Corinth also had a variety of stalls and taverns for retailing crafts and specialty products like pottery, textiles, and furniture, as well as high-frequency periodic markets for the sale of basic provisions, the sorts of market spaces found throughout the Roman Mediterranean.[75] But these macella, marketplaces, and urban shops and stalls were primarily retail spaces that constituted different sorts of marketplaces than we find in Corinth's ports, and there is no reason to think that surpluses produced in the countryside would have necessarily filtered through urban markets.[76]

The emporion in the harbors was central to Corinth's regional trade. When Strabo notes that the emporion facilitated trade between Italy and Asia,[77] he is representing the harbors of the Isthmus as the sites of marketing and economic connection where traders concentrate. In Strabo's

---

[70] *Kenchreai* I, 36–38.

[71] *Kenchreai* I, 17–22; Rothaus 2000, 66–69.

[72] *Kenchreai* I, 23–35, 43.

[73] Williams 1993.

[74] De Ruyt 1983; Frayn 1993.

[75] On high-frequency retail markets like macella, fora, agoras, and marketplaces in the Roman Mediterranean, see Frayn 1993; De Ligt 1993, especially 106–54; Morley 2007b, 79–81. Alciphron comments snidely on the cheap fruits and bread sold at a market in Corinth's Kraneion district: Alciphron *Letters of Parasites* 3.60.

[76] See Paterson 1998; Morley 2007a, 580–87, for different scenarios for the distribution of agricultural goods for local consumption and trade.

[77] Strabo 8.20.

conception, merchants from the east did not need to travel all the way to Italy to exchange their wares but could simply unload at Kenchreai; merchants from the west did not sail around the Peloponnese but could put in at Lechaion. The harbors on either end of the Isthmus formed centralized trading depots and meeting points between east and west, places for exchange and the redistribution of goods.[78]

It is unfortunate that Strabo and other authors leave so much unexplained in how exchange actually occurred and the mechanisms by which goods were redistributed within and between harbors. The passage from Strabo noted above indicates that he viewed Corinth as a kind of entrepôt, which would give the Corinthians some role in the movement of goods across the Isthmus. It is possible, of course, that Strabo believed that individual traders redistributed goods by procuring luxury items from east (Asia) or west (Italy) for consumers in the opposite gulfs. Whatever ancient authors may have believed about the redistribution of goods across the land bridge, archaeological evidence indicates that the overland movement of goods was little more than a trickle. Indeed, ceramic patterns from places east and west of the Isthmus indicate that most trade involved local or regional wares within eastern and western gulfs, not long-distance exchange between Italy and Asia.[79]

The Corinthian Economy and the Question of Inequality

We can turn in this concluding discussion to the question of the economy of Roman Corinth. Recognizing that ancient writers regarded the emporion as the primary commercial basis for the city's wealth provides insight into how the Corinthian Isthmus generated wealth and created economic inequality. Scholars have often highlighted the urban center itself as the center of trade in the region and urban markets as the mechanism for the redistribution of goods to rural dwellers and visitors to the city center.[80] While there were certainly different kinds of markets in Corinth, the emporion places the harbors at the center of the region's commercial economy. Kenchreai and Lechaion, at least, were the places of large-scale trade in the territory.

Harbors fostered an environment of economic activity and created opportunities through a wide range of productive and commercial activities

---

[78] Cf. Ael. Ar. *Or.* 46.22–27.

[79] Pettegrew 2011b.

[80] One prominent example is Engels 1990.

in both the countryside and town: money lenders and merchants negotiating loans, merchants buying up craft in the town for exporting abroad, land owners seeking markets for their surplus olive oil and wine, and retailers and peddlers redistributing imported goods in the city's more specialized markets, fora, and fairs. As such, Kenchreai and Lechaion created the economic space for business for a wide range of individuals linked to trade:[81] wholesaler dealers, financiers, ship owners, traders, landowners, middle men, retailers, craft specialist, sailors and rowers, and many others.

In ancient conceptual frameworks, emporia also 'created' the right condition for dramatic profits through trade in goods produced both locally and abroad – the 'rags to riches' scenario problematized by Millis's contribution to this volume.[82] In the Early Roman era, anecdotes still circulated about wealthy Corinthians of the former Greek city, like the rich man Moerichus, who owned an entire fleet of merchant vessels,[83] and Demaratus, who had grown wealthy by making cargo runs between Lechaion and ports in southern Italy.[84] In the 4th century CE, Libanius tells of a detestable dealer in garum named Heliodorus who, in the course of his trade came to Corinth, sat in on law proceedings, mastered oratory, and eventually made a killing between his legal activities and his trade in fish sauce.[85] Such anecdotes reflect the ancient conception that long-distance trade provided the means of generating spectacular profits and upward social mobility, and that the harbors of Corinth in particular seemed to be fitting environments for profit-making. The reality, of course, is that most people who were tied to commercial activity in any way were low-status individuals not typically made wealthy through the process.[86]

Corinth's harbors, in any case, did create numerous opportunities to make a living. The initial construction of the harbor facilities, along with occasional refurbishments, required many hundreds of laborers who could operate cranes, complete masonry, excavate the basins, and dredge the mouths.[87] The construction of the monumental buildings at the harbors – the warehouses, temples, and churches – fostered needs for architects,

---

[81] Paterson 1998.
[82] See Millis this volume.
[83] Lucian *D. Mort.* 21.1.2.
[84] Dion. Hal. 3.46.3–5.
[85] Libanius *Or.* 62.46.
[86] See Reed 2003, for example, who argues that most maritime traders (*emporoi*) in classical Athens were poor, low status, and foreign. Cf. Morley 2007b, 88.
[87] Rickman 1985; Oleson 1988.

carpenters, porters, and a myriad of unskilled workmen.[88] The numerous private apartments, villas, houses in the districts surrounding both Lechaion and Kenchreai required a supply of construction workers from the 1st to 7th centuries.

The commercial activities occurring during sailing season likewise employed a myriad of workers at the sea front.[89] Hundreds of people were needed to manage the arrival of ships and movement of goods at the quays and storehouses: stevedores and porters, custom officials and clerks, inspectors, crane operators, lightermen, shipwrights, ballast handlers, and divers and dredgers. Transferring goods from farm estates to harbors and from harbors to towns demanded many muleteers and wagon drivers. And the services provided to arriving merchants, sailors, and passengers put to work retailers, shopkeepers, tavern and bar owners, innkeepers, craftsmen, and prostitutes. In the varied economic activities that occurred at harbors, there was a large demand for seasonal laborers both skilled and unskilled.[90]

If the harbors created opportunities, they also inscribed a series of striking contrasts in the landscape through the principal economic activity, wholesale trade. On the one hand, commercial exchange reflected the interests of the land-owning wealthy and powerful, who undertook trade directly or managed it through dependents, selling their produce to itinerant merchants or outfitting their own ships.[91] The elite individually or collectively (through the civic council) financed the construction of the buildings at the ports, maintained harbor facilities, and administered the commerce and duties on exported or imported goods.[92] The Bacchiadae in old Corinth, Strabo believed, grew wealthy from the duties on the emporion.[93]

---

[88] See Brunt 1980 for a discussion of this issue in the context of Rome.

[89] Rougé 1966, 162–64; Casson 1971, 366–370; Oleson 1988, 147.

[90] For Ostia and Puteoli, we know from epigraphic evidence that many harbor specialists were organized into collegia of divers, ballast men, porters, and dredgers, among others, but the evidence from other Italian ports does not indicate that this was necessarily typical; see Houston 1980.

[91] On elite attitudes to and involvement in trade, see D'Arms 1980; Paterson 1998, 158; Morley 2007a, 580–87; Morley 2007b, 85–86.

[92] See Houston 1980 for the Italian context; Rickman 1988, 264–65. The development of the harbor of Lechaion in the 1st century may have been partially funded by the emperors, but locals would have paid for maintenance, refurbishments, and new construction. As Purcell has noted (2005b, 204), "In both the emporion and the regime of taxes on mobility, we are dealing with the structures with which the powerful manage the consequences of the Mediterranean environment."

[93] Strabo 8.6.20; Purcell 2005b, 209.

With funds for purchasing, of course, the elite also benefited from merchandise imported for consumption.[94]

On the other hand, the labor force that operationalized the harbors was either materially poor or socially marginal. These laborers were not necessarily the peasant farmers who found markets for their small surpluses in the retail spaces of town and countryside,[95] but were more likely the "motley throng" of seasonal workers of every stripe,[96] foreign merchants and sailors, the peddlers and retailers, the ass-drivers and muleteers, the tax and customs collectors, among so many others. These individuals lacked real social and economic security (land), and depended for their livelihood on the consistency of work and fairness of the employer.[97] These low-status laborers may have identified with other workers through associations and their forms of employment,[98] but they assumed occupations universally despised by Roman, Jewish, and eventually Christian elite.[99]

The contrasts between landed elite and landless laborers are physically visible in the architecture adorning the marine seafront at the harbors. Beyond the quays and warehouses themselves funded by the elite and the city council, the monumental public architecture of temples, churches, and monuments bespoke the munificence of individuals. The waterfront properties of both Kenchreai and Lechaion included ornate seaside villas of Roman date. The apparent permanency of these buildings and habitations can be contrasted with the essentially ephemeral character of seasonal employment of the laborers at the harbors.

Today, one can imagine from the ruins at Kenchreai and Lechaion the contrast between these wealthy few responsible for the visible remains of commercial facilities, public buildings, and private residences, and the invisible workmen, porters, retailers, and sailors of differing levels of wealth and connection who formed the dynamic force that brought to life the harbors. Such contrasted spaces marked the medium through which Paul, Aquila, Priscilla, Phoebe, and their associates entered and exited the city of Corinth. But more problematically, they formed the economic and social environment that shaped and divided their Christian communities.

---

[94] Morley 2007b.
[95] De Ligt 1993, 106–54; Morley 2007a, 580–87.
[96] Conzelmann 1975, 12.
[97] Brunt 1990, 90–91.
[98] Joshel 1992.
[99] On the elite disdain for manual labor, manufacturing, and trade, see Grant 1977, 66–95.

CHAPTER EIGHT

THE AMBIVALENT LANDSCAPE OF CHRISTIAN CORINTH: THE ARCHAEOLOGY OF PLACE, THEOLOGY, AND POLITICS IN A LATE ANTIQUE CITY

William Caraher

Introduction

The political, economic, and ecclesiastical position of Corinth during the middle decades of the 6th century CE created an environment with the potential for dynamic contrasts between Corinthian residents and imperial authority. Corinth and its territory represented a liminal zone between the more prosperous east and the less stable west, stood amidst conflicting political and ecclesiastical jurisdictions during shifts in the nature of imperial authority, and endured a systematic campaign of external investment by the ambitious and expansionistic emperor Justinian I (527–565 CE), who sought not only to expand imperial power institutionally, but symbolically as well.

This chapter argues that the textual and archaeological evidence for imperial involvement in the Corinthia provides faint traces of what Elsner has called "internal friction" in the manifestation of imperial and Corinthian authority in the region.[1] For Elsner, internal friction represented a cultural response to the presence of Romanness at the periphery of the empire. While Corinth is rarely regarded as a peripheral region, the political situation in the 6th century placed it at the limits of imperial control over ecclesiastical affairs, and the monumental building campaign attributed to the emperor Justinian suggests that the territory represented a significant focal point for imperial policy. At the same time, there were contemporary changes in the region that cannot be attributed directly to external involvement. The architectural and epigraphic evidence preserve traces of the kind of internal frictions that Elsner associated with practices of resistance and domination. Evidence for such practices suggests an ambivalence in Late Antique Corinth and the bishops of Illyricum

---

[1] Elsner 2007, 255.

toward imperial overtures throughout the 5th and into the 6th century. The methods employed by the emperor to project political and ecclesiastical power into the Corinthia suggest efforts both to entice and cow local residents into recognizing imperial authority. Exploring possible local responses to imperial projects cannot reveal whether local resistance or imperial policy carried the day in the 6th century, but it carves out interpretative space to consider economic, political, and even social inequality in the ancient world.

The historical circumstances of the 5th and 6th century in the Corinthia present a good vehicle for considering asymmetrical power relations in the region. The tensions between the political authority of the East and the religious authority of the West under Justinian presented a crucial phase in the conflicts that played out all across the Balkans beginning in the 5th century. The political and ecclesiastical controversies that engulfed the Balkans began with the Acacian schism (484–519) which placed most of the bishops of Illyricum and Epiros at odds with the Patriarch and Emperor in Constantinople.[2] The resolution of this conflict in 519, shortly after the accession of Justin I, marked only a momentary break in the divisive politics of Chalcedon. The ascendance of Justinian and his well-documented and ambitious policies had a significant impact on the political and religious life of the empire, and Corinth did not escape the impact of these policies in its political position as the capital of Achaea and its ecclesiastical position as the seat of the powerful Bishop.[3] The location of Corinth – between East and West, imperial power and papal authority – provided a dynamic space for both resistance and accommodation.

My effort to excavate evidence for power relations and inequality in the Corinthia focuses on three relationships which capture the ambivalent nature of imperial authority in 6th-century Greece. The first section considers the relationship between ecclesiastical architecture and authority in the Corinthia. I argue that monumental religious architecture played an important role in projecting imperial power in the region and created a monumentalized discourse of political and religious authority, but also offered opportunities to resist this authority. The next section extends this discussion to consider how imperial efforts to project authority in the Corinthia shaped production, settlement, and fortification in the

---

[2] For the best discussion of the Acacian Schism in Greece, see: Charanis 1974. See also Pietri 1984.

[3] Rothaus 2000; Gritsopoulos 1972, 77–84.

6th century. In this discussion, I focus on the impact that the monumentalized discourse of power and resistance had on the local economy and settlement as well as through the physical labor and experiences of ancient Corinthians. The final section of this chapter considers the theological aspect of the imperial presence in the region and argues that the expression of imperial policy manifested itself in a pair of theologically ambivalent texts and ritually-encoded architecture that manifest traces of internal friction between the goals of an imperial state and the understanding of power on the local level. The interplay between imperial patronage and the local response did not create a neatly organized binary between imperial power and local resistance. The interplay between evidence for local reception and imperial authority reinforced the ambivalent position of Corinth in the political and religious world of the 6th century situated between the crafty ambition of Justinian and persistent local interests.

Monumentalizing the Discourse of Power

Monumental architecture represents one of the most visible and significant means to project authority.[4] Not only does monumental architecture make a visually impressive statement, but it also provides a space to articulate complex ideas, condition behavior, and generate emotional responses even in landscapes crowded with meaning. Monumental architecture has the additional benefit of being relatively well-preserved in the archaeological record. Although the architecture of even such well-documented regions as the Corinthia remains only fragmentary, sufficient evidence nevertheless exists to offer some informed speculation on the relationship between various contemporary monumental buildings.

The relationships between the 6th-century buildings in Corinth provide some of the only evidence for the local impact of large-scale, imperially-funded construction. A whole series of 6th-century buildings coincide with Justinian's growing influence over religious institutions and his efforts to advertise his authority through church building. The six major Late Antique basilicas arrayed around the city of Corinth represent part of a monumentalized discourse of authority contemporary with imperial involvement in the region (Map 1).[5] Based on the present state of our

---

[4] Given 2004; Kardulias 1995.
[5] Pallas 1990. For more recent summaries and discussion see Gregory 2010; Sanders 2005a.

knowledge, these buildings appear to represent a roughly contemporary phase of large scale, monumental, 'Early Christian' type architecture in the Corinthia. There is little convincing evidence for earlier Christian buildings, and later Early Byzantine structures were either on a much smaller-scale or were simply the later phases of 6th-century monuments.[6]

This section will consider the context and implications of the 6th-century building boom around the city of Corinth and make three interrelated arguments. First, I suggest that the construction of numerous churches was less a functional response to a growing Christian population and more of a response to increased imperial investment in the region. Then, I show how this investment makes it possible to trace the aesthetic influences between ecclesiastical architecture and other contemporary buildings around Corinth. Finally, I argue that some decorative and architectural choices in the 6th-century churches may indicate efforts to produce local distinction or even to manifest resistance to imperially funded monuments.

The size and architecture of the 6th-century churches represents one of the more obvious characteristics of the 6th-century Christian city and its territory. It seems probable that these churches replaced a less monumental group of earlier structures dedicated to Christian worship. Earlier phases of Christian architecture may have stood in the countryside, perhaps associated with the property of the local elite, rather than clustered around the urban core. In fact, work across the Corinthia over the past 50 years has produced evidence for at least a half-dozen unexcavated Early Christian period churches which could have a 5th century date.[7]

The 5th-century Christian community may have relied on modest rural churches or even less imposing structures for their ritual and social needs. The presence of known, but unexcavated Christian buildings throughout the countryside provides sufficient evidence to discourage arguments that see the absence of churches as a sign of a small or underdeveloped Christian community.[8] The presence of small Christian sites may, in fact, provide evidence to support the recent work of Bowes on the role of villa and private churches in the Christian communities in the Late Antique Mediterranean.[9] Based on evidence from across in the

---

[6] The obvious examples of probable late 6th or early 7th-century buildings in the Corinthia are the basilica on Temple Hill and the small church on Acrocorinth.

[7] Gregory 2010.

[8] Sanders 2005a, 441; Sweetman 2010, 207–10, 241–44.

[9] Bowes 2008.

Mediterranean, Bowes has observed that Late Antique local aristocrats cultivated Christian communities in their extra-urban and sub-urban villas which typically stood apart from the political space of the ancient city's urban core, the church's institutional authority, and the need for monumental, public architecture.[10] While there is no specific evidence for this practice in Greece, the prevalence of villas in the countryside provides at least one necessary precondition for this kind of arrangement. From the 4th century, the significant number of Late Roman villas in the Corinthia suggests that a kind of villa culture existed in the region. A similar shift of political, social, and economic capital to the countryside also occurred in the neighboring province of Epiros where Bowden demonstrated that rural villas were particularly common,[11] and, at the same time, that monumental Christian architecture largely postdated other evidence for the appearance of Christianity.[12] While the evidence for a villa-based Christianity in Epirus or the Corinthia remains circumstantial, the practice elsewhere reminds us that the appearance of monumental Christian architecture is as likely to represent the changing fortunes of the institutional church as it is to represent the expansion of the size or significance of local Christian communities. In other words, the construction of monumental churches around the urban core at Corinth could well mark out a shift in how Christianity was expressed locally rather than the growth of the Christian community in absolute terms. Monumental churches could, for example, demonstrate an interest among the local ecclesiastical elite in appropriating the traditional, monumental urban core as a challenge to less centralized expressions of Christian authority.

In this context, then, the 6th-century Corinthian basilicas with their imposing size, opulent decoration, and distinctive architecture present an architectural conversation extending beyond the basic functional needs of Christian community.[13] These buildings would have likely stood out in size and decoration from their 5th century predecessors and may have represented the emergence of monumental architecture to manifest authority in Corinthian society.

---

[10] Pettegrew 2006, 331–52; Rothaus 1994.

[11] Bowden 2003, 59–82.

[12] Bowden 2003, 110; Rothaus 2000, 96; see Trombley (2001, 283–32) for a more guarded assessment of the growth of the Christian community in Athens and Attica and its relationship to church building.

[13] Pallas 1977, 165–71 for a brief summary; Slane and Sanders 2005.

The large-scale expansion of monumental Christian architecture in the 6th century Corinthia provides a basis for reconsidering the most impressive of the 6th-century churches, the Lechaion Basilica, which stood in the center of Corinth's western harbor town (fig. 8.1). This building is particularly significant because its extensive use of Proconnesian marble, elaborately decorated column capitals and floor treatments, and vast size suggests that the church was an imperial foundation.[14] Initially dated by the excavator Pallas to the late 5th to early 6th century, the revised ceramic chronology offered by Slane and Sanders recommends a mid to late 6th century date for this building's construction.[15] The combination of a mid to late 6th century date and opulent décor makes it possible to see this building as part of Justinian's larger building project both in the region and across the empire.

Despite the size and significance of this building, there is no contemporary textual evidence for the church. As a result, the only evidence for the impact of this building on local residents comes from its influence on the architecture of nearly contemporary structures in the region. Sanders has suggested that some aspects of the Panayia Bath as well as other small bathing establishments in the city of Corinth show similarities to the baptistery at Lechaion Basilica.[16] The Lechaion baptistery and the

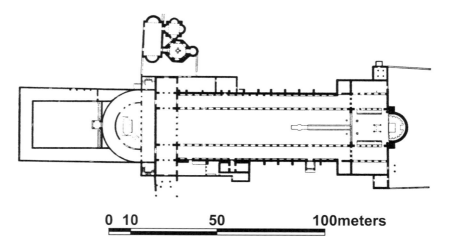

0 10   50   100meters

Fig. 8.1. Plan of the Lechaion Basilica. Drawing by J. Herbst after Dimitrios Pallas.

---

[14] Sanders 2005a, 439. Pallas 1979, 95–96.
[15] Sanders 2005a, 439; Pallas 1977, 171.
[16] Sanders 1999, 474–75.

Panayia Bath are probably close contemporaries (fig. 8.2), and baptism and bathing share longstanding symbolic and architectural associations.[17] As a result, an audience might have been predisposed to recognize the similarities between the two buildings; both have apsidal halls that led to two-chambered spaces, and both feature an octagonal core which opens onto additional chambers on four of its sides.

While finding parallels for octagonal baptisteries in Late Antiquity is not a particularly challenging task, it is worth noting that there are also clear parallels between the Lechaion baptistery and the perhaps contemporary 'Small Baptistery' at Agia Sophia in Constantinople.[18] In Corinth itself, an octagonal structure associated with the so-called amphitheater church just inside the Kraneion gates of the city might be another baptistery. Pallas identified an ionic impost capital similar to those at Lechaion nearby and concluded that this might be a church or martyrium. Until this building is documented by excavation, its architectural and chronological

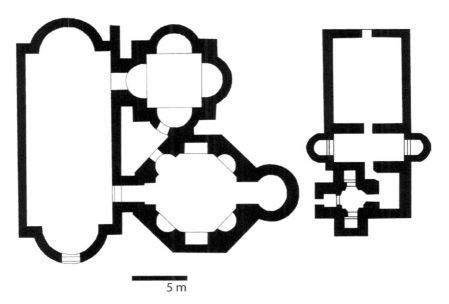

5 m

Fig. 8.2. Plans of the Lechaion baptistery (left) and the Panayia bath (right). Drawings by author (after Sanders 1999, fig. 18).

---

[17] Ristow 1998, 20–23.
[18] Dark and Kostenec 2006.

relationship to other buildings in the region will remain obscure. The octagonal shape, however, and fragmentary architectural sculpture makes it tempting to imagine another 6th-century basilica in the area.[19]

The influence of the Lechaion Basilica also extended to a nearby nymphaion situated just over a kilometer to the northeast of the building.[20] The initial phase of this structure appears to date to the Roman period, but coins of Justinian and Justin date a significant rebuilding to the 6th century.[21] There are clear similarities between the opus sectile floors preserved at the nymphaion and those present at Lechaion. Another parallel comes from the architectural marble associated with the 6th-century rebuilding of the nymphaion. Both buildings featured impressive *verde antico* columns, and more importantly, there are at least three well-preserved ionic impost capitals from the site that look identical to those at the Lechaion Basilica. The similarities with the decoration of the nymphaion suggest that some of the marble architectural elements may have been produced by the same crews who worked on the Basilica. This is particularly significant for the appearance of three unpublished ionic impost column capitals from the nymphaion, a type which is exceedingly rare in non-ecclesiastical contexts.[22] In fact, in Vemi's catalogue of published ionic impost capitals from Greece, there is only one such capital from a non-ecclesiastical building. While the precise function of the nymphaion remains unclear,[23] the similarities in decoration between the two sites hints that the nymphaion enjoyed some relationship with the grandiose nearby church. It may be that the nymphaion served to advertise the imperial connections of a wealthy local resident, to support the prestige of the ecclesiastical hierarchy, or to serve as a stopping point for travelers along the coastal road on the approach to the church at Lechaion. In any context, the Justinianic date of the nymphaion coincides with the revised dates of the Lechaion Basilica and provides another example of the influence of this monumental building.

The most obvious buildings to reflect the function and architecture of the Lechaion Basilica are the other 6th-century basilicas around Corinth. While the chronological relationship between these buildings remains

---

[19] Sanders 2004, 185.
[20] Philadelpheus 1918; Stikas 1957.
[21] Stikas 1957, 93–94.
[22] Yegül (1974, 266) noted that the impost capitals from non-ecclesiastical context at Sardis and from the Palace in Constantinople did not feature crosses; the ones in Thessaly and the Corinthia do.
[23] Vemi 1989, no. 116; Soteriou 1939, 59–60.

difficult to assess, Pallas argued that the Corinthian churches, nevertheless, shared sufficiently similar features to be considered as a group.[24] He based his arguments on the cluster of possible liturgical annexes around their western end, their similar proportions of length to width, and their vaguely anthropomorphic shape. Even without Pallas's typological arguments, it is certainly possible to see the great Lechaion Basilica in the plans of both the Kodratos and Skoutelas Basilicas, and to a somewhat lesser extent in the preserved remains of the Kraneion Basilica.

Architectural similarities among the 6th-century Corinthian basilicas also highlight the differences between them. In this region, the Kraneion Basilica stands out as a notable exception to local patterns (fig. 8.3). At the Kraneion Basilica, heavy piers separated the aisles from the main nave (1.80 m wide × 0.85 m deep; against 1.80 m wide openings).[25] This difference in how the nave was separated from the flanking aisles almost certainly had an impact on a visitor to a Corinthian basilica. The Lechaion Basilica, in contrast, followed a more traditional pattern by separating the nave from the aisles by a series of columns supporting arches that sprung from ornate ionic impost capitals. It appears that most of the columns in this nave colonnade were imperially-sourced Proconnesian marble with its imperial connections and the ionic impost capitals are sufficiently regular in design to suggest an imperial work crew. The absence, then, of a marble colonnade at Kraneion would have marked this church as distinct from its near contemporary at Lechaion. If we regard the use of Proconnesian marble and carefully-wrought ionic impost capitals in the nave colonnade at Lechaion as markers of the building's imperial funding, then the absence of such a colonnade at Kraneion may have served to distinguish this church and perhaps its source of patronage from the massive Lechaion Basilica.

This inconsistency in one of the primary areas for display in Late Roman basilica-type churches may have had particular significance in the context of the Greek liturgy. In most reconstructions of the Greek liturgy, the congregation stood in the aisles leaving the main nave open for liturgical movements by the clergy.[26] The importance of clerical processions to the early Byzantine liturgy influenced the basic design of basilica-style churches and transformed the long axis of the church into a processional

---

[24] Pallas 1979, 93–142.
[25] Shelley 1943, 172.
[26] Matthews 1971, 123–25; Sanders 2005a, 440–41.

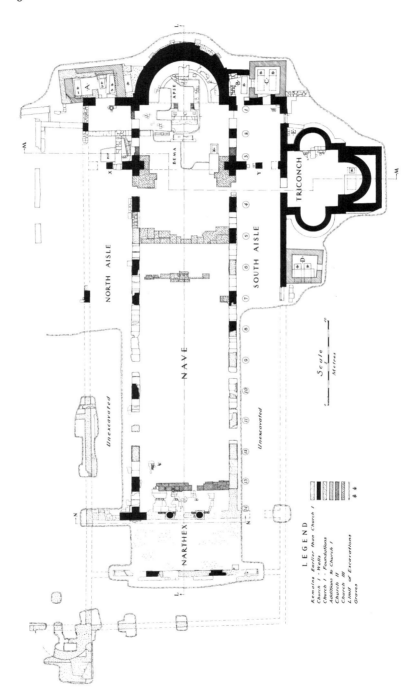

Fig. 8.3. Plan of the Kraneion Basilica (Shelley 1943, pl. 12). Drawing by J.M. Shelley.

way. The colonnades and other barriers that separated the central nave from the flanking aisles structured the experience of viewing the processions and likely separated the clergy, who processed toward the more sacred eastern end of the church building, from the congregation who watched the progress of the clergy.

Thus, in a ritual context, the colonnade served to frame the perspective of the congregation as they watched the liturgical proceedings. The contrasting perspectives offered by the Lechaion Basilica and the church at Kraneion would not have been lost on even the most casual observer. Moreover, the importance of the processions to most Late Antique liturgies made the processional axis of the church a particularly important area for display. This accounts for the imposing colonnade of imported marble columns at Lechaion which represented a major commitment of resources, wealth, and decorative flourish. In contrast, the absence of an elaborate nave colonnade at Kraneion, then, literally reframed the viewing of the liturgy and suggested that the wealth and privilege communicated by the Lechaion colonnade formed just one part of a monumentalized discourse of religious status.

The appearance of monumental basilica-style churches in the neighborhood of Corinth in the 6th century had a clear impact on local architecture across the region. The architectural influence of the Lechaion Basilica extended to include buildings without clear religious functions, suggesting that church buildings represented more than merely ritual space for the community, but also served to shape local ideas of prestige as well. If the Lechaion Basilica was built with imperial funding, then its local impact is clear evidence for the effect of imperial building policy in the Corinthia and suggests that some individuals or groups in the Corinthia saw associating with a prestigious manifestation of imperial policy to be a good thing and extended the influence of the emperor's authority into the nearby landscape. In contrast, the difference between the Lechaion Basilica and the apparently contemporary Kraneion Basilica might well represent one limit to imperial influence in the vicinity of Corinth.

Labor, Production, and Power in the 6th-Century Landscape

While the elaborate basilicas that dotted the 6th-century landscape were architectural focal points of the Late Antique Corinthia, the influence of the 'building boom' extended beyond efforts to emulate ecclesiastical architecture. Procopius tells us that Justinian repaired the Hexamilion fortification which had fallen into ruins. Justinian may have also repaired or refortified the city wall of Corinth.[27] Survey archaeology has documented what appear to be contemporary developments in the construction across the Corinthian countryside. The material present in the countryside suggests that the rural zone of the Isthmus saw a new wave in elite rural habitation perhaps associated with the intensification of agriculture and local prosperity. The large-scale 6th-century investment in the region by both the imperial authorities and local residents must have made a significant impact on the economy, settlement, and experience of life in the Corinthia.

The 6th-century building boom across the Corinthia demonstrated the use of monumental architecture to communicate imperial authority and resistance across the region. As I have argued, fragments of this monumentalized discourse of authority are visible in the influence of the Lechaion Basilica, but its effects extended beyond stylistic or architectural influences and contributed to the productive and experiential landscape of the region as well. The construction of such imposing buildings, whether in collaboration with the emperor or in response to imperial initiatives, undoubtedly taxed the resources of the local elite and involved the labor of numerous ordinary Corinthians. Traditionally, the study of large-scale building projects has emphasized the role that it played in communicating identities and structuring relationships among both local elite and external authority. While there is little doubt that elite motives played a central role in structuring the ancient architecture of a region, the act of constructing the physical monuments also engaged the physical bodies of a significant number of Corinthians. The economic impact of the monumentalization of authority on both elite and non-elite Corinthians linked patterns of labor, production, and consumption to the experience of an increasingly monumentalized landscape. The result was a dynamic, heterogeneous landscape laced with the potential for accommodation and resistance.[28] The construction of power and authority was not monolithic and provided new opportunities for Corinthians to use imperial investment in the region to promote their own position in society.

The most ambitious non-ecclesiastical project in the region was likely the work to repair or reinforce both the Hexamilion and the city wall of Corinth. Inscriptions associated with the Hexamilion Fortress and Procopius's account of Justinian's work in the area make clear that these

---

[27] Procop. *Aed.* 4.2.27–28; 4.1.2; Gregory 2000, 105–15.
[28] Paynter and McGuire 1991.

projects represented imperial interest in the Corinthia. While we will consider the Justinianic inscriptions in greater detail in the final section of the chapter, these texts named the emperor specifically and alluded to the deployment of an official named Victorinus who may have been a specialist in fortifications in the Balkans and beyond.[29] Even if the 6th-century wall around the city itself was, as Sanders has argued, much smaller than previously suggested, the refortification of the city nevertheless represented a serious and highly visible commitment to the community.[30] Kardulias and Gregory have both shown that the financing and personnel required for these projects would have provided employment to local laborers, influenced the distribution of wealth in the local economy, and likely brought troops or skilled workmen into the region.[31] The scale of the undertakings, particularly those associated with the repair of the Hexamilion, suggests that these refortification projects would have affected almost the entire Corinthia. Moreover, the presence of monumental inscriptions associated with at least some of these fortifications tied imperial munificence to important and highly visible features in the Corinthia. Finally, city walls and the massive structure of the Hexamilion shaped how residents of the Corinthia experienced travel through the region in highly visible and tactile ways.

The renewed fortification walls across the Corinthia were not merely spectacles designed to impress local residents with the presence of the imperial authority.[32] Local Corinthians, irrespective of political or religious predilections would have contributed to the physical construction of the Hexamilion Wall and the maintenance of any associated garrisons. Epigraphical evidence shows that laborers in the Late Antique Corinthia were organized as they were elsewhere in the empire.[33] The organization of labor into guilds or less formal groups linked individual identity, at least in part, to participation in the local economy and local politics. It may be that this organization left faint traces across the monuments of the Corinthia suggesting that the building boom of the 6th century did more than simply project elite power into the region, but also provided a space for more ordinary Corinthians to negotiate their own place within the monumental discourse of authority. As possible evidence for this process,

---

[29] Feissel 1990, 136–46.
[30] Slane and Sanders 2005, 193.
[31] Kardulias 1995 and 2005.
[32] For recent work on this topic in the west, see Dey 2010.
[33] M.B. Walbank 2010 for the most recent summary.

Sanders has reported that graffiti of fish were made in the wet mortar of the Lechaion Basilica, the Panayia Bath in the city of Corinth proper, the Hexamilion Wall, as well as several other places in the vicinity of Corinth.[34] These markers in the mortar of the exterior wall of the basilica would have been visible for only a short period of time as they would have almost certainly been covered with either a layer of finer stucco or the surrounding ground level when the building was completed. The symbol of the fish may have religious significance as it was one of the earliest symbols associated with Christianity. We have no idea whether these symbols were set to mark out these buildings as 'Christian' (as if this was necessary for the Lechaion Basilica), to serve some kind of as apotropaic function or to mark the work of a particular crew of laborers. These modest graffiti might well suggest that the same groups of workers or, perhaps, the same organization provided labor for both buildings.

Whatever their function, however, it is clear that the monumental architecture of the Corinthia not only projected power across the region and onto (and through) the bodies of laborers, but it also provided a new context for the everyday actions of Corinthian workers. The subtle traces left by individuals working on the walls provide a glimpse of the physical labor responsible for the construction of imperial authority on the Isthmus. The appearance of the graffiti fish in inconspicuous places on a number of contemporary buildings suggests a division between the explicit message made by the architecture and decoration and the simpler, hidden graffito. The understated character of these graffiti would be consistent with subtle expressions of resistance from individuals in highly asymmetrical power relations.[35] Even if these graffiti are not the marks of resistance, they demonstrate how the local investment in imperial authority created a heterogeneous space for the expression of corporate identities.

Additional evidence for the impact of imperial influence on labor and production on the Isthmus of Corinth comes from Procopius. Procopius was clearly aware that building and providing garrisons for Greece had an impact on labor and production. For example, he praised Justinian for constructing granaries near Thermopylae to provide food for garrisons stationed there.[36] As Given has noted, the act of collecting or contributing taxes in kind represents a highly visible and physical means to link the

---

[34] Sanders 2005a, 428; Athanasoulis 1998.
[35] For more on the archaeology of resistance see: Paynter and McGuire 1991; Silliman 2001; Scott 1985, 1986.
[36] Procop. *Aed.*, 4.2.14.

act of agricultural production to the power of the dominant authority.[37] It seems reasonable to conclude that the stationing of garrisons around Corinth would have required a similar investment in granaries to supply the forces. While Procopius tells us nothing in his *De Aedificiis* of the local response to the creation of granaries or the construction of fortifications across Greece, he is less charitable in his *Historia Arcana*. In this text, Procopius blames Justinian and his lieutenant Alexander 'the Scissors' for taxing Greece so heavily to pay for garrisons that no public buildings could be constructed or games held even in Athens.[38] Local responses to Justinian's investment in Greece likely fell between the neutral view presented in the *De Aedificiis* and the critical view of the *Anecdota*. The increased involvement of the emperor in the affairs of the provinces, nevertheless, makes it difficult to avoid Dunn's conclusions that the economic reorganization of Greece begun under Justinian had a significant impact on production and settlement in the region.[39]

Evidence that connects specific policies with settlement changes, shifts in patterns of agricultural exploitation, and other short-term economic changes often goes undetected in archaeological work conducted on the regional scale. Ceramic chronologies, particularly for the coarse and utility wares that played a key role in the regional economy, remain generally too imprecise to provide evidence for short-term shifts in economic activity. The Eastern Korinthia Archaeological Survey, however, produced several suggestive concentrations of 6th-century fine ware on the Isthmus that may hint at changes in the local settlement and consumption patterns by local residents (fig. 8.4).[40] These concentrations consist of three of the most common middle to late 6th- century pottery forms: Phocaean Red Slip (or Late Roman C) Form 10 and African Red Slip Forms 103–105 and 99, which usually date to after 533 and the Byzantine reconquest of North Africa. These sherds appear in several clear concentrations of artifacts suggesting that they reflected some kind of cohesive activity areas. Moreover, the survey units with 6th-century pottery tend to lack diagnostic fine ware from earlier periods in Late Antiquity. This would seem to indicate that these areas saw an increase in investment or a change in function during the mid 6th century. Perhaps earlier, more industrial uses

---

[37] Given 2004, 93–195.
[38] Procop. *Anecdota*, 26.
[39] Dunn 2004.
[40] Pettegrew 2006 for the most detailed discussion of the Late Roman landscape.

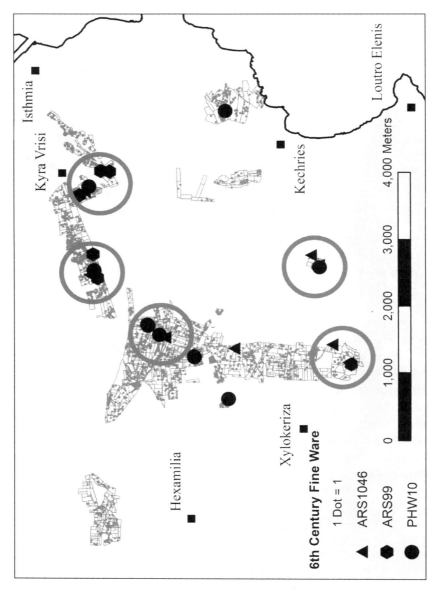

Fig. 8.4. 6th-century material from the Eastern Korinthia Archaeological Survey. Drawing by author.

of the city's territory gave way to domestic activities where imported fine wares were more appropriate.

The evidence from this survey complements evidence from better-documented sites, such as the villa at Akra Sophia published by Gregory and the Southeastern Korinthia Exploration Project.[41] Gregory dated the elaborate Akra Sophia villa to the second half of the 6th century on the basis of a fragment of amphora embedded in the mortar of a foundation and associated material.[42] Like many of the concentrations discovered in the survey, there was little evidence to suggest that this villa was part of an expansion of earlier large-scale activity at the site, although the villa's foundations set into the bedrock may have obscured or obliterated evidence for earlier activity. While these scattered pottery finds do not provide us with enough evidence for our functional, political, or religious arguments, they do show that settlement patterns experienced some modest shift contemporary with a time of increased imperial and local investment in the monumental architecture of the region.

To sum up, the economic impact of the 6th-century building boom provides visible traces both of imperial involvement in the region and local responses in the rural territory and labor market of the Corinthia. Unlike the relationships among monumental buildings, which remained highly visible in the Corinthia landscape, the impact of imperial involvement on everyday life may have penetrated areas barely visible in the archaeological record but very much present in the daily experiences of Corinthians. In this context, subtle traces like the graffiti of fish or changes in settlement may represent acts of accommodation or resistance to external pressures.

*Ambivalence, Control, and Compromise
in Inscriptions and Architecture*

The imperial investment in a building like the Lechaion Basilica and the particular attention to ritual space is consistent with imperial interests in liturgical space across the empire. Justinian's involvement in the affairs of the institutional church, however, did not end at the funding of

---

[41] Gregory 1985, 416–19.
[42] The associated pottery includes fragments of an imitation of a Phocaean Red Slip or Late Roman C bowl, a Phocaean Red Slip or Late Roman C Form 10B, and an African Red Slip Form 99; all of which support a date in the later 6th century CE.

monumental architecture, but extended to what Cameron and Nelson have referred to as the "liturgification" of society.[43] This interest in expanding the role the liturgy in Late Roman society coincided with Justinian's efforts to seek political and theological compromise. Procopius's *De Aedificiis*, for example, emphasized the strong religious dimension to Justinian's building projects, and Justinian's own writing showed a commitment to theological and ecclesiastical affairs that finds parallels with his increasingly public and monumentalized discourse of authority.[44] Moreover, as this final section will show, these texts walk a fine and intentionally ambivalent line between potentially divisive statements of religious policy and a willingness to compromise with potential local practices.

The language present in the two Corinthian inscriptions associated with Justinian demonstrates how he brought together theology, the liturgy, and monumental architecture. While these texts are discussed in greater detail elsewhere,[45] both texts used theologically loaded language to ask God and the Virgin to protect the emperor, his colleague Victorinus, and Greece.[46]

The first text likely comes from a gate in the Hexamilion Wall:[47]

+Φῶς ἐκ φωτός, θεὸς
ἀληθινὸς ἐκ θεοῦ ἀληθινοῦ,
φυλάξῃ τὸν αὐτοκράτορα
Ἰουστινιανὸν καὶ τὸν
πιστὸν αὐτοῦ δοῦλον
Βικτορῖνον ἅμα τοῖς
οἰκούσειν ἐν Ἑλάδι τοὺς κ(α)τ(ὰ) Θεῶν
ζῶντας.+

Light of Light, True God of True God, guard the emperor Justinian and his faithful servant Victorinus along with those who dwell in Greece living according to God.

The second text, now in Verona, comes either from the wall of the city of Corinth, or perhaps more plausibly, from another gate in the Hexamilion:[48]

[43] Nelson 1976, 101–5; Cameron 1979, 15–17.
[44] Fowden 1995, 549–67; Cameron 1985; Gray 1979.
[45] Caraher forthcoming.
[46] *IG* IV 204; *IG* IV 205.
[47] *IG* IV 204; *Corinth* VIII.3. no. 508, 168–69; *Isthmia* V, 12–13, no. 4.; Feissel and Philippidis-Braat 1985, 279–80, no. 16; Monceaux 1884, 277–78; Skias, 1893, 123; Lambros 1905, 268–69; Lampakis 1906, 46–47; Groag 1949, 79; Bees 1941, 1–5, no. 1.
[48] *IG* IV 205; Bees 1941, 5–9, no. 2; Feissel and Philippidis-Braat 1985, 281–82, no. 18; Guarducci 1978, 327–30, no. 2; *Isthmia* V, 14 no. 5.

+ Ἀγ(ία) Μαρία Θεοτόκε, φύλαξον
τὴν βασιλείαν τοῦ
φιλοχρίστου Ἰουστινιανοῦ
χαὶ τὸν γνησίως
δουλεύοντα αὐτῷ
Βικτωρῖνον σὺν τοῖς
οἰκοῦσιν ἐν Κορίνθῳ κ(ατὰ) Θεὼν
ζῶντας. +

Holy Mary, Theotokos, safeguard the empire of the Christ-loving Justinian
and his faithful servant Victorinus, along with those who dwell in Corinth
living according to God.

The texts are inscribed in tabula ansata fields, and the size, content, and
shape of the inscriptions suggest that they were probably built into a gate,
perhaps above the arch, as was common elsewhere in the Mediterranean
during the Justinianic period.[49] Scholars have generally dated these texts
to the early 550s based on the absence of Theodora from the texts.

A date in the mid 6th century places these inscriptions amidst a series
of increasingly hostile political and theological clashes with the church in
the West which ultimately emerged over the course of the Three Chapters
Controversy in the 540s and 550s and culminated in the Second Council
of Constantinople (553).[50] This environment may provide a context both
for the text's refusal to name any local elites and for its clear reference to
contemporary theological controversies. Even under Justinian, local elites
regularly appeared in texts commemorating monumental construction in
the provinces.[51] In the Corinth texts, the absence of any mention of local
elites might well imply that these inscriptions indicate projects spon-
sored directly by the emperor. This casts light, then, on references to the
Theotokos and the Nicene-Constantinopolitan Creed, which both evoked
some of the emperor's theological imperatives and suggested the con-
comitant spread of the imperially-sponsored Constantinopolitan liturgy.
The presence of the Nicene-Constantinopolitan Creed in the inscription
discovered at Isthmia likely evokes the Constantinopolitan liturgy where

---

[49] There are particularly close parallels from North Africa: Pringle 1981, 319 no. 4, 327 no.
29; and from Syria: *IGLSyr* I.145, 146, 147. See also an inscription of similar date originally
in the city wall of Byllis in Albania, *SEG* 35.530–33 naming Viktorinos and inscribed with
similarly sized letters.

[50] For a good summary of issues related to the Three Chapters controversy, see Chazelle
and Cubitt 2007.

[51] Pringle 1981, 89–91; Croke and Crow 1983, 147–48.

the Creed was regularly read by the 6th century.[52] The reference to the Theotokos in the second contemporary inscription from the Isthmus may represent a theological extension of the references in the Isthmia text. In fact, these texts may have worked together to embed a theological argument within the physical space and monuments of the Corinthia. After all, if Christ was "Light from light, true God from true God," then it made some sense to see Mary as the Theotokos.

The link between Mary as the Theotokos and the Creed transferred concepts from Justinian's own theological writings to the Corinthia. The same link between the Creed and the Theotokos appears in his own writings. The clearest example of this comes from Justinian's Letter on the Three Chapters which E. Schwartz suggested was a response to a poorly known 'synod' of Eastern Illyricum held in the mid-540s.[53] This text responded, in particular, to letters from a bishop alleging that Justinian's rejection of the Three Chapters was a form of Nestorianism. Justinian's response took pains to demonstrate how Mary's status as the Theotokos was inseparable from the incarnation of the Divine Logos as Christ which he explicitly articulated as "Light of Light." He then reversed the charge and argued that the author of the letter was himself a Nestorian, and this represented the dangers of the work of Theodore of Mopsuestia whose texts he condemned amidst the Three Chapter debates. Justinian's work followed closely the work of the called Neo-Chalcedonian theologians who drew heavily on the works of Cyril of Alexandria.[54]

This debate, however, extended beyond theological polemics, and appeared in less theological texts like the near contemporary encomium of Corripus, *In Laudem Iustini Augusti minoris*. This text celebrated Justin II's ascension to the throne in 565, encapsulated many of the efforts at theological reform by Justinian I. It began with a vision of the Theotokos, and concluded with long passage describing Agia Sophia in Constantinople in terms of the Creed.[55] The tendency to link Mary as Theotokos to an argument for the incarnation using the Nicene-Constantinopolitan Creed provides a context for the invocations of both the Corinth inscriptions and relates these texts clearly to the ongoing debate concerning the status of the Three Chapters.

---

[52] Kelly 1950, 348–49.
[53] Schwartz 1939, 115.
[54] *PG* 86.1048; Gray 1979; Justinian, *On the Person of Christ: The Christology of Emperor Justinian*. Translation by Wesche 1991, 119–20 and throughout.
[55] Cameron 1976.

By foregrounding theologically sensitive language in these two Corinthian inscriptions, Justinian emphasized a growing interest not only in extending imperial authority over matters of theology, but specifically in exerting a concerted influence over the church in the West.[56] Neither of the texts referenced above would fit within the theological context of Western, that is Papal, theology. In fact, the Roman church neither venerated Mary as the Theotokos nor saw the Nicene-Constantinopolitan Creed as an important public text until its inclusion in the liturgy in the 10th century.[57] At the same time, these texts drew upon concepts on which there was general agreement in the West and East, and in particular reinforced the imperial loyalty to ecumenical symbols of Chalcedon, Ephesos, and ultimately Nicaea.

The Constantinopolitan and imperial liturgy also made its presence felt locally through the position of the centrally placed ambo in the church at Lechaion. The ambo was an elevated pulpit from which the presiding clergy read the Gospels. The central placement of this feature is unusual in Greece and was incompatible with the organization of the early liturgy in the West.[58] In Constantinople, the solea, a walkway protected by balustrades, provided access to the ambo. It allowed the clergy to move freely to the ambo without being crushed by the press of congregation in the main nave.[59] Ambos in Greece, in contrast, were offset to either the north or south of a church's main axis and generally lacked the solea.[60] In fact, the solea was redundant in Greece, and at the Lechaion Basilica in particular, because intercolumnar parapet screens set atop a high stylobate separated the aisles from the main nave and the congregation from the main processional space of the clergy. In this arrangement, the specific function of the centrally-placed ambo and the solea, as well as its relationship to specific liturgical movements is perhaps less significant than the architectural allusion to the Constantinopolitan liturgy in the arrangement of the nave at Lechaion. The use of Proconnesian marble, as we noted above, completed the architecture experience by framing the scene of the liturgy with imperial opulence.

---

[56] Markus 1979, 277–306; Sotinel 1992, 2005, 267–90.
[57] Kelly 1950, 356–57.
[58] For the liturgy in Greece see: Soteriou 1929; Orlandos 1957; Pallas 1979/1980; Pallas 1984; Mathews 1971, 119–21.
[59] Jakobs 1987, 255–56; Xydis 1947; Mathews 1971, 110.
[60] Jakobs 1987.

The textual sources for the church of Corinth are particularly scant, but perhaps in the context of the epigraphy and architecture they can contribute slightly to our picture. The Corinthian church was probably out of communion with the Bishop of Constantinople until the early decades of the 6th century and the resolution of the Acacian schism. The aftershocks of this controversy probably echoed and ensured that the emperor's religious policies did not garner enthusiasm at least among the ecclesiastical elite. In 536, the bishop of Corinth overtly supported a visit of Pope Agapitus to the Capital to depose the monophysite-leaning Patriarch Anthimus by sending two deacons presumably to represent his See.[61] In a more circumstantial association, Pseudo-Gregory in his Dialogues has militantly pro-Chalcedonian Bishop Datius of Milan stop through Corinth on his way to the Capital in 544.[62] It should go without saying that a major route from the West passed through Corinth in Late Antiquity;[63] so it may be significant that the city of Corinth is mentioned by name. By the Council of Constantinople in 553, only four bishops attended from the province of Achaea: Megara, Opus, Aigio, and Porthmos on Euboea.[64] While the subscription list for the council remains problematic, the absence of Corinth – the metropolitan church of Achaea – suggests that support for the Council's decision did not necessarily follow along the lines of the ecclesiastical hierarchy.

The textual sources, the inscribed texts from the Isthmus, and the arrangement of liturgical furnishings presented an ambivalent message regarding the relationship between the emperor and the local community. On the one hand, imperial interests and the allusions to imperial liturgy of Constantinople are unmistakable; on the other hand, references to local practice and sensitivities to local beliefs grounded imperial authority in a Corinthian context. The ambivalence in the sources of the imperial attitude toward Corinth may capture precisely the kind of 'internal friction' that Elsner identified as traces of resistance.

Conclusions

The political position of the Corinthia in the 6th century gives us reason to consider the archaeology of the territory in a new light. The increased

---

[61] *ACO* III, 29.16, 127.39, 163.13, 171.30.
[62] Ps.-Gregory, *Dialogues*, 3.4.
[63] McCormick 2000, 69–72.
[64] Price 2009, 294; Chrysos 1966.

imperial investment in the territory and the corresponding building boom reflects the emergence of a monumental discourse of authority during a time when imperial policy toward the Western empire took on an expansionist posture. Evidence from inscriptions confirms that imperial interest in the Corinthia was not free from theological and, most likely, ecclesiological interests, and this position seems appropriate considering Corinth's status as the seat of the bishop of Achaia.

At the same time, the energy expended to present imperial authority in the region preserved subtle traces of what might be local critique. The text of the inscriptions and the organization of liturgical space within the Lechaion Basilica communicated an ambivalence that charted a course between a brash assertion of imperial policy and the accommodation of local practices. The graffiti made in the external walls of local buildings, the responses of the local economy to the requirement of monumental construction and garrisons, and the influence of important buildings across the Corinthia present subtle clues as to how the Corinthian community responded to increased imperial involvement. While none of this provides explicit and incontestable evidence for traditional or widespread forms of resistance in the Corinthia, it opens up space to consider the limits of imperial authority and local accommodation during times of conflict.

Mediterranean archaeology has traditionally emphasized artifacts associated with the economic elite. Monumental architecture, fine table wares, epigraphy, and the long shadow of literary texts, has produced a world where evidence for inequality and resistance will appear only in the margins. By reading against the grain of both existing scholarship and evidence, it is possible to identify the potential for resistance in the Late Antique Corinthia. Only continued archaeological work and careful study of texts can determine whether this space for potential resistance is ultimately filled with the activities of autonomous human agents.

CHAPTER NINE

REGILLA STANDING BY: RECONSTRUCTED STATUARY AND RE-INSCRIBED BASES IN FOURTH-CENTURY CORINTH

Daniel N. Schowalter

While Annia Appia Regilla Caucidia Tertulla, the wife of Herodes Atticus, graces the title of this paper, she (and her statues) are really just innocent bystanders. This paper is about two statue base inscriptions and a rather convoluted tale of interpretation based on readings and re-readings of these inscriptions over the last 100+ years. The paper also considers the social fabric of ancient Corinth in different periods, and finally it asks the question why Regilla might have been honored long after her death and by whom. In a collection of essays on inequality, we are accustomed to expect that wealthy people will be honored for beneficence shown toward their city and other residents, but how does this equation change when the financial stakes no longer matter, and honors are bestowed for other reasons? As might be expected, even these secondary honors continue to reflect a fundamental inequality of Roman society.

The Inscriptions

One of the two bases bears an inscription that praises Regilla's *sōphrosynē*, goes on at some length about her husband Herodes who is said to have set up the statue, addresses Regilla as if she were Tyche, and notes that the statue stands before a sanctuary.[1] Hereafter, I will refer to this as the Regilla-Tyche base (fig. 9.1).

> ['Ρηγίλλας τ]όδ' ἄγαλμα. φυὴν δ' ἐχάραξε τεχνείτης
> [πᾶσαν σ]ωφροσύνην ἐς λίθον ἀραμένην.
> ['Αττικ]ὸς Ἡρώδης μέγας ὤπασεν, ἔξοχος ἄλλων,
> [παντ]οίης ἀρετῆς εἰς ἄκρον εἰκόμενος,
> [ὅν π] ὅσιν Ἑλλήνων ἔλαχεν περίβωτον ἁπάντων
> [κρέσ]σογα δ' αὖτε π⟨ά⟩ϊν ἄνθος 'Αχαιϊάδος
> ['Ρηγίλ]λα ἡ Βουλή σε Τύχην ὡς εἰλάσκουσα,
> [εἰκόωα π]ρ⟨ὸς⟩ τεμένι στήσατο λαϊνέην.

---

[1] *Corinth* VIII.3 no. 128; *SEG* 13.226; Corinth Excavations Inventory No. I 1658.

Fig. 9.1. The Regilla-Tyche base (I 1658). Photo by I. Ioannidou and L. Bartzioti.

This is a statue of Regilla. An artist carved her nature
extolling all of her moderation in stone. It was given by
Herodes Atticus the Great whom she took as a companion,
he stands out from all others in all virtues,
much talked about among the Hellenes,
a most excellent son (of Greece), the flower of Achaia.
O Regilla, the Boule as if calling you Tyche,
has set up your statue before the sanctuary.

The second example is found on a reused statue base from the Peirene Fountain.[2] It too describes Regilla as an image of sōphrosynē, but instead of reference to a sanctuary, this example places her "beside the streams of the source." Hereafter, I will refer to this as the Regilla-Peirene base (fig. 9.2).

[N]εύματι Σισυφίης βουλῆς παρὰ χεύματι πηγῶν
Ῥηγίλλαν μ' ἐσορᾷ(ι)ς, εἰκόνα σωφροσύνης
Ψ(ηφίσματι) β(ουλῆς)

By the command of the Sysiphian Boule, beside the streams of the source,[3]
You see me, Regilla, an image of moderation,
By decree of the Boule.

The Regilla-Tyche base was found on the west side of the Forum on March 22, 1935.[4] According to the field notebook, the block was taken

---

[2] *Corinth* VIII.1 no. 86; *IG* IV, 1599; Corinth Excavations Inventory No. I 62.

[3] B.A. Robinson uses the phrase "streams of the source" to great effect in her translation and discussion; 2011, 79.

[4] Scranton 1935, 41–44.

Fig. 9.2. The Regilla-Peirene base (I 62). Photo by I. Ioannidou and L. Bartzioti.

from a Byzantine wall near the foundations of what would eventually be labeled as Temple F. Because the inscription addresses Regilla as Tyche, and mentions that the statue was set up in front of a sanctuary (*temenos*), this inscribed block has been used as evidence for identifying Temple F as the Temple of Tyche.[5] The Regilla-Peirene base was found in the fountain complex in 1899, "lying on the marble floor, – halfway between the basin and the front of the eastern apse."[6] Richardson speculates that the base is "perhaps not *in situ*" but assumes from the beginning that it carried a statue of Regilla.[7]

---

[5] Kent mentions that the base was found near the foundation of Temple F, but laments that this find spot has been used (by Scranton) to support the identification of Temple F as dedicated to Tyche. Kent (*Corinth* VIII.3, 22) calls it "unfortunate" that both Regilla blocks "have been so heavily relied upon for topographical evidence;" referring to Scranton 1951, 68–69. In his study of Tyche at Corinth (1990, 537), Edwards locates the find spot for the base as "near the foundations of Temple F, and points out that Regilla was honored as priestess of Agathe Tyche in Athens" (*IG* II², 3607). On other grounds, Williams (1975, 27) has identified Temple D as dedicated to Tyche. He mentions a fragmentary statue of Tyche, found "north of Temple D," and this may be why Tobin misidentifies the find spot of the Regilla-Tyche inscription as "north of Temple D" (Tobin 1997, 298). Brown (2008, 122) argues that the use of the word *temenos* on the inscription rules out any of the smaller stand-alone temples on the west end of the Forum for Tyche. She also ignores the find spot and tries to make a case for connecting both Regilla and the Tyche Temple with Temple E.

[6] Richardson 1900, 235.

[7] On the basis of this identification, Richardson assigns what he calls "the second marble period" of the fountain to the time and benefaction of Herodes (1900, 236–37).

In cataloging the former base in 1966, and commenting on the latter, J. Kent posited that the inscriptions are recuts which should be seen as having been crafted at least 100 years after the death of Regilla around 160 CE. So Kent places these inscriptions along with three others as examples of 3rd to 4th-century recuts of earlier inscriptions.[8]

From the moment I first read this claim, I was struck by what seemed to be the odd historical image of someone in the late 3rd or 4th century taking the time and effort to recreate a dedication for Regilla, the long dead wife of one of the wealthiest men of the mid 2nd century CE. Is it possible that someone in the late 3rd or early 4th century would have made such a dedication, and under what circumstances might this have happened? In order to evaluate Kent's argument, it is necessary to consider the relationship between the family of Regilla and Herodes and the Corinthia, to review the epigraphic evidence for and against the claim that the inscriptions were recut, and then to consider the social realities that might explain how this re-inscribing could have happened. In the end, I believe that Kent's case for re-inscribing cannot be sustained. My negative judgment must remain hypothetical, but working toward that conclusion also yields insights on the Late Antique city and social relations within it.

---

[8] Kent identifies two statue bases for P. Caninus Agrippa (published by West in *Corinth* VIII.2, nos. 65–66) as recuts. In support of this claim, Kent points out, "West has already noted (nos. 65, 66) the incompetence of the letter cutter, who was evidently quite unfamiliar with the Latin language" (*Corinth* VIII.3, 22 n. 15). West does comment with regard to no. 65, "The peculiarities of this line are to be explained by the assumption that the inscription was cut by an inexperienced workman, presumably a Greek," and for no. 66, "Considering the curious errors of the contemporary dedication (no. 65), one may be justified in assuming that this inscription also was cut by an ignorant Greek workman" (*Corinth* VIII.2, 45–46). In West's description, however, there is no mention of this Greek workman doing his engraving long after the life of P. Caninius Agrippa, and in fact, regarding no. 65, West specifically rejects the suggestion by Dean (1919, 271) that the last two lines are later additions. Kent also argues that a fifth inscription (*Corinth* VIII.3, no. 129) is also a later recut. This statue base was found in the central area of the South Stoa in 1936, and an additional fragment of it turned up in 1948. Although the subject of the statue is not named in the surviving portion of the inscription, Kent argues that there "seems little doubt that ... this base contained a dedication to Herodes Atticus himself" (*Corinth* VIII.3, 59). He argues for this conclusion with similarities in lettering and wording with the Regilla-Tyche base, but Kent's reconstruction of the text and his attempt to connect it to Herodes Atticus are challenged by Robert and others (Robert 1966, 742–43). *Corinth* VIII.3 no.129 may somehow be connected with the two Regilla bases, but there is enough doubt about the identification with Herodes to exclude it from consideration in this chapter.

Regilla and the Corinthia

The connection between Regilla and the Corinthia must be traced through her husband Herodes.[9] A. Spawforth thinks that the family of the mother of Herodes settled in Corinth no later than the time of Augustus, and suggests that Herodes's maternal grandfather, L. Vibullius Rufus might have been a brother or cousin of the distinguished L. Vibullius Pius.[10] E. Perry points out that Herodes's second child, a daughter Elpinike and the only child to survive after his own death, was married to Lucius Vibullius Hipparchus II, great-grandson of L. Vibullius Rufus.[11]

Connections with Herodes's paternal line can also be traced back in Corinth. Since the boule voted a statue of a young Herodes to be erected in Eleusis, it is obvious that they were interested in positive connections with the family.[12] In the early 2nd century, the father of Herodes, Tiberius Claudius Atticus Herodes, was honored by the city with at least two inscriptions at the time of his restoration to prominence and reception of the *ornamenta praetoria*.[13] T. Martin suggests that these identical inscriptions for Atticus may have been set up on opposite ends of the Forum "upon his reception of the *ornamenta praetoria*."[14]

Evidence for benefactions from the family of Regilla and Herodes in the Corinthia is substantial, although not as abundant as it is for Athens. According to Philostratus (*VS* 2.551), the benefactions of Herodes to Corinth included the construction of a "roofed theater" or odeion in the city. Tobin equates this work with the second phase or Marble Period of the Odeion, which dates to the second half of the 2nd century CE.[15]

While Richardson originally used the Regilla-Peirene base to argue that Herodes was also responsible for a late 2nd-century refurbishment of the

---

[9] Regilla is specifically named as the donor of a water source and grand fountain in Olympia. On her Roman family background and activities, see Gleason 2010, and also, with caution, Pomeroy 2007.

[10] Spawforth 1978, 252.

[11] Perry (2001, 486) argues that the couple should be associated with an elaborately decorated sarcophagus found in Kephisia.

[12] *IG* II² 3604b. Mentioned in Tobin (1999, 73).

[13] *Corinth* VIII.2 no. 58 and Corinth Inventory No. I 74–5 were published by Martin (1977, 185–86). Martin posits that I 74–5 is a twin to the former inscription, and that both were set up in to honor Ti. Claudius Atticus. Unfortunately, *Corinth* VIII.2, no. 58 has been lost.

[14] Martin 1977, 185. The suggestion is based on secondary find spots.

[15] Tobin, 1997, 301–2.

Peirene Fountain,[16] Herodes's sponsorship of such a project has been questioned by a number of scholars, and the notion of a major 2nd-century
renovation has been dismissed by B. Robinson's careful work.[17] Robinson
does, however, suggest that Regilla and/or Herodes could have set up the
Scylla statue group which she places in the central *hypaithros krene* of
the Peirene Fountain.[18] Graindor argues for a connection between Herodes
and the statue of Armed Aphrodite on Acrocorinth, but Tobin rejects this
idea as speculative.[19]

Both Pausanias (2.1.8) and Philostratus (*VS* 2.551) mention multiple
offerings made by the family in Isthmia, especially a "large statue group
in gold and ivory of Poseidon and Amphitrite in a chariot pulled by four
horses and flanked by Tritons."[20] The placement of these gifts in the
Posei-don sanctuary has been debated,[21] but in any case they attest to the
relation between Herodes's family and the Corinthia. Two portrait heads
of Polydukeion, the favorite student of Herodes, were found in or near the
bath complex at Isthmia,[22] and J. Reinhard has suggested that the 2nd-
century bath complex at Isthmia and the huge mosaic floor – also featur-
ing Poseidon and Amphitrite – might be given by Herodes as a tribute to
Polydukeion.[23] Some level of involvement by Regilla and Herodes with
this bath is certainly plausible.

In response to these benefactions, it is certain that the city erected
many tributes to Regilla, Herodes and their family, but unfortunately
few of these survive. There is the aforementioned inscription to the child
Herodes at Eleusis,[24] and an inscribed herm of Herodes found near New
Corinth.[25] A bust of Polydeukion was found in the area of the Kraneion,

---

[16]   Richardson 1900, 236.

[17]   Robinson 2011, 252–75.

[18]   Robinson 2011, 247–48. According to Robinson, the Scylla group was a subject that
necessitated a wealthy donor(s) familiar with the decoration of imperial dining facilities
in Italy, a requirement that is met by both Herodes and Regilla. The *hypaithros krene*,
mentioned by Pausanias (2.3.3), was "an open-air fountain with running water" taking the
form of "a quadrangular depression in the floor of the court" (Robinson 2011, 188).

[19]   Graindor 1930, 213; Tobin 1997, 300.

[20]   Tobin 1997, 312.

[21]   Sturgeon 1987, 76–113.

[22]   Isthmia Inventory Nos. IS 437 and IS 78–12 respectively. Discussed by Tobin (1997, 312).

[23]   Reinhard 2005, 36–69, 250.

[24]   N. 11 above.

[25]   Ἡρώδης ἐνθάδε περιεπάτει, "Herodes used to walk here" (Corinth Inventory No. S 1219;
SEG II 52; *Corinth* VIII.1 no. 85, 63–64; Tobin 1997, 297–99).

but this may have been set up by Herodes himself.[26] The latter two are on
display in the Corinth museum today. In addition, we have the two Regilla
bases under consideration in this paper.[27] Of course, the Regilla-Tyche
statue is said to have been donated by Herodes while the Regilla-Peirene
statue was set up by decree of the boule. Such honors are to be expected
during or immediately after the lifetime of benefactors, but Kent's argument that Regilla was honored with statue bases recut more than a century after her death must be tested both on epigraphic grounds and in the
context of Late Antique Corinth.

The Epigraphic Argument

With regard to the Regilla-Tyche base, Kent argues that "the lunate sigma,
uncial omega, and the clumsy shapes of rho and other letters indicate that
the text was engraved at least a century after Regilla's death."[28] Elsewhere
Kent specifies that for both Regilla bases "the lettering is of later third or
fourth century date, with phonetic errors in spelling that are characteristic
of early Byzantine gravestones."[29] It is obvious that the lettering of both
Regilla bases is significantly different from the one sure epigraphic reference to Herodes from Corinth – the herm with the head of Herodes found
near new Corinth (S1219).[30] It is also important to recognize that cuttings
on both of the blocks indicate that they were reused, at least twice in the
case of the Regilla-Peirene block.[31] For the most part, Kent's brief argument
for recutting of these inscriptions has been accepted. Robert questioned
aspects of Kent's reading of the alleged recuts, but agrees with Kent and
places both Regilla bases in the 4th century.[32] In her collection of material
related to Herodes, Tobin admits that the bases seem to have been recut

---

[26] Corinth Inventory No. S 2734. The Kraneion was "the ancient park of the city where
philosophers spent time" (Tobin 1997, 299).

[27] Tobin agrees with Robert (1966, 742–43) that the third recut base cited by Kent
should not be identified as holding a statue of Herodes (Tobin 1997, 298–99).

[28] *Corinth* VIII.3, 59.

[29] *Corinth* VIII.3, 22, n. 15.

[30] Tobin 1999, 299. The fact that this text appears on a herm shows a classicizing intention, and based on the letter forms this inscription could be read as coming from a time
significantly earlier than the 2nd century CE if the image were not of a known figure.

[31] Robinson (2011, 253 n. 12) citing Hill (*Corinth* I.6, 102–3) summarizes the evidence for
the three phases of use, including two cuttings for bronze statues, "the second of which
stood above a shallow relief carved into one face of the base." The phase associated with
the Regilla inscription "probably was a marble figure on a plinth."

[32] Robert 1966, 742–43.

"at some later time." She also speculates on possible explanations for recreating the inscriptions.[33] For Robinson, the late dating for the Regilla-Peirene base fits very well with her dating of a major renovation and redecoration of the fountain between the 4th and mid 6th centuries CE.[34]

In opposition to Kent's claim for late recutting based on letter forms, there is a large body of scholarship that considers dating based on paleography to be unreliable. B. McLean summarizes the case: "[T]he dating of Hellenistic and Roman inscriptions according to allegedly key developments of particular letter forms is notoriously difficult and unreliable because older letter forms persist alongside new forms . . . In the absence of more studies like Tracy's, it is not possible to date inscriptions precisely on the basis of letter forms."[35] The images of inscriptions related to Herodes collected by Tobin reveals not a consistent letter style, but a wide variety of hands, letter sizes, and spacing.[36] Overall, the evidence seems to indicate a wide divergence of letter forms in the corpus of inscriptions which date to the lifetime of Herodes.[37] In response to the initial presentation of this chapter, R. Stroud also expressed concern about dating inscriptions based on letter forms. He acknowledged Kent's great abilities as an epigrapher, but he did not believe that letter forms could be used as a reliable basis for dating.[38]

Thus Kent's proposed recutting and re-dating of the inscriptions based on epigraphic analysis cannot be accepted uncritically. The remainder of this paper will seek to apply other criteria to test Kent's proposal for recutting. The following questions will be explored: In what circumstances

---

[33] Tobin 1997, 299.

[34] Robinson 2011, 281–82. Pomeroy (2007, 113) misrepresents Robinson's position, while citing her in support of her attempt to move the marble phase of Peirene to a 2nd century date, and thereby to posit that Regilla (not Herodes) was responsible for the remodeling. She also refers to the musical instrument relief on the right side of the block, and suggests that it was chosen especially from "plenty of other bases available" to "draw attention to Regilla's accomplishments in the musical arts." Unfortunately, Pomeroy fails to mention that the instrument relief is upside down in relation to the Regilla inscription, something that cannot be seen in the accompanying illustration since it features a drawing of the top and bottom of the base, not the side that actually shows the relief frieze. J. Wiseman finds the characterization of the inverted relief as musical instruments to be erroneous and misleading. Rather, he sees these as cultic symbols that need to be reconsidered in a ritual context (personal communication, March 23, 2011).

[35] McLean 2002, 42–43. Although McLean's examples pertain mostly to the persistence of older forms, his caution about dating based on paleography still applies in this case.

[36] Tobin 1999, figs. 5, 6, 7, 9, 10, 13–19, 21–23, 35.

[37] Kent seems rather romantic in his reluctance to "imagine that Herodes would have tolerated such a slipshod memorial to his beloved wife" (*Corinth* VIII.3, 59–60).

[38] Stroud, personal communication, Oct. 1, 2010.

could such a base have been recut? Who might have had the motivation to do so? Where did the text on the inscription come from? Where did the re-erected bases/statues stand? When could a hypothetical recutting have taken place?

Why Recut the Bases?

In order to sustain Kent's argument for recut statue bases in the late 3rd or early 4th century, one must argue for a situation in which statues are being re-erected. Since the Regilla-Peirene base was found on the floor of the Peirene Fountain, within and around which multiple statuary fragments were found, it is not hard to imagine such a circumstance. In discussing the Late Antique phases of Peirene, Robinson refers to extensive evidence for re-erected statues in the area. Citing parallels from Aphrodisias and Ephesos, she sees examples of pieces of statuary from different periods put together as "temporal hybrids" set up in and around the Fountain. "Statuary finds around Peirene, including Roman portrait bodies, Late Antique bases naming earlier individuals, new and recut portrait heads, and traditional pagan figures, suggest a nostalgic, museum-like arrangement in and near the fountain in late antiquity."[39]

Specifically, Robinson suggests that the statue body of a Roman matron (Corinth Inventory No. S 55) found near the Peirene Fountain might have been combined with a Late Antique head of a woman with large eyes and snood (Corinth Inventory No. S 986), and placed on top of the Regilla-Peirene base.[40]

J. Alchermes has pointed out that in the 4th and 5th century there was administrative and even imperial impetus for reconstruction and reuse of Classical material including sculpture. According to Alchermes, "legislation that called for the installation in new contexts of prized, often recognizably reused, architectural and sculptural elements sought to maintain the traditional appearance of the civitas and to stimulate positive reactions of civic solidarity among the residents of late imperial municipalities."[41]

---

[39] Robinson 2011, 281.

[40] Robinson 2011, 282. Robinson asks "would the late antique *boule* (and a hired sculptor) have worried about the close replication of the likeness of Annia Appia Regilla, and was her appearance even still known?" (2011, 281–82). Her answer to both questions is no. Whoever put up the statues was content to use available fragments in a kind of jigsaw puzzle reconstruction. This would seem to make it less likely that they would make the effort of re-inscribing old decrees on the base.

[41] Alchermes 1994, 178.

Robinson sees the attitude behind this legislation as a large part of the motivation for the Late Antique Phase 1 of the Peirene Fountain. She points out that "regional officials must attend to the maintenance and restoration of 'old illustrious buildings,'" among which, Peirene was certainly numbered. If local officials were enjoined to make use of sculptural fragments as part of the urban renewal programs of the late 4th century, then it is certainly understandable that old bases (like the two on which the Regilla inscriptions appear) and statues would have been reused, but this mandate for architectural and decorative recycling does not imply that the correct statue would have to be placed on the right base. Neither would it require the re-inscription of a dedication on a statue base. It would be perfectly possible to reconstruct a statue on any base, unless someone specifically wanted the base to refer to Regilla. So 4th-century norms could explain why a block would be reused, but they do not explain why the same dedication would be maintained.

Who Would Recut a Base of Regilla?

The question of who might have spent the time and money to re-inscribe these bases is a vexing one. Such an act requires either an individual or a community body with both the means and the inclination to recreate an honor for Regilla. Tobin suggests that the putative recuts may be associated with descendants of Herodes and Regilla who still lived in the area. "It is possible that there were still Vibullii in Corinth who felt it prestigious to continue the connection with Herodes, particularly at a time when circumstances might make it desirable to look back on the more prosperous past of the city."[42]

There are, however, problems with this suggestion. As detailed above, we know that the benefactions of Regilla and Herodes to Corinth were based on a longstanding relationship between the family and the city. It does not necessarily follow that the family would still have been a force in the city after more than a century of political vicissitudes, economic setbacks, and natural disasters following the deaths of Regilla and Herodes. Since among their children only Elpinike is known to have had any offspring, the chances of such long-term prominence seem slight.[43] The fact that neither inscription includes any family names beyond Regilla or

---

[42] Tobin 1997, 299.
[43] Tobin 1997, 85.

Herodes, also decreases the likelihood that the statues were re-erected by descendants. If there were still relatives in the region by the late 3rd or 4th century, and if they paid to have inscriptions recut, then they surely would have wanted their own names or at least family names to be included on the stone.

Another suggestion as to who might have paid for the putative Regilla recuts was alluded to above. Kent argues that any inscription which incorporates the terminology Ψηφίσματι βουλῆς ("by decree of the city council"), or, as in the case of the Regilla-Peirene base, the psi/beta abbreviation should be taken to indicate that "official approval of the city council was obtained before a new monument was erected."[44] Kent further insists that this approval amounted to an authorization that was very specific and that made the statue the official property of the city. As such it fell to the boule to see that such statues "were adequately protected and maintained."[45] In the event of damage to any of these civic dedications, Kent implies that the city would actually have been obligated to reconstruct it. While Kent's proposal is plausible, one must at least question whether such requirements applied over 100 years later.

So if it is unlikely that 4th-century descendants of Regilla paid to have a statue base re-inscribed and if we cannot be certain that the boule would have taken on the task, who else would have picked up the tab? Robinson observes that the Late Antique remodeling of the Peirene Fountain could be the result of poetic or philosophical inspiration. In the 4th century, she sees a renewed rhetorical interest in Corinth and the Fountain. References to Peirene in "Themistius, Libanius, and the emperor Julian, as well as a clear allusion by Himerius . . . reveal that the fountain was still well-known and well-appreciated, probably not only for its water, but as a symbol of poetic or philosophical inspiration."[46]

One could argue that the same inspiration led to the re-erection of statues, and the need to recut bases. Some 4th-century benefactor could have wanted to honor Regilla specifically, not because of her or her husband's benefactions to the city, but because of Herodes's contributions to rhetoric and education. This kind of appreciation of Herodes as teacher

---

[44] *Corinth* VIII.3, 22. Most likely, this category would include for Kent an example like the Regilla-Tyche base where the boule is said to have "set up" the statue, even if the official decree wording is missing.

[45] *Corinth* VIII.3, 22.

[46] Robinson 2011, 62–63, 274–75.

is displayed in the early 3rd-century writing of Philostratus, so it is not unreasonable that he continued to be influential in learned circles.

A Late Antique appreciation for philosophical tradition is discussed at length by R.R.R. Smith in his treatment of "Late Roman Philosopher Portraits from Aphrodisias." Smith highlights the elevated role of philosophers and their art in the late 4th and early 5th centuries CE. Leading philosophers were "prominent, influential, even glamorous figures," who were also "the radical defenders of pagan religion."[47] In Aphrodisias, this high regard for philosophy also translated into a tendency to portray philosophers in sculpture, some well-known and long dead, others unknown and probably more recent.[48]

This practice of commemorating long dead teachers is seen in many contexts across the empire in Late Antiquity, as Smith makes clear. One Corinthian example, however, stands out. Smith cites "the remarkable glass panels from Cenchreai, the port of Corinth (mid-fourth century, probably from Alexandria)."[49] Due to some kind of mishap, it appears that these images never made it out of the shipping crates until modern times, but they may have been imported in the same spirit and perhaps by the same individuals who wanted to see marble statues re-erected as a reminder of the philosophical past of Greece, and probably a re-enforcement for the on-going battle with the Church for the soul of Greek and Roman culture.[50]

L. Stirling has also considered these glass panels in her study of *The Learned Collector: Mythological Statuettes and Classical Taste in Late Antique Gaul*. She points out that in the panels, "the sages and the divinities are shown as statues standing on bases, reflecting continuing interest in that medium." She concludes that "the patron evidently found that these subjects went together well to illustrate a life of contemplation, good taste, and high status."[51]

So a good hypothetical case can be built to give credit to unnamed literati of Late Antique Corinth for re-erecting statues to their rhetorical

---

[47] Smith 1990, 127.
[48] Smith 1990, 142–50. The philosopher portraits in Aphrodisias are very different, yet instructive. The medallion portraits were newly carved and described by Smith as "superbly finished" (1990, 132). Some of them are inscribed, but only with the name of the subject. The focus is clearly on the image. These would not support Kent's argument for re-inscribed bases.
[49] Smith 1990, 151.
[50] Smith 1990, 154–55.
[51] Stirling 2005a, 154.

heroes. If the re-erection of the statues was motivated by a desire to high-light one of the philosophical heroes of Greek culture, then a recut base might have been important.[52] But unlike the Aphrodisian sculptures or the Kenchreai images, the bases in question refer to statues not of the beloved thinker, but of his wife. The Regilla-Peirene base does not even mention Herodes, so it becomes more difficult to ascribe the recutting to people who want to highlight the contributions of the great rhetorician.[53]

Whence the Texts?

As we have seen, it is difficult to identify an agent who is likely to have played the role of Kent's recutter. A further difficulty comes from under-standing the practical situation that would have allowed these texts to be recut. For Kent's suggestion to be feasible, one must posit that the original base for a Regilla statue was no longer usable, but that the text of the original inscription was somehow still available. Each of these assertions presents difficulties.

A statue base is usually a large block of stone that is not easily destroyed. The processes that might typically demolish a base – cutting it up for building blocks or breaking it up for the lime kiln – would obviously ren-der the block unreadable.[54] Between the time of Regilla and the putative recutting of the base, the most likely causes of damage to the statue would have been violent human attack or an earthquake. While either of these options could have certainly toppled and damaged the statue, it is less likely that a rampaging invader or a seismic tremor would have led to the destruction of a base. Unless we imagine the recutter gathering and reas-sembling fragments to read, it is doubtful that either human activity or an earthquake would have destroyed the base. Even if such a rare scenario occurred in the case of one or two bases, it seems overly simplistic to use this explanation for all five recut bases mentioned by Kent.

---

[52] In that case, the elaborate language used to praise Herodes on the Regilla-Tyche base might make sense: "It was given by Herodes Atticus the Great whom she took as a companion, he stands out from all others in all virtues, much talked about among the Hellenes, a most excellent son (of Greece), the flower of Achaia."

[53] Both bases ascribe the virtue of sōphrosynē to Regilla, but is that alone justification for carving a new inscription? See p. 181 below.

[54] If a base had simply cracked over time, the principle of least effort would suggest that it would have been mended, rather than recreated, if possible.

It is possible to imagine that the statues had been toppled and the original bases were built into another structure where the text was still visible.[55] Or perhaps, in the spirit of the times, the original bases had already been reused as bases for other statuary. In this case, the creators of these hypothetical reconstructions could have decided not to erase the earlier inscriptions, but rather to spin it so that a new inscription could be applied to a blank side, and so the old inscription might still be visible.

If, for some reason, the original bases were unavailable, there are at least three potential scenarios to explain the source for the text of a recut inscription. One is to suggest that records of the inscriptions were kept in some kind of civic archive. Since both inscriptions make mention of the boule, perhaps the council kept records that could have been consulted 100 plus years later. Such remarkable record keeping might seem very Roman, and it coheres nicely with the argument discussed above that the boule was somehow involved in producing the recuts. On the other hand, there has to be some skepticism about this level of civic efficiency over a period of a century or more.

A second explanation for the availability of the text arises if the bases were destroyed in the lifetime of those who chose to recut them, and human memory could then have served as the source for the text. Even the eight lines of the Regilla-Tyche inscription would have been well within the memory capacity for that time.

Finally, it is possible that Kent's 4th-century bases with their "decadent lettering" were not recuts at all, but whole-cloth creations by representatives of a late 3rd or 4th-century Roman elite who were trying to hang on to a centuries-old tradition. The florid language of the two Regilla bases, would certainly be at home in such a context. But the overall tone of the inscriptions would also be quite compatible with the Second Sophistic and the lifetime of Regilla and Herodes.

While it is possible that one of these scenarios might explain the availability of the texts for a hypothetical 4th-century recutter, each one requires a great deal of special pleading. If Robinson is right about the eclectic nature of the "temporal hybrids" occupying the Late Antique

---

[55] There are plenty examples of the latter occurring in the Roman period, notably, the library of Pantainos inscriptions built into the Post-Herulian wall in Athens (Agora Inventory No. I 848; Meritt 1946, 233). While the Herulian invaders are no longer thought to have reached Corinth, that does not mean that the city would not have tried to improve defenses in light of what A. Frantz describes for Athens as "an uneasy peace, under constant threat of further attack, until the last decade of the 4th century" (Agora XXIV, 13).

fountain space, the plausibility of these explanations is further reduced. It is hard to imagine making the effort to re-inscribe a base to Regilla when whoever commissioned the project fashioned a "temporal hybrid" to stand upon it. The circumstances under which the inscription would be available are not decisive in evaluating Kent's proposal.

Where Did the Bases Stand?

Both Regilla inscriptions make reference to location. The Regilla-Tyche base states that the statue was set up "before the sanctuary (of Tyche)," and the Regilla-Peirene base says that it stood "beside the streams of the source." Since the latter was found on the floor of the Peirene Fountain between the basin and the front of the eastern apse, it makes sense to posit both original and secondary location in or around the Fountain. In its final incarnation, whether or not the base was recut, this statue would have been part of the "nostalgic, museum-like arrangement" that Robinson posits in and around the fountain.[56] Conversely, since the Regilla-Tyche base was found reused in a Byzantine wall, there can be no certainty about the place or places it stood while bearing a statue. As mentioned above (n. 4), this uncertainty has not stopped scholars from using the block as a topographical indicator, but it is not possible to know from where the Regilla-Tyche base was moved for reuse in the Byzantine wall. Certainly, it also could have been part of the "nostalgic, museum-like arrangement" envisioned by Robinson, but there is no way to confirm this. In fact, apart from Kent's theory of recutting, there is no reason to suppose that this base was used in the 4th century for any purpose other than a wall block.

When Could a Recutting Have Occurred?

When statues of Regilla or Herodes were put up during or immediately after their lifetimes, they stood as part of a complicated social interaction between their family and various municipalities and groups that they chose to support.[57] By the late 4th century, the city might still appreciate these contributions, and someone might be led to re-inscribe dedications, but it is instructive that the neither inscription refers to a specific benefaction from

---

[56] Robinson 2011, 281.
[57] In the case of Corinth, this relationship is detailed above pp. 170–72.

Regilla or her family.[58] If statues of Regilla were set up in the 4th century, and if the bases were re-inscribed especially for the occasion, the motivation must go beyond the traditional patron-client model of benefaction. The possibility that these statues honor Herodes as a famous teacher was discussed and rejected above, but perhaps it is Regilla herself who strikes a chord within the Late Antique city.

The common denominator between the two bases is reference to the sōphrosynē ("moderation") of Regilla. The concept of sōphrosynē would have fit nicely into the 4th-century world of both Christian and Greco-Roman values. Perhaps the inscriptions were featured as a way to build bridges between polytheistic and Christian residents of the city. In her analysis of pagan statuettes from the Panayia Domus, Stirling discusses the tense religious situation found in the city at that time. She points out that in a speech to the emperor Julian, the orator Libanius (Oratio 14) depicted Corinth as a city harshly divided on religious lines, with pagan cult waning in influence and under attack by Christian partisans.[59] In light of this "chilly climate for pagan worship," tributes to Regilla could be set up specifically to honor her sōphrosynē.

Based on this hypothesis, one could argue that the Regilla-Peirene base was tolerated and reused with a new occupant while the Regilla-Tyche statue, with its explicit connection to the goddess, was removed and used as a wall block. This context provides a plausible explanation of why a tribute to Regilla might have been re-established, but it actually works against Kent's argument for the recuts.

In the 4th century, various groups in Corinthian society were vying for power and influence. The boule of the city was most likely, a mixed group of Christians and followers of Greco-Roman cults by this time. If the remodeling of Peirene is seen as a needed improvement/repair of an important civic space, useful to people from all walks of life, the re-erection of a statue of Regilla within it serves the purpose of both decoration and education. Her story evokes a time and place where Corinth and all of the empire were at their height, perhaps for the last time. Her sōphrosynē stands as a commendable virtue regardless of one's religious orientation. In this context, however, it becomes more difficult if not impossible to

---

[58] On the Regilla-Peirene base, Herodes is given credit only for setting up the statue of his wife.

[59] Stirling 2008, 138. She suggests that "in the polarized environment that Libanius describes, the owner of the Panayia Domus may have felt uneasy about openly displaying a domestic shrine."

imagine that someone would recarve an inscription that explicitly refers to an important goddess of the city, and expect that it could be displayed in a public place.

Conclusions

Kent's argument for a later recutting of these two bases mentioning Regilla cannot be sustained. The argument, that someone went to the trouble of re-inscribing a base for what may have been a composite statue, is not plausible. The argument that they did it twice, and included a potentially inflammatory reference to a goddess is even less likely. While the context of the 4th century, the legal injunctions to restore ancient structures and statues, and the revival of poetic and philosophical study in Corinth and elsewhere, makes it likely that statues were re-erected on these bases as part of a "nostalgic, museum-like arrangement,"[60] that context does not require that the bases were re-inscribed. Even if we posit that the boule of Corinth or some other interested party decided to re-erect two statues representing Regilla, we cannot assume that they also commissioned the cutting of two new inscriptions for the bases on which those images stood.

It seems much more likely that the original 2nd-century bases, perhaps repurposed already, along with fragmentary statues would have been used to establish the kind of "museum-like" display described by Robinson. The overall effect of such a display would have depended much more on the statues than on what was written on the bases.

In the process of evaluating Kent's argument, we can also learn from a comparison between a display of Regilla in the 2nd century and one involving her name, at least, in the 4th century. In their original contexts, the Regilla statues would have been of a living or recently deceased person who, in spite of what either inscription said, had to be best known for her wealth and generosity. These original statues reflected a dynamic relationship between Regilla and Herodes and the elites of Corinth, in which honor was offered in exchange for favor, and benefaction was offered in exchange for prestige and publicity. While this exchange usually takes place almost completely between elites and super-elites in the city, it can be argued that some of the benefactions for which Regilla was honored in the second century could have been enjoyed by anyone in the town.

---

[60] Robinson 2011, 281. The find spots make this much more likely for the Regilla-Peirene base than the Regilla-Tyche base.

In addition, construction and maintenance of these contributions would have provided jobs for at least some people in the community.

By the time statues might have been re-erected on these bases in the 4th century, the typical patronage relationships cannot explain their presence. We cannot be sure what shape the Odeion was in by the mid 4th century, but if it was still functioning it must surely have been renovated, perhaps several times, since Regilla and Herodes had done their work. If there were family members still living in the area, and if they still controlled enough wealth to be potential or actual patrons of the city, why is there no mention of their benefaction, and why are relevant family names not included in either inscription?

In the 4th-century reconstructions, Regilla is honored not as a donor, but as an image of a past reality. Those who could read the inscription might comment on her sōphrosynē, or her magnificent husband. Some might raise an eyebrow at the stated connection to a goddess. Some people might look at the statue display and see a symbol of "civic solidarity," as Alchermes suggested, or a connection to 'ancient' rhetoric and philosophy à la Robinson. But all of these reactions would come only from the elite in the city. Without benefaction as part of the equation, the majority of people in the city would have no point of connection to the statue of this woman, whatever she looked like, and however virtuous she might have been. Most 4th-century Corinthians who stopped at Peirene to fetch water did not have time to appreciate "civic solidarity" or rhetoric. Unlike the 2nd-century audience, people who did glance at the statue in the 4th century had no idea what Regilla looked like. If they took further time to ask about the inscription, her name would not ring a bell, and the virtue of moderation would be less important than the more pressing issues of everyday life. Any contributions of Regilla from the 2nd century were not likely to impact the lives of common people in the 4th century.[61] For the vast majority of Corinthians in the 4th century this kind of elite re-display of nobility would serve only to highlight the inequality of the society in which they lived.

---

[61] An exception would be a water system such as the one Regilla dedicated at Olympia, provided it was still functioning and the inscription still stood.

PART THREE

INEQUALITIES IN GENDER AND RELIGION IN ROMAN CORINTH

CHAPTER TEN

RELIGION AND MAGIC IN ROMAN CORINTH

Ronald S. Stroud*

In this paper I explore some aspects of the interplay of religion and magic in Roman Corinth. My focus will rest primarily on the Sanctuary of Demeter and Kore on the northern slopes of Acrocorinth beginning in the early years of the newly-founded Roman colony.[1] We will also briefly consider other literary and archaeological evidence for magical practices in the city and its adjacent territory.

Visitors to the central part of the city were confronted with a grim reminder of Corinth's dark legendary past in the form of a large statue of a woman named 'Terror' (Δεῖμα) that stood near the Roman Odeion. It formed part of a cenotaph for the murdered children of Medea, the most notorious witch in the ancient Greek world. She was brought to Corinth by her husband Jason and here worked some of her spells and brewed her lethal potions. First she rescued Corinth from a devastating drought and later she poisoned the princess Glauke, who had been promised to Jason as a royal bride. According to the version of the legend followed by Euripides in his *Medea*, her next move was to murder her own children to increase Jason's suffering. Later as a form of expiation, the Corinthians erected a memorial to this latter event in the form of the statue of Terror, described by Pausanias after the middle of the 2nd century CE.[2]

Also at Corinth, in the fashionable eastern suburb of Kraneion, near a cemetery that housed the grave monuments of Diogenes, the Cynic philosopher, and Lais, Corinth's most renowned courtesan, visitors were shown a notorious haunted house. The essayist Lucian tells us the gripping

* I wish to thank N. Bookidis and H.C. Stroud for reading and significantly improving an earlier draft of this paper.

[1] For the foundation of the colony in 44 BCE and some of the main players in the early years of its government and administration, see the chapter by Millis in this volume.

[2] Paus. 2.3.7. Almost all aspects of the legends, representations in art, and connections of Medea with archaeological remains are admirably collected and critically examined in Claus and Johnston 1996. The chapter by Johnston (1996) provides a good *envoi* into this specific question.

story of how a man called Arignotos had once famously exorcised a ghost in this house.[3]

Tales of miraculous transformations, hauntings, and evil spirits fill the literature on Roman Corinth. Even the terrain of the Isthmus itself was thought to be full of demons, for when the workmen of the Emperor Nero – no stranger to magic – first struck the earth to dig a canal across it in 67 CE, αἷμά τε γὰρ ... ἀνέβλυσεν καὶ οἰμωγαὶ μυκηθμοί τινες ἐξηκούοντο καὶ εἴδωλα πολλὰ ἐφαντάζετο, "blood spurted up, groans and bellowing were heard, and many phantoms appeared."[4]

The most abundant physical evidence for the practice of magic in Roman Corinth, however, is provided by numerous lead tablets inscribed with magical spells, curses, and prayers to the gods and spirits of the underworld. These have turned up in excavations in several parts of the ancient city and its territory in wells, graves, and especially in sanctuaries. They are predominantly Roman in date, written almost exclusively in Greek, and echo the message of our literary sources regarding the prevalence of magic in Corinth. In fact, after Athens, Corinth is represented by the largest collection of such objects in the Greek mainland.[5]

Recent investigations by the American School of Roman tombs on the Isthmus near the eastern port of Kenchreai have produced to date four lead curse tablets, which Joseph Rife briefly presented in *Corinth in Context*.[6] The writers of these tablets curse named individuals, calling for their dismemberment and destruction and invoking the powers of the underworld. The tablets add striking physical evidence for the practice of magic at Kenchreai, which itself already possessed an aura of mystery through literary references to secret rites of both Dionysos and Isis,[7] the latter made famous by Apuleius in his *Metamorphoses*. We know also that Paul spent time in Kenchreai; he had followers there and probably founded a church in this port city.[8]

Excavation in another sector of Roman Corinth has revealed evidence that the practice of magic in this city continued at least into late antiquity.

---

[3] On Kraneion, see Paus. 2.2.4; on the haunted house, Lucian, *Philops.* 30–31. Stroud (forthcoming) collects other literary and archaeological evidence for magic in Roman Corinth.

[4] According to Dio Cassius 62.16.

[5] For compilations of lead curse tablets found in Greece, see Jordan 1985, 2000; for those from Corinth, see Stroud forthcoming.

[6] Rife 2010, 421–23.

[7] For the cults of Kenchreai, see Rife 2010, 400–21, with earlier bibliography.

[8] Acts 18:18; Romans 16:1–2; see also Rife 2010, 423–31.

Representing the University of Texas at Austin, James Wiseman in 1967/8 and later found evidence at Corinth for pagan and Christian magic alike in his excavations of the Gymnasium Area in the northern part of the city and also in the Fountain of the Lamps near the Asklepieion and Lerna.[9] In the former, four lead curse tablets came to light and four more turned up among the thousands of votive clay lamps in the underground bath complex. Although these tablets remain unpublished, they probably indicate that rituals involving curses inscribed on lead continued into the 3rd and 4th centuries CE. These texts on lead appear to be uniformly pagan. Some of the lamps, however, carry incised prayers invoking supernatural figures from Jewish and Christian traditions.[10]

We now turn to a shrine, which provides more evidence for the practice of magic than any other part of the ancient city. High up on the steep northern slope of Acrocorinth (Map 1), excavations of the American School have exposed the substantial remains of a major sanctuary that was active from at least the early 7th century BCE and probably earlier. Its heyday was in the Archaic, Classical, and early Hellenistic periods. Like many other parts of the city, it did not remain active during the century following the Roman sack of Corinth in 146 BCE, although excavation revealed no trace of violent destruction at this time.[11] Soon after 44 BCE the settlers of the new Roman *Colonia Laus Iulia Corinthiensis* revived this sanctuary and it remained an important cult center until the end of the 4th century after Christ. Using contemporary inscriptions and the character of the votive offerings, the excavators have identified it as the Sanctuary of Demeter and Kore visited by Pausanias ca. 160 CE.[12]

In addition to her protection of crops as goddess of the harvest, Demeter also presided over mystery cults at several places in the Greek world and there is evidence to suggest that mysteries may also have been celebrated here on Acrocorinth in the Greek period.[13] In other parts of the city of Corinth, the early colonists lost little time after 44 BCE in putting important religious centers into working order. This was clearly the case with the shrine of the healing god Asklepios, the cult of Apollo on Temple Hill,

---

[9] Wiseman 1970, 1972a, 1972b.

[10] Wiseman 1972b, 26–33. See, however, Jordan's new readings reported in *SEG* XLIV 293–96.

[11] *Corinth* XVIII.3, 434. This is the period of Corinth's history that forms one of the main topics of the chapters of James and Sanders in the present volume.

[12] Paus. 2.4.6. For the identification of this shrine, its topography, history, and cult, see *Corinth* XVIII.3 and n. 14 below.

[13] *Corinth* XVIII.3, 2 and other passages collected on 489.

the Temple of Aphrodite on the top of Acrocorinth, and several smaller
temples and shrines at the west end of the Corinthian Forum.[14] In the
Sanctuary of Demeter and Kore, however, there was a time lag of some
decades before the construction of canonical temples, a propylon, and a
stoa in the area previously occupied by Demeter's shrine. It was probably
not until after a serious earthquake in the middle 70s CE that the rebuild-
ers of the shrine constructed the latter two buildings and three flanking
temples at the top of the site, dedicated to the Fates, Persephone, and
Demeter.[15]

A brief review of the plan of the shrine in the Greek period provides an
understanding of the physical setting for magic in the Roman Sanctuary of
Demeter and Kore (fig. 10.1). The main Greek cult buildings in this earliest
period lay at the upper, southern part of the site as they did in the Roman
period, while the lower, northern sector was the home of a large collection
of dining rooms devoted to ritual meals closely connected with worship of
the goddesses. We have inferred from the form and large number of these
dining rooms and from inscribed pottery found in them that they accommodated many women diners probably on festival days, perhaps for rites
resembling the women's Thesmophoria.[16]

In the mid 1st century CE, however, most of these dining rooms had
been abandoned and filled in with earth. This lower part of the site appears
at this time to have remained relatively free of construction (fig. 10.2).
If, as seems possible, there was also a Thesmophoria festival in Roman
times, the large number of women attending on festival days was then
more casually accommodated. At Athens, as we learn from Aristophanes,
women at the Thesmophoria camped out in tents.[17] It is possible, then,
that festival celebrations of this nature took place here before the construction of canonical temples in the sanctuary after ca. 70 CE.

---

[14] For the Corinthian Asklepieion, see Wickkiser 2010. For the other cults, see also
Bookidis 2003, 257–58.

[15] For arguments in favor of the identification of this sanctuary as that of Demeter,
Kore, and the Fates described in Paus. 2.4.6, see *Corinth* XVIII.3 and Stroud forthcoming.
The latter argues in detail that the Building of the Tablets (Building K) is an integral part
of this sanctuary. He finds no convincing support in favor of either the presence of the
Egyptian deity Nephthys in the central temple or the view that this was a strictly Roman
shrine dedicated to Ceres, Liber, and Libera, as proposed by Spaeth, cited by Økland 2010,
215–20.

[16] For discussion of these dining rooms see *Corinth* XVIII.3, 393–421. For the inscriptions, see Stroud forthcoming.

[17] Ar. *Thesm.* 624, 658.

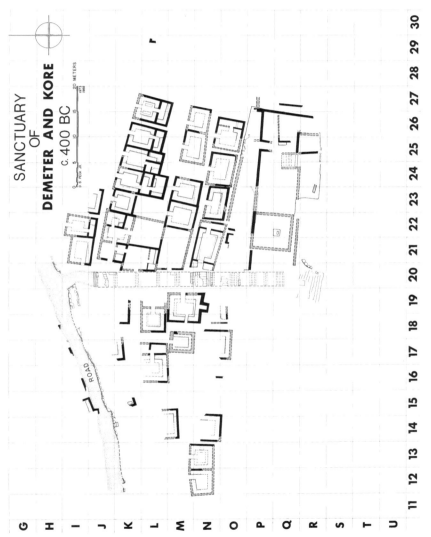

Fig. 10.1. Plan of the Sanctuary of Demeter and Kore, ca. 400 BCE. Drawing by D. Peck.

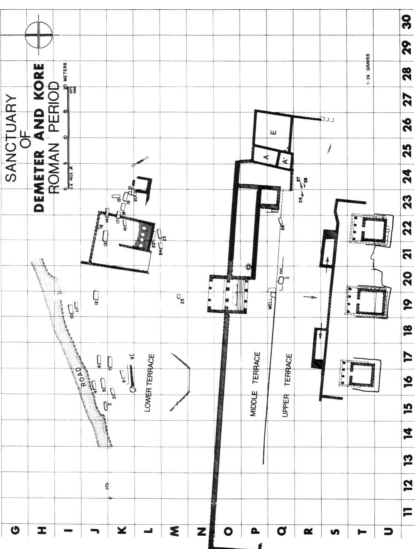

Fig. 10.2. Plan of the Sanctuary of Demeter and Kore in the Roman Period. Drawing by D. Peck.

Fig. 10.3. Roman thymiaterion (C 1971 182) from the Sanctuary of Demeter and Kore. Photo by I. Ioannidou and L. Bartzioti.

For our purposes, however, it is important to note that not all the old dining rooms had been covered over and filled in by this time. Some of their walls were still standing and they apparently attracted people to this old sacred site in the early years of the new Roman colony. For instance, on the Lower Terrace, in L-M:28, one of the old abandoned dining rooms had been slightly renovated into a kind of shack. Excavating within this shack, my colleague Nancy Bookidis found two large complete clay incense burners, probably early Roman in date, one of them sitting upright (fig. 10.3).[18] Burning of incense was a regular accompaniment of most ancient magical spells and it is very likely that this particular incense burner was used for that purpose because found nearby were two lead curse tablets. They both target the same person, significantly in this shrine, a woman, Maxima Pontia, and although the message is short, its aim is not in doubt: ἐπὶ κατεργασίᾳ "for total destruction" (fig. 10.4).[19]

That a magician or sorceress was using this renovated dining room to practice her craft in the first century CE gains credence from the excavations of Bookidis in another contemporary renovated dining room in K-L:21–22,

---

[18] For these vases, *Corinth* XVIII.2, 66–71, nos. 146–47; *Corinth* XVIII.3, 274–76; Bookidis 2003, 256–58. The associated finds in this context indicate a date in the early 1st century CE.

[19] This discussion of the lead tablets supersedes some information in Økland 2010, which drew on early unpublished descriptions. For a full publication of these tablets, see Stroud forthcoming.

Fig. 10.4. Drawing of two lead curse tablets from the Sanctuary of Demeter and
Kore. Drawing by author.

which we have labeled the Building of the Tablets (fig. 10.5).[20] Though very
poorly preserved, these remains provide both more architectural evidence
for the form of the structure and some excellent stratification. Here in
Room 7 were excavated ten lead curse tablets, many of them clustered
around four low bases, all written in Greek, the earliest of which was in a
layer dated roughly in the mid 1st century CE and the latest probably falling in the 3rd century CE.

In addition, more fragments of incense burners and over two hundred
fragments of clay lamps were found here, indicating that most activity in
this room was nocturnal. The lamps, like the one in figure 10.6 were all
unglazed and dull gray in color.[21] Many of the prescriptions for spells in
the Greek Magical Papyri specify that the lamps should be simple, undec-
orated lamps, and not glazed red. The lighting of lamps itself formed an
essential part of some magical rituals. Lead curse tablets, lamps, incense
burners, dark rooms, nocturnal gatherings are all prominent features in the
Greek Magical Papyri, which constitute our best written evidence for
the practice of magic in antiquity. Even the setting for all these finds, the
Room of the Tablets closely matches some of the prescriptions in these
papyri; for instance:

> In a room on ground level, in which no one has died during the past year
> have the door facing west. Now setting up in the middle of the room an

---

[20] This structure also appears in Corinth XVIII.3 as Building K.

[21] The assertion that the excavators were reluctant "to reflect on the amounts, quality
and gendered implications of the pottery found in the Roman layers of the sanctuary"
(Økland 2010, 225) is not reflected in *Corinth* XVIII.3 (e.g. 10, 15, 22–24, 32, 37, 134, 211–21,
289–290, 351, 357, 374, and the detailed index of pottery lots on 493–497). Moreover, no
pottery or lamps of any period were discarded before analysis (contra Wire as cited by
Okland 2010, 226) and indeed all of the lamp fragments were saved.

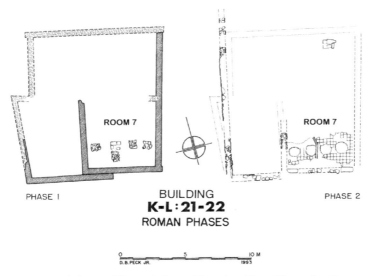

Fig. 10.5. Plan of the Building of the Tablets (Building K) in the Sanctuary of Demeter and Kore. Drawing by D. Peck.

Fig. 10.6. Roman lamp (L 1969 409) from the Sanctuary of Demeter and Kore. Photo by I. Ioannidou and L. Bartzioti.

earthen altar and [having ready] cypress wood, ten pinecones full of seed,
two white roosters uninjured and without blemish, and filling two lamps
with good olive oil, each holding an eighth of a pint, then when you come
to the [appropriate] day, in the middle of the night at about eleven o'clock
when there is quiet, light the altar fire and have at hand the two roosters
and the two lamps, lighted.[22]

Of the eighteen lead curse tablets from the Demeter and Kore Sanctuary,
six are written against women and three are almost certainly written by
women. The most complete surviving example is a very unusual double
tablet consisting of two rolls pierced and joined by an iron spike (fig. 10.7).
The text (fig. 10.8), which continues from one tablet to the other, reads:[23]

παραθίτομα[ι] καὶ καταθί[το]μα[ι] Καρπί –
μην Βαβίαν στεφανηπλόκον Μοίραις π-
ραξιδίκαις ὅπως ἐγδεικ[ήσ]ωσι τὰς ὕβρ{ι}εις,
4 Ἑρμῇ Χθονίῳ, Γῇ, Γῆς παισίν, [ὅ]πως κατεργά-
σων⟨τ⟩αι καὶ διεργάσωνται ψ[υ]χὴν αὐτῆς κα-
ὶ καρδίαν καὶ νοῦ⟨ν⟩ αὐτῆς [καὶ] φρένες v
Καρπίμης Βαβίας σ⟨τ⟩εφανη[π]λόκου. ὁρκίζ-
8 ω σε καὶ ἐναρῶμαί σε καί ἐνεύχομαί σ-
⟨σ⟩οι, Ἑρμῇ Χθόνιε, τὰ μεγάλα *vacat* 0.05 m
ὁ[νύ]ματα τῆς Ἀνάνκης ΝΕΒΕΖΑΠ
ΑΔΑΙΕΙΣΕΝ[.]ΓΕΙΒΕΒΗΩΗΕΡΑ κάρπισαί
12 με, τὸ μέγα ὄν[υ]μα τὸ ἐπάνανκον, ὃ οὐκ εὐ-
χερῶς ὀνυμάζεται, ἂν μὴ ἐπὶ μεγάλαις ἀν-
ανκαίαι⟨ς⟩, ΕΥΦΕΡ, μέγα ὄνυμα, κ⟨άρ⟩πισαί με κα-
ὶ κατέργασαι Καρπίμην Βαβίαν στεφ[α]-
16 νηπλόκον ἀπὸ κεφαλῆς μέχρι ἰχνέων
ἰ⟨ς⟩ ἐπιμήν⟨ι⟩ον κατεργασ[ί]αν. *vacat* 0.064 m

I entrust and consign Karpime Babbia, weaver of garlands, to the Fates who
exact Justice, so that they may punish her acts of insolence, to Hermes of the
Underworld, to Earth, to the children of Earth, so that they may overcome
and completely destroy her soul and heart and her mind and the wits of
Karpime Babbia, weaver of garlands. I adjure you and I implore you and I
pray to you, Hermes of the Underworld, that the mighty names of Ananke,
Nebezapadaieisen[.]geibebeohera, make me fertile; that the mighty name,
the one carrying compulsion, which is not named recklessly unless in dire
necessity, EUPHER, mighty name, make me fertile and destroy Karpime

---

[22] *PGM* VII 727.
[23] Full publication of this tablet with apparatus criticus, illustrations, and commentary
will appear in Stroud forthcoming as no. 125/126.

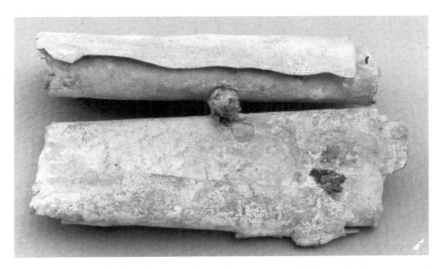

Fig. 10.7. Two rolled lead curse tablets (MF 1969 294/5) from the Sanctuary of Demeter and Kore. Photo by I. Ioannidou and L. Bartzioti.

Babbia, weaver of garlands, from her head to her footsteps with monthly destruction.

The writer invokes the gods of the Underworld, Hermes, Ge, the children of Ge, and the Fates (who exact Justice), the Moirai Praxidikai (who occupied the easternmost of the three temples on the Upper Terrace of the Demeter and Kore Sanctuary), the mighty names of Ananke, and an exotic Egyptian spell, Eupher. She prays to them to exact vengeance on Karpime Babbia, weaver of garlands, who has insulted her, by inflicting crippling injuries. She prays also to be made fertile. The text thus combines elements of two common categories of lead tablets, cursing and prayers for justice.

Perhaps the weaver of garlands, who may herself have been a mother, had mocked the writer because she was barren. In a sanctuary of Demeter, which may have hosted an annual Thesmophoria festival of women, the writer's plight may have been more conspicuous, especially if she were no longer a young bride. Barbette Spaeth's proposal that in Roman times women at the Thesmophoria were divided into *matrones* and *virgines* would have put our writer in a very difficult position to say the least.[24]

---

[24] Spaeth 1996, 104–13.

Fig. 10.8. Transcribed text of the lead curse tablets in Figure 10.7. Drawing by author.

Other tablets from this same building include two more curses against this same woman, Karpime Babbia, another curse against opponents in a lawsuit, and a love charm aimed at a woman named Secunda Postumia. Another curious curse was scratched into the floor of a circular lead receptacle that resembles a small modern pillbox (fig. 10.9). Recognizable is the verb κατεργάζομαι, denoting total destruction or obliteration (fig. 10.10). The object is ca. 0.086 m in diameter with low vertical walls. A very badly battered fragment of lead of the same size that probably formed the lid was found nearby. A small, covered, circular receptacle of this form somewhat resembles five roughly oval lead boxes or 'coffins' of the early 4th century BCE found in the Kerameikos at Athens.[25] Their inner lids were inscribed with curses and four of the little boxes once contained a crudely shaped lead male doll, also inscribed. Our circular box could also have housed a similar doll or perhaps some other magical items such as human hair, nail clippings, etc. Similar 'voodoo dolls' of lead, and some

---

[25] See the discussion in Gager 1992, 127–29.

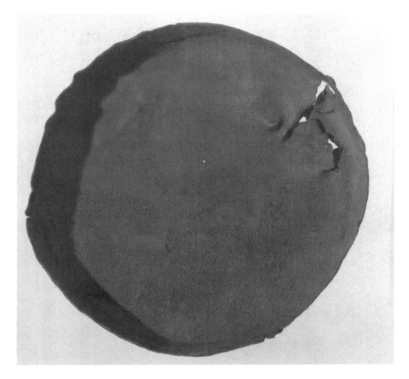

Fig. 10.9. Circular lead receptacle (MF 1969 296) from the Sanctuary of Demeter and Kore. Photo by I. Ioannidou and L. Bartzioti.

even of wax, have been found in the excavations of Marina Piranomonte in the underground Fountain of Anna Perenna in Rome.[26]

The presence of the curse tablets, the incense burners, the lamps, and four low bases in one end of the room all suggest that the magical paraphernalia were not just dumped in this building but that they were most probably used there in nocturnal magical rituals probably conducted by professional sorceresses. Lead curse tablets were also excavated in other parts of the Roman Demeter and Kore Sanctuary indicating that the practice of magic was not limited to this lower sector of the sanctuary. One of these found at the top of the sanctuary explicitly calls upon Kyria Demetra, "Lady Demeter."

---

[26] Piranomonte 2002, 38–45.

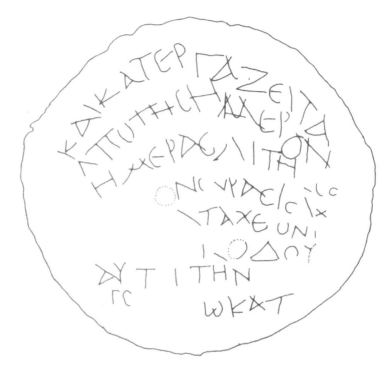

Fig. 10.10. Transcribed text of the inscription on the circular lead receptacle (Figure 10.9). Drawing by author.

In my view the fact that our earliest excavated evidence for activity at this site in the Roman period concerns the practice of magic permits the inference that it was sorcerers and their clients – not priestesses or religious officials – who first returned to this steep and remote site in the early years of the new Roman colony. They were probably 'in residence' so to speak before the construction of canonical temples and cult buildings. Such practitioners may have been drawn to this site because they knew that this spot had once been the home of Persephone, the Queen of the Underworld, and the Moirai Praxidikai, the Fates who exact Justice. Sorcerers sought the aid of these divinities in practicing their craft.

It is striking that this magical activity continued in the Sanctuary of Demeter and Kore long after the site assumed the form of a typical religious center of the Roman period. It is here that we can best observe the interaction of canonical religion and magic. That is, on the basis of the excavated finds we can be sure that at least until the 3rd century CE (and perhaps later) nocturnal incantations accompanied by the burning of incense, the deposition of lead curse tablets, ritual lightings of lamps, communal drinking of potions, and other activities of this sort went on at the same time and in virtually the same place as religious processions, prayers, animal sacrifices, dedications of votive objects, probably festive gatherings like the women's Thesmophoria, and other typical forms of worship of the two goddesses and the Fates. It might not be surprising to find some of the same women engaged in both of these kinds of activities.

As scholars we all love to classify and modern scholars have expended millions of words in books and articles seeking airtight definitions of magic as opposed to religion.[27] In my view, the quest has seldom been successful. Some of the outward distinctions are obvious but to the women in the Demeter and Kore Sanctuary on the slopes of Acrocorinth, who sought solutions to real life problems, such as the infertile writer of our longest tablet, some of these scholarly distinctions would probably not have meant much. These women appear to have tried, with all their hearts, to enlist all the superhuman powers they could, be they the gods who dwell on Mt. Olympos or those who occupy the realm of Hades and his Queen, Persephone.

Lest this sound too far-fetched, there is a close parallel from the Sanctuary of Demeter at Knidos. Within the confines of this sanctuary and even inside a cult building, Sir Charles Newton in the nineteenth century excavated thirteen lead curse tablets. They were all written by women and many against women. These women used the altars, temples, and other typical installations of normal religious worship in this shrine but at the same time they practiced magic in the sanctuary to attack their enemies. From time to time they even invited into the sanctuary professional sorceresses, who, for a fee, would help them cast a spell upon their husbands.[28]

In a paper, which she generously shared with me before publication, Laura Nasrallah has written movingly about some of the anxieties facing pagan women in Corinth in the mid 1st century CE, particularly regarding life expectancy, the birth and death rate of infants, and the precariousness of a relatively normal family life.[29] Antoinette Wire has written about this

---

[27] On this vast topic see, e.g. Versnel 1991; Fowler 1995; Cunningham 1999.
[28] For the Demeter Sanctuary at Knidos and the curse tablets, see among others, Stroud forthcoming.
[29] Nasrallah 2012.

topic[30] as has Jorunn Økland.[31] Some of these anxieties are reflected in the finds from the Demeter and Kore Sanctuary. They are private, rather than public concerns, more the affair perhaps of a chapel than of a grand basilica, anxieties played out in a small hillside shrine rather than in a great temple. They demonstrate to my mind how closely entwined were both magic and religion in Roman Corinth.

I close with what to me is an intriguing question: while many of these nocturnal rituals and secret rites were being practiced on the slopes of Acrocorinth, Paul was preaching his new doctrine probably down in the lower city. After they tried prayers, processions, and sacrifices to Demeter and Kore, after they tried sniffing incense, lighting lamps, and scratching curses on lead tablets in a dark room, did any of these troubled women on Acrocorinth feel inclined to come down into the lower city to try Paul's solution for their problems?

---

[30] Wire 1990.
[31] Økland 2010, 199–229.

CHAPTER ELEVEN

JUNIA THEODORA OF CORINTH: GENDERED INEQUALITIES IN THE EARLY EMPIRE

Steven J. Friesen

Scholars have long agreed that women appear more frequently in Roman imperial period inscriptions from the eastern Mediterranean than they do in earlier inscriptions from that same region. The agreement breaks down, however, when specialists discuss reasons for the prominence of women, with the argument often dividing over two options: is the increasing number of references to women a sign of empowerment[1] or exploitation?[2] In other words, were women afforded more equality in the early imperial period, or were they simply subject to a new kind of oppressive public practice?

During the late 20th century, Junia Theodora of Corinth became a subject in this debate as an example in support of the argument for empowerment.[3] I think that trend is mistaken. The broader question about women in the early Empire cannot be solved in a chapter-length study, but we can establish that Junia Theodora was at best an ambivalent example of the sort of power women might exercise in the Roman Empire. Careful analysis of an inscription found at Corinth leads to the conclusion that Junia Theodora is known to us only because she used her unusual position in society to support Roman domination of the eastern Mediterranean region. Thus, in Junia we have an example of a woman who promoted a particular configuration of inequality, to the detriment of many other women and men. In that disturbing sense she showed that some Roman women "achieved status and prominence equal to that of many men."[4]

---

[1] Pomeroy 1975; Boatwright 1991.
[2] Gardner 1986, 256–66; Bremen 1996.
[3] Kearsley 1999; Campbell 2009; Osiek 2005, 357 adds more nuance to the picture. Bremen disagreed with Kearsley, but Junia did not fit easily into Bremen's thesis that wealthy Roman women appeared in public primarily as wives or daughters, and so Junia was relegated to the footnotes of Bremen's study (1996, 164 n. 73, 165 n. 78, 198 n. 11).
[4] Boatwright 1991, 263; but used there more optimistically than my use of the quote.

The Junia Theodora Inscription

Our only information about Junia Theodora comes from an 85-line Greek inscription[5] found in 1954 near the village of Solomos, along the road from Corinth to Argos about 5 km from the Roman Forum at Corinth. The location where the inscription was originally displayed is unknown because it was discovered in secondary use in a late Roman tomb where the inscribed stone was recycled as a door.[6] The 85 lines include five separate texts in which Junia Theodora was praised by the Lycian koinon, and by city officials from Myra, Patara, and Telmessos. This anthology of laudatory texts was probably compiled and inscribed near the end of Junia's life, for the two koinon decrees offer gifts for her (eventual) funeral (l. 10–11, 43–45, 63–66) and mention her will (l. 7, 59). This suggests that the inscribed marble stele may have originally adorned her grave somewhere near the findspot. My translation of the inscription appears in the appendix to this chapter.

The content of the five texts revolves around Junia and her efforts in Corinth on behalf of Lycia and its inhabitants. She is described as a Roman living in Corinth (l. 13, 22–23, 63, 67, 73) and also as πολεῖτις ὑμῶν ("your citizen," with "your" referring to Corinthian officials; l. 16–17). She is said to be καλή ("noble"), ἀγαθή ("good"), and εὔνους ("benevolent") toward the nation (ἔθνος; l. 2–3, 13, 47–48, 68); σωφρόνως ("living with discretion") and φιλολύκιος (apparently a neologism[7] meaning "a friend of the Lycians," l. 23–24). Her actions on behalf of Lycia are described in general terms as σπουδή ("zeal") and φιλοτιμία ("nobility," l. 3–4, 7, 49), συμπαθῶς ("having empathy," l. 4, 50), εὐεργεσία ("benefaction," l. 26, perhaps also 74), and φιλοστοργία ("affection," l. 69).

More specifically, Junia is praised for three kinds of activities.[8] First, she intervened with οἱ ἡγούμενοι/ἡγεμόνες ("the authorities;" l. 5–7, 51–53)

---

[5] *RP* I COR 359.

[6] Corinth Inventory No. I 2486; Pallas, Charitonidis, and Venencie 1959, 496–498; *SEG* XVIII (1962) no.143 (note that the Corinth Inventory Number is erroneously given as I 2476 in this publication); Wiseman 1978, 90. The stele was found broken into two large fragments. Other small fragments are lost. The combined dimensions of the two extant fragments are 0.84 m height, 1.260–1.265 m width, and 8 cm depth (maximum). The excavators' conclusion that the tomb comes from 4th century CE is possible but not proved. Since the bodies in the tomb would not have faced eastward, the excavators assumed that the tomb must have been built before Christianity influenced the disposition of corpses, which is a tenuous basis for dating the structure; Mary E. Hoskins Walbank, personal communication, August 2010.

[7] Robert 1960, 326.

[8] See Robert 1960, 326–30.

Fig. 11.1. The Junia Theodora inscription (I 2486). Photo by I. Ioannidou and L. Bartzioti.

on behalf of Lycia. These would certainly have been Roman authorities,[9] rather than the Corinthian municipal ἄρχοντες ("magistrates") mentioned in l. 15 and 42. Second, Junia is praised because she made Lycia a beneficiary in her will (l. 7–8, 59).[10] A certain Sextus Julius[11] would have been another beneficiary, for he is called her successor (διάδοχος, l. 53–54) and also the representative (ὁ φροντιστής, l. 11–12) for the Lycian koinon in Corinth. Third, Junia's exceptional hospitality is noted several times: providing for newly-arrived visitors from Myra (l. 18–19); hosting many citizens from Patara and other Lycians in her own home (l. 27–29); helping ambassadors from Lycian cities and from the nation (l. 49–51); welcoming many Lycians who were in exile (l. 58–59); and bringing citizens of Telmessos into her home (l. 75–77).

Because of her activities, the five texts cast Junia as a patron of Lycia and its cities, with the Patarians referring explicitly to her benefaction on their behalf (l. 26). So one of the several functions of these documents is to describe how the Lycians hold up their end of the relationship through asymmetrical reciprocity. The regional koinon voted two honorary decrees, set up two other inscriptions (different from the texts in the extant Junia inscription; l. 12–14, 66–69), promised to send a gold crown (l. 10–11, 63–64) and 5 minas of saffron for her funeral (l. 64), and dedicated a painted, gilded statue of her for display in Corinth (l. 67–68). The cities, on the other hand, responded only with texts. The leaders of Myra sent a letter to the Corinthian city officials, notifying them of their regard for her and their gratitude. Patara and Telmessos also praised her, but they did so by voting decrees and sending copies to Corinth. Those two decrees remind us that another function of these five documents was to elicit further gifts from Junia, for the Patara and Telmessos texts overtly urged her to continue her beneficent actions toward their respective cities, promising to praise her even more for future gifts.

Junia's hospitality, however, was not simply a matter of social entertainment or obligation. It came at an unspecified period of urgent social disruptions. The wide-ranging exchanges between Junia and Lycia, the references to imperial diplomacy, and the sheltering of exiles all point to an unusual political context for her activities. These indicators have led to two proposals about the dates of her activities.

---

[9] Robert 1960, 329–30.
[10] The reference to using her life or livelihood for Lycia (l. 24–25) may also be an allusion to this provision in her will.
[11] *RP* I COR 336.

The most plausible proposal is that Junia was active in Lycian politics in the second quarter of the 1st century CE, when Lycia became part of a province of the Roman Empire.[12] During the early Empire, Lycia was not a province but rather functioned as an officially independent region within the sphere of Roman influence, organized as cities participating in a regional league known as the koinon (κοίνον). The koinon would have been the primary regional institution for mediating Roman influence. In 43 CE, when Claudius formalized Roman authority over the region by creating the province of Lycia and Pamphylia, the koinon remained in this powerful position.

According to Suetonius, the creation of the province was an imperial response to a power struggle among Lycian factions for control of the region.[13] A monumental inscription from Patara from 46 CE contributes to our understanding of the period by giving us an official imperial interpretation of this difficult period in Lycia. The inscription comes from a 5 m high square tower with a dedication to the emperor Claudius, whose titles provide the date. The results of his Lycian policies are described in glowing terms.

> To Tiberius Claudius, son of Drusus, Caesar Augustus Germanicus...the savior of their nation; the Lycians, Rome- and Caesar-loving [φιλορώμαιοι καὶ φιλοκαίσαρες], faithful, allied, freed from faction, lawlessness and brigandage through his divine foresight, having recovered concord, the fair administration of justice and the ancestral (?) laws, the conduct of affairs having been entrusted to councilors drawn from among superior people by the incompetent majority, in return for the many benefits they have received from him (?)...[14]

If this mid 1st century CE date is accurate, Junia was a prominent member of Corinth's social elite in a relatively stable period during the second quarter of the 1st century CE, more than a half-century after the colony became Achaia's capital. During Lycia's intraregional turmoil, Junia's household with

---

[12] First proposed in Pallas, Charitonidis, and Venencie 1959, 508; followed by Robert (1960, 331–32) and most others. The other significant proposal dates Junia's activities in the late 40's BCE; Behrwald 2000, 120–128; Kolb 2002, 211. I consider this option possible but less likely. Kearsley (1999, 191–92) proposed 57 CE as a third possible date, when the Lycians' charges against their proconsul were dismissed and some accusers were punished with exile (based on Tac. *Ann.* 13.33.5). This third date seems least likely for two reasons: the exiles were punished for misusing Roman law and so Roman Corinth is an unlikely place for them to go into exile; and it is also unlikely that Junia would be publicly praised for taking care of them.

[13] Suet. *Claud.* 5.25.9.

[14] From the reconstructed text with translation in Jones 2001, 161–63.

its social network centered in Corinth would have sided with Roman interests. The exiles whom she assisted would therefore have been pro-Roman Lycian elites, who went into exile in Corinth until they could return after 43 CE when Claudius imposed provincial status on Lycia.[15]

Intersectional Method

The synopsis of the inscription's contents and the indications of its probable historical setting indicate that Junia Theodora was an individual of extraordinary accomplishments. We should also note that there are no references in these texts to a husband, brother, or children, and only one brief reference to her father Lucius (l. 16–17) which is for the purpose of identification. So it is not surprising that she has been portrayed in the secondary literature as an example of the remarkable advances of women in the Roman imperial period.[16] In this chapter, however, I make the case that Junia shows what influence a woman could have if she had the necessary resources – wealth, status, etc. – and if she used them to support Roman domination.

   To advance the argument I utilize distinctions that have been developed under the rubric of intersectionality. Intersectionality is an approach developed in gender studies that focuses on the lives of African American women. It is based on the conclusion that "subjectivity is constituted by mutually reinforcing vectors of race, gender, class, and sexuality."[17] One advantage of this approach is that it moves beyond analysis based on a simple binary category such as male/female (or privileged/oppressed, rich/poor, etc.). Instead, intersectionality complicates the analysis by looking at the ways in which all these factors (and others) perpetuate inequality in particular historical contexts. This is not intended as a retreat from gender analysis, but rather as a recognition that a single category like gender describes only one of the crucial factors at work. It attempts to address gender in conjunction with other indicators so that our analysis better accounts for the complexity of lived experience that includes phenomena

---

[15] These conclusions would describe Junia even if the minority view for the date of her activities (i.e., the early years of the colony) is accepted. The main difference would be that the Corinthian and eastern Mediterranean settings were much less settled at that time.

[16] For example, Kearsley 1999, 189–211, esp. 191–98.

[17] Nash 2008, 2. See also McCall 2005.

such as race, ethnicity, and class. To this list I would also add religion, which tends to be neglected in intersectional studies.[18]

Another advantage of this approach is that it forces us to consider the interaction of social constraints and human agency. Intersectional analysis starts from the axiom that humans live within multifaceted, pre-existing structural parameters. But this approach also takes seriously the role of the subject in accepting and challenging various aspects of their own structural position. Thus, in an exploration of inequality one looks for the interaction of structural position and agency, which generates subject positions.[19]

Third, intersectionality has its origins in the analysis of the experiences of women of color in America, and so marginalization is a central concept. Moreover, the rejection of binary analysis means that this theoretical framework allows us to explore that marginalization with more nuance. For example, an intersectional analysis helps us think about the way in which a factor like ethnicity might increase a woman's marginalization, or a factor like wealth might decrease certain aspects of her marginalized subject position. Intersectional theorists note that the interaction of these factors are not additive but rather multiplicative, for each new factor does not simply add to the marginalization; it also amplifies the effects of the others.[20]

In the case of Junia Theodora, we do not have nearly as much information as we would like for this sort of analysis, but we can certainly utilize the existing information better to understand the multiplicative structures of inequality at work in her social context. In order to do so, I organize the discussion using the categories of structural parameters and subject position affecting Junia Theodora.[21] By 'structural parameters' I refer to a range of externally imposed discourses that frame – but do not completely control – the way one thinks and acts. With 'subject position' I refer to the evolving product of the ongoing interaction of an individual with those structural parameters. Moreover, I take both of these terms

---

[18] Religion is absent even from this expanded list, which describes intersectionality as "a critical analytic lens to interrogate racial, ethnic, class, physical ability, age, sexuality, and gender disparities;" Dill and Zambrana 2009, 1.

[19] Nash (2008, 11) rightly notes that this interaction has not been sufficiently theorized, but the general orientation is sufficient for the purposes of this study. For an attempt to develop the theory with a practical intersectional research design, see Hancock 2007.

[20] Hancock 2007; Schüssler Fiorenza 2007, 14–15; 2009.

[21] I am indebted to Schüssler Fiorenza 2009 (esp. 10–18) for these categories, which I have adapted somewhat for this analysis.

to be concepts in the mind of the theorist rather than discrete objective entities to be observed and measured. By using these concepts, I hope to negotiate the divide between scholars who seek for the lived experience of ancient women and those who look only for ancient discourses about women.[22] In other words, structural parameters and subject position are metaphors that could be useful in avoiding the choice between an exclusive focus on either 'referential women' (the historical women behind the texts) or 'representational women' (the crafted portrayals of women in the texts).[23]

Junia Theodora and the Reproduction of Inequalities

Structural Parameters in the Life of Junia Theodora

Based on the five texts about her, we can describe at least six factors related to Junia's structural position in 1st-century CE imperial society, starting with the three that are relatively clear and then working on those about which we have less information. Even the clearer factors in the structural description, however, leave us with questions. For example, the first factor is citizenship. It is clear that Junia Theodora was a Roman citizen because of her name and because of several references in the texts to her as a Roman (l. 13, 22, 63, 67, 72). She was, however, also referred to as a Corinthian citizen in the letter from the boule and demos of the Myrians (l. 17). It is possible that both statements are correct since citizens of the Roman colony would have been Roman citizens. But the implication that she was a Corinthian citizen does not match up well with other descriptions of her as "living in Corinth" (κατοικοῦσα ἐν Κορίνθῳ, l. 1–2, 47); "a Roman living in Corinth" (l. 63, 67); one "who lives alongside you [Corinthians]" (κατοικούσῃ παρ' ὑμεῖν, l. 45); and "a Roman among those living in Corinth" ('Ρωμαία τῶν κατοικουσῶν ἐν Κορίνθῳ, l. 22–23). So the decree from the Myra boule appears to be worded imprecisely. Junia probably was not a citizen of the colony, even though her household was located in Corinth and this served as the center of her social, political, and economic network.[24]

---

[22] Milnor 2010, 816.

[23] The terms used by Dixon 2001, 3–15.

[24] Pallas, Charitonidis, and Venencie 1959, 503; contra Kearsley (1999, 192–93) who suggests that Junia was a Corinthian citizen as well, perhaps as the offspring of a marriage between a Roman male and a woman from a prominent Corinthian family.

She was, rather, a high profile and influential Roman with regional influence who was based in Corinth.

A second factor in Junia's structural position involved gender and we can already begin to see how these various factors intersect with each other to reinforce institutional inequity. As a female citizen, Junia would not have had all the same rights as male citizens. She would not have been given (among other things) the right to vote, to hold elected office, to engage in certain kinds of prosecutions, to hold *potestas* (legal control) over other free citizens (including *patria potestas* for her family), to adopt, to serve as guardian (*tutor*) or financial overseer, nor to act as a guarantor for the loans of other wealthy citizens.[25] Legal parameters and gender thus defined her structural position in a way that created disadvantages in relation to some other citizens at the top of the socio-economic hierarchy, even though she occupied a more privileged position than nearly all of the inhabitants of the colony.

The gender differential is especially pronounced if we consider the ratio of men and women involved in the creation and reception of the five texts that comprise this inscription. There are only four named individuals: Junia Theodora; her father Lucius (l. 16–17); Lycia's representative Julius Sextus (l. 12, 54); and the eponymous priest Dionysophanes at Telmessos (l. 70).[26] The number of representatives who made up the Lycian koinon is unknown but a conservative estimate of 100 members is reasonable,[27] all of whom were men from the wealthiest families in Lycia. Four boulai are involved in these texts, for each of which we might estimate 200–300 members, all men from wealthy families in the municipal elites of those cities.[28] Thus, the creation and reception of this inscription involved approximately 1000 individuals. Among the 1000 or so members

---

[25] Gardner 1993, 85–109.

[26] The damaged right side of l. 71 probably named two prytaneis from Telmessos as well.

[27] A surviving letter indicates that the koinon of Asia included 150 representatives in 4 BCE; Deininger 1965, 143.

[28] Two of the five texts came from the boulai of Myra and Telmessos, and the boule of Patara is implied but not mentioned; the boule (= senate) of Corinth was the named recipient of decrees from Patara and the Lycian koinon, and the magistrates of Corinth were the addressees of the Myra letter. Again, the exact numbers are unknown. One rough average for empire-wide calculations uses 100 members for a boule of a large city and 30 members for a boule of a small city, admitting that eastern boulai may have been larger than this; Scheidel and Friesen 2009, 77–78. For Roman Asia Minor, a recent study estimates 200–400 representatives per boule, noting that the Lycian city of Oinoanda had 500 members; Zuiderhoek 2009, 29 n. 13.

of the Lycian and Corinthian elites involved in these transactions, Junia Theodora was the only female. The others were all men.[29]

At least as important as the numbers, however, is the point of view. All five of these texts were at least approved – and probably composed – by male members of the ruling elites of Lycia, which means that we have no direct testimony from Junia herself.[30] All of our information about her is mediated to us by elite males from Roman Lycia operating according to elite patriarchal norms.

The third relatively clear factor was Junia's considerable wealth. We have no way of measuring this precisely but we do not need exact numbers. Anyone who intervened with Roman authorities, who entertained visiting dignitaries in Corinth, and who left part of her estate as a bequest to a koinon would be well within the wealthiest one percent of the imperial population.[31] Her economic standing is confirmed by the socio-economic level of the men who praised her in these five texts. We can be certain that any activities Junia wished to pursue would be well-funded.

The fourth factor is marriage and family formation, and this takes us into the structural factors that require more speculation on our part, but that are nevertheless crucial for understanding the multiplicative structures of domination in play. Regarding Junia's status, we do not know whether she was single, married, divorced, or widowed. I consider it most likely that she was single (or perhaps divorced) since there is no reference to a husband or to offspring in this long inscription. Stated conversely, if she had been married or a widow at the time these texts were written, one would expect some reference to the husband.[32]

Junia's family of origin is unknown to us except through names. The letter from Myra mentions her father Lucius. In all likelihood Junia received her name from him, rather than from a husband,[33] which means that her father's full name was probably Lucius Junius Theodoros. Neither Junia's

---

[29] The inscription refers to Junia's hospitality toward Lycians in Corinth, and this probably involved some women accompanying the male ambassadors and some female refugees.

[30] It is possible that Junia selected these five texts for the inscription. If that was the case, that selection process would constitute at least some indirect testimony of her agenda.

[31] Scheidel and Friesen 2009, 82–88.

[32] Robert thought Junia was either single or a widow (1960, 329). In the case of widowhood, however, her husband would also have been a significant figure and so the absence of any reference to him in the five texts would be unusual.

[33] Some married women took the names of their husbands, but this is doubly unlikely in Junia's case since she we have no evidence that she was married.

father nor her mother (not mentioned in the inscription) are given any attention in these texts, suggesting that Junia's heritage was not illustrious.[34] This impression may be misleading, however, since her family of origin was probably the source for her wealth, and so the absence of family information may simply be an accident of composition or preservation.

Inheritance can be considered as a fifth factor in Junia's structural position even though it is intimately related to the other factors already mentioned. While her own inheritance was perhaps the source of her wealth, her ability to name her heirs provided a legal mechanism for her to influence political affairs beyond her own death (discussed further below). In relation to her structural position we only need to note that the extension of her political activities through the disposition of her estate was made possible by her wealth, by her standing as a female citizen, and by the legal right to name her heirs. She probably did not need the approval of a male tutor since the ethos of these five texts, while admittedly oleaginous, suggests that Junia operated *sui iuris* (in her own right), without legal interference of father, husband, or guardian. If her father was dead or had released her from his *manus* (paternal power of a father or marital power of a husband) while alive, she would be able to make financial decisions on her own without requiring clearance from a legally responsible male.[35]

A sixth and final feature of Junia's structural position was her ethnicity, which is unknown.[36] Her Greek cognomen Theodora indicates that she was almost certainly not Italian, and thus the references in the inscription to her as a Roman were legal and perhaps cultural indicators rather than ethnic ones. In other words, she matches up well with Millis's description of the sorts of individuals who dominated the Roman colony – Roman citizens with a Greek heritage and with economic connections to the eastern Mediterranean.[37]

Junia's Lycian connections have led some to conclude that she was probably Lycian or that part of her family came from Lycia.[38] While this

---

[34] The assertion in Pallas, Charitonidis, and Venencie (1959, 505) that Sextus Julius must have been Junia's relative was corrected by Robert (1960, 330–31 n. 5). They may have been related, but this is not required by the text.

[35] Even if Junia was married, in the early Empire it is unlikely that she would have come under her husband's *manus*; Grubbs 2002, 20–23.

[36] Kearsley (1999, 193, 196) describes Lycia as Junia's homeland, but this runs contrary to the rhetoric of the decrees.

[37] Millis 2010a, 13–35. Note also that Roman citizenship was rare in Lycia even among elite families until the mid 2nd century CE; Sherwin-White 1973, 408–11.

[38] *RP* 1, 339 COR 359; Kearsley 1999, 193.

is possible, there are also features of the inscription that speak against Lycian family ties. None of the five Lycian texts in the inscription claims Junia for their own nor attempts to draw ethnic or family ties to her. On the contrary, the rhetoric of the letters and decrees imply that she was a benevolent outsider to Lycians. The term φιλολύκιος ("friend of the Lycians, loyal to the Lycians," l. 24) is particularly important here in its implication that the person so described is an outsider who is well-disposed toward insiders. It is a neologism built by analogy with φιλορώμαιος, "friend of the Romans,"[39] which was used for non-Romans who supported Roman interests.

This leads to two significant observations. First, it is still possible that there were some Lycian connections in Junia's family line, but the important point is that the public rhetoric did not identify her as Lycian. Discursively, she was Roman. The second observation is this. If Junia had no significant ethnic or familial ties to Lycia (which I think is probable), then her ties to that region were mostly economic and commercial.[40] Her primary connection, then, would have been due to landholdings in Lycia and/or trade involving Lycia,[41] placing her in the milieu of the negotiatores and their backers who were an important segment of the colony's ruling class.[42] The fact that she lived in Corinth suggests that her Lycian interests were only one part of her financial network that spread far beyond that mountainous region on the southwestern coast of Asia Minor.

So the factors of citizenship, gender, wealth, family, inheritance, and ethnicity intersected in various ways that defined the boundaries within which someone like Junia could operate. These and other factors set up parameters that would normally be upheld, but which could conceivably be violated if an individual was willing to take the risk. What can we say about Junia's initiatives in this context?

Subject Position: Junia's Agenda

One way to analyze Junia's activism is to think carefully about the pre-history of the inscription that praises her. There had to be at least two phases of activities in order for this inscription to be executed. One phase

---

[39] Robert pointed out that φιλορώμαιος had also been constructed by analogy to φιλα-θήναιος for people who displayed goodwill toward Athens and its inhabitants; 1960, 326. He did not mention the other important analogous descriptor – φιλόκαισαρ.

[40] Purcell 2005a, 97.

[41] Robert 1960, 330; Kearsley 1999, 194.

[42] Spawforth 1996, 171–73; the chapter by Millis in this volume.

Table 11.1. Comparison of the two decrees regarding Junia Theodora from the koinon of the Lycians.

	First Decree (l. 1–14)	Second Decree (l. 47–69)
Praised for	Generous toward nation: both toward individuals and toward collective. Made many friends for nation from among [Roman] rulers. Bequest for Lycia in her will.	Generous toward nation: both individuals and *emissaries from cities or from koinon.* Influenced [Roman] rulers to be most *benevolent* toward Lycia. Bequest for Lycia in her will. *Welcomed many exiles.*
Reciprocity	Offer 'testimonials.' Recognition and praise. Gold crown for her approach to the gods. Dedicatory inscription [on crown?].	Offer 'testimonials' and *'gracious acts.'* Recognition and praise. Gold crown and *5 minas of saffron* for her approach to the gods. *Painted gilded statue of Junia. Inscription that mentions crown and statue* [on statue base?].

Italics indicate significant new features in second decree. Square brackets enclose my comments.

was a period of indeterminate length – a matter of years or even decades – during which Junia engaged in an ongoing relationship with Lycian leaders and institutions. This relationship involved acts of patronage on her part, while the role of the Lycians was to request assistance, to praise her when assistance occurred, to record their praise, and to protect her interests when they had the opportunity. The second phase was much shorter – perhaps a matter of weeks or even days, and involved the selection of these five texts for inclusion in the inscription.

In the quest to illuminate Junia's subject position, we can look more deeply into the first period, that of reciprocity and patronage, because there are two koinon decrees in the inscription.[43] These two decrees from

---

[43] There has been a tendency in the secondary literature to overlook the important differences between the two koinon decrees, differences regarding themes, praise, gifts of reciprocity, and the wording of commissioned inscriptions. These differences require us to treat them as distinct documents. Since the two decrees were public political documents involving regional relations and imperial politics that were crafted and approved by assembled representatives, we must assume that the wording is precise and deliberate.

the same Lycian institution imply some historical development in the relationship that helps us understand Junia's agenda.

The first koinon decree praises Junia for three things in her relationship with Lycia: her generosity toward individuals and toward the nation; her interventions with Roman authorities on behalf of Lycia; and the inclusion of a bequest to Lycia in her will. The bequest was mentioned in both decrees, but in the second decree two more items appear differently and one new praiseworthy deed was added. One of the differences is that her generosity toward Lycia was expanded in the second decree to mention ambassadors from cities and from the koinon. While it is possible that these emissaries may have been implied in the phrasing of the first decree, at least the rhetoric of the second decree has changed. The new focus emphasized official Lycian delegations to Corinth on missions authorized by their cities or region. The second difference is in Junia's intervention with the Roman authorities. In the first decree she was praised for having established friends for Lycia among the authorities (φίλους κατεσκεύακεν, l. 5), but in the second decree she was commended for influencing the authorities to be (or become) most benevolent toward Lycia (συνκατα-σκευάζουσα τούς ἡγ[ε]μόνα[ς ε]ὐνο[υστάτο]υς⁴⁴ ἡμεῖν γείνεσθαι, l. 52–53). Finally, a new praiseworthy deed is mentioned: Junia welcomed Lycian exiles in magnificent fashion.

Taken together, these new developments in the rhetoric of the second decree point toward Junia's alignment with Roman interests. Her importance for the official Lycian delegations was not simply hospitality, but rather her role in promoting their relationship with Roman authorities. Her support of the Lycian exiles is another sign of her pro-Roman agenda, since only exiles who supported Roman influence would have sought refuge in Corinth. The second decree was probably issued after the Lycian situation was resolved and after the exiles could return, while the first decree was issued earlier, perhaps during the difficulties or before they arose. In any event, one aspect of Junia's agenda is clear. From her base in Corinth she worked to support Roman control of Lycia.

The expanded reciprocity in the second decree supports the argument that the decree reflected a resolution of the tensions that sent some Lycians into exile in Corinth. The first decree recognized Junia with

---

⁴⁴ This lacuna could also be reconstructed with a comparative ([ε]ὐνο[υστέρο]υς, "more benevolent") rather than a superlative, but a superlative is more appropriate for the rhetorical aims of the koinon regarding their relations to imperial institutions.

testimonials, a gold crown for her funeral, and a dedicatory inscription with Junia in the dative case and no explicit verb. This dedicatory formula (l. 12–14) indicates that the inscription was probably meant to go on the crown itself. This placement of the dedication inscription would also explain why the text does not mention the crown: it assumed that a viewer would be reading from the crown. In the second decree the reciprocity of the Lycians was significantly upgraded. They again offered testimonials and a gold crown, but added five minas of saffron and a painted, gilded statue of Junia. In this second decree, however, the koinon's inscription (l. 66–69) follows a standard statue base formula with the subject of the portrait in the accusative case. The inscription goes out of its way to mention both the statue and the crown, which might mean that the crown was now meant to be worn by the statue.[45]

If we now consider all five texts in the inscription, we can draw some other conclusions about Junia's agenda. As she pursued a policy of supporting Roman imperialism, she operated primarily at the regional level rather than at the municipal level. She wrote the koinon into her will, but there is no evidence that she supported the cities in that way. Moreover, the koinon is the only institution known to have responded with physical gifts beyond letters and decrees. Examination of the three city documents support that conclusion: the cities only praise Junia for benefactions to the koinon and for housing their municipal representatives in Corinth (l. 16–19, 27–30, 75–78). In fact, the decrees from Patara and Telmessos overtly encourage Junia to do more for their cities and promise to repay her with appropriate praise if she directs benefactions toward them (l. 33–36, 82–85). Thus, the five texts reflect competition among the cities of Lycia and also competition between the cities and the koinon in the efforts of the Lycian elites to attract some of Junia's resources. In this intra-regional battle over her resources, Junia chose to operate through the koinon at the regional level.

In the descriptions of Junia's benefactions in the texts there are two curious gaps that may also speak to her agenda.[46] One has to do with religious office. Nowhere in these five texts is there any reference to Junia serving in a priesthood, in a high priesthood, or in any other religious office either in Lycia or in Corinth. This absence of information about

---

[45] See also l. 43–44. The statue and the saffron must be new gifts offered at the time of the second koinon decree, since it is unthinkable that these would have been forgotten or left out of the first decree.

[46] These anomalies were noted also by Kearsley; 1999, 196.

religious offices may be explicable. If Junia did not live in Lycia she would have had few opportunities to undertake such responsibilities, and if she held religious offices in Corinth there would be no reason for the Lycians to mention it. But it is also possible that she chose not to engage in such service to the communities and their deities.

A second curious gap is more difficult to explain: the absence of references to building projects by Junia. It was not unusual for extremely wealthy women of her standing to underwrite such projects, and it would have been appropriate for her to do so both in Lycia and in Corinth. In fact, it would probably have been expected of her and it would be the sort of thing that would be noted in the types of texts that make up the Junia Theodora inscription. Without further evidence, however, it is not possible to draw solid conclusions about this.

Thus, the five laudatory texts that comprise the Junia Theodora inscription depict a wealthy, female Roman citizen who appears to have acted independently without supervision of a male relative. She lived in Corinth as a resident Roman and from there supervised a regional network with economic and political interests involving Lycia. She actively supported Roman control of Lycia and acted as an intermediary between Roman imperial officials and Lycian pro-Roman elites. As far as we can tell, she was not interested in underwriting the physical infrastructure of the Lycian cities nor in filling their religious offices. Rather, her Lycian benefactions went primarily to the koinon, suggesting that Junia was particularly interested in nurturing a centralized Lycian institution that would enhance Roman control of the area.

The Funeral of Junia Theodora

Robert calls our attention to one important implication of the preparations for Junia's funeral. The second koinon decree referred to a gift of saffron for the ceremony. Saffron was a specialty of Lycia and so it made an appropriate gift for the koinon to offer. Five minas was a large amount of saffron, about 3 kg in weight and the product of 100,000–300,000 flowers.[47] For Greek funerary rituals, however, this perfume would have been an unusual choice. Aromatics are known to have been part of Roman funerals but not of Greek funerals. Robert noted an important exception that actually proves the rule: the Pergamene hymnodes of Rome and Augustus – a

---

47 Robert 1960, 336.

Romanizing association from the Hadrianic period in Pergamon – used incense in their regular memorial services for members. So in their choice of gifts for Junia's funeral, the Lycians thought it proper to recognize her as a Roman woman of distinction.[48]

The repeated references to the future death of an honorand is an unusual facet of this inscription, for honorary decrees do not normally draw attention to the mortality of the benefactor. In these five texts, however, we have several references to Junia's funeral. It suggests that she was advanced in years when the texts were composed, but not on death's door since the exhortations from Patara and Telmessos to expand her benefactions toward them would then make little sense. So the texts probably reflect a time late in her life near the end of her activities as patron of the institutions of Lycia and Corinth.

Those ongoing relationships with Lycian institutions reflected the first important phase of the inscription's pre-history. The second phase was shorter and involved the compilation of these five texts. It is quite possible that there were other decrees and letters from other cities of Lycia honoring Junia that were not included in this inscription. But even if these were the only texts available, there was at some point a decision to compile these five for display on one marble plate. Who made that decision? Perhaps Junia herself commissioned the inscription as a record of her generosity and of Lycia's gratitude toward her. If that is the case, then her decision is the one – admittedly indirect – piece of written evidence from Junia Theodora about her life. It is also possible, however, that a relative, employee, or client commissioned the inscription as a way of honoring her memory.[49]

One person with urgent interests in Junia's legacy was Sextus Julius. Perhaps he is the one who compiled the texts and commissioned the inscription. He is known to us from the two koinon decrees, where we glimpse an important development in his status. In the first koinon decree he is mentioned near the end of the text as the koinon's representative who will procure the gold crown and dedicatory inscription (l. 11–12). In the second koinon decree, however, he is no longer referred to as the

---

[48] Robert 1960, 333–342.

[49] Given the references in the texts to Junia's funeral, the inscription may have been displayed originally on her tomb. The rough finish on the back of the marble suggests that the stone could have been part of the façade of a small tomb. If that is the case, Junia's tomb was probably near the findspot at Solomos where the inscription was reused in a different tomb.

koinon's representative, but rather as Junia Theodora's successor and heir
(l. 53–56).[50] In addition, his placement in the text has changed. He is no
longer mentioned at the end as the one who executes the will of the koinon. In the second koinon decree he has been moved up to the mid section of the decree where he is honored along with Junia as someone who
shares her zeal and benevolence toward Lycia. He even receives his own
copy of the second decree (l. 56–57).

The rising fortunes of Sextus Julius also reveal a good deal about the
agenda and role of Junia Theodora. The rise of this elite male to become
her successor suggests that her significant accomplishments were possible
because she dedicated herself to the promotion of dominant imperial interests. Her powerful regional network could function with a female or male
at the helm. Gender still mattered, but the disadvantages of womanhood
were mitigated by the advantages of family, wealth, and legal standing.
For Junia crafted a subject position well within the patriarchal parameters
of her social context. When it came time for her to approach the gods,
elite men took over her imperial project. The Lycian koinon received part
of her estate, and Sextus Julius must have received a good portion as well.
Her deification and departure (l. 44) apparently made little difference in
the reproduction of inequalities.

Junia Theodora and Corinth

In the secondary literature Junia is rarely examined in relation to her role
in Corinth. Studies about the inscription usually deal with what the inscription tells us about Lycia[51] or how Junia might provide a comparison for
understanding Phoebe of Kenchreai (mentioned in Romans 16:1–2).[52] Much
of the information about Junia in the inscription deals with her relationship to Lycia, but the dynamics of gender, wealth, family, ethnicity, and
religion in Corinth would have been similar to those manifested in the
Lycian connections. In addition, however, the Junia materials provide
the basis for four observations about Corinth.

The first is simply a reminder that our information about the social hierarchy and population of Corinth is quite fragmentary. Junia's household
must have been among the wealthiest in Corinth. Her influence reached
up into the levels of Roman imperial administration and stretched out

---

[50] Robert 1960, 330–31.
[51] Behrwald 2000, 120–128; Kolb 2002, 211.
[52] Kearsley 1999; Klauck 2000.

at least as far as Lycia, but we had no inkling of her existence until this inscription came to light on a stone reused as the door of a tomb in an unexplored outlying sector of ancient Corinth. The fact that we have such random information about the high end of the socio-economic scale, emphasizes how little we know about the other 99% of the population.[53]

Second, Junia's social profile fits easily within recent reconstructions of Corinth as a colony dominated especially by the commercial interests of wealthy negotiatores. So a statement like the following provides a concise summary of the small but powerful segment of the population, the "families with business interests," in which Junia Theodora operated.

> The picture which emerges from this study is of a colony which in its early years was dominated socially by wealthy men of freedman stock and by Roman families with business interests in the east . . .[54]

Millis's discussion of the hybrid Greek/Roman culture of the colony's elite adds nuance to this picture.[55] While we have no clear evidence that she came from a freedman family, our inscription does portray the public image and *romanitas* of Junia Theodora. We should complement this image by hypothesizing also the Hellenistic layers of her identity that are implied by her cognomen, by her connections to Lycia, and by the language of the inscription itself.

A third observation: the Junia Theodora materials provide us with an important example of a way in which Corinth functioned as a 'bridgehead city.' The term comes from Alcock and describes urban centers that "can serve . . . in the promulgation of imperial ideology and control."[56] Alcock's concern was with the way in which Corinth might function as a unifying center for the province of Achaia, and she suggested that personal and legal connections with Rome (freedmen with former owners, veterans, etc.), western architecture and iconography, and imperial religious trends might be the primary ways in which the province was bound to Rome through Corinth.[57] In the Junia Theodora inscription, the mechanism is not so much iconography, religion, or fashion, but rather the personal and legal ties that provided access to Roman officials in Corinth and were mediated by individuals like Junia. Also in this case the geographical

---

[53] On Junia and the invisibility of most women, Økland 1998.
[54] Spawforth 1996, 174. See also Rizakis 2001, 41–46; and the chaper by Millis in this volume.
[55] Millis 2010a.
[56] Alcock 1993, 166.
[57] Alcock 1993, 166–69.

scope was broader: in the Junia Theodora inscription we see Corinth as a bridgehead for Roman control beyond the boundaries of the province, playing an important role in the consolidation of Roman control of the eastern Mediterranean region.

Finally, the Junia Theodora inscription suggests that Corinth was not only a bridgehead for the spread of Roman domination, but also a competitor for the acquisition of economic resources in the region. Why would the Lycian koinon and cities send official letters and decrees about Junia Theodora to the magistrates of Corinth? One factor was certainly the desire to enhance their benefactor's status in Corinth, which would in turn enhance their own power and prestige. But the official correspondence also established Lycia's claim on some of her resources. In this sense, Corinth was a threat to the Lycian leaders. With the passing of Junia into the presence of the gods, what would happen to her economic holdings? There must have been requests in Corinth for Junia to construct Corinthian buildings, to serve in Corinthian offices, to establish Corinthian endowments, and to support athletic and artistic competitions like the Isthmian Games. The five extant texts from Lycia would also have been at least in part an effort to minimize the possibility that Corinth might siphon off Junia's resources. The Lycians did this by asserting Lycia's own claims to her benefactions and by encouraging her to direct more of them their way. Corinth was both a bridgehead and a threat in a high-stakes, zero-sum game of elite patronage.

Conclusion

Most of the data from antiquity have been lost, and the evidence that survives has normally been filtered through the biases of ancient patriarchal institutions. The 85-line inscription about Junia Theodora is an example. It provides us with an important trove of information about an extraordinary woman who oversaw regional economic interests from her home in Corinth, who was probably not a Corinthian but rather a resident Roman who wielded more influence than most other inhabitants of the colony. All of that information about her is mediated to us through elite male perspectives.

When we read the inscription against the grain, however, and look for Junia's role in the Roman 'system of inequality'[58] we see an ambigu-

---

[58] Garnsey and Saller 1987, 125.

ous example of empowerment for women. Junia negotiated the complex
structural parameters set by gender, wealth, family, marriage, ethnicity,
inheritance, and religion, and fashioned a subject position that extended
Roman domination of the eastern Mediterranean. From a systemic perspective, her achievements as a woman were a victory for patriarchy, and
at her passing the male-dominant system of elite rule easily assimilated
the products of her lifelong labors.

In this sense, Junia played out one important theme in the story of
Roman Corinth. The colony was certainly a vibrant urban center with
abundant natural resources, a strategic location, and an enviable heritage.
It was also a conduit for Roman exploitation of the province and of the
region, a bridgehead for Roman ideology and control. In this system, Junia
Theodora and other elite men and women played important roles in the
ongoing, structural inequalities that defined the early Roman Empire.

Appendix: The Junia Theodora Inscription

This translation renders in English the five documents that comprise the Junia
Theodora inscription.[59] The translation attempts to convey the fulsome style of
the decrees and letters, and preserves the lineation of the inscription whenever
possible. Parentheses denote important editorial additions and square brackets
reflect the size of the larger lacunae. Small lacunae are not indicated in order
to enhance the readability of the translation. The Greek text comes from *SEG*
XVIII.143; it can also be found in Pleket 1969, 20–26.

1. Decree of Lycian Koinon (lines 1–14)

Decided by the [koino]n of the Lycians: whereas Junia Theodora, living
in Corinth, a woman noble and good and benevolent
toward our nation, continually displays zeal on behalf of our nation
4   and munificence, being sympathetically disposed both toward each of the
       Lycians individually and jointly toward all;
and (whereas) she has made from among the authorities a great many friends
for our nation, assisting in all the affairs that pertain especially
to all Lycians; and (whereas) through the will that she has made she has
       displayed toward our
8   nation attentiveness; and (since) it is quite fitting that our nation also with
       the appropriate
testimonials repay her; (therefore,) it has been decided by the koinon of the
       Lycians to

---

[59] I thank Ronald Stroud and Benjamin Millis for their suggestions on the translation.
Any problems that remain are my responsibility, not theirs.

recognize and to praise Junia Theodora, and to send her a crown of
gold when she draws near to the gods; and our representative
12 Sextus Julius will also be certain to inscribe the following inscription:
"The koinon of the Lycians (dedicated this) to Junia Theodora, a Roman,
    a woman noble and good and benevolent
toward our nation."

2. *Letter from Myra's Boule and Demos (lines 15–21)*

The boule and the demos of the Myrians, to the magistrates of the Corinthians,
    greetings. A great many of
16 our (citizens), having been in your area, have offered testimonials about your
    citizen Junia
Theodora, daughter of Lucius, regarding the benevolence and zeal that she
    exhibited
on their behalf, continually providing for our (citizens), even when they had
    just arrived
in your city. We, therefore, acknowledging her for the
20 benevolence which she has toward our city, hold her in the highest regard,
    and we have
decided also to write to you, so that you may be aware of the gratitude of our
    city.

3. *Decree of the Demos of the Patarians (lines 22–41)*

Decided by the demos of the Patarians: whereas Junia Theodora, a Roman
    among those living
in Corinth, is a woman among those established with the highest honor,
    living
24 with discretion and being a friend to the Lycians, having dedicated her own
    livelihood
to (gaining) the gratitude of all Lycians; and (whereas) she has provided
    many things for a great many of
our own citizens as a benefaction; and (whereas) she, showing the
    magnanimity
of her soul, out of benevolence does not cease providing her
28 hospitality toward all Lycians, even receiving them in her home, and espe-
    cially toward
our own citizens she does not cease excelling in her gracious acts toward all,
because of which also a great many of our citizens, coming before the
    assembly
have testified about her; therefore, it is appropriate also for our demos,
32 being grateful, both to praise Junia and to testify about her
regarding the recognition and benevolence which she has from our native
    city, and that it encourages
her to expand further her benevolence toward the demos, knowing that our
    demos also

will in no way fall short in its benevolence and grace toward her, but
36 will do everything for her pertaining to excellence and glory; for which reason, by Good Fortune, it has
been decided to praise her for everything written above; and furthermore, in
order that both Junia herself
and the city of the Corinthians might learn about the benevolence of our city
toward her
and about the existing decree for her, the secretary of the boule will send
40 the copy of this decree, sealed with the official seal,
to the demos of the Corinthians.

4. Letter of the Koinon and Officials of Lycia
Containing a Second Decree of the Koinon (lines 42–69)

The koinon and magistrates of the Lycians, to the magistrates, boule, and
demos of the Corinthians, greetings.
Of the existing, heartfelt decree and the crowning with a
44 gold crown and the dedication of a statue for her deification after the
[de]p[a]rture
(of) Junia Theodora, who lives alongside you, we have sent you this copy,
having
sealed it with the official seal, so that you may be awar[e] of th[ese things].
Decided by the koinon of the Lycians: whereas Junia Theodora, living in
Corinth,
48 a woman noble and good and benevolent toward the nation of the Lycians,
has contin[ual]ly
displayed zeal on behalf of the nation and munificence toward all
visitors, being sympathetically disposed toward both private individuals and
ambassadors sent
either by the nation or separately by a city; (and whereas) she has found
52 favor with everyone, influencing the authorities to be [most b]enev[ole]nt
toward us, since she finds favor with them in every way; [and] (whereas) her
s[uc]cessor Sectus[60] Julius, a Roman, be[i]n[g] a good man [......with
s]urpassing
benevolence (he) possess[es the same] zeal toward [o]u[r] nation corre-
56 sponding to the aforementioned benevolence of Junia toward us, to him at
the [same] time
will be sent the[61] decree from the nation of the Lycians regarding Ju[nia
Theodo]ra;
and (whereas) a great many of [ou]r (citizens) who were in exile she already
welc[omed spl]en-
didly, and through the will that she has made she has displayed her [own
benevole]nce;

---

60 The inscription misspells ΣΕΧΤΥΣ as ΣΕΚΤΥΣ.
61 The ἡ appears to be an incorrect definite article for (τὸ) ψήφισμα.

60 and (since) it is quite fitting also that our koinon, in return for these things
        which [she] contin[uing.....]
    does [well] to repay her with testimonials and gracious acts; (therefore,) it
        has been decided by the [k]oinon [of the] L[ycians]
    to recognize and to praise, for all the aforem[entioned reasons, Ju]nia
    Theodora, a Roman living in Corinth, and to send for her both a crown of
64 gold and five minas of saffron whi[ch can be s]to[red in her home so that it
        will be re]ady[62]
    whenever she draws near to the gods an[d......]T[....with a painted,
        g]ilded [statue],
    and to inscribe th[is] inscription: [The koinon and magistrates of the Lycians]
    [honored] Junia Theodora, a Roman living in Corinth, with a [cro]wn
68 and a painted, gilded statue, a woma[n no]ble and [g]oo[d a]nd
        be[nevolent],
    because of her continual affection for our nation an[d.........]ΕΙΣΛΛ[....]

        5. Decree of the boule and demos of Telmessos (lines 70–85)

    In the 40th year, when the priest was Dionysopha[n]es (son) o[f..]
        A[............ Decided]
    by the boule and the demos of the Telmessians, (the) prytanei[s..]O[......
        ....]
72 resolution. Whereas[63] Junia Theodora, a Roman, a woman who initiate[d
        with the greatest benevolen]ce
    for both the koinon of the Lycians and for our city man[y.... benefacti]ons,
    has completed both for the koinon and for our native city [................
        .....]
    ΩN to the city, the visitors from among the Lycians and from [our]
        cit[izens.......she welc]omed
76 in her own home, providing for the[m every]thing [......................]
    [di]s[playing] (her) responsibility[64] for those present [... ....]
    own distinction and earnestness [.]A[...]O[..]AΘ[............ .....]
    and (since) it is [quite] fitting that our city also should repay h[er the proper
        testim-]
80 onial; (therefore,) by Good Fortune, it has been decided by the demos of the
        Telm[es]s[ians to re]c[ognize and]
    [to p]raise the [afore]mentioned Junia Theodora for all the aforementioned
        reasons,
    and to encourage her, remaining in the same disp[osition,]
    to be always the source of something good for us all, knowing that our [city
        also,]
84 being thankful, will again repay her the appropri[ate]
    testimonials.

---

    [62] The restoration at the end of line 64 was proposed by Robert (1960, 332).
    [63] The ΕΠΙ on the stone is a misspelling of ΕΠΕΙ.
    [64] The noun προστασία could also mean "sponsorship" or "patronage" here. The damage
in this part of the inscription makes it difficult to be precise.

CHAPTER TWELVE

'MIXED MARRIAGE' IN EARLY CHRISTIANITY:
TRAJECTORIES FROM CORINTH

Caroline Johnson Hodge

In the sixth decade of the 1st century CE, a conversation took place between
Paul, a Jew who believed in Christ, and a group of gentile believers in
Corinth. Some aspects of this conversation survive for us in a series of
letters written by Paul. In this correspondence, we get a sense of some
of the issues encountered by this community of newly baptized gentiles,
attempting to live as a people of the God of Israel. Through these letters,
the various dilemmas and choices that the Corinthians encountered – both
within the community and relating to outsiders – echoed around the empire
for centuries to come. Although the historical situation changed drastically
as Christianity itself took shape after Paul wrote, believers asked the same
questions: How do we live with our non-believing neighbors? How can we
protect the integrity of the body of Christ and the bodies of its members?
How do we define ourselves as different from others?

In this study, I focus on one particular topic for which all of these
questions were relevant: marriage between believers and unbelievers. In
1 Corinthians 7:12–16, Paul addressed a question that was perhaps asked
of him by the Corinthians: how will a marriage work when one spouse
is baptized and another is not? Paul's response was remarkably tolerant
and not terribly specific, and thus lent itself to multiple interpretations.
Later church writers, the first of whom was Tertullian, expanded on Paul's
comments, and, with some creative exegesis, filled in details to develop a
condemnation of mixed marriages. Specifically, Tertullian, writing in the
early 3rd century, used the purity language of 1 Corinthians 6 to interpret
1 Corinthians 7:12–14, thus taking Paul's language about the whole community and applying it specifically to Christian wives. This exegetical move
took hold, I suggest, because it meshed with a larger discourse of protecting and controlling women's bodies. I explore the possibility, however, that
Christian writers, 'published Christians' like Tertullian, were not the only
ones interpreting Paul. We have evidence of 'unpublished Christians' –
those whose opinions are not represented by their own extant texts, but

whose views might be recovered in the published arguments of others –
who read Paul differently. These Christians capitalized on Paul's tolerant
attitude to validate their own mixed households.

To trace these contrasting interpretations, I first discuss 1 Corinthians
7:12–16. Next I turn to Tertullian, who is the first extant published author
to use 1 Corinthians to talk about mixed marriages. Then I focus on evidence of unpublished Christians and their interpretations of Paul in order
to demonstrate how the apostle's ideas are used in creative ways to support different positions on mixed marriage.

Paul's Letter to the Corinthians[1]

In 1 Corinthians 7, Paul wrote about topics related to sexual morality and
marriage. In the middle of this discourse, he turned to the topic of 'mixed
marriages,' or believers being married to unbelievers.

> To the rest I say (I and not the Lord): if a brother has an unbelieving wife
> and she agrees to live with him, let him not leave her. And if a woman has
> an unbelieving husband and he agrees to live with her, let her not leave her
> husband. For the unbelieving husband is made holy (ἡγίασται) by the wife
> and the unbelieving wife is made holy by the brother. Otherwise your chil-
> dren are unclean (ἀκάθαρτα); but now they are holy (ἅγια). If an unbelieving
> man separates, let him separate; neither a brother or a sister is enslaved in
> cases such as these. God has called you in peace. For how do you know,
> woman, if you will save your husband? Or how do you know, man, if you
> will save your wife? (1 Cor 7:12–16)[2]

This advice is in keeping with Paul's larger theme in chapter 7, which is
to remain as you are (1 Cor 7:17–20). Whether motivated by apocalyptic
views, by an interest in preventing social upheaval, or perhaps both, Paul
expressed a fairly tolerant and flexible set of instructions for believers married to unbelievers: if it works, stay together. Paul called for harmony and
accommodation on the part of both male and female believers. After all, as
Paul wrote to the Corinthians, "God has called you in peace" (1 Cor 7:15).

Paul's admonition is striking for two reasons. On the one hand, his
approach shows little regard for the social context he addressed, and on
the other hand, Paul justified his position with an unexpected argument
about contagious holiness. The first point becomes apparent in light of the

---

[1] For a fuller treatment of this passage, see Johnson Hodge 2010a.
[2] Translations of biblical texts are by the author unless otherwise noted.

social context for these relationships, the ancient household. Households in the Roman period were hierarchical social units, with a head of the household (usually, but not always, a man) at the top and subordinate members under him. Religious practices were important in maintaining and expressing this hierarchical relationship, as wives, slaves, children, and other dependents were expected to worship the gods that protected the household, specifically the gods worshipped by the head of the household.[3] Whether or not these hierarchies were practiced universally, the ideology of household order was ubiquitous in ancient writings, where there is a close connection between proper obedience and proper devotion to the gods.[4]

In dealing with the question of mixed marriage, Paul did not recognize these domestic social expectations at all. He seems unconcerned about whether the wishes of the head of the household will be followed, regardless of whether that head is a believer or an unbeliever. In the case of a believing man who is the head of his household, Paul's advice assumed that his wife and other household members have not followed his religious preferences, but have kept their own. In the case of a believing wife in Corinth, Paul's words implied that she should not obey her polytheistic husband, and should continue to be a believer. For a slave, who often has the least power in the household,[5] loyalty to the God of Israel instead of to the household gods creates an even more complex dilemma.

Any believer's situation was made more difficult by the fact that ancient households were religious spaces. Daily offerings were made at meals in households, sacrifices were held there, prayers were spoken upon entering and leaving. Images of the gods in the form of statuettes or paintings populated many homes. Devotion to the gods was interwoven into the details of daily life. Did Paul expect believers to follow the household practices and to participate in these ritual activities, or to ignore social expectations and somehow to avoid them?

A second striking component of this passage is Paul's use of purity language in verse 14: "For the unbelieving husband is made holy by the wife and the unbelieving wife is made holy by the brother. Otherwise your children are unclean; but now they are holy." In this tantalizing tidbit,

---

[3] This is the same concept that underlies the imperial cult: devotion to the deities of your ruler shows obedience and demonstrates membership in the larger community; Johnson Hodge 2010a, 9–13.

[4] Johnson Hodge 2010a, 10–12.

[5] See the chapter by Nasrallah in this volume.

a kind of 'contagious holiness' seems to make the situation work, but Paul's solution has puzzled generations of scholars. Did the original audience comprehend Paul's instructions, or did they scratch their heads over this verse as we do?

Paul never explained how this system of holiness worked. Much scholarly ink has been spilled on the question of why the children were holy, or how holiness passed from one spouse to another.[6] Although answers elude us, it is clear that Paul relied on notions of purity to explain why these mixed marriages worked. In some way, the holiness of the believer transforms other family members, so it is not a defiling situation for the believer, but a sanctifying situation for the non-believers. We can reason backwards from the solution (contagious holiness sanctifies family members) that perhaps the initial concern – whether raised by Paul or the Corinthians – was fear of contamination from someone outside the community. This would fit with Paul's understanding of the Corinthian *ekklesia* as a holy, bounded community, set apart for God.

Indeed, typically in Paul, purity language was used to create and maintain barriers between believers and non-believers, and to describe the transformation that occurs when one goes from not believing to believing.[7] Gentiles, by definition, worshipped the wrong gods and were prone to *porneia* (sexual immorality). As I have argued elsewhere, this was a theological condition of those who do not worship the God of Israel.[8] Gentiles-in-Christ, however, were transformed, sanctified, and changed into a holy people who worshipped the right God and reject porneia. After describing their former lives, Paul described this new people: "But you were washed, you were sanctified (ἡγιάσθητε), you were justified in the name of the Lord Jesus Christ and in the Spirit of our God" (6:9b-11).[9] Holiness characterized this new identity for gentiles-in-Christ.

This new holy state, however, required vigilance; its boundaries had to be protected like the holy spaces of the temple (1 Cor 3:16–17; 6:19).[10] Using

---

[6] Some have speculated that it has to do with married intercourse or the intimacy of living together. For discussion of these issues, see Conzelmann 1975, 121–23; Collins 1999, 262–73; MacDonald 1996, 189–95; Johnson Hodge 2010a, 14–15.

[7] See Johnson Hodge 2010a, 15; Knust 2006, 51–87; Newton 1985; Klawans 2000, 150–56.

[8] See Johnson Hodge 2007, 49–51.

[9] See also Rom 6:19b: "For just as you once presented your members as slaves to impurity and to greater and greater iniquity, so now present your members as slaves to righteousness for sanctification."

[10] This kind of purity and holiness language is reminiscent of discussions of the temple among Jewish authors. Paula Fredriksen discusses this and argues, "Jerusalem's

the example of a male believer uniting with a prostitute, Paul warned that such porneia ("sexual immorality") had dire consequences: it could infect the whole community. He invoked Genesis 2:24 to argue that sexual intercourse created 'one flesh,' so that sex with a prostitute made 'members of Christ' 'members of a prostitute' (1 Cor 6:16). Purity language served Paul's larger effort to construct boundaries around this new community, to encourage them to live up to their new identities as God's people. Their responsibility, according to him, was to maintain the integrity of these boundaries.

We can see how marriage to an unbeliever could raise some concerns, especially if one agreed with Paul's 'one flesh' idea.[11] Yet Paul, as if responding to such concerns among the Corinthians, explicitly states in chapter 7 that mixed marriage is not vulnerable to contagious pollution. Instead, contagious holiness prevails.[12] Non-believing members of the household are sanctified, and we can assume that the sanctity of the larger community, the body of Christ, is preserved. Indeed, this concept of contagious holiness raises some interesting questions about the boundaries of the community that elsewhere Paul is at pains to protect. If spouses and children were 'made holy' by the believing family member, did this grant entry into the ekklesia?[13]

As we will see in the remainder of this study, the questions surrounding Paul's words on mixed marriage allowed for a variety of interpretations by later Christians. One possible understanding is that believing wives, even as subordinate members of the household, might have the power to sanctify their families and protect themselves and their fellow believers from the taint of unbelievers. This intriguing idea runs counter the notion that a wife would follow her husband's religious loyalties. While some Christians may have found this openness appealing, others, like Tertullian, argued vehemently against it.

---

temple, traditionally conceived, gave Paul his chief terms for conceptualizing the Gentiles' inclusion in Israel's redemption;" 2010, 232; also see 244–49.

[11] As we will see when we turn to Tertullian, this notion, as well as other concepts in 1 Corinthians 6, are critical to his own condemnation of mixed marriages.

[12] This concept of contagious holiness is unusual in Jewish texts, where it is typically pollution that is contagious; Hayes 2002, 251 n. 13; see also 145–63 for a discussion of rabbinic exceptions. As I will argue below, it is also unusual in Christian texts after Paul.

[13] See Mitchell 1991, 121–23; and Johnson Hodge 2010a, 18.

Tertullian and Other 'Published Christians'

Paul's advice to the Corinthians reverberated around the empire in the centuries that followed. New historical moments – indeed, the development of Christianity itself – created a variety of interpretations of Paul. The first surviving explicit treatment of Paul's advice in 1 Corinthians is found in the writing of Tertullian at the turn of the 3rd century. In the second book of his treatise *ad Uxorem* ("To His Wife"), Tertullian soundly condemned marriages between believers and unbelievers and used 1 Corinthians to support his position. Since 1 Corinthians 7:12–16 did not give Tertullian enough support for his prohibition of mixed marriages, he had to turn elsewhere.[14] He found the support he needed in the language from 1 Corinthians 6, where Paul, talking about the new identities of gentile believers, warned them of the dire consequences of porneia. Tertullian seized upon this discussion to define mixed marriage as sexual immorality and to warn Christian women against it.

Tertullian opened his argument by explaining that he had recently heard of several occasions of Christian women taking non-Christian husbands. Shocked by this behavior and by the collusion of their advisors, he suggested the possibility that such people justify their behavior by citing 1 Corinthians (*ad Uxorem* 2.2.1), and especially 1 Cor 7:12–14, where Paul asserted that believing men and women make their spouses holy.[15] Lest anyone think that this passage actually condoned mixed marriages, Tertullian attempted to explain what Paul must have meant here. The apostle did not say, "if a believer *takes* a wife," but, "if a believer *has* a wife;" so clearly the couple was already married (*ad Uxorem* 2.2.2). Therefore, according to Tertullian, the only situation condoned by Paul was an already-established marriage of non-Christians in which conversion

---

[14] Cohen (2011) also examines this exegetical move in his recent article on mixed marriage in early Christianity. I am grateful to Cohen for sharing his pre-publication draft with me. His survey of early Christian responses to mixed marriages and how they compare to Paul's has been most helpful to my study.

[15] Tertullian's rendering of 1 Corinthians 7:12–14: "If any of the brethren has an unbelieving wife, and she consents to the matrimony, let him not dismiss her; similarly, let not a believing woman, married to an unbeliever, if she finds her husband agreeable (to their continued union), dismiss him: for the unbelieving husband is sanctified by the believing wife, and the unbelieving wife by the believing husband; else were your children unclean" (translation by Thelwall 1913, 44; Latin text for *ad Uxorem* throughout is from Munier 1980, 124–26).

of one spouse takes place. By no means does this passage allow for Christians to initiate marriage with 'gentiles.'[16]

Let us examine how Tertullian supported this narrow application of spousal sanctification. He explained: "those who are seized (*deprehenduntur*) by the faith" while already married to an unbeliever are not defiled, because others are sanctified along with them (*ad Uxorem* 2.2.9; referring to 1 Cor 7:14). Marriage guarantees a two-for-one deal: should one spouse be 'seized' or 'apprehended' by faith after the marriage is established, sanctification of the non-believing spouse occurs. If, however, a marriage occurs between one who is already a Christian and one who is not, sanctification cannot happen:

> Without doubt, they who have been sanctified *before* marriage, if they mix (*commisceantur*) themselves with foreign flesh (*extraneae carni*), cannot sanctify that (flesh) in (union with) which they were not apprehended. The grace of God, moreover, sanctifies that which it *finds*. Thus, what has not been able to be sanctified is unclean; what is unclean has no part with the holy (*sancto*), unless to defile and slay it by its own (nature). (*ad Uxorem* 2.2.9)[17]

If the believer is apprehended by faith before marriage, Tertullian argued, then the believer's holiness has no effect on the unbelieving spouse. In fact, it operates the other way around: the unbeliever, marrying and uniting in body with the Christian, sullies and destroys the holy body. Of course, Tertullian's temporal distinction – before marriage or after marriage – is not found in 1 Corinthians 7:12–16.

Tertullian accentuated the boundary between the believer and the unbeliever by calling the non-Christian 'foreign flesh' (*extranea caro*). Earlier in *ad Uxorem*, Tertullian referred to an unbelieving wife as *aliena* and *extranea* (2.2.2); throughout the text, Tertullian used 'gentiles' (*gentiles*) to refer to non-Christians (while Paul used ἔθνη to refer to non-Jews). This ethnic and political language, which casts believers and unbelievers as opposing peoples – one 'us' and the other 'them' – echoes Jewish texts on intermarriage.[18] Combined with the term 'flesh', it signals that Tertullian

---

[16] According to Tertullian, this latter point was made crystal clear by 1 Corinthians 7:39, where Paul instructs widows that they may marry again, "only in the Lord" (*ad Uxorem* 2.3.3–4). Tertullian insisted that the phrase 'in the Lord' carries a specific and unambiguous meaning: only marry a Christian. As Cohen has shown, this is not an inevitable interpretation, as other contemporary writers read it differently; 2011, 264–67.

[17] Translation amended from Thelwall 1913, 45; emphasis in original translation.

[18] See Yarbrough 1985, 8–25, and Cohen 1999, 241–62. A similar cluster of ideas is found in Jude 7: "Likewise, Sodom and Gomorrah and the surrounding cities, which, in the same

was concerned with bodily practices and unseemly mixing between two unrelated peoples, Christians and non-Christians.[19]

Tertullian's logic depends on a 'one flesh' argument that he appropriated from elsewhere in Paul, and that Paul had already appropriated from Genesis. As mentioned above, in 1 Corinthians 6:16, Paul warned against the dangers of porneia, in this case of a male believer uniting with a female prostitute, using Genesis 2:24 to explain that with sexual intercourse the bodies of the participants become one: "Do you not know that whoever is united to a prostitute becomes one body with her? For it is said, 'The two shall become one flesh'" (1 Cor 6:16; Gen 2:24). This union has serious consequences for the believer and for the community. The believer's body, according to Paul, was transformed from a sinful one to a holy one, and illicit sex, like that with a prostitute, pollutes it. Paul argued that the stakes are high, because these newly baptized gentiles were members of Christ's body (1 Cor 6:15). Therefore, porneia committed by one believer could pollute the whole body of Christ. In 1 Corinthians 6, Paul used the one flesh argument to warn against the dangers of sexual immorality as he attempted to draw boundaries around this new community of baptized gentiles.

Tertullian took the one flesh theory of 1 Corinthians 6 and applied it specifically to his analysis of mixed marriage in 1 Corinthians 7. This explains the idea that spouses can sanctify each other (1 Cor 7:14): if you share a body with a spouse, the sanctification of your body is also the sanctification of your spouse's body. Tertullian also used this one flesh theory to argue that spousal sanctification will not work if the believer is not already married: their bodies are separate when the believer is seized by faith. God's grace, because it sanctifies that which it finds, cannot extend to bodies that unite later with Christian bodies.[20] Spousal sanctification or pollution hinges upon whether or not the bodies were united upon seizure.

---

manner as they, indulged in sexual immorality (ἐκπορνεύσασαι) and went after other flesh (σαρκὸς ἑτέρας), serve as an example by undergoing a punishment of eternal fire" (NRSV). Like the author of Jude, Tertullian is just about to argue that uniting with 'foreign flesh' constitutes sexual immorality.

[19] Tertullian found this ethnic language useful here, despite his argument elsewhere that Christians do not comprise a new *genus*; *ad Nationes* 1.8. See Buell 2005, 155.

[20] This language is reminiscent of Paul's assertion in 1 Corinthians 7:17–24 that God calls people as they are. Tertullian has adopted a similar idea, but applied it to sanctifying, which serves his larger aim of limiting the effectiveness of spousal sanctification.

With this use of the one flesh theory, Tertullian's exegetical strategy emerges. He borrowed concepts from 1 Corinthians 6, where Paul spoke about the boundaries of the community, to construct a condemnation of mixed marriage. Admonitions like "shun fornication," aimed at the newly baptized gentiles in 1 Corinthians 6, became, in Tertullian's hands, proscriptions for the Christian spouse, and specifically the Christian wife. Tertullian creatively applied the instructions in 1 Corinthians 6 (and in one case, 1 Corinthians 5) to 1 Corinthians 7:12–16, so that marrying an unbeliever itself became sexual immorality:

> If these things are so, it is certain that believers (*fideles*) contracting marriages with gentiles (*gentilium*) are guilty of fornication (*stupri*), and are to be excluded from all communication with the brotherhood, in accordance with the letter of the apostle, who says that "with persons of that kind there is to be no taking of food even" (1 Cor 5:11)...That which is prohibited, is it not adultery (*adulterium*)? Is it not fornication (*stuprum*)? Does not the admission of a foreign man (*extranei hominis*) (to your couch) violate "the temple of God" (1 Cor 3:16; 6:19), does it not mix (*comiscet*) "the members of Christ" with the members of an adulteress (1 Cor 6:15)? So far as I know, "We are not our own, but bought with a price" (1 Cor 6:19, 20); and what kind of price? The blood of God. In hurting this flesh of ours, therefore, we hurt Him directly. (*ad Uxorem* 2.3.1)[21]

In these few sentences, which represent the climax of his condemnation of mixed marriages, Tertullian quoted three times from 1 Corinthians 6 and once from 1 Corinthians 5 (noted above). In each of these texts, Paul discussed porneia, which for him is often an immoral sexual act connected to a lack of self-mastery and a tendency toward idolatry that is characteristic of gentiles (e.g., 1 Cor 6:9; 1 Thess 4:3–5).

In 1 Corinthians 6:15 in particular, Paul spoke of porneia in terms of a wrong kind of mixing that triggers impurity: "Do you not know your bodies are members of Christ? Should I therefore take the members of Christ and make them members of a prostitute (πόρνης)? Never!" For Paul, this violation occurred because during intercourse, the two bodies become one (the one flesh idea). In Tertullian's rendering, however, Paul's 'prostitute' in 6:15 became an 'adulteress' (*adultera*), which was a rhetorical sleight of hand that focused Paul's condemnation on a different kind of wrong mixing of bodies, one that violated the bonds of marriage.[22] Tertullian

---

[21] Translation amended from Thelwall 1913, 45–46.
[22] Cohen comments on this as well; 2011, 269 n. 26.

reworked Paul so that he could condemn mixed marriage with the same vehemence and authority projected by the apostle about porneia.

Furthermore, Tertullian not only appropriated the language of 1 Corinthians 6 to prohibit mixed marriage in general, but he applied it specifically to women. Although his argument to this point did not focus specifically on women – perhaps because Paul's advice explicitly addressed both men and women – it is clear that women were Tertullian's concern.[23] This focus is not surprising, given his efforts elsewhere to control women's bodies.[24] He began *Ad Uxorem II* by explaining that he was writing about women who had disregarded the apostle's admonition to "marry in the Lord" (2.1.1) and then cited specific examples of women who married "gentiles" in order to show that the threat was not just theoretical (2.2.1). For the rest of this treatise, Tertullian detailed the particular problems faced by Christian women married to unbelievers.

Many of these problems, Tertullian argued, were created by conflicting practices between the husband and wife. Living with an unbelieving husband, a Christian wife "has by her side a slave of Satan" who will hinder the wife's efforts to carry out her duties as a Christian (2.4.1). Tertullian gave many examples: if you must keep a station, your husband will take you to the baths; if you must fast, your husband will prepare a feast on that day; how will you ever get permission from your husband to go out at night to evening meetings, to call on the brothers, to assist at the Lord's Supper, to host a traveling brother (2.4.1–2)?[25]

These conflicting practices were particularly problematic for the wife, as Tertullian recognized, because of the asymmetrical power relationship in marriage. As discussed above, the societal expectation was that the wife be subordinate to her husband, signaled in part by her worshipping of his gods. Tertullian agreed with this prescription and recognized that the aberration of this power relationship was one of the problems with mixed marriage. He wrote, "Every believing woman must obey God. Yet how can she serve two masters, the Lord and her husband?" (2.3.4).[26] Tertullian here articulated the crux of the problem for women in mixed

---

[23] Some have argued that Paul was primarily concerned about women in 1 Corinthians 7 (e.g., MacDonald 1990), despite his explicit mention of both wives and husbands in certain verses.

[24] See texts such as *de Cultu Feminarum* and *de Virginibus Velandis*. For analysis, see Daniel-Hughes 2011.

[25] More examples follow in 2.6.1–2, where Tertullian laments that a wife will have to endure pagan holidays, decorated doorways, sitting with her husband in a tavern.

[26] Translation amended from Thelwall 1913, 46.

marriages: they were responsible to two conflicting 'masters,' each requiring obedience.[27] Furthermore, if she obeys a 'gentile,' Tertullian reasoned, she will behave like a gentile as well (2.3.4). Thus her marriage threatens her Christian identity.

Like the "one flesh" argument, this point about subordination to the Lord also comes from 1 Corinthians 6. Paul argued that gentiles-in-Christ were subordinate to the larger body of Christ. He invoked the language of slavery, warning them that they "are not their own," but "have been bought with a price" (1 Cor 6:19–20).[28] When Tertullian warned Christian women not to admit 'foreign men' lest they violate the 'temple of God,' he loosely quoted these verses, "We are not our own, but bought with a price" (2.3.1). This rhetoric worked beautifully because women (in Tertullian's text) and gentiles-in-Christ (in Paul's text) occupied similar positions. Their bodies were subjected to another, more powerful body; they both were governed by an authoritative entity. Both belonged to God and are therefore holy, yet both were vulnerable to invasion by a foreign, polluting source. Therefore, gentiles and women both needed, according to Paul and Tertullian, respectively, to be protected and controlled. These similarities allowed Tertullian to develop his slippery argument, applying admonitions for one to the other.

The net result of Tertullian's interpretation, in which he borrowed heavily from 1 Corinthians 6, was that he was able to argue the opposite of what Paul said in 1 Corinthians 7:14. Whereas Paul's purity language made mixed marriages unproblematic (believing spouses make their families holy; 1 Cor 7:14), in Tertullian, purity language was used to condemn these unions. Paul offered no caveats based on when the marriage took place; for Tertullian this made all the difference. For Paul contagious holiness was at work in mixed marriages, but for Tertullian the contagious pollution of 1 Corinthians 6 took over. Paul did not count mixed marriage as sexual immorality; Tertullian adamantly declared that it is. Paul explicitly addressed men and women in 1 Corinthians 7:12–16; Tertullian focused on women.

Of these two models for understanding mixed marriage, Tertullian's is the one that was followed by later Christian writers who, for the most part, soundly condemned marriages contracted between believers and

---

[27] This would be a problem for any subordinate member of a household, including slaves. The power dynamics of the household may help explain why Christian authors after Paul focus on wives more than husbands in mixed marriages.

[28] On this topic see the chapter by Nasrallah in this volume.

non-believers. First, as Shaye Cohen has shown, many authors followed Tertullian in limiting the use of spousal sanctification and in citing passages other than 1 Corinthians 7:12–16 to condemn mixed marriages.[29] Second, they focused on the polluting dangers of mixed marriage. For example, Cyprian wrote that Christians who marry non-believers "have prostituted the members of Christ to the Gentiles."[30] Paul's notion of contagious holiness did not take hold; instead, the fear of contagious pollution overwhelmed the discussion.[31]

Third, whereas Paul explicitly balanced his instructions for wives and husbands in this situation, other Christians, like Tertullian, focused on wives. This was not universally true, but it was far more common for Christian texts to be concerned about women in mixed marriages than about men.[32] This trend began even before Tertullian, with 1 Peter's advice to women in unbelieving households (3:1–6).[33] In keeping with other household management discourses of the time, this author urged wives to obey their husbands, encouraging them to win them over by their behavior. Like Tertullian, the author of 1 Peter saw these Christian women as holy, set apart from their unbelieving spouses. Also like Tertullian, this author recognized the power dynamics of the household.[34]

---

[29] Cohen discusses these authors, which include Cyprian, Ambrosiaster, Chrysostom, Jerome, Theodoret; 2011, 274. In *Homily* 19 on 1 Cor 7:39, Chrysostom equivocates a bit, recognizing that spousal sanctification makes the unbeliever at least partially holy. The exception to this general trend is Augustine, who argues that Paul cannot be used to argue against mixed marriage; *De adulterinis coniugiis* 1.21, 25–26; see Cohen 2011, 262–63.

[30] Cyprian, *De Lapsis* 6. Translation: Deferrari 1958, 61.

[31] One exception is 1 Clement, written forty or so years after Paul: "For it is written, 'Unite with the holy ones (κολλᾶσθε τοῖς ἁγίοις), for those who unite with them shall be made holy (ἁγιασθήσονται)'" (46:2). The language of "uniting" and "being made holy" or being "sanctified" echoes Paul's language in 1 Corinthians 6:16–17 and 6:11 (respectively). It is notable that contagious holiness in general does not take hold in the imaginations of Christian writers. One might imagine the theory of spousal sanctification could be considered quite useful, especially to the extent that wives might be evangelists in the household. The few references I have seen to the evangelizing potential of wives focus on their model behavior as a persuasive tool (as in 1 Pt 3:1–2; Justin Martyr, *Second Apology* 2.2), but not the sanctifying power of her body for other household members.

[32] An exception to this preoccupation with Christian wives in mixed marriages is found in the *Apostolic Tradition* 41.11–12, where a Christian man is advised to say his midnight prayers in a separate room from a non-Christian wife.

[33] See Johnson Hodge 2010b, 9–14.

[34] Other early examples of authors discussing Christian wives in mixed marriages are Justin's Second Apology 2.1–6 and The Apocryphal Acts of the Apostles. This latter group of texts chronicled the disruption of households when the apostle comes through town, and focused on women who convert to Christianity and then leave their unbelieving husbands behind.

The 4th-century *Canons of Elvira* also illustrate this phenomenon. Three of these canons dealt directly with marriages between believers and unbelievers (or between "catholics" and "heretics"), and each one focused on protecting Christian women. None of them addressed Christian men in mixed marriages. For example, Canon 15 states: "Christian girls are not to marry gentiles (*gentilibus*), no matter how few eligible men there are, for such marriages lead to adultery (*adulterium*) of the soul."[35] We hear echoes of Tertullian's language, referring to unbelievers as 'gentiles' and marriage with them as a kind of 'adultery' or wrong mixing.

Finally, Jerome, writing at the end of the 4th and the beginning of the 5th centuries, spoke specifically about wives who "are joined to gentile (*gentilibus*) husbands, and prostitute the temples of Christ to idols."[36] He used the very same purity language of 1 Corinthians 6 – aimed to protect the integrity of newly baptized bodies, as well as the body of Christ, against porneia – to circumscribe the bodies of Christian brides. Such a marriage violated the holy space that is the Christian wife's body, changing it through prostitution from God's temple to an idol's temple.

What might explain this preoccupation with Christian women, and not Christian men, in mixed marriages? Tertullian suggested that it had to do with the gendered power dynamics of the household: as a subordinate member of an unbelieving household, the Christian wife was in a tricky position, obligated to 'two masters.' On the contrary, a male head of household who converted to Christianity would not have this problem since presumably the rest of the household would convert with him. This power relationship seems to have motivated the author of 1 Peter as well.

I would also suggest that the ethnic and purity language of protecting the community of believers, first used by Paul and then reworked by Tertullian, gained traction because it overlapped with a larger societal discourse aimed at managing women's bodies. In ancient gender ideologies, women's bodies needed protecting and controlling because they were perceived to be particularly vulnerable to their passions and were

---

[35] Canon 16: "Heretics shall not be joined in marriage with catholic girls unless they accept the catholic faith. Catholic girls may not marry Jews or heretics, because they cannot find a unity when the faithful and the unfaithful are joined. Parents who allow this to happen shall not receive communion even at the time of death." Canon 17: "If parents allow their daughter to marry a pagan priest, they shall not receive communion, even at the time of death." Translations amended from Womer 1987, 76. My thanks to Paula Fredriksen for calling my attention to this text.

[36] *Against Jovinianus* 1.10; translation amended from *NPNF* 4.353.

therefore more likely not only to sin themselves, but also to cause men to sin.[37] The virtue (or lack thereof) of wives and daughters was perceived to determine the honor (or shame) of the family. This view is illustrated by ancient moralists who typically encouraged the subordination of wives to their husbands, which signaled good order, virtue, and honor in ancient households.[38] Margaret MacDonald shows how a parallel dynamic influenced the development of Christianity, as the church responded to accusations from outsiders that it did not keep its women in line and was thus morally suspect.[39]

In the context of 1st-century Corinth, Paul's language feminized and subordinated the newly baptized believers: they were not their own, but they belonged to the Lord and were vulnerable to invasion and pollution by outsiders. Their bodies were problematic sites to be managed. In the centuries that followed, as Christianity emerged and defined itself in the larger cultural register of the Roman world, it was not difficult for Tertullian and others to apply this language to wives.

Responses of 'Unpublished Christians'

These elite 'published Christians' – church fathers whose writings are preserved for us – were not the only ones who responded to Paul's text or weighed in on the topic of marrying unbelievers. If we listen carefully to the evidence examined above, and if we allow ourselves to use some imagination, we can say something about how other, unpublished Christians reacted to the discussions that occurred in 1st century Corinth. After all, the Corinthian believers themselves were Paul's correspondents: what did they think of his advice? Presumably they were the ones who experienced these situations and perhaps brought the subject up in the first place. What did they write in their letters to Paul?

Some believers must have found it difficult to live as baptized gentiles in a polytheistic household, perhaps because of the logistical difficulties

---

[37] Again, Tertullian himself had plenty to say about this in texts such as *de Cultu Feminarum* and *de Virginibus Velandis*. See Daniel-Hughes 2011 and scholarship discussed there.

[38] For an introduction to the discourse of household management, see Pomeroy 1994, 41–90; and Balch 1981.

[39] MacDonald 1996. MacDonald argues that these accusations arise precisely because women were active leaders in the early Christian movement. This exposed Christians to critique by writers such as Celsus. Christians had to manage the tension created by the cultural norms that subordinated women and the roles played by women in the church.

of incompatible practices and power relationships, such as those enumerated by Tertullian in *ad Uxorem* (discussed above).[40] These believers might have resisted Paul's admonition to "stay as you were called." Some Corinthians, in keeping with the logic of 1 Corinthians 6, may have thought that marriage to an unbeliever would pollute their holy status and were thus leaving their households. Others may have thought that their baptism dissolved prior family ties, freeing them to live the celibate, single life that Paul models (1 Cor 7:7–8).[41] Such views could have prompted Paul to encourage them to stay.

Others may have embraced the idea of spousal sanctification, and the freedom and power it gave them. Whether Paul intended it or not, this verse opened up intriguing possibilities for Christian bodies to sanctify whole households, spouses, and children. Indeed, believers might have seen themselves as evangelists in the household (like the wives in 1 Peter), hoping to fully convert their spouses.[42] Some believers may have liked their mixed households so well that they did not want to leave, prompting Paul's advice to take the unbeliever's wishes into consideration: if the unbeliever desires to separate, let him go (1 Cor 7:15).

Less imagination is required in retrieving the views of unpublished Christians in Tertullian's *ad Uxorem*, for Tertullian offered a reconstruction of their position. As mentioned above, Tertullian launched his argument with the admission that he had heard of Christian women who had married non-Christians. He also suggested the possibility that they use 1 Corinthians 7:14 to justify this decision, and he alluded to 'advisors' – some sort of spiritual directors – who supported their decision and interpretation of Paul (*ad Uxorem* 2.2.1). Finally, Tertullian complained, there is one man who said that to marry a 'stranger' was indeed a fault, but only a small one (*ad Uxorem* 2.3.2). Clearly, there were Christians who disagreed with Tertullian's position and his reading of Paul.[43]

Furthermore, Jerome complained that "many women, despising the apostle's command, are joined to gentiles." He spoke vehemently against

---

[40] For a more detailed consideration of Corinthian views, see Johnson Hodge 2010a.

[41] Schüssler Fiorenza 1991, 155–56.

[42] In my view, Paul expresses skepticism about this option in 1 Corinthians 7:16: "For how do you know, woman, if you will save your husband? Or how do you know, man, if you will save your wife?" Others translate this verse in a more optimistic sense, "Wife, for all you know you might save your husband. Husband, for all you know you might save your wife" (NRSV). For a discussion and references, see Johnson Hodge 2010a, 19 n. 69.

[43] It seems likely that those who supported mixed marriage would have had an easier time arguing on the basis of Paul's writing.

this practice, knowing that "crowds of matrons will be furious" at him.[44] Who were these Christian women? The term 'matron' indicates that they were probably elite women who were responsible, along with their husbands, for managing their households. Were they themselves married to unbelievers? Were they Christian mothers who wanted to find a good match for their daughters, even if he was a 'gentile'? These household responsibilities seem, according to Jerome, to have conflicted with their duties as Christians.

Maybe the *Canons of Elvira*, discussed above, responded to a group like these furious matrons when they warn that Christian girls are not to marry pagan men, no matter how few eligible Christian men there are (Canon 15), or that Christian parents will be punished for allowing their daughters to marry Jews, heretics (Canon 16) or pagan priests (Canon 17). Judith Evans Grubbs points out that church rulings such as those in the *Canons of Elvira*, more so than treatises on marriage written by and for the elite, address issues of daily life for 'ordinary' Christians.[45] They represent the efforts by church officials to police the behavior of their parishioners, which gives us insight into what these parishioners were up to. In the early 4th century, Spanish clerics were clearly concerned about Christian girls and women marrying non-Christians.

Given the patriarchal structure of the household, how might these Christian women married to 'gentiles' manage their dual loyalties to God and husband? Perhaps some Christian women performed their rituals in secret, so as not to appear insubordinate. Others may have incorporated their Christian practices into the daily activities in the household. From what we know about household worship, neither option is difficult to imagine. Household religious practices appear to have been fluid and diverse, and were often tied to daily activities (such as eating and drinking, coming and going).[46] As John Bodel argues, this is the type of environment in which multiple types of worship are possible.[47] Indeed, we can imagine that both wives and slaves might import traditions from their prior households and homelands, or new religions they adopt, into their current households, perhaps without the notice of the head of household. Thus, if

---

[44] *Against Jovinianus* 1.10; translation amended from *NPNF* 4.353.

[45] Grubbs 1994, 399.

[46] Johnson Hodge 2010b, 6–7.

[47] Bodel 2008, 260–62, 265. Bodel argues that the variety of deities and objects found in household shrines indicates that the household cult could accommodate not only the individual tastes and needs of particular households, but of even individuals or small groups within households.

religious practices offer one way to express loyalty and subordination to the head of the household, worshipping in secret might be a way to resist the social hierarchy or maintain a different identity.

Ironically, Tertullian is one of our best sources on the topic. In his rant over how disastrous a mixed marriage would be for a Christian wife, he offered tantalizing clues as to how women might have protected themselves, and perhaps their households, from defilement: "Shall you escape notice when you sign your bed, (or) your body; when you blow away some impurity; when even by night you rise to pray?" (*ad Uxorem* 2.5.3).[48] To "sign oneself" is to trace the shape of the cross on one's body or on another object (like the bed here).[49] This might be seen as a ritual of protection, especially if a Christian wife is about to share the bed with her non-Christian husband. Similarly, "blowing away some unclean thing" refers to ritual insufflation, in which the believer blows on her hand, catching saliva which is understood to replicate baptismal water.[50] These rituals recall the metaphor of protecting sacred space and the community of believers that Paul articulated in 1 Corinthians 6. Tertullian would have agreed that rituals like this are necessary for the unfortunate situation of mixed marriages, but would have had doubts that the Christian wife would get away with them. The wives, however, through these acts, may have perceived that they were maintaining their sanctified Christian bodies, and even sanctifying the household, in keeping with Paul's ideas in 1 Corinthians 7:12–16.

A striking feature of the evidence for unpublished Christians reviewed here is the persistence of unions between Christians and non-Christians, despite the many prohibitions against this practice on the part of published Christians.[51] Perhaps they used Paul as their authority for doing so, as did Tertullian's interlocutors. According to Tertullian a mixed marriage household would be a disaster. Recall the vivid picture he painted of all the inconveniences of trying to perform Christian duties at the same time

---

[48] Translation amended from Thelwall 1913, 46.

[49] Le Saint 1956, 129 n. 116.

[50] Le Saint 1956, 129 n. 116. A later manual of Christian rituals, the *Apostolic Tradition*, mentions this practice: "Through consignation with moist breath and catching your spittle in your hand, your body is sanctified down to your feet. For when it is offered with a believing heart, just as from the font, the gift of the Spirit and the sprinkling of washing sanctifies him who believes;" 41.17; translated in Bradshaw 2002, 200. See Johnson Hodge 2010b, 16.

[51] Hayes documents canons addressing this issue through the 7th century; 2002, 255 n. 32.

that your husband is dragging you off to the baths and such (*ad Uxorem* 2.4.1). Yet it seems that not all were bothered by this. The "crowds of matrons" that Jerome dreads clearly value their marriages – or those of their daughters – to gentile men. Thus, while it might be difficult to serve two masters, the voices of these unpublished Christians indicate that at least some were making it work.

Conclusion

The tolerance and flexibility of Paul's short-term advice to the Corinthians – believers and unbelievers just stay together as long as the unbelievers agree – was unacceptable to Tertullian and other writers in a later historical moment. Tertullian's creative interpretation of 1 Corinthians 7:14 served to correct the problem, offering constraints on the contagious holiness Paul asserted. Other Christian writers, concerned both with the boundaries of the community of believers and with the behavior of Christian women, condemned mixed marriages and accused Christian wives married to non-Christians of sexual immorality, adultery and idolatry.

Whether they meant to or not, published Christians such as Tertullian, Jerome and the authors of the *Canons of Elvira* preserved for us the opinions of unpublished Christians who read Paul differently. These Christians recognized in 1 Corinthians 7:12–16 a scriptural warrant for their mixed marriages, and attempted to integrate their faith and practices into their polytheistic households. Furthermore, the ancient household – the context in which all of these texts, opinions and practices need to be considered – may have lent itself to the sort of mixing of religious traditions that would have been involved in such marriages. Both the voices of these unpublished Christians, just barely audible in these texts, and the vociferous objections of the published Christians, signal that boundaries were not always clear between Christians and non-believers. For some, this was just fine; for others, it was a threat to the faith. Both sides, it seems, could find support for their positions from Paul's letter to believers in Corinth.

BIBLIOGRAPHY

For the abbreviations used here, readers should refer to the list of abbreviations in the front matter of this volume.

Abad Casal, L. 1982. *La pintura romana en España*. Alicante: Universidad de Alicante.

Abadie-Reynal, C. 1995. "Céramique et romanisation de la Grèce: Argos aux Ier s. av. et ap. J.-C." In *Hellenistic and Roman Pottery in the Eastern Mediterranean: Advances in Scientific Studies*, 1–5. Edited by H. Meyza and J. Mlynarczk. Warsaw: Research Center for Mediterranean Archaeology.

———. 2005. "Trade Relations in the Aegean Sea: the ceramic evidence from Argos from the 1st c. B.C. to the 2nd c. A.D." In *Trade Relations in the Eastern Mediterranean from the Late Hellenistic Period to Late Antiquity*, 37–49. Edited by M. Briese and L.E. Vaag. Odense: University Press of Southern Denmark.

Adams, J.N. 2003. *Bilingualism and the Latin Language*. Cambridge: Cambridge University Press.

Alabé, F. 1987. "Guirlandes déliennes en 'stripes de palmier.'" In *Peinture murale romaine: Actes du Xe séminaire de L'AFPMA, Vaison-la-Romaine, 1–3 Mai*, 171–80. Edited by C. Allag. Vaison-la-Romaine: AFPMA.

———. 1991. "Peintures apparentées au deuxième style pompéien découvertes à Delos." *Köln Jahrbuch für Frühgeschichte* 24: 33–34.

———. 1995. "Intérieurs de maisons hellénistiques. Les murs peints à Delos." *RA* 191–97.

———. 1999. "'Un deuxième style' des peintures déliennes." *RA* 185–186.

Alchermes, J. 1994. "Spolia in Roman Cities of the Late Empire: Legislative Rationales and Architectural Reuse." *DOP* 48: 167–78.

Alcock, S. 1993. *Graecia Capta: The Landscapes of Roman Greece*. Cambridge: Cambridge University Press.

———. 2005. "Roman Colonies in the Eastern Empire: A Tale of Four Cities." In *The Archaeology of Colonial Encounters: Comparative Perspectives*, 297–330. Edited by G.J. Stein. Santa Fe: School of American Research Press.

Alexander, Patrick H., John F. Kutsko, James D. Ernest, Shirley A. Decker-Lucke, and David L. Petersen (eds.) 1999. *The SBL Handbook of Style for Ancient Near Eastern, Biblical, and Early Christian Studies*. Peabody, MA: Hendrickson Publishers.

Allbaugh L.G. 1953. *Crete. A Case Study of an Under-Developed Area*. Princeton: Princeton University Press.

Allison, P.M. 1991. "'Workshops' and 'Patternbooks.'" *KölJb* 24: 79–84.

Amandry, M. 1988. *Le monnayage des duovirs Corinthiens*. Athens: École française d'Athènes.

Anderson, V. 2002. *Creatures of Empire: How Domestic Animals Transformed Early America*. Oxford: Oxford University Press.

Andreades, M. 1996. *Η Κορινθία την Οθωνική περίοδο 2: 1833–1862*. Athens.

Andreou, A. 1989. "Griechische Wanddekorationen." Ph.D. Dissertation, University of Mainz.

Apostolaki, Ch., V. Perdikatsis, E. Repuskou, H. Brekoulaki, and S. Lepinski. 2006. "Analysis of Roman Wall Paintings from Ancient Corinth/Greece." Paper presented at the Second International Conference on "Advances in Mineral Resources Managements and Environmental Geotechnology," Hania, Greece.

Appadurai, A. 1986. "Introduction: Commodities and the Politics of Value." In *The Social Life of Things: Commodities in Cultural Perspective*, 3–63. Edited by A. Appadurai. Cambridge: Cambridge University Press.

Arzt-Grabner, P., M. Ernst, R.E. Kritzer, A. Papathomas, F. Winter, G. Schwab, and A. Bammer. 2006. *1. Korinther: Papyrologische Kommentare zum Neuen Testament 2.* Göttingen: Vandenhoeck & Ruprecht.

Asimenos, K. 1978. "Technological observations on the Thera wall-paintings." In *Thera and the Aegean World: Proceedings of the Second International Scientific Congress, Santorini, Greece, August 1978.* Edited by C. Doumas, 571–78. London: Thera and the Aegean World.

Athanasoulis, D.H. 1998. "Λουτρική εγκατάσταση στην Κοκκινόκρραχι Σπάρτης." *Πρακτικά τοῦ Ε' Διεθνούς Συνεδρίου Πελοποννησιακών Σπουδών* 2: 209–44.

Avramea, A. 1997. *Le Péloponnèse du IVe au VIIIe siècle: Changements et persistances.* Paris: Publications de la Sorbonne.

Bagdikian, A. 1953. "The Civic Officials of Roman Corinth." M.A. Thesis, University of Vermont.

Bagnall, R.S. and B.W. Frier. 1994. *The Demography of Roman Egypt.* Cambridge: Cambridge University Press.

Balch, D.L. 1981. *Let Wives Be Submissive: The Domestic Code in 1 Peter.* Chico, CA: Scholars Press.

Balzat, S.-J. and B.W. Millis. Forthcoming. "M. Antonius Aristocrates: Provincial Involvement with Roman Power in the Late 1st century B.C." *Hesperia.*

Barbet, A. 1981. "Les bordeurs ajourées dans le IVe style de Pompéi. Essai de Typologie." *MEFRA* 93: 917–98.

——. 1982a. "La diffusion du IIIe Style Pompéien en Gaule: Premiere Partie." *Gallia* 40: 53–82.

——. 1982b. "The Diffusion of the Third Pompeian Style in Gaul." In *Roman Provincial Wall Painting of the Western Empire,* 75–81. Edited by J. Liversidge. Oxford: BAR-IS.

——. 1983. "La Diffusion du IIIe Style Pompéien en Gaule: Deuxième Partie." *Gallia* 41: 111–65.

——. 1987. "La diffusions des Ier, IIe et IIIe styles pompéiens en Gaule." In *Pictores per Provincias: Aventicum,* 7–27. Edited by V.H. Bögli, W. Drack and D. Paunier. Avenches: Cahiers d'Archéologie Romande and Association Pro Aventico.

——. 1990. "L'emploi des couleurs dans la peinture murale romaine antique." In *Pigments et Colorants de l'Antiquité et du Moyen Age: Peinture, enluminure, études historiques et physico-chimiques,* 255–71. Paris: Éditions du Centre National de la Recherche Scientifique.

——. 2005. *Zeugma II. Peinture murales romaines.* Varia Anatolica XVII. Istanbul: Georges Dumézil, Institut français d'études anatoliennes.

Barbet, A. and C. Allag. 1972. "Techniques de préparation des parios dans la peinture murale romaine." *MEFRA* 84: 935–1069.

Barbet, A. and C. Lahanier. 1983. "L'emploie de la feuille d'or dans la peinture murale romaine." In *Les methods physico-chimiques d'analyse des œuvres d'art,* 260–76. Athens: Nouvelles de l'Archéologie.

Bartchy, S.S. 1973. Μᾶλλον χρῆσαι: *First-Century Slavery and the Interpretation of 1 Corinthians 7:21.* Atlanta: Scholars Press.

Béarat, H., M. Fuchs, M. Magetti, and D. Paunier. 1997. *Roman Wall Painting: Materials, Techniques, Analysis, and Conservation.* Fribourg: Institute of Mineralogy and Petrography Press.

Bees, N.A. 1941. *Die Griechisch-christlichen Inschriften Des Peloponnes.* Athens: Christlich-Archäologische Gesellschaft.

Behrwald, R. 2000. *Der Lykische Bund: Untersuchungen zu Geschichte und Verfassung.* Bonn: Habelt.

Bennett, J. 2010. *Vibrant Matter: A Political Ecology of Things.* Durham: Duke University Press.

Bergmann, B., S. De Caro, J.R. Mertens, and R. Meyer. 2010. "Roman Frescoes. The Villa of Publius Fannius Synistor in Reality and Virtual Reality." *The Metropolitan Museum of Art Bulletin* 67.4: 11–32.

Betz, H.D. 1992. *The Greek Magical Papyri in Translation.* 2nd ed. Chicago: University of Chicago Press.

Bezerra de Meneses, U.T. 1970. "Les revetments murale." In *L'ilot de la Maison des Comédiens: Exploration archéologique de Délos. Delos 27.* Edited by T. Homolle and M. Holleaux. Paris: Fontemoin et Cie.

——. 1983. "Les Peintures." In *Guide de Délos*, 81–87. Edited by P. Bruneau and J. Ducat. Paris: École Française d'Athènes.

——. 1999. "Un 'deuxième style' à Délos? Réflexions à partir des peintures murales figurées." *RA* 186–91.

Biers, W.R. and D.J. Geagan. 1970. "A New List of Victors in the Caesarea at Isthmia." *Hesperia* 39: 79–93.

Blackman, D.J. 1982. "Ancient harbours in the Mediterranean." *IJNA* 11: 79–104, 185–211.

——. 2008. "Sea Transport, Part 2: Harbors." In *The Oxford Handbook of Engineering and Technology in the Classical World*, 638–70. Edited by J.P. Oleson. Oxford: Oxford University Press.

Blanck, H. 1992. *Das Buch in der Antike.* Munich: C.H. Beck.

Blitzer, H. 1990a. "Koroneika: Storage Jar Production and Trade in the Traditional Aegean." *Hesperia* 59: 675–711.

——. 1990b. "Pastoral Life in the Mountains of Crete." *Expedition* 32: 23–41.

——. Forthcoming. *The Traditional Industries of Greece: their History, Technology, Raw Materials and Trade.*

Boatwright, M.T. 1991. "Plancia Magna of Perge: Women's Roles and Status in Roman Asia Minor." In *Women's History and Roman History*, 249–72. Edited by S.B. Pomeroy. Chapel Hill: University of North Carolina Press.

Bodel, J. 2008. "Cicero's Minerva, *Penates*, and the Mother of the *Lares*: An Outline of Roman Domestic Religion." In *Household and Family Religion in Antiquity*, 248–75. Edited by J. Bodel and S.M. Olyan. Malden, MA: Blackwell.

Bookidis, N. 2003. "The Sanctuaries of Corinth." In *Corinth XX*, 247–59.

——. 2005. "Religion in Corinth: 146 B.C.E. to 100 C.E." In *URRC*, 141–64.

Bórhy, L. (ed.). 2004. *Plafonds et voûtes á l'époque antique. Actes du VIIIe Colloque international de l'Association International pour la Peinture Murale antique (AIPMA), 15–19 mai 2001, Budapest-Veszprém.* Budapest: Pytheas Kiade és Nyomda.

Boserup, E. 1965. *The Conditions of Agricultural Growth: The Economics of Agrarian Change under Population Pressure.* Chicago: Aldine Press.

——. 1981. *Population and Technological Change: A Study of Long Term Trends.* Chicago: University of Chicago Press.

Bowden, W. 2003. *Epirus Vetus: The Archaeology of a Late-antique Province.* London: Duckworth.

Bowersock, G.W. 1961. "Eurycles of Sparta." *JRS* 51: 112–18.

Bowes, K. 2008. *Private Worship, Public Values, and Religious Change in Late Antiquity.* Cambridge: Cambridge University Press.

Bradshaw, P.F. 2002. *The Apostolic Tradition: A Commentary.* Minneapolis: Fortress Press.

Brekoulaki, H. 1997. "La couleur dans la peinture grecque antique de Macédoine." *Histoire de l'art* 39: 11–21.

——. 2006. *La peinture funeraire de Macedoine: emplois et fonctions de la couleur IVe–IIe siècles av. J.-C.* Athens: De Boccard.

Bremen, R. van. 1996. *The Limits of Participation: Women and Civic Life in the Greek East in the Hellenistic and Roman Periods.* Amsterdam: J.C. Gieben.

Briggs, S. 1989. "Can an Enslaved God Liberate? Hermeneutical Reflections on Philippians 2:6–11." *Semeia* 47: 137–53.

——. 2000. "Paul on Bondage and Freedom in Imperial Roman Society." In *Paul and Politics: Ekklesia, Israel, Imperium, Interpretation*, 110–23. Edited by R.A. Horsley. Harrisburg: Trinity Press International.

——. 2004. "Slavery and Gender." In *On the Cutting Edge: The Study of Women in Biblical Worlds*, 171–92. Edited by J. Schaberg, A. Bach, and E. Fuchs. New York: Continuum Press.

Broneer, O. 1935. "Excavations in Corinth, 1934." *AJA* 39: 53–75.

Brooten, B. (ed.). 2010. *Beyond Slavery: Overcoming Its Religious and Sexual Legacies*. New York: Palgrave Macmillan.

Brown, A. 2008. "The City of Corinth and Urbanism in Late Antique Greece." Ph.D. Dissertation, University of California, Berkeley.

Brown, B. 2001. "Thing Theory." *Critical Inquiry* 28: 1–22.

Bruno, V.G. 1969. "Antecedents of the Pompeian First Style." *AJA* 73: 305–17.

Brunt, P.A. 1971. *Italian Manpower 225 B.C.–A.D. 14*. Oxford: Oxford University Press.

———. 1980. "Free Labour and Public Works at Rome." *JRS* 70: 81–100.

Buell, D.K. 2005. *Why This New Race: Ethnic Reasoning in Early Christianity*. New York: Columbia University Press.

Bulard, M. 1908. *Peintures murales et mosaïques de Délos*. Paris: E. Leroux.

Buraselis, K. 2000. *Kos: Between Hellenism and Rome*. Philadelphia: American Philosophical Society.

Calamiotou, M., M. Siganidou, and S.E. Filippakis. 1983. "X-ray Analysis of Pigments from Pella, Greece." *Studies in Conservation* 28: 117–22.

Caley, E.R. and J.F.C. Richards. 1956. *On Stones: Theophrastus. Introduction, Greek Text, English Translation, and Commentary*. Columbus: Ohio State University Press.

Callahan, A. 2001. *Semeia 83–84: Slavery in Text and Interpretation*. Atlanta: Society for Biblical Literature.

Cameron, A. 1976. *Corippus, Flavius Cresconius: In Laudem Iustini Augusti Minoris*. London: Athlone Press.

Cameron, Av. 1979. "Images of Authority: Elites and Icons in Late Sixth-Century Byzantium." *PastPres* 84: 3–35.

———. 1985. *Procopius and the Sixth Century*. London: Duckworth.

Caputo, G. 1948. *Lo scultore del grande bassorilievo con la danza delle Menadi in Tolemaide di Cirenaica*. Rome: L'Erma.

Caraher, W.R. Forthcoming. "Epigraphy, Liturgy, and Imperial Policy on the Justinianic Isthmus." In *A Half Century on the Isthmus*. Edited by T.E. Gregory and E.R. Gebhard. Princeton: American School of Classical Studies at Athens.

Casevitz, M. 1993. *"Emporion*: Emplois Classiques et Histoire du mot." In *L'Emporion*, 9–22. Edited by A. Bresson and P. Rouillard. Paris: Centre Pierre Paris.

Casson, L. 1971. *Ships and Seamanship in the Ancient World*. Princeton: Princeton University Press.

———. 1978. "Unemployment: the building trade and Suetonius *Vesp.* 18." *BASP* 15: 43–51.

Campbell, J.C. 2009. *Phoebe: Patron and Emissary*. Collegeville, MN: Liturgical Press.

Chandler, R. 1776. *Travels in Greece, or an Account of a Tour Made at the Expense of the Society of Dilettanti*. Oxford: Clarendon.

Charanis, P. 1974. *Church and State in the Late Roman Empire: the Religious Policy of Anastasius the First, 491–518*. Madison: University of Wisconsin Press.

Charitonidis, S. 1966. "Ἀνάσκαφες εθνίκι οδου. Χρονίκα." *ArchDelt* 21: 121–123.

Chase, W.T. 1971. "Egyptian Blue as a Pigment and Ceramic Material." In *Science and Archaeology*, 80–90. Edited by R.H. Brill. Cambridge: Massachusetts Institute of Technology Press.

Chazelle, M.C. and C. Cubitt (eds.). 2007. *The Crisis of the Oikoumene: the Three Chapters Controversy and the Failed Quest for Unity in the Sixth-Century Mediterranean*. Turnhout: Brepols.

Christopoulou, P.F. 1971–72. "Η Περί τον Κορινθιακόν περιοχή κατά τά τελή ΙΗ αιώνος." *Επετηρίς Εταιρείας Στερεοελλαδικών Μελετών* 3: 439–71.

Chrysos, E. 1966. *Die Bischofslisten des V. Ökumenische Konzils (553)*. Bonn: Rudolf Habelt.

Churchin, L.A. 1990. *The Local Magistrates of Roman Spain*. Toronto: University of Toronto Press.

Clark, C. and M. Haswell. 1967. *The Economics of Subsistence Agriculture*. 2nd ed. London: MacMillan.

Clarke, J. 1991. *The Houses of Roman Italy, 100 B.C.–A.D. 250: Ritual, Space, and Decoration.* Berkeley: University of California Press.
Claus, J.J. and Johnston, S.I. (eds.). 1996. *Medea: Essays on Medea in Myth, Literature, Philosophy, and Art.* Princeton: Princeton University Press.
Cohen, S.J.D. 1999. *The Beginnings of Jewishness.* Berkeley: University of California Press.
———. 2011. "From Prohibition to Permission: Paul and the Early Church on Mixed Marriage." In *Paul's Jewish Matrix*, 259–92. Edited by T.G. Casey and J. Taylor. Rome: Gregorian and Biblical Press.
Collins, R.F. 1999. *First Corinthians.* Collegeville, MN: Liturgical Press.
Conzelmann, H. 1975. *1 Corinthians: A Commentary on the First Epistle to the Corinthians.* Translated by J.W. Leitch. Philadelphia: Fortress Press.
Cook, R.M. 1986. "A Further Note on the *Diolkos.*" In *Studies in Honour of T. B. L. Webster*, Volume 1, 65–68. Edited by J.H. Betts, J.T. Hooker and J.R. Green. Bristol: Bristol Classical Press.
Counillon, P. 1993. "L'Emporion des Géographes Greces." In *L'Emporion*, 47–57. Edited by A. Bresson and P. Rouillard. Paris: Centre Pierre Paris.
Cristofori, A. 2001. "The maritime city in the Graeco-Roman perception: Carthage and Alexandria: Two Emblematic Examples." In *The Sea in European History*, 1–24. Edited by L. Francois and A.K. Isaacs. Pisa: Edizioni Plus.
Croke, B. and J. Crow. 1983. "Procopius & Dara." *JRS* 73: 143–59.
Crook, J.A. 1967. *Law and Life of Rome.* Ithaca: Cornell University Press.
Cunningham, G. 1999. *Religion and Magic: Approaches and Theories.* Edinburgh: Edinburgh University Press.
Curtius, E. 1851–52. *Peloponnesos; eine historisch-geographische Beschreibung der Halbinsel.* Gotha: J. Perthes.
———. 1868. *The History of Greece.* Translated by A.W. Ward. London: R. Bentley.
D'Arms, J.H. 1980. "Senator's involvement in commerce in the Late Republic: some Ciceronian evidence." In *The Seaborne Commerce of Ancient Rome: Studies in Archaeology and History*, 77–89. Edited by J.H. D'Arms and E.C. Kopff. Rome: American Academy in Rome.
D'Ambra, E. 1993. *Roman Art in Context: An Anthology.* Englewood Cliffs: Prentice Hall.
Daniel-Hughes, C. 2011. *The Salvation of the Flesh in Tertullian of Carthage: Dressing for the Resurrection.* New York: Palgrave Macmillan.
Dark K. and J. Kostenec. 2006. "The Byzantine Patriarchate in Constantinople and the Baptistery of the Church of Hagia Sophia." *Architectura* 36: 113–30.
Daux, G. 1968. "Chronique des fouilles et découvertes archéologiques en Grèce en 1967: Isthmia, fouilles américains." *BCH* 9: 773–86.
Davey, N. and R. Ling. 1982. *Wall-Painting in Roman Britain.* Gloucester: Allan Sutton.
Davies, G.S. 1877. *St. Paul in Greece.* London: SPCK.
Dawes, G.W. 1990. "But if you can gain your freedom (1 Corinthians 7:17–24)." *CBQ* 52: 681–97.
De Ligt, L. 1993. *Fairs and Markets in the Roman Empire: Economic and Social Aspects of Periodic Trade in a Pre-Industrial Society.* Amsterdam: J.C. Gieben.
De Ruyt, C. 1983. *Macellum: marché alimentaire des Romains.* Louvain-la-Neuve: Institut supérieur d'archéologie et d'histoire de l'art, Collège Érasme.
De Waele, F.J. 1931. "The Greek Stoa North of the Temple of Apollo." *AJA* 35: 394–423.
Dean, L.R. 1919. "Latin Inscriptions from Corinth II." *AJA* 23: 163–74.
Deferrari, R.J. (ed.). 1958. *The Fathers of the Church. Saint Cyprian: Treatises.* New York: The Fathers of the Church.
Deininger, J. 1965. *Die Provinziallandtage der römischen Kaiserzeit von Augustus bis zum Ende des dritten Jahrhunderts n. Chr.* Munich: C.H. Beck.
Deissmann, A. 1927. *Light from the Ancient East: The New Testament Illustrated by Recently Discovered Texts of the Graeco-Roman World.* Rev. ed. Translated by L.R.M. Strachan. New York: George H. Doran.

DelPlace, C. 1986. "Publications récent sur la peinture murale romaine." *RBArch* 64: 86–98.
———. 1989. "Nouvelles publications récentes sur la peinture murale romaine." *RBArch* 67: 161–70.
Department of Commerce, 1949. "Income of Families and Persons in the United States: 1947." *Bureau of the Census, Current Population Reports Consumer Income, Series P-60.5.* Washington D.C. Online at: http://www2.census.gov/prod2/popscan/p60-005.pdf. Accessed 1 May 2011.
Dey, H. 2010. "Art, Ceremony, and City Walls: The Aesthetics of Imperial Resurgence in the Late Roman West." *Journal of Late Antiquity* 3: 3–37.
Dill, B.T., and R.E. Zambrana. 2009. "Critical Thinking about Inequality: An Emerging Lens." In *Emerging Intersections: Race, Class, and Gender in Theory, Policy, and Practice*, 1–21. Edited by B.T. Dill and R.E. Zambrana. New Brunswick, N.J.: Rutgers University Press.
Diop, B. 1989. "Spirits." In *The Negritude Poets*, 152–54. Edited by E. Kennedy. New York: Thunder's Mouth Press.
Dixon, S. 2001. *Reading Roman Women: Sources, Genres, and Real Life*. London: Duckworth.
Dodwell, E. 1819. *A Classical and Topographical Tour through Greece, During the Years 1801, 1805, and 1806, Volume 2*. London: Rodwell & Martin.
Donderer, M. 2005. "Und es gab sie doch! Ein neuer Papyrus und das Zeugnis des Mosaiken belegen die Verwendung antiker 'Musterbücher.'" *AntW* 36: 59–68.
Donohue, A.A. 1998–1999. "Ai Bakchai Chorenousi: The Reliefs of the Dancing Bacchantes." *Hephaistos* 16/17: 7–49.
Doukellis, P.N. 1994. "Le territoire de la colonie romaine de Corinthe." In *Structures rurales et sociétés antiques. Actes du colloque de Corfou, 14–16 mai 1992*, 359–90. Edited by P.N. Doukellis and L.G. Mendoni. Paris: Diffuse par Les Belles Lettres.
Doursther, H. 1840. *Dictionnaire universel des poids et mesures*. Brussels: M. Hayez.
Dow, S. 1951. "The Latin Elegiacs of ca. 101 B.C." *HSCP* 60: 81–96.
DuBois, P. 1991. *Torture and Truth*. New York: Routledge.
———. 2003. *Slaves and Other Objects*. Chicago: Chicago University Press.
Duchêne, H. 1986. "Sur la Stèle d'Aulus Caprilius Timotheos, Sômatemporos." *BCH* 110: 513–30.
Duell, P. 1964. "The Painted Decoration." In *Corinth* I.6, 110–16.
Dunn, A. 2004. "Continuity and change in the Macedonian countryside, from Gallienus and Justinian." In *Late Antique Archaeology 2. Recent Research on the Late Antique Countryside*, 535–86. Edited by W. Bowden and L. Lavan. Leiden: Brill.
Eastaugh, N., V. Walsh, T. Chaplin, and R. Siddall. 2004. *The Pigment Compendium: A Dictionary of Historical Pigments*. Amsterdam: Elsevier Butterworth-Heinemann.
Edwards, C.M. 1981. "Corinth 1980: Molded Relief Bowls." *Hesperia* 50: 189–210.
———. 1994. "The Arch over the Lechaion Road at Corinth and Its Sculpture." *Hesperia* 63: 263–308.
Ehrhardt, W. 1987. *Stilgeschichtliche Untersuchungen an Römischen Wandmalereien von der späten Republik bis zur Zeit Neros*. Mainz am Rhein: Philipp von Zabern.
Eibner, A. 1926. *Entwicklung und Werkstoffe der Wandmalerei vom Altertum bis zur Neuzeit*. Munich: B. Heller.
Elsner, J. 2007. *Roman Eyes: Visuality and Subjectivity in Art and Text*. Princeton: Princeton University Press.
Engels, D. 1990. *Roman Corinth. An Alternative Model for the Classical City*. Chicago: University of Chicago Press.
Étienne, R. 1993. "*L'Emporion* chez Strabon: A. Les *Emporia Strabioniens: Inventaire, Hiérarchies et Mécanismes Commerciaux*." In *L'Emporion*, 23–34. Edited by A. Bresson and P. Rouillard. Paris: Centre Pierre Paris.
Evans, J.K. 1981. "Wheat Production and its Social Consequences in the Roman World." *CQ* 31: 428–42.

Farrar, F.W. 1879. *The Life and Work of St. Paul.* New York: Dutton.

Feissel, D. 1988. "L'architecte Viktôrinos et les fortifications de Justinien dans les provinces balkaniques." *Bulletin de la société nationale des antiquaires de France*: 136–46.

Feissel, D. and A. Philippidis-Braat. 1985. "Inventaires en vue d'un recueil des inscriptions historique de Byzance. III. Inscriptions du Péloponnèse." *Travaux et Mémoires Byzance* 9: 267–395.

Filippakis, S.E., B. Perdikatsis, and T. Paradellis. 1976. "An Analysis of Blue Pigments from the Greek Bronze Age." *Studies in Conservation* 21: 143–53.

Finley, M.I. 1964. "Between Slavery and Freedom." *Comparative Studies in Society and History* 6: 233–49.

Fitzmyer, J.A. 2008. *First Corinthians: A New Translation with Introduction and Commentary.* New Haven: Yale University Press.

Fowden, G. 1995. "Late Roman Achaea Identity and Defence." *JRA* 8: 549–67.

Fowler, R.L. 1995. "Greek Magic. Greek Religion." *Illinois Classical Studies* 20: 1–22.

Frayn, J.M. 1993. *Markets and Fairs in Roman Italy: Their Social and Economic Importance from the Second Century BC to the Third Century AD.* Oxford: Clarendon.

Fredriksen, P. 2010. "Judaizing the Nations: The Ritual Demands of Paul's Gospel." *NTS* 56: 232–52.

Friesen, S.J. 2004. "Poverty in Pauline Studies: Beyond the So-called New Consensus." *JSNT* 26: 323–61.

——. 2005. "Prospects for a Demography of the Pauline Mission: Corinth among the Churches." In *URRC*, 351–70.

——. 2010. "The Wrong Erastus: Ideology, Archaeology, and Exegesis." In *CCxt*, 231–56.

Gadbery, L. 1993. "Roman Wall-Painting at Corinth: New Evidence from East of the Theater." In *The Corinthia in the Roman Period (JRA Sup 8)*, 47–64. Edited by T.E. Gregory. Ann Arbor: JRA.

Gager, J.G. 1992. *Curse Tablets and Binding Spells from the Ancient World.* Oxford: Oxford University Press.

Gallant, T. 1991. *Risk and Survival in Ancient Greece, Reconstructing the Rural Domestic Economy.* Stanford: Stanford University Press.

Gallazzi, C., B. Kramer, and S. Settis (eds.). 2008. *Il Papiro di Artemidoro (P. Artemid.).* Milano: LED Edizioni Universitairie di Lettere Economia Diritto.

Gardner, J.F. 1986. *Women in Roman Law and Society.* Bloomington: Indiana University Press.

——. 1993. *Being a Roman Citizen.* London: Routledge.

——. 2011. "Slavery and Roman Law." In *The Cambridge World History of Slavery, Volume 1: The Ancient Mediterranean World*, 414–37. Edited by K. Bradley and P. Cartledge. Cambridge: Cambridge University Press.

Gargola, D.G. 1995. *Lands, Laws & Gods: Magistrates & Ceremony in the Regulation of Public Lands in Republican Rome.* Chapel Hill: University of North Carolina Press.

Garland, R. 1987. *The Piraeus: From the Fifth to the First Century B.C.* Ithaca: Cornell University Press.

Garnsey, P. 1983. "Grain for Rome." In *Trade in the Ancient Economy*, 118–30. Edited by P. Garnsey, K. Hopkins, and C.R. Whittaker. London: Chatto & Windus.

——. 1988. *Famine and Food Supply in the Graeco-Roman World.* Cambridge: Cambridge University Press.

——. 1996. *Ideas of Slavery from Aristotle to Augustine.* Cambridge: Cambridge University Press.

Garnsey, P. and R. Saller. 1987. *The Roman Empire: Economy, Society and Culture.* Berkeley: University of California Press.

Geagan, D.J. 1968. "Notes on the Agonistic Institutions of Roman Corinth." *GRBS* 9: 69–80.

Gebhard, E.R. 1993. "The Isthmian Games and the Sanctuary of Poseidon in the Early Empire." In *The Corinthia in the Roman Period (JRA Sup 8)*, 78–94. Edited by T.E. Gregory. Ann Arbor: JRA.

Gebhard, E. and M. Dickie. 2003. "The View from the Isthmus, ca. 200 to 44 B.C." In *Corinth* XX, 261–78.

Gee, R. 2010. "Fourth-Style Responses to 'Period Rooms' of the Second and Third Styles at Villa A ('of Poppaea') at Oplontis." Paper presented at Antike Malerei zwischen Lokal stil und Zeitstil. XI. Internationales Kolloquium der AIPMA, 13–17 September 2010, Ephesos-Selçuk/Türkei, Turkey.

Gettens, R.J. and G.L. Stout. 1966. *Painting Materials: A Short Encyclopaedia.* New York: Dover Publications.

Gill, D. 1993. "In Search of the Social Elite in the Corinthian Church." *TynBul* 44: 323–37.

Given, M. 2004. *The Archaeology of the Colonized.* London: Routlege.

Glancy, J. 2002. Slavery in Early Christianity. Oxford: Oxford University Press.

Gleason, M. 2010. "Making Space for Bicultural Identity: Herodes Atticus commemorates Regilla." In *Local Knowledge and Microidentities in the Imperial Greek World,* 125–62. Edited by Tim Whitmarsh. Cambridge: Cambridge University Press.

Graindor, P. 1930. *Un milliardaire antique: Herode Atticus et sa famille.* Cairo: Imprimerie Misr, Société anonyme égyptienne.

Grant, M. 1946. *From Imperium to Auctoritas.* Cambridge: Cambridge University Press.

Grant, R.M. 1977. *Early Christianity and Society: Seven Studies.* San Francisco: Harper & Row.

Gray, P.T.R. 1979. *The Defense of Chalcedon in the East (451–553).* Leiden: Brill.

Gregory, T.E. 1985. "An Early Byzantine Complex at Akra Sophia near Corinth." *Hesperia* 54: 411–28.

———. 2000. "Procopius on Greece." *Antiquité Tardive: revue internationale d'histoire et l'archéologie* 8: 105–15.

———. 2010. "Religion and Society in the Roman Eastern Corinthia." In *CCxt*, 433–76.

Gritsopoulos, T. 1972. "Ἐκκλησιαστικὴ Ἱστορία Κορινθίας." *Peloponnesiaka* 9: 77–84.

Groag, E. 1949. *Die Reichsbeamten von Achaea in spatromischer Zeit.* Budapest: Magyar Nemzeti Múzeum.

Grubbs, J.E. 1994. "'Pagan' and 'Christian' Marriage: The State of the Question." *JECS* 2: 361–412.

———. 2002. *Women and the Law in the Roman Empire: A Sourcebook on Marriage, Divorce, and Widowhood.* New York: Routledge.

Guarducci, M. 1978. *Epigrafia Greca IV: Sacre Pagane e Cristiane.* Rome: Istituto poligrafico dello Stato.

Gustafsson, G. 2000. *Evocatio Deorum: Historical and Mythical Interpretations of Ritualised Conquests in the Expansion of Ancient Rome.* Uppsala: Uppsala University Press.

Hafemann, S.J. 2000. *2 Corinthians: The NIV Application Commentary, from Biblical Text – to Contemporary Life.* Grand Rapids: Zondervan.

Hancock, A-M. 2007. "When Multiplication Doesn't Equal Quick Addition: Examining Intersectionality as a Research Paradigm." *Perspectives on Politics* 5: 63–79.

Hansen, M.H. 1997. "*Emporion.* A Study of the Use and Meaning of the Term in the Archaic and Classical Periods." In *Yet More Studies on the Ancient Greek Polis,* 83–105. Edited by T.H. Nielsen. Stuttgart: F. Steiner.

———. 2006. "*Emporion.* A Study of the Use and Meaning of the Term in the Archaic and Classical Periods." Updated edition of Hanson 1997. In *Greek Colonisation: An Account of Greek Colonies and Other Settlements Overseas. Volume 1,* 1–39. Edited by G.R. Tsetskhladze. Leiden: Brill.

Haraway, D. 2009. "Staying with the Trouble: Becoming with Creatures of Empire." Paper presented at the California College of the Arts, 20 October 2009, San Francisco, CA.

Harper, K. 2010a. "Slave Prices in Late Antiquity (And in the Very Long Term)." *Historia* 59: 206–38.

———. 2010b. "The SC Claudianum in the Codex Theodosianus: Social History and Legal Texts." *CQ* 60: 610.

——. 2011a. "Review Article: Knowledge, Ideology, and Skepticism in Ancient Slave Studies." *AJP* 132: 160–68.

——. 2011b. *Slavery in the Late Roman World, AD 275–425.* Cambridge: Cambridge University Press.

Harrill, J.A. 1995. *The Manumission of Slaves in Early Christianity.* Tübingen: Mohr Siebeck.

——. 2006. *Slaves in the New Testament: Literary, Social, and Moral Dimensions.* Minneapolis: Fortress Press.

Hatzfeld, J. 1919. *Les trafiquants italiens dans l'Orient hellénique.* Paris: De Boccard.

Hauser, F. 1889. *Verzeichnis der neuattischen Reliefs.* Stuttgart: Konrad Wittwer.

Hauvette-Besnault, A. 1888. "Statue d'Athéné trouvé à Athènes, prés du Varvakeion." *BCH* 5: 54–63.

Hayes, C. 2002. *Gentile Impurities and Jewish Identities: Intermarriage and Conversion from the Bible to the Talmud.* Oxford: Oxford University Press.

Hohlfelder, R.L. 1985. "The Building of the Roman Harbour at Kenchreai: Old Technology in a New Era." In *Harbour Archaeology: Proceedings of the First International Workshop on Ancient Mediterranean Harbours, Caesarea Maritima, 24–26.6.83*, 81–86. Edited by A. Raban. Oxford: *BAR-IS.*

Hohlfelder, R.L. and R.L. Vann. 2000. "Cabotage at Aperlae in Ancient Lycia." *IJNA* 29: 126–35.

Honoré, T. 2002. *Ulpian: Pioneer of Human Rights.* 2nd ed. Oxford: Oxford University Press.

Hooper, W.D. and H.B. Ash. 1934. *Cato and Varro: On Agriculture.* Cambridge, MA: Harvard University Press.

Hopkins, K. 1978. "Between Slavery and Freedom: On Freeing Slaves at Delphi." In *Conquerors and Slaves*, 133–71. Edited by K. Hopkins. Cambridge: Cambridge University Press.

Hornblower, Simon and Antony Spawforth (eds.) 2012. *The Oxford Classical Dictionary.* 4th ed. Oxford: Oxford University Press.

Horrell, D.G. and E. Adams. 2004. "Introduction: The Scholarly Quest for Paul's Church at Corinth: A critical Survey." In *Christianity at Corinth: The Quest for the Pauline Church*, 1–47. Edited by E. Adams and D.G. Horrell. Louisville: Westminster John Knox Press.

Horsley, R.A. 1998. *1 Corinthians.* Nashville: Abingdon Press.

Houston, G.W. 1988. "Ports in Perspective: Some Comparative Materials on Roman Merchant Ships and Ports." *AJA* 92: 553–64.

——. 1980. "The Administration of Italian Seaports during the First Three Centuries of the Roman Empire." In *The Seaborne Commerce of Ancient Rome*, 157–71. Edited by J.H. D'Arms and E.C. Kopff. Rome: American Academy in Rome.

Howego, C. 1989. "After the Colt Has Bolted: A Review of Amandry on Roman Corinth." *NC* 149: 99–208.

Hull, M. 2005. *Baptism on Account of the Dead (1 Cor 15:29): an Act of Faith in Resurrection.* Leiden: Brill.

Hurst, H. 2007. "Doing Archaeology in the Classical Lands: Roman." In *Classical Archaeology*, 69–85. Edited by S.E. Alcock and R. Osborne. Malden, MA: Blackwell.

Hykin, A. 1993. *A Survey of Pigments Found in Roman Wall Painting at Corinth.* Unpublished Study.

Jakobs, P.H.F. 1987. *Die Frühchristlichen Ambone Griechenlands.* Bonn: Reihe Klassische Archäologie.

Jaksch, H., W. Siepel, K.L. Weinger, and A. El Goresy. 1983. "Egyptian Blue-Cuprorivaite: A Window to Ancient Egyptian Technology." *Die Naturwissenschaften* 70: 525–35.

James, S.A. 2010. "The Hellenistic Pottery from the Panayia Field, Corinth: Studies in Chronology and Context." Ph.D. Dissertation, The University of Texas at Austin.

——. Forthcoming. "Bridging the Gap: Reconsidering local pottery production in Corinth 146–44 BC," In *Pottery, Peoples and Places*. Edited by P. Bilde and M. Lawall. Aarhus: Centre for Black Sea Studies.

——. In preparation. "A Typology and Chronology of Sikyonian Ceramic Production during the Hellenistic Period."

Jardé, A. 1925. *Les céréales dans l'antiquité grecque*. Paris: Ecole de Boccard.

Johnson Hodge, C. 2007. *If Sons, then Heirs: A Study of Kinship and Ethnicity in the Letters of Paul*. Oxford: Oxford University Press.

——. 2010a. "Married to an Unbeliever: Households, Hierarchies and Holiness in 1 Corinthians 7:12–16." *HTR* 103: 1–25.

——. 2010b. " 'Holy Wives' in Roman Households: 1 Peter 3:1–6." *Journal of Interdisciplinary Feminist Thought*: 4: 1–24.

Johnson-DeBaufre, M. and L.S. Nasrallah. 2011. "Beyond the Heroic Paul: Toward a Feminist and Decolonizing Approach to the Letters of Paul." In *The Colonized Apostle: Paul through Postcolonial Eyes*, 161–74. Edited by C. Stanley. Minneapolis: Fortress Press.

Johnston, S.I. 1996. "Corinthian Medea and the Cult of Hera Akraia." In *Medea: Essays on Medea in Myth, Literature, Philosophy, and Art*, 44–68. Edited by J.J. Claus and S.I. Johnston. Princeton: Princeton University Press.

Jones, C.P. 2001. "The Claudian Monument at Patara." *ZPE* 137: 161–168.

Jongman, W. 2003. "Slavery and the Growth of Rome: The Transformation of Italy in the Second and First Centuries BCE." In *Rome the Cosmopolis*, 100–122. Edited by C. Edwards and G. Woolf. Cambridge: Cambridge University Press.

Jordan, D.R. 1985. "A Survey of Greek *Defixiones* Not Included in the Special Corpora." *GRBS* 26: 151–97.

——. 1994. "Inscribed Lamps from a Cult at Corinth in Late Antiquity." *HTR* 87: 223–29.

——. 2000. "New Greek Curse Tablets (1985–2000)." *GRBS* 41: 5–46.

Joshel, Sandra R. 1992. *Work, Identity, and Legal Status at Rome: A Study of the Occupational Inscriptions*. Norman: University of Oklahoma Press.

Kakoulli, I. 2009. *Greek Painting Techniques and Materials from the Fourth to the First Century B.C.* London: Archetype Publications.

Kallet-Marx, R. 1995. *Hegemony to empire: the development of the Roman Imperium in the East from 148 to 62 B.C.* Berkeley: University of California Press.

Kardulias, P.N. 1995. "Architecture, Energy, and Social Evolution at Isthmia, Greece: Some Thoughts about Late Antiquity in the Korinthia." *JMA* 8: 33–59.

——. 2005. *From Classical to Byzantine: Social Evolution in Late Antiquity and the Fortress at Isthmia, Greece*. Oxford: *BAR-IS*.

Kearsley, R.A. 1999. "Women in Public Life in the Roman East: Junia Theodora, Claudia Metrodora, and Phoebe, Benefactress of Paul." *TynBul* 50: 189–211.

Kelly, J.N.D. 1950. *Early Christian Creeds*. London: Longmans, Green, & Co.

Kelsey, F. 1926. *Excavations at Carthage 1925, a Preliminary Report*. New York: Macmillan.

Kittredge, C. 2000. "Corinthian Women Prophets and Paul's Argumentation in 1 Corinthians." In *Paul and Politics: Ekklesia, Israel, Imperium, Interpretation*, 103–109. Edited by R.A. Horsley. Harrisburg: Trinity Press International.

Klauck, H-J. 2000. "Junia Theodora und die Gemeinde von Korinth." In *Kirche und Volk Gottes: Festschrift für Jürgen Roloff zum 70. Geburtstag*, 42–57. Edited by M. Karrer, W. Kraus, and O. Merk. Neukirchen-Vluyn: Neukirchener.

Klawans, J. 2000. *Impurity and Sin in Ancient Judaism*. Oxford: Oxford University Press.

Kleiner, F.S. 1977. "Artists in the Roman World: An Itinerant Workshop in Augustan Gaul." *MÉFRA* 89: 661–96.

Klinkert, W. 1957. "Bemerkungen zur Technik der pompejanischen Wanddekoration." *RM* 64: 111–48.

Klynne, A. 2002. "Terra Sigillata from the Villa of Livia, Rome. Consumption and Discard in the Early Principate." Ph.D. Dissertation, Uppsala University.

Knust, J. 2006. *Abandoned to Lust: Sexual Slander and Ancient Christianity*. New York: Columbia University Press.

Koester, H. 2005. "Corinth General Information 1." In *Cities of Paul: Images and Interpretations from the Harvard New Testament Archaeology Project.* CD-ROM. Minneapolis: Fortress Press.

Kolb, F. 2002. "Lykiens Weg in die Römische Provinzordnung." In *Widerstand Anpassung – Integration. Die griechische Staatenwelt und Rom: Festschrift für Jürgen Deininger zum 65. Geburtstag,* 207–21. Edited by N. Ehrhardt and L-M. Günther. Stuttgart: Steiner.

Kopytoff, I. 1989. "The Cultural Biography of Things: Commoditization as Process." In *The Social Life of Things: Commodities in Cultural Perspective,* 64–94. Edited by A. Appadurai. Cambridge: Cambridge University Press.

Kostakis, K. 1998. "The Past Is Ours: Images of Greek Macedonia." In *Archaeology under Fire: Nationalism, Politics and Heritage in the Eastern Mediterranean and Middle East,* 44–67. Edited by L. Meskell. London: Routledge.

Laird, M.L. 2010. "The Emperor in a Roman Town: The Base of the Augustales in the Forum at Corinth." In *Ccxt,* 67–116.

Lake, K. (trans.). 1912. *The Apostolic Fathers. Volume I.* Cambridge: Harvard University Press, 1912.

Lambros, S.P. 1905. "Τὰ τείχη το ἰσθμοῦ Κορίνθου κατὰ τοὺς μέσους αἰῶνας." *Νέος Ἑλληνομνήμων* 2: 268–69.

Lampakis, G. 1906. "Ἑτέραι Χριστιανικαὶ ἀρχαιότητες, 3ων." *Deltion tes Christianikes Archaiologikes Hetaireias* 6: 46–47.

Lawall, M. 2006. "Consuming the West in the East: Amphoras of the Western Mediterranean in Athens before 86 BC." In *Old pottery in a new century: innovating perspectives in Roman pottery studies,* 265–86. Edited by M. Malfitana, J. Poblome, and J. Lund. Catania: Istituto per i beni archeologici e monumentali.

Le Saint, W.P. 1956. *Tertullian: Treatises on Marriage and Remarriage.* Westminster: The Newman Press.

Leach, E.W. 1982. "Patrons, Painters, and Patterns: The Anonymity of Romano-Campanian Painting and the Transition from the Second to the Third Style." In *Roman Literary and Artistic Patronage in Ancient Rome,* 158–67. Edited by B. Gold. Austin: University of Texas Press. Reprinted in *Roman Art in Context: An Anthology,* 133–60. Edited by E. d'Ambra, 1993. Englewood Cliffs, N.J.: Prentice Hall.

——. 2004. *The Social Life of Painting in Ancient Rome and on the Bay of Naples.* Cambridge: Cambridge University Press.

Leake, W.M. 1830. *Travels in the Morea: Volume 1.* London: J. Murray.

Lemprière, J. and C. Anthon. 1831. *A Classical Dictionary.* 3rd ed. New York: Harper & Brothers.

Lepinski, S. 2008. "Roman Wall Paintings from Panayia Field, Ancient Corinth, Greece: A Contextual Study." Ph.D. Dissertation, Bryn Mawr College.

——. Forthcoming. "A Diachronic Perspective of Roman Paintings from Ancient Corinth, Greece: Period Styles and Regional Traditions." Association International pour la Peinture Murale Antique. *Antike Malerei zwischen Lokal stil und Zeitstil.* Vienna: Verlag der Österreichische Akademie der Wissenschaften.

Lepinski, S. and H. Brekoulaki. 2010. "Painting Practices in Roman Corinth: Contextualizing Analytical Studies on Wall Paintings from Panayia Field and the Area East of the Theater." Paper read at the 111th Annual Meeting of the Archaeological Institute of America, 7–10 January, Anaheim, CA.

Lewis, M.J.T. 2001. "Railways in the Greek and Roman World." In *Early Railways. A Selection of Papers from the First International Early Railways Conference,* 8–19. Edited by A. Guy and J. Rees. London: Newcomen Society.

Liddell, H.G. and R. Scott. 1996. *A Greek-English Lexicon.* Oxford: Clarendon.

Limberis, V. 2005. "Ecclesiastical Ambiguities: Corinth in the fourth and fifth centuries." In *URRC,* 443–57.

Ling, R. 1991. *Roman Wall Painting.* Cambridge, MA: Harvard University Press.

Linton, H. 1881. *The First (second) Epistle to the Corinthians, with Notes and Appendix,* London: George Philip & Sons.

Lintott, A. 1992. *Judicial Reform and Land Reform in the Roman Republic*. Cambridge: Cambridge University Press.

Llewelyn, S.R. 1989. *New documents illustrating early Christianity: a review of the Greek inscriptions and papyri published in 1980–81*. North Ryde: Ancient History Documentary Research Centre, Macquarie University.

Lohmann, H. Forthcoming. "Der Diolkos von Korinth – eine antike Schiffsschleppe?" In *The Corinthia and the Northeast Peloponnesus: Topography and History from Prehistory Until the End of Antiquity*. Edited by N. Kissas.

Lolos, Y. 2011. *Land of Sikyon: Archaeology and History of a Greek City-State*. Princeton: American School of Classical Studies at Athens.

Lund, J. 2005. "An Economy of Consumption. The Eastern Sigillata A Industry in the Late Hellenistic period." In *Making, Moving and Managing: The New World of Ancient Economies*, 233–52. Edited by Z. Archibald, J. Davies and V. Gabrielsen. Oxford: Oxbow.

MacDonald, B.R. 1986. "The Diolkos." *JHS* 106: 191–95.

MacDonald, M.Y. 1990. "Women Holy in Body and Spirit: the Social Setting of 1 Corinthians 7." *NTS* 36: 161–81.

———. 1996. *Early Christian Women and Pagan Tradition: The Power of the Hysterical Woman*. Cambridge: Cambridge University Press.

Marchal, J. 2011. "The Usefulness of an Onesimus: The Sexual Use of Slaves and Philemon." *JBL* 130: 749–70.

Markus, R.A. 1979. "Carthage – Prima Justiniana – Ravenna: an Aspect of Justinian's Kirchenpolitik." *Byzantion* 49: 277–306.

Martin, A. 1997. "Roman and late antique fine wares at Olympia." *RCRFActa* 35: 211–15.

Martin, D.B. 1990. *Slavery as Salvation: The Metaphor of Slavery in Pauline Christianity*. New Haven: Yale University Press.

———. 2001. "Review Essay: Justin J. Meggitt, Paul, Poverty and Survival." *JSNT* 84: 51–64.

Martin, T. 1977. "Inscriptions at Corinth." *Hesperia* 46: 178–98.

Mason, H.J. 1971. "Lucius at Corinth." *Phoenix* 25: 160–65.

Mathews, T.F. 1971. *The Early Churches of Constantinople: Architecture and Liturgy*. University Park, PA: Pennsylvania State University Press.

McCall, L. 2005. "The Complexity of Intersectionality." *Signs* 30: 1771–800.

McCormick, M. 2000. *Origins of the European Economy: Communications and Commerce AD 300–900*. Cambridge: Cambridge University Press.

McGrew, W.W. 1985. *Land and Revolution in Modern Greece, 1800–1881: The Transition in the Tenure and Exploitation of Land from Ottoman Rule to Independence*. Kent, OH: Kent State University Press.

Mckenzie, J. 1990. *The Architecture of Petra*. Oxford: Oxford University Press.

McLean, B.H. 2002. *An Introduction to Greek Epigraphy of the Hellenistic and Roman Periods from Alexander the Great down to the Reign of Constantine (323 B.C.–A.D. 337)*. Ann Arbor: University of Michigan Press.

Meeks, W. 1983. *The First Urban Christians: The Social World of the Apostle Paul*. New Haven: Yale University Press.

Meggiolaro, V., U. Pappalardo, and P.P. Vergerio. 1995. "Pitture romana a Corinto: Southeast Building." In *I temi figurativi nella pittura parietale antica (IV sec. a.C.–IV sec. d.C.). Atti del VI Convegno Internazionale sulla Pittura Parietale Antica*, 241–396. Edited by D.S. Corlàita. Bologna: University Press.

Meggiolaro, V., G.M. Molin, U. Pappalardo, and P.P. Vergerio. 1997. "Contribution to Studies on Roman Wall Painting. Materials and Techniques in Greece: Corinth, The Southeast Building." In *Roman Wall Painting: Materials, Techniques, Analysis, and Conservation; Proceedings of the International Workshop Fribourg 7–9 March 1996*, 105–18. Edited by H. Béarat, M. Fuchs, M. Maggetti, and D. Paunier. Fribourg: Institute of Mineralogy and Petrography.

Meggitt, J.J. 1998. *Paul, Poverty and Survival*. Edinburgh: T&T Clark.

Meiggs, R. 1973. *Roman Ostia*. 2nd ed. Oxford: Clarendon.

Meritt, B.D. 1946. "Greek Inscriptions." *Hesperia* 15: 169–253.

Mielsch, H. 2001. *Römische Wandmalerei.* Darmstadt: Wissenschaftliche Buchgesellschaft.

Milanovic, B., P. Lindert, and J. Williamson. 2007a. "Measuring Ancient Inequality." Policy Research. The World Bank Development Research Group Poverty Team Working Paper Series 4412. Online at: http://www-wds.worldbank.org/servlet/WDSContentServer/WDSP/IB/2007/11/28/000158349_20071128113445/Rendered/PDF/wps4412.pdf. Accessed 3 November 2010.

———. 2007b. "Pre-Industrial Inequality: An Early Conjectural Map." Online at: http://www.economics.harvard.edu/files/faculty/62_Pre-Industrial_Inequality.pdf. Accessed 3 November 2010.

Miller, S.G. 1989. "Macedonian Tombs: Their Architecture and Architectural Decoration." In *Macedonia and Greece in Late Classical and Early Hellenistic Times,* 153–71. Edited by B. Barr-Sharrar and E.N. Borza. Washington, DC: National Gallery of Art.

Miller-Collett, S.G. 1993. *The Tomb of Lyson and Kallikles: A Painted Macedonian Tomb.* Mainz am Rhein: Philipp von Zabern.

Millis, B. 2006. "'Miserable Huts' in Post-146 B.C. Corinth." Hesperia 75: 397–404.

———. 2010a. "The Social and Ethnic Origins of the Colonists in Early Roman Corinth." In *CCxt,* 13–36.

———. 2010b. "Corinthians in Exile 146–44 BC." In *Onomatologos: Studies in Greek Names Presented to Elaine Matthews,* 244–57. Edited by R. Catling and F. Marchand. Oxford: Oxbow.

Milnor, K. 2010. "Women." In *The Oxford Handbook to Roman Studies,* 815–26. Edited by A. Barchiesi and W. Scheidel. New York: Oxford University Press.

Mitchell, M.M. 1991. *Paul and the Rhetoric of Reconciliation: An Exegetical Investigation of the Language and Composition of 1 Corinthians.* Louisville: Westminster John Knox Press.

Möller, A. 2007. "Classical Greece: Distribution." In *The Cambridge Economic History of the Greco-Roman world,* 362–84. Edited by W. Scheidel, I. Morris, and R. Saller. Cambridge: Cambridge University Press.

Mommsen, T. and P. Krüger (eds.). 1905. *Theodosiani libri XVI cum Constitutionibus Sirmondianis et Leges novellae ad Theodosianum pertinentes.* 3 vols. Berlin: Apud Weidmannos.

Monceaux, P. 1884. "Fouilles et recherches archéologiques au sanctuaire des Jeux Isthmique." *Gazette archéologique:* 273–85, 354–63.

Moormann, E. 1993. *Functional and Spatial Analysis of Wall Painting: Proceedings of the Fifth International Congress on Ancient Wall Painting.* Leiden: BABesch.

Mora, P., L. Mora, and P. Philippot. 1984. *Conservation of Wall Paintings.* London: Butterworth.

Moreno, P. 1979a. "La pittura in Macedonia." *Storia e Civiltà dei Greci* 6: 703–21.

———. 1979b. "La pittura tra classicità ed ellenismo: La pittura Macedonia." *Storia e Civiltà dei Greci* 6: 458–89.

Morley, N. 2007a. "The Early Roman Empire: Distribution." In *The Cambridge Economic History of the Greco-Roman World,* 570–91. Edited by W. Scheidel, I. Morris, and R. Saller. Cambridge: Cambridge University Press.

———. 2007b. *Trade in Classical Antiquity.* Cambridge: Cambridge University Press.

Morris, I. 2011. "Archaeology and Greek Slavery." In *The Cambridge World History of Slavery, Volume 1: The Ancient Mediterranean World,* 176–93. Edited by K. Bradley and P. Cartledge. Cambridge: Cambridge University Press.

Morrison, J.S. and J.F. Coates. 1989. *An Athenian Trireme Reconstructed: the British Sea Trials of Olympias.* Oxford: BAR-IS.

Morrison, J.S., J.F. Coates, and N.B. Rankov. 2000. *The Athenian Trireme: the History and Reconstruction of an Ancient Greek Warship.* 2nd ed. Cambridge: Cambridge University Press.

Mouritsen, H. 2011. *The Freedman in the Roman World*. Cambridge: Cambridge University Press.

Munier, C. 1980. *Tertullien: A Son Epouse*. Paris: Les Editions du Cerf.

Murphy-O'Connor, J. 2002. *St. Paul's Corinth: Texts and Archaeology*. 3rd ed. Collegeville, MN: Liturgical Press.

Nash, J.C. 2008. "Re-thinking Intersectionality." *Feminist Review* 89: 1–15.

Nasrallah, L. 2010. *Christian Responses to Roman Art and Architecture: The Second-Century Church amid the Spaces of Empire*. Cambridge: Cambridge University Press.

———. 2012. "Grief in Corinth: The Roman City and Paul's Corinthian Correspondence." In *Contested Spaces: Houses and Temples in the Roman Empire and the New Testament*, 109–40. Edited by D. Balch and A. Weissenrieder. Tübingen: Mohr Siebeck.

Nelson, J. 1976. "Symbols in Context: Rulers Inauguration Rituals in Byzantium and the West in the Early Middle Ages." *Studies in Church History* 13: 97–119.

Newton, M. 1985. *The Concept of Purity at Qumran and in the Letters of Paul*. Cambridge: Cambridge University Press.

Økland, J. 1998. "'*In Publicum Procurrendi*': Women in the Public Space of Roman Greece." In *Aspects of Women in Antiquity: Proceedings of the First Nordic Symposium on Women's Lives in Antiquity, Göteborg 12–15 June 1997*, 127–41. Edited by L.L. Lovén and A. Strömberg. Jonsered: Paul Åströms Förlag.

———. 2010. "Ceres, Κόρη, and Cultural Complexity: Divine Personality Definitions and Human Worshippers in Roman Corinth." In *CCxt*, 199–229.

Oleson, J.P. 1988. "The technology of Roman harbors." *IJNA* 17: 147–57.

Orlandos, A. 1957. *Η Ξυλόστεγος Παλαιοχριστιανική Βασιλική Της Μεσογειακής Λεκάνης: Μελέτη Περί Της Γενέσεως, Της Καταγωγης, Της Αρχιτεκτονικής Μορφής Και Της Διακοσμήσεως Των Χριστιανικών Οίκων Λατρείας Από Των Αποστολικών Χρόνων Μέχρις Ιουστινιανού*. Athens: Bibliothiki tis en Athinais Archaiologikis Etaireias.

Osborne, R. and S.E. Alcock. 2007. "Introduction." In *Classical Archaeology*, 1–10. Edited by S.E. Alcock and R. Osborne. Malden, MA: Blackwell.

Osiek, C. 2005. "*Diakonos* and *prostatis*: Women's patronage in Early Christianity." *Hervormde Teologiese Studies* 61: 347–70.

Palinkas, J. and J.A. Herbst. 2011. "A Roman Road Southeast of the Forum at Corinth: Technology and Urban Development." *Hesperia* 80: 287–336.

Pallas, D.I. 1957. "Προτοχριστιανίκι Κόρινθος." *Peloponnesiaki Protochronia* 52–62.

———. 1969. "Νεκρικόν Υπογέιον εν Κόρινθο." *Prakt*: 121–34, vPin.137–44.

———. 1975. "Investigations sur les monuments chrétiens de Grèce avant Constantin." *CahArch* 24: 1–19.

———. 1977. *Les Monuments Paléochrétiens De Grèce Découverts De 1959 À 1973*. Vatican: Pontificio Istituto di Archaeologia Cristiana.

———. 1979. "Corinth et Nicopolis pendant le haut moyen-âge." *Felix Ravenna* 18: 93–142.

———. 1979/80. "Monuments et texts: rémarques sur la liturgie dans quelques basiliques paléochrétiens." *Επετηρίς Εταιρείας Βυζανινών Σπουδών* 44: 37–116.

———. 1984. "L'édifice culturel chrétien et la liturgie dans l'Illuricum oriental." *Studi Antichita Cristiana* 1: 544–57.

———. 1990. "Korinth." In *Reallexicon zur Byzantinischen Kunst 4* s.v., 745–811. Stuttgart: A. Hiersemann.

Pallas, D.I., S. Charitonidis, and J. Venencie. 1959. "Inscriptions Lyciennes trouvées a Solômos près de Corinthe." *BCH* 83: 496–508.

Papafotiou, A.E. 2007. *Ο δίολκος στον ισθμό της Κορίνθου*. Corinth: [s.n.].

Pappalardo, U. 2000. "Pittura Romana a Corinto: il 'south-east building'." *ASAtene* 76–8: 315–74.

Paterson, J. 1998. "Trade and Traders in the Roman World: Scale, Structure and Organization." In *Trade, Traders and the Ancient City*, 149–67. Edited by P. Helen and C. Smith. London: Routledge.

Paynter, R. and R.H. McGuire. 1991. "The Archaeology of Inequality: Material Culture, Domination and Resistance." In *The Archaeology of Inequality*, 1–27. Edited by R. Paynter and R.H. McGuire. Oxford: Blackwell.

Peña, J.T. 2007. *Roman Pottery in the Archaeological Record*. Cambridge: Cambridge University Press.

Perry, E. 2001. "Iconography and the Dynamics of Patronage: A Sarcophagus from the Family of Herodes Atticus." *Hesperia* 70: 461–92.

Petersen, L. 2006. *The Freedman in Roman Art and Art History*. Cambridge: Cambridge University Press.

Petropoulos, E.K. 2005. *Hellenic Colonization in Euxeinos Pontos. Penetration, Early Establishment and the Problem of the "Emporion" Revisited*. Oxford: Archaeopress.

Pettegrew, D.K. 2006. "Corinth on the Isthmus: Studies of the End of an Ancient Landscape." Ph.D. Dissertation, Ohio State University.

———. 2011a. "Niketas Ooryphas Drags his Fleet: Crossing the Corinthian Isthmus in 872 AD." Paper presented at the annual meeting of the Archaeological Institute of America, San Antonio, TX.

———. 2011b. "The *Diolkos* and the Commercial Facility of the Isthmus of Corinth." *AJA* 115: 549–74.

Pharr, C. 1952. *The Theodosian Code and Novels, and the Sirmondian Constitutions. The Corpus of Roman Law 1*. Princeton: Princeton University Press.

Philadelpheus, A. 1918. "᾿Αραία ᾿επαυλὶς μετὰ νυμφαίου ἐν Λεχαίῳ τῆς Κορινθίας." *ArchDelt* 4: 125–35.

Pickersgill, C. 2009. "Transitional periods in Roman Sparta observed in the pottery assemblages." In *Sparta and Laconia: From Prehistory to Pre-Modern. British School at Athens Studies: Vol. 16*, 293–300. Edited by W. Cavanaugh, C. Gallou, and M. Georgiadis. London: British School of Archaeology at Athens.

Pietri, C. 1984. "La géographie de l'Illyricum ecclésiastique et ses relations avec l'Églize de Rome (Vᵉ–VIᵉ siècles)." In *Villes et peuplement dans l'Illyricum protobyzantin: actes du colloque organisé par l'École française de Rome*, 21–59. Rome: École française de Rome.

Piranomonte, M. 2002. *Il santuario della Musica e il Bosco Sacro di Anna Perenna*. Milano: Electa.

Pleket, H.W. 1983. "Urban Elites and Business in the Greek Part of the Roman Empire." In *Trade in the Ancient Economy*, 131–44. Edited by P. Garnsey, K. Hopkins, and C.R. Whittaker. London: Chatto & Windus.

Pomeroy, S.B. 1975. *Goddesses, Whores, Wives, and Slaves: Women in Classical Antiquity*. New York: Schocken.

———. 1994. *Xenophon: Oeconomicus: A Social and Historical Commentary*. Oxford: Clarendon.

———. 2007. *The Murder of Regilla: a Case of Domestic Violence in Antiquity*. Cambridge, MA: Harvard University Press.

Pomey, P. and A. Tchernia. 1978. "Le tonnage maximum des navires de commerce romains." *Archaeonautica* 2: 233–51.

Preisendanz, K. (ed.). 1928–1931. *Papyri Graecae Magicae: Die Griechischen Zauberpapyri*. 2 vols. 2nd ed. Leipzig: B.G. Teubner.

Price, R. 2009. *The Acts of the Council of Constantinople of 553*. Liverpool: Liverpool University Press.

Pringle, D. 1981. *The Defence of Byzantine Africa from Justinian to the Arab Conquest: An Account of the Military History and Archaeology of the African Provinces in the Sixth and Seventh Centuries*. Oxford: BAR-IS.

Purcell, N. 2005a. "Romans in the Roman World." In *The Cambridge Companion to the Age of Augustus*, 85–105. Edited by K. Galinsky. Cambridge: Cambridge University Press.

———. 2005b. "The Ancient Mediterranean: The View from the Customs House." In *Rethinking the Mediterranean*, 200–32. Edited by W.V. Harris. Oxford: Oxford University Press.

Raban, A., M. Artzy, B. Goodman, and Z. Gal. 2009. *The Harbour of Sebastos (Caesarea Maritima) in its Roman Mediterranean Context*. Oxford: Archaeopress.

Raepsaet, G. 1993. "Le Diolkos de l'Isthme à Corinthe: son Tracé, son Fonctionnement." *BCH* 117: 233–56.

———. 2008. "Land Transport, Part 2: Riding, Harnesses, and Vehicles." In *The Oxford Handbook of Engineering and Technology in the Classical World*, 580–605. Edited by P. Oleson. Oxford: Oxford University Press.

Ratzan, D. 2011. "Getting to Yes: The Institutional Context of Economic Divination in Roman Egypt." Paper presented at Princeton University, 12 November 2011, Princeton, NJ.

Reber, K. 1998. *Eretria Ausgrabungen und Forschungen X: Die Klassischen und hellenistischen Wohnhäuser im Westquartier*. Lausanne: Editions Payot.

Reed, C.M. 2003. *Maritime Traders in the Ancient Greek World*. Cambridge: Cambridge University Press.

Reinhard, J.P. 2005. "The Roman Bath at Isthmia: Decoration, Cult, and Herodes Atticus." Ph.D. Dissertation, University of Minnesota.

Richards, L.E. (ed.). 1909. *Letters and Journals of Samuel Gridley Howe*. Boston: Estes.

Richardson, R.B. 1900. "Pirene." *AJA* 4: 204–39.

Rickman, G.E. 1985. "Towards a Study of Roman Ports." In *Harbour Archaeology*, 105–14. Edited by A. Raban. London: *BAR-IS*.

———. 1988. "The archaeology and history of Roman ports." *IJNA* 17: 257–67.

Ridgway, B.S. 1981. "Sculpture from Corinth." *Hesperia* 50: 422–48.

Ridley, R. 1986. "To be Taken with a Pinch of Salt." *CP* 81: 140–46.

Rife, J.L. 2010. "Religion and Society at Roman Kenchreai." In *CCxt*, 391–432.

Rife, J.L., M. Moore Morison, A. Barbet, R.K. Dunn, D.H. Ubelaker, and F. Monier. 2007. "Life and Death at a Port in Roman Greece: The Kenchreai Cemetery Project, 2002–2006." *Hesperia* 76: 143–82.

Ristow, S. 1998. *Frühchristliche Baptisterien*. Münster: Aschendorfsche Verlagsbuchhandlung.

Rizakis, A. 2001. "La cite grecque entre la periode hellenistiques et l'Empire." In *Recherche recentes sur le monde hellenistique*, 75–96. Edited by R. Frei-Stolba and K. Gex. Bern: Peter Lang.

Robert, L. 1960. "Recherches épigraphiques." *REA* 62: 276–361.

———. 1966. "Inscriptions de l'antiquité et du Bas-Empire à Corinthe." *REG* 79: 733–70.

Robinson, B.A. 2001. "Fountains and the Culture of Water at Roman Corinth." Ph.D. Dissertation, University of Pennsylvania.

———. 2005. "Fountains and the Formation of Cultural Identity at Roman Corinth." In *URRC*, 111–40.

———. 2011. *Histories of Peirene: a Corinthian Fountain in Three Millennia*. Princeton: American School of Classical Studies at Athens.

Robinson, H. 1963. "Excavations at Corinth. Chronika." *ArchDelt* 18: 77–80.

———. 1965. "Excavations at Ancient Corinth, 1959–1963." *Klio* 46: 289–305.

Rohn, A.H., E. Barnes, and G.D.R. Sanders. 2009. "An Early Ottoman Cemetery at Ancient Corinth." *Hesperia* 78: 501–615.

Romano, D.G. 1993. "Post-146 B.C. Land Use in Corinth, and Planning of the Roman Colony of 44 B.C." In *The Corinthia in the Roman Period (JRA Sup 8)*, 9–30. Edited by T.E. Gregory. Ann Arbor: JRA.

———. 2003. "City Planning, Centuriation, and Land Division in Roman Corinth: Colonia Laus Iulia Corinthiensis & Colonia Iulia Flavia Augusta Corinthiensis." In *Corinth XX*, 279–301.

———. 2005. "Urban and Rural Planning in Roman Corinth." In *URRC*, 25–59.

Romano, I.B. 1994. "A Hellenistic Deposit from Corinth: Evidence for Interim Period Activity (146–44 B.C.)." *Hesperia* 63: 57–104.

Roselaar, S.T. 2008. "Public land in the Roman Republic: a Social and Economic History of the *Ager Publicus*, 396–89 BC." Ph.D Dissertation, Leiden University.

Rosenfeld, Ben-Zion, and J. Menirav. 2005. *Markets and Marketing in Roman Palestine.* Leiden: Brill.

Rothaus, R. 1994. "Urban Space, Agricultural Space and Villas in Late Roman Corinth." In *Structures rurales et sociétés antiques,* 391–96. Edited by P.N. Doukellis and L.G. Mendoni. Paris: Belles Lettres.

———. 1995. "Lechaion, Western Port of Corinth: A Preliminary Archaeology and History." *OJA* 14: 293–306.

———. 2000. *Corinth, the First City of Greece: An Urban History of Late Antique Cult and Religion.* Leiden: Brill.

Rotroff, S.I. 1997. "From Greek to Roman in Athenian Ceramics." In *The Romanization of Athens,* 98–116. Edited by M. Hoff and S.I. Rotroff. Oxford: Oxbow.

Rougé, J. 1966. "Recherches sur l'organisation du commerce maritime en Méditerranée sous l'Empire Romain." Ph.D. Dissertation, Impr. nationale.

Rouillard, P. "L'Emporion chez Strabon: B. Les Emporia Strabioniens: Fonctions et Activités." In *L'Emporion,* 35–46. Edited by A. Bresson and P. Rouillard. Paris: Centre Pierre Paris.

Rozenberg, S. 1996. "The Wall Paintings of the Herodian Palace at Jericho." In *Judaea and the Greco-Roman World in the Time of Herod in Light of Archaeological Evidence,* 121–28. Edited by K. Fittschen and G. Foerster. Göttingen: Vandenhoeck & Ruprecht.

———. 2004. "The Role of Colour in Herod's Palace at Jericho." In *Colour in the Ancient Mediterranean World,* 22–31. Edited by L. Cleland, K. Stears, and G. Davies. Oxford: BAR-IS.

Sackett, L.H., 1992. 'Section 6: The Roman Pottery." In *Knossos: From Greek City to Roman Colony. Excavations at the Unexplored Mansion II,* 148–78. Edited by L.H. Sackett. London: British School of Archaeology at Athens.

Sallares, R. 1991. *The Ecology of the Ancient Greek World.* Ithaca: Cornell University Press.

Salmon, J. 1984. *Wealthy Corinth: A History of the city to 338 B.C.* Oxford: Clarendon.

Sanders, G.D.R. 1996. "Portage of Ships Across the Isthmus" In *7th International Symposium on Ship Construction in Antiquity: Tropis VII: Pylos, 26, 27, 28, 29 August 1999: Proceedings,* 423–28. Edited by H. Tzalas. Athens: Hellenic Institute for the Preservation of Nautical Tradition.

———. 1999. "A Late Roman Bath at Corinth: Excavations in the Panayia Field, 1995–1996." *Hesperia* 68: 441–80.

———. 2000. "New Relative and Absolute Chronologies for 9th to 13th Century Glazed Wares at Corinth: Methodology and Social Conclusions." In *Byzanz als Raum. Zu Methoden und Inhalten der historischen Geographie des östlischen Mittelmeerraumes im Mittelalter,* 153–73. Edited by K. Belke, F. Hild, and J. Koder. Vienna: Verlag der Österreichische Akademie der Wissenschaften.

———. 2004. "Problems in Interpreting Rural and Urban Landscape in Southern Greece AD 365–700." In *Landscapes of Change: Rural Evolutions in Late Antiquity and the Early Middle Ages,* 163–93. Edited by N. Christie. Aldershot: Ashgate Press.

———. 2005a. "Archaeological Evidence for Early Christianity and the End of Hellenic Religion in Corinth." In *URRC,* 419–42.

———. 2005b. "Urban Corinth: An Introduction." In *URRC,* 11–24.

Sanders, G.D.R., S.A. James, I. Tzonou-Herbst, and J. Herbst. Forthcoming (2014). "An Overview of the Panayia Field Excavations at Corinth: The Neolithic to Hellenistic Phases." *Hesperia* 83.

Sanders, G.D.R. and I.K. Whitbread. 1990. "Central Places and Major Roads in the Peloponnese." *BSA* 85: 333–61.

Scahill, D. 2012. "The South Stoa at Corinth: Design, Construction, and Function of the Greek Phase." Ph.D. Dissertation: University of Bath.

Schaff, P. and W. Henry (eds.). 1994. *Jerome: Letters and Select Works. Nicene and Post-Nicene Fathers. Volume VI.* Peabody, MA: Hendrickson.

Scheidel, W. 2008. "The Comparative Economics of Slavery in the Greco-Roman World." In *Slave Systems: Ancient and Modern,* 105–26. Edited by E. Dal Lago and C. Katsari. Cambridge: Cambridge University Press.

——. 2011. "The Roman Slave Supply." In *The Cambridge World History of Slavery, Volume 1: The Ancient Mediterranean World*, 287–310. Edited by K. Bradley and P. Cartledge. Cambridge: Cambridge University Press.

Scheidel, W., and S.J. Friesen. 2009. "The Size of the Economy and the Distribution of Income in the Roman Empire." *JRS* 99: 61–91.

Scheper-Hughes, N. and L. Wacquant (eds.). 2002. *Commodifying Bodies*. London: SAGE.

Schneider, G. 2000. "Chemical and Mineralogical Studies of Late Hellenistic to Byzantine Pottery Production in the Eastern Mediterranean." *RCFActa* 36: 526–35.

Schüssler Fiorenza, E. 1999. *Rhetoric and Ethic: the Politics of Biblical Studies*. Minneapolis: Fortress Press.

——. 2007. *The Power of the Word: Scripture and the Rhetoric of Empire*. Minneapolis: Fortress Press.

——. 2009. "Introduction: Exploring the Intersections of Race, Gender, Status, and Ethnicity in Early Christian Studies." In *Prejudice and Christian Beginnings: Investigating Race, Gender, and Ethnicity in Early Christian Studies*, 1–23. Edited by L.S. Nasrallah and E. Schüssler Fiorenza. Minneapolis: Fortress Press.

Schwartz, E. 1939. *Drei domatische Schriften Iustinians*. Munich: Verlag der Bayerischen Akademie der Wissenschaften.

Scott, J.C. 1985. *Weapons of the Weak: Everyday Forms of Peasant Resistance*. New Haven: Yale University Press.

——. 1986. "Everyday Forms of Peasant Resistance." In *Everyday Forms of Peasant Resistance in South-East Asia*, 5–35. Edited by J.C. Scott and D.J. Kerkvliet. London: Frank Cass.

Scranton, R.L. 1935. "Corinth Excavation Notebook" 150.

Segré, M. (ed.). 1944–45. *Tituli Calymnii. Annuario della Scuola Archeologica di Atene. Volume 22/23*. Roma, Scuola archeologica italiana di Atene.

Shaner, K. 2012. "Religious Practices of the Enslaved: A Case Study in Roman Ephesos." Th.D. Dissertation, Harvard University: The Divinity School.

Shaw, J.W. 1972. "Greek and Roman harbourworks." In *A History of Seafaring Based on Underwater Archaeology*, 87–112. Edited by G. Bass. London: Thames & Hudson.

Shear, T.L. 1925. "Excavations at Corinth in 1925." *AJA* 29: 381–87.

——. 1931. "The Excavation of Roman Chamber Tombs at Corinth in 1931." *AJA* 35: 424–41.

Shelley, J.M. 1943. "The Christian Basilica Near the Chenchrean Gate at Corinth." *Hesperia* 12: 166–89.

Sherwin-White, A.N. 1973. *The Roman Citizenship*. Oxford: Clarendon.

Shoe, L.T. 1964. "Roman Ionic Base in Corinth." In *Essays in Memory of Karl Lehmann*, 300–303. Edited by L.F. Sandler. New York: New York University Press.

Siganidou, M.K. 1981. " Ἀνασκαφές Πελλας." *Prakt*: 42–54.

——. 1982. " Ἡ ἰδιοτίκι κατικία στην αρχαία Πελλας." *Archaiologia* 2: 31–36.

——. 1990. "Πολεοδομίκα προβλέματα της Πελλας." *Polis kai Xora* 167–74.

Silliman, S.W. 2001. "Theoretical Perspectives on Labor and Colonialism: Reconsidering the California Missions." *JAnthArch* 20: 379–407.

Skias, A. 1893. " Ἐπιγραφαὶ Κορίνθου." *AEph*: 123.

Skinner, E.B. 2008. *A Crime So Monstrous: Face-to-Face with Modern-Day Slavery*. New York: Free Press.

Slane, K.W. 1978. "Early Roman Terra Sigillata and its local imitations from the post-war excavations at Corinth." Ph.D. Dissertation, Bryn Mawr College.

——. 1986. "Two Deposits from the Early Roman Cellar Building, Corinth." *Hesperia* 55: 271–318.

——. 1989. "Corinthian Ceramic Imports: Changing Patterns of Provincial Trade in the First and Second Centuries." In *The Greek Renaissance in the Roman Empire. Papers from the Xth British Museum Classical Colloquium (British Institute of Classical Studies Supplement 55, 1989)*. Edited by S. Walker and A. Cameron, 219–25. London: University of London, Institute of Classical Studies Press.

——. 2000. "East-West Trade in Fine Wares and Commodities: The View from Corinth." *RCRFActa* 36: 299–312.

——. 2012. "Corinth as context: more contributions on Corinthian society, cults and the Isthmus." *JRA* 25: 858–63.

Slane, K.W. and G.D.R. Sanders. 2005. "Corinth: Late Roman Horizons." *Hesperia* 74: 243–97.

Small, J.P. 2003. *The Parallel Worlds of Classical Art and Text.* Cambridge: Cambridge University Press.

Smith, R.R.R. 1990. "Late Roman Philosopher Portraits from Aphrodisias." *JRS* 80: 127–55.

——. 2006. *Aphrodisias II: Roman Portrait Statuary from Aphrodisias.* Mainz am Rhein: Philipp von Zabern.

Sommerstein, Alan H. (ed. and trans.). 1994. *Thesmophoriazusae.* Warminster: Aris & Phillips.

Soteriou, G.A. 1929. "Αἱ παλαιοχριστιανικαὶ βασιλικαὶ τῆς Ἑλλάδος." *AEph*: 161–254.

Sotinel, C. 1992. "Autorité pontificale et pouvoir impérial sous le règne de Justinien: Le Pape Vigile." *MÉFR* 104: 439–63.

——. 2005. "Emperors and Popes in the Sixth Century: The Western View," In *The Cambridge Companion to the Age of Justinian*, 267–90. Edited by M. Maas. Cambridge: Cambridge University Press.

Sotiropoulou, S., K. Andrikopoulos, and V. Chrissikopoulos. 2003. "The Use of Tyrian Purple in the Wall Paintings of Thira." Paper presented at the 4th Symposium of the Hellenic Society for Archaeometry, National Hellenic Research Foundation, 28–31 May 2003, Athens, Greece.

Spaeth, B.S. 1996. *The Roman Goddess Ceres.* Austin: University of Texas Press.

Spar, D. 2006. *The Baby Business: How Money, Science, and Politics Drive the Commerce of Conception.* Boston: Harvard Business School Press.

Spawforth, A.J. 1978. "Balbilla, the Euryclids and Memorials for a Greek Magnate." *BSA* 73: 249–60.

——. 1996. "Roman Corinth: The Formation of a Colonial Elite." In *Roman Onomastics in the Greek East: Social and Political Aspects*, 167–82. Edited by A.D. Rizakis. Athens: Research Center for Greek and Roman Antiquity.

Sreenivasa, I.N. and L. Ram Jain. 1974. "A Method of Estimating Income Distributions." *Economic and Political Weekly* 9: 2103–09.

Stansbury, H.A. 1990. "Corinthian Honor, Corinthian Conflict: A Social History of Early Roman Corinth and its Pauline Community." Ph.D. Dissertation, University of California, Irvine.

Stevens, S. 1988. "A Legend of the Destruction of Carthage." *CP* 83: 39–41.

Stewart, P. 2008. *The Social History of Roman Art.* Cambridge: Cambridge University Press.

Stikas, E.G. 1957. "Ἀνασκαφὴ νυμφαίου καὶ κρήτης παρὰ τὸ Λέχαιον Κορινθίας." *Prakt*: 89–94.

Stillwell, R. 1936. "Excavations at Corinth." *AJA* 40: 21–45.

Stirling, L. 2005a. *The Learned Collector: Mythological Statuettes and Classical Taste in Late Antique Gaul.* Ann Arbor: University of Michigan Press.

——. 2005b. "The Goddess Roma in a Late Roman Villa at Corinth." Paper presented at Roman Sculpture Session. 106th Annual Meeting of Archaeological Institute of America, 6–9 January, 2005, Boston, MA.

——. 2008. "Pagan Statuettes in Late Antique Corinth: Sculpture from the Panayia Domus." *Hesperia* 77: 89–161.

Straus, J.A. 2004. *L'achat et la vente des esclaves dans l'Egypte Romaine: contribution papyrologique à l'étude de l'esclavage dans une province orientale de l'Empire Romain.* Munich: K. G. Saur.

Strocka, V.K. 2007. "Painting and the 'Four Styles.'" In *The World of Pompeii*, 302–22. Edited by J.J. Dobbins and P.W. Foss. London: Routledge.

Stroud, R.S. Forthcoming. *The Sanctuary of Demeter and Kore: The Inscriptions.* Princeton: American School of Classical Studies at Athens.

Sturgeon, M. 1987. *Sculpture I: 1952–1967.* Princeton: American School of Classical Studies at Athens.

Sweetman, R. 2010. "The Christianization of the Peloponnese: The Topography and Function of Late Antique Churches." *Journal of Late Antiquity* 3: 203–61.

Sweetman, R. and G.D.R. Sanders. 2005. "A New Group of Mosaics from Corinth in Their Domestic Context and in the Context of the Colony." In *La mosaïque gréco romaine IX. Actes du IX e Colloque international pour l'étude de la mosaïque antique et médiévale organisé à Rome, 5–10 novembre 2001 (CÉFR 352),* 359–69. Edited by H. Morlier. Rome: École française de Rome.

Syme, R. 1958. *Tacitus.* Oxford: Clarendon.

Taylor, L.R. and A.B. West. 1928. "Latin Elegiacs from Corinth." *AJA* 32: 9–22.

Temin, P. 2004. "The Labor Market of the Early Roman Empire." *Journal of Interdisciplinary History* 34: 513–38.

Thelwall, S. 1913. *Ante-Nicene Fathers. Volume IV.* Edited by A. Roberts and J. Donaldson. New York: Charles Scribner's Sons.

Thomas, C.M. 2005. "Placing the Dead: Funerary Practice and Social Stratification in the Early Roman Period at Corinth and Ephesos." In *URRC,* 281–306.

———. 2010. "Greek Heritage in Roman Corinth and Ephesos: Hybrid Identities and Strategies of Display in the Material Record of Traditional Mediterranean Religions." In *CCxt,* 117–47.

Tobin, J. 1997. *Herodes Attikos and the City of Athens (APXAIA EΛΛAΣ 4),* Amsterdam: Gieben.

Tompkins, D.P. 1990. "Review of Donald W. Engels, *Roman Corinth.*" *BMCR.*

Toynbee, J.M.C. 1951. *Some Notes on Artists in the Roman World.* Brussels: Latomus.

Treggiari, S. 1969. *Roman Freedmen during the Late Republic.* Oxford: Clarendon.

———. 1991. *Roman Marriage: Iusti Coniuges from the Time of Cicero to the Time of Ulpian.* Oxford: Clarendon.

Trombley, F.R. 2001. *Hellenic Religion and Christianization c. 370–529.* 2 vols. Leiden: Brill.

Trümper, M. 2009. *Graeco-Roman Slave Markets: Fact or Fiction?* Oxford: Oxbow.

Tsotsoros, S. 1986. Οικονομικοί και κοινωνικοί μηχανισμοι στον ορεινο Χώρο : Γορτυνια, 1715–1828. Athens: Historiko Archeio, Emporikē Trapeza tēs Hellados.

Vemi, V. 1989. *Les Chapiteaux Ioniques à Imposte de Grèce à L'Époque Paléochrétienne.* Athens: École française d'Athènes.

Verdelis, N.M. 1956a. "Συνέχισις τῆς ἀνασκαφῆς τοῦ Διόλκου." *AEph*: Chronika 1–3.

———. 1956b. "Der Diolkos am Isthmos von Korinth." *AthMitt* 71: 51–59.

———. 1957. "How the Ancient Greeks Transported Ships over the Isthmus of Corinth; Uncovering the 2550-year-old *Diolcos* of Periander." In *Illustrated London News* (October 19, 1957), 649–51. London: William Little.

———. 1958. "Die Ausgrabung des Diolkos während der Jahre 1957–1959." *AthMitt* 73: 140–45.

———. 1960. " Ἀρχαιότητες Ἀργολιδοκορινθίας." *ArchDelt* 16: 79–82.

———. 1960 (1966a). " Ἀνασκαφή τοῦ Διόλκου." *Prakt*: 136–43.

———. 1962 (1966b). " Ἀνασκαφή τοῦ Διόλκου." *Prakt*: 48–50.

Versnel, H. S. 1976. "Two Types of Roman *Devotio.*" *Mnemosyne* 29: 365–410.

von Blanckenhagen, P.H. and C. Alexander. 1990. *The Augustan Villa at Boscotrecase.* Mainz am Rhein: Philipp von Zabern.

von Reden, Sitta. 1995. "The Piraeus – A World Apart." *GaR* 42: 24–37.

Walbank, M.E.H. 1989. "Pausanias, Octavia and Temple E at Corinth." *BSA* 84: 361–94.

———. 1997. "The Foundation and Planning of Early Roman Corinth." *JRA* 10: 95–130.

———. 2002. "What's in a Name? Corinth under the Flavians." *ZPE* 139: 251–64.

———. 2010. "Image and Cult: The Coinage of Roman Corinth." In *CCxt,* 151–97.

Walbank, M.B. 2010. "Where Have All the Names Gone? The Christian Community in Corinth in the Late Roman and Early Byzantine Eras." In *CCxt,* 256–96.

Wallert, A. 1995. "Unusual Pigments on a Greek Marble Basin." *Studies of Conservation* 40: 177–88.

Walter, J. and R. Schofield. 1989. "Famine, Disease and Crisis Mortality in Early Modern Society." In *Famine, Disease and the Social Order in Early Modern Society*, 1–73. Edited by J. Walter, R. Schofield, and A. Appleby. Cambridge: Cambridge University Press.

Walters, J. 2005. "Civic Identity in Roman Corinth and its Impact on Early Christians." In *URRC*, 397–418.

Watson, A. 1985. *The Digest of Justinian*. 4 vols. Translated by T. Mommsen and P. Krueger. Philadelphia: University of Pennsylvania Press.

——. 1987. *Roman Slave Law*. Baltimore: Johns Hopkins University Press.

Weber, R. 1972. *Corpus Christianorum Series Latina. Volume III. Sancti Cypriani Episcopi Opera*. Turnholt: Brepols.

Weitzmann, K. 1970. *Illustrations in Roll and Codex: A Study of the Origin and Method of Text Illustration*. Princeton: Princeton University Press.

Welborn, L.L. 2005. *Paul, the fool of Christ: a Study of I Corinthians 1–4 in the Comic-Philosophic Tradition*. London: T & T Clark International.

Werner, W. 1997. "The Largest Ship Trackway in Ancient Times: the Diolkos of the Isthmus of Corinth, Greece, and Early Attempts to Build a Canal." *IJNA* 26: 98–119.

Wesche, K.P. 1991. *On the Person of Christ: the Christology of Emperor Justinian*. Crestwood, NY: St. Vladimir's Seminary Press.

Wesenberg, B. 1990. "Wanddekorationen des zweiten pompejanischen Stils in Griechenland." In *Akten des XIII Internationalen Kongresses für Klassische Archäologie*, 576–77. Mainz am Rhein: Philipp von Zabern.

Westermann, W.L. 1945. "Between Slavery and Freedom." *American Historical Review* 40: 213–27.

——. 1948. "The Freedmen and Slaves of God." *PAPS* 92: 55–64.

Whitehouse, D. 1991. "Glassmaking at Corinth: A Reassessment." In *Ateliers de verriers de l'antiquité à la période pré-industrielle*, 23–30. Edited by D. Foy and G. Sennequier. Rouen: Association Française pour l'Archéologie du Verre.

Wikkiser, B.L. 2010. "Asklepios in Greek and Roman Corinth." In *CCxt*, 37–66.

Will, E.L. 1982. "Greco-Italic Amphoras." *Hesperia* 51: 338–56.

Williams, C.K. 1977. "Corinth 1976: Forum Southwest." *Hesperia* 46: 40–81.

——. 1979. "Corinth, 1978: Forum Southwest." *Hesperia* 48: 105–44.

——. 1980. "Corinth Excavations, 1979." *Hesperia* 49: 127–31.

——. 1989. "A Re-evaluation of Temple E and the West End of the Forum at Corinth." In *The Greek Renaissance in the Roman Empire* (*BICS* Suppl. 55), 156–62. Edited by S. Walker and A. Cameron. London: University of London, Institute of Classical Studies Press.

——. 1993. "Roman Corinth as a commercial center." In *The Corinthia in the Roman Period* (*JRA Sup 8*), 31–46. Edited by T.E. Gregory. Ann Arbor: JRA.

——. 2005. "Roman Corinth: The Final Years of Pagan Cult Facilities along East Theater Street." In *URRC*, 221–48.

Williams, C.K. and J.E. Fisher. 1975. "Corinth, 1974: Forum Southwest." *Hesperia* 44: 1–50.

Williams, C.K. and P. Russell. 1981. "Corinth: Excavations of 1980." *Hesperia* 50: 1–44.

Williams, C.K. and O.H. Zervos. 1984. "Corinth, 1983: The Route to Sikyon." *Hesperia* 53: 83–108.

——. 1986. "Corinth, 1985: East of the Theater." *Hesperia* 55: 129–63.

——. 1987. "Corinth, 1986: Temple E and East of the Theater." *Hesperia* 56: 1–46.

——. 1988. "Corinth, 1987: South of Temple E and East of the Theater." *Hesperia* 57: 95–131.

——. 1989. "Corinth, 1988: East of the Theater." *Hesperia* 58: 1–36.

Willis, W. 1991. "Corinthusne deletus est?" *BZ* 35: 233–41.

Wilson, A.J.N. 1966. *Emigration from Italy in the Republican Age of Rome*. Manchester: Manchester University Press.

Wire, A.C. 1990. *The Corinthian Women Prophets: A Reconstruction through Paul's Rhetoric*. Minneapolis: Fortress Press.

——. 2006. Response to Jorunn Økland's book *Women in their Place*. Paper read at the Society of Biblical Literature Annual Meeting, Washington, DC.

Wirth, F. 1931. "Wanddekorationen ersten Stils in Athens." *AM* 56: 33–58.

Wiseman, J.R. 1970. "The Fountain of the Lamps." *Archaeology* 23: 130–37.

——. 1972a. "Excavations in Corinth: The Gymnasium Area 1967–68." *Hesperia* 38: 64–106.

——. 1972b. "The Gymnasium Area at Corinth, 1969–1972." *Hesperia* 41: 1–42.

——. 1978. *The Land of the Ancient Corinthians*. Göteborg: Paul Åströms.

——. 1979. "Corinth and Rome I: 228 B.C.–A.D. 267." *ANRW* 2.7.1: 438–548.

Wiseman, T.P. 1971. *New Men in the Roman Senate 139 B.C.–A.D. 14*. London: Oxford University Press.

Womer, J.L. (ed. and trans.). 1987. *Morality and Ethics in Early Christianity. Sources on Early Christian Thought*. Philadelphia: Fortress Press.

Woolf, G. 2004. "Becoming Roman: The Origins of Provincial Civilization in Gaul." In *Roman Imperialism: Readings and Sources*, 231–42. Edited by C.B. Champion. Malden, MA: Blackwell.

Wyse, W. (ed.). 1865. *An Excursion in the Peloponnesus in the Year 1858*. London: Day Press.

Xydis, S.G. 1947. "The Chancel Barrier, Solea, and Ambo of Hagia Sophia." *ArtB* 29: 1–24.

Yarbrough, O.L. 1985. *Not Like the Gentiles: Marriage Rules in the Letters of Paul*. Atlanta: Scholars Press.

Yegül, F. 1974. "Early Byzantine Capitals from Sardis. A Study on the Ionic Impost Type." *DOP* 28: 265–74.

Zarinebaf, F., J. Bennet, and J. Davis, 2005. *A Historical and Economic Geography of Ottoman Greece. The Southwestern Morea in the 18th Century*. Princeton: Princeton University Press.

Zimmerman, N. 2005. "Wandmalerei." In *Hanghaus 2 in Ephesos: Die Wohneinheit 4; Baubefund, Ausstattung, Fund*, 105–31. Edited by H. Thür, I. Adenstedt, S. Jilek, and U. Stipanits. Vienna: Verlag der Österreichischen Akademie der Wissenschaften.

Zimmermann, N. and S. Ladstätter. 2010. *Wandmalerei in Ephesos von hellenistischer bis in byzantinische Zeit*. Vienna: Phoibos.

Zuiderhoek, A. 2009. *The Politics of Munificence in the Roman Empire: Citizens, Elites and Benefactors in Asia Minor*. Cambridge: Cambridge University Press.

INDEX

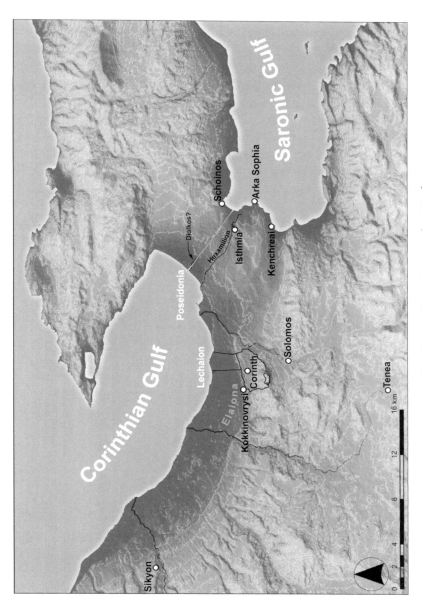

Map 1. Corinth and the Isthmus. Drawing by J. Herbst.

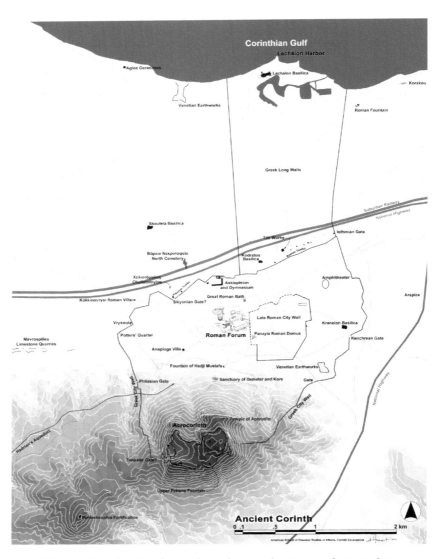

Map 2. Corinth: City plan with modern roads. Drawing by J. Herbst.

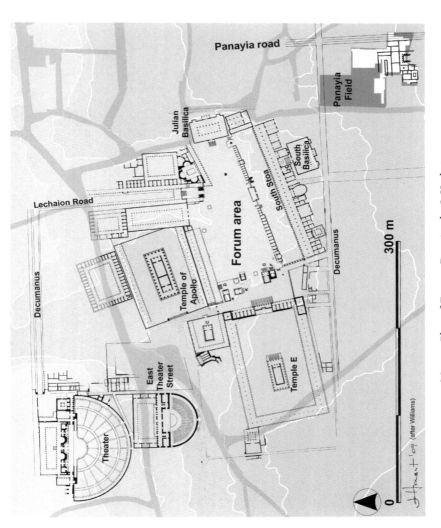

Map 3. Plan of Forum. Drawing by J. Herbst.